Goal!

A CULTURAL AND SOCIAL
HISTORY OF MODERN
FOOTBALL

Goal!

CHRISTIAN KOLLER AND
FABIAN BRÄNDLE

Translated by David S. Bachrach

The Catholic University of America Press
Washington, D.C.

Originally published as *Goal! Kultur- und Sozialgeschichte des modernen Fussballs.*
© Orell Fuessli 2002

English translation copyright © 2015
The Catholic University of America Press
All rights reserved
The paper used in this publication meets the minimum requirements
of American National Standards for Information Science—
Permanence of Paper for Printed Library Materials,
ANSI Z39.48-1984.
∞

Design and typesetting by Kachergis Book Design

Library of Congress Cataloging-in-Publication Data
Bachrach, David Stewart, 1971–
[Goal! Kulture- und Sozialgeschichte des modernen Fussballs.
English.]
Goal! : a cultural and social history of modern football /
Christan Koller and Fabian Braendle ; translated by
David S. Bachrach.
pages cm
"Originally published as Goal! Kulture- und Sozialgeschichte
des modernen Fussballs. Orell Fuessli 2002"—T.p. verso.
Includes bibliographical references and index.
ISBN 978-0-8132-2727-6 (paper : alk. paper)   1. Soccer—
Social aspects.   2. Soccer fans.   I. Koller, Christian, 1971–
II. Brändle, Fabian.   III. Title.
GV943.9.S64B34 2015
796.33409—dc23   2015009767

CONTENTS

Preface to the English Edition   vii

1 | Introduction   1

2 | A Game for the Elite   8

3 | The People's Game   43

4 | Football and Money   71

5 | Football and Emotion   107

6 | Football and the Nation   139

7 | Football and Class Struggle   175

8 | Football and Dictatorship   200

9 | Football and War   238

10 | Football and Gender   264

11 | Conclusion: Autonomy
and Context   295

Bibliography   297

Index   337

PREFACE TO THE ENGLISH EDITION

This book was first published in German in 2002, after many of the arguments presented here had been discussed extensively with students in a course we jointly taught at the University of Zurich during the winter term 1999–2000. In view of the scholarly and popular reception the German edition received, we were delighted when the Catholic University of America Press asked if we would be interested in working on an English translation. The text, however, had to be thoroughly revised and updated for two reasons: on the one hand, the cultural and social history of football during the past decade has continued, with many of the trends we described in the 2002 edition—such as the commercialization and the increasing role of the media as well as criticism against it—having accelerated, while others, such as the tendency toward more gender equality, are still rather sluggish. On the other hand, academic research into the history of football, whose limitations we lamented in the 2002 edition, has become a rapidly expanding, legitimate avenue for academic enquiry. Even outside the United Kingdom, it has become fashionable for academic historians to work on this topic. This development has resulted in a number of scholarly conferences and a multitude of new publications. As a consequence, it is now quite challenging to keep up with the multifarious ongoing debates in the field. In view of this trend toward specialization, the need for syntheses appears even more urgent. Therefore, we are delighted to be able to present our book to an English-language audience.

Goal!

1 | *Introduction*

In 1901 a thoughtful observer of city life in Glasgow wrote that the best thing about football was that it gave workers something to talk about.[1] Football is fundamentally about communication. It provides the context for energetic debates about the proper strategies that the coach of the home team should pursue, wistful memories of a past golden age, as well as apocalyptic visions of decline in the next season. However, discussions about football do not take place in a vacuum. Rather, these conversations are deeply imbedded in their societal context. In Glasgow, for example, the rivalry between Celtic and the Rangers reflects the religious and ethnic conflict between Protestants and Irish Catholics. In other places there are social, regional, or ideological conflicts. Games between countries can become issues of national honor, as is demonstrated by the eruption of emotion in the Islamic Republic of Iran following a victory over the United States of America in the World Cup in 1998. On the other hand, identity-creating conversations about football can also paper over societal fault lines because they produce loyalties that are not based on social conditions or ideological convictions.

In this context, it is not surprising that the French writer and existentialist philosopher Albert Camus, who was a goalkeeper in his youth on the team Racing Universitaire d'Alger and a lifelong supporter of Racing Paris,[2] would write that everything he knew about human morality was due to football. This would be reason enough, one would think, for the historical discipline to investigate the most important pasttime in the world. British social history has been engaged in this topic for more than a (scholarly) generation. Since the 1970s, British scholars have in-

---

1. James Hamilton Muir, *Glasgow in 1901* (Glasgow: White Cockade, 2001), 193.

2. See Patrick McCarthy, *Camus: A Critical Study of his Life and Work* (London: Hamilton, 1982), 17 and 112.

vestigated the history of sport in general, and football in particular, in the context of the general development of industrial society.[3] In other places, however, such as in the German-speaking world, the topic did not lose its reputation as being unserious until the 1990s. It was only after the turn of the millennium that sport became an actual topic of academic history.[4]

This book is intended to provide an overview of the results of international investigations into the history of football, and at the same time identify interesting questions and problems of social and cultural history that would benefit from additional scholarly research. Our own research has addressed, on a selective basis, those phenomena that were of interest to us. Consequently, there is a certain concentration on western and central Europe. We are very well aware that this region encompasses just a small part of the global football community. We have only touched on individual questions regarding some regions that are central to football, such as southern Europe and Latin America, although there is a growing body of historical literature dealing with these regions.[5] This is also true of eastern Europe and the increasingly important continent of Africa.[6] However, a systematic investigation of these regions would go far beyond the boundaries of this book.

3. For a synthesis of the scholarship, see Richard Holt, *Sport and the British: A Modern History* (Oxford: Clarendon Press, 1989).

4. See Pascal Delhaye (ed.), *Making Sport History: Disciplines, Identities and the Historiography of Sport* (London: Routledge, 2014).

5. For older scholarship, see *An Annotated Bibliography of Latin American Sport: Pre-Conquest to the Present*, ed. Joseph Arbena (Westport, Conn.: Greenwood Press, 1989). For newer scholarship, see, for example, Edoardo P. Archetti, "In Search of National Identity: Argentinian Football and Europe," *International Journal of the History of Sport* 12 (1995): 201–19; Archetti, "Playing Styles and Masculine Virtues in Argentine Football," in *Machos, Mistresses, Madonnas: Contesting the Power of Latin American Gender Imagery*, eds. Marit Melhuus and Anne Stølen (London: Verso, 1996), 34–55; *Sport and Society in Latin America*, ed. Joseph Arbena (Westport, Conn.: Greenwood Press, 1988); Osvaldo Bayer, *Fútbol argentine* (Buenos Aires: Editorial Sudamericana, 1990); Leonardo Affonso de Miranda Pereira, *Uma historia social do futebol no Rio de Janeiro, 1902–1938* (Rio de Janeiro: Nova Fronteira, 2000); and Ronaldo César de Oliveira Silva, *Uma caixinha de surpresas: Apropriação do futebol pelas classes populares (1900–1930)* (Londrina: Editora UEL, 1998). For a brief sketch, see William Rowe and Vivian Schelling, *Memory and Modernity: Popular Culture in Latin America* (London: Verso, 1991), 138–42.

6. See Eva Apraku and Markus Hesselmann, *Schwarze Sterne und Pharaonen: Der Aufstieg des afrikanischen Fussballs* (Göttingen: Werkstatt, 1998); Paul Darby, *Africa, Football, and FIFA: Politics, Colonialism, and Resistance* (London: Taylor & Francis, 2001); and Peter C. Alegi, "Keep Your Eyes on the Ball: A Social History of Soccer in South Africa, 1910–1976," PhD diss. Boston University, 2000.

Introduction

We gave this book the subtitle "A Cultural and Social History of Football." What does this mean? First, it must be stressed that we will not be discussing results and rankings, nor will we be offering a history of the world and European championships, of the most exciting decisive games and impressive championship goals. Certainly, we will discuss individual games or tournaments. However, these examples will be placed within broader social and cultural-historical contexts. The cultural anthropologist Clifford Geertz once defined "culture" as "self-spun webs of significance" in which man is suspended.[7] The world of football is teeming with significant threads that, in part, are understood only in this world, but that in part also are closely connected with the world "outside." This is true on both macro and micro levels. The British historiography dealing with football, for example, stresses the importance of the street and of pubs in the creation of local identities. In classical working-class culture, a football team belongs to a single neighborhood. Boys learn the rules of the game and the rough, manly bonding customs of their elders on the streets and in back lots. These customs create what is, fundamentally, a pre-modern popular culture. In the stadium, the boy identifies with the heroes of the local league. He measures them against the rivals from the neighboring cities in northern England. The already well-developed sporting culture arouses his emotions, and the boy's ties to the "we-group" are strengthened by "face-to-face" connections in the stadium. The identification with the "local hero" and with "the lads," grounded as it is in a context of the common identity as workers, is often deeper than the solidarity felt with striking colleagues in a distant city.

However, it is not only identity but also alterity that is constructed through football. In many cases, one's view of the world is strongly influenced by football. The German cabaret performer Dieter Hildebrand once described this phenomenon aptly in the following manner:[8]

7. Clifford Geertz, *Dichte Beschreibung: Beiträge zum Verstehen kultureller Systeme* (Frankfurt: Suhrkamp, 1997), 9. A similar definition of culture is found in Jürgen Kocka, *Sozialgeschichte: Begriff-Entwicklung-Probleme* (Göttingen: Vandenhoeck & Ruprecht, 1986), 133; Hans Medick, "Missionare im Ruderboot? Ethnologische Erkenntnisweisen als Herausforderung an die Sozialgeschichte," *Geschichte und Gesellschaft* 10 (1984): 309; and Umberto Eco, *Zeichen: Segno* (Milan: ISEDI, 1973).

8. Dieter Hildebrand, *Über die Bundesliga: Die verkaufte Haut oder Ein Leben im Trainingsanzug* (Frankfurt: Ullstein, 1981), 122.

If you ask a couple of thousand people what comes to mind when they think of Liverpool, is it the Beatles or Kevin Keegan? Is there a wall in Berlin or Hertha BSC? What came first in Turin, Fiat or Juventus? What does a West German think of when it comes to the GDR? Honecker, Biermann, Bahro? Or do they focus on Sparwasser? Sparwasser shot that damned goal against us when the badly paid football players from the GDR won 1–0 against the well-paid (fatally high) football players of the Federal Republic. They stick to Sparwasser. Bonn? Bonn does not have a team any more, but Cologne is right next door, and Cologne has already won two national championships.

It was only a small step from identifying with the local club to identifying with the national team.[9] The connection between nationalism and football is a worldwide success story. The game is well suited to the confirmation of stereotypes. This is true with regard both to self-image and to the image of others. What politically correct reader has not been caught ranting about the will to win of the Germans? Who has not wondered at the "tackling" of the unlucky Scots? On the other hand, the Italian winger rolls about after a supposed foul like a tenor in a Verdi opera, while his colleague on defense, like Baldassare Castiglione's Hoffmann, does not show the slightest emotion when he breaks free following a nutmeg. Do the Brazilian fans not take pleasure in the agility of their players as contrasted with the blocky Britons? Do the Italians not take pleasure in the *fare bella figura* of their favorites?

An important reason for the success of football is its tight integration into trans-regional competition. Fans quickly recall this or that noteworthy cup final. Newspapers are quick to report on the sensational hat trick of the middle forward in the last international match. Certain football games are actual "sites of memory" (Pierre Nora). Deeply anchored in popular cultural memory, they are enriched with myths and become legendary and intangible.[10] Football can create identities. It is a religion awaiting its saints and villains, offering a forum for rituals and ceremonies. A match can take an unbelievable turn, and decades later fans will still be clapping in rhythm. This is the case, for example, with

9. See also *Doppelpässe: Fussball und Politik*, ed. Norbert Seitz (Frankfurt: Eichborn, 1997).

10. For a discussion of the concept of "sites of memory," see *Les lieux de mémoire*, ed. Pierre Nora (7 vols.) (Paris: Gallimard, 1984–92); and Nora, "Das Abenteuer der *Lieux de mémoire*," in *Nation und Emotion: Deutschland und Frankreich im Vergleich, 19. und 20. Jahrhundert*, eds. Etienne François et al. (Göttingen: Vandenhoeck & Ruprecht, 1995), 83–92.

Rapid Vienna and the quarter hour of the turn, the "Rapid quarter hour." A calendar with yearly high points, with preferences for Easter or Whit Monday, provides for the weekly grind and periodic happiness. Favorites fall. The ball found its way into the net via the back of a head or rather the hand of God. After an important victory, the players, just like heroes, make their way toward the galleries, accompanied by lofty music, for a victory ceremony. The media played and play an important role in the development of this knowledge of the past that is quite exceptional, particularly in comparison to what people know about politics. From a very early stage, journalists and reporters utilized a quasi-religious language: "Toni Turek, football god." Television, in particular, recalls previous glorious moments in football history leading up to the World Cup. After every tournament, montages comprising ebullient celebrations of goals and the desolation following missed penalty shots are standard fare on every television broadcast and every illustrated magazine.

In view of the almost continuously triumphant advance of the sport of football, it is necessary to explain the spaces that are empty of football. From the perspective of football, the most important empty space is the "other" half of humanity, that is women. Certainly, in Britain, women's football did experience rapid growth in the period immediately after the First World War. Benefit matches with women's and mixed teams attracted large audiences. However, these games could not escape the sense of being exotic, and even unserious, and consequently the Football Association issued a general prohibition on women's football in 1921. Women's football faced prohibitions, discrimination, hostility, and condemnation in other nations as well. This situation only began to change slowly at the end of the twentieth century.

The United States represents a second important empty space. Here, "soccer" has had very limited opportunities. The most beloved game in the world still has not achieved complete breakthrough as a commercial magnet for the public. The traditional advantage of competitive sports such as American football, baseball, ice hockey, and basketball played an important role in its failure. The fact that women's football faced comparatively limited opposition in the United States is closely connected to the fact that other sports provided an outlet for masculine heroic identification, though there were also other cultural factors in play.

However, we do not wish to limit our investigation to these cultural-historical factors. The history of football makes clear, contrary to a trend in historical studies that was popular at end of twentieth century, that the issues of social and economic inequality cannot be resolved completely through a close examination of "cultural practices" and "gendered discourses." The history of football is and remains fundamentally a history of social inclusion and exclusion, a history of the struggle of the underprivileged for material well-being, and a history as well of the maximization of profits by clever businessmen and anonymous marketing firms. In sum, it is an important part of social and economic history.

The fact that a game that originated among elite students in Great Britain could become the premier team sport in the world is based upon hard economic facts, including the early professionalization of the game in the face of resistance by the wealthy middle class and aristocratic founders of the sport. It was this factor that allowed members of the lower social classes to mix in at the highest levels of the sport. Crucial here was the patronage of the first professional clubs by small and middling entrepreneurs. Men of this type were proper kings of small towns and neighborhoods. Engaged in local politics, these men were happy to be celebrated by the mass audience. The same pattern emerged several decades later in continental Europe. Football first spread on the continent as the game of technical-mercantile intelligentsia who, at the *fin de siècle* indulged in the liberal capitalist "English way of life" as Grasshoppers or Young Boys on the green turf. The game quickly diffused down to the lower classes, and consequently no longer was able to create a "profitable distinction" (Pierre Bourdieu) for the academic youth.[11] Increasingly, it was derided as a plebeian sport without becoming, as proponents of the workers movement hoped, a locus of socialist class consciousness.

Finally, social and cultural history cannot be divided from each other. Rather, they are engaged in a constant process of exchange. Consequently, the individual chapters of this book cannot be identified as distinctly social or cultural history. Both perspectives play out together in the history, with one and then the other dominating. It is self-evident

11. With regard to the sociological concept of distinction, see Pierre Bourdieu, *Distinction: A Social Critique of the Judgement of Taste* (Cambridge, Mass.: Harvard University Press, 1987).

that this account also frequently deals with political matters as well. The following chapters follow the establishment of modern football from the adoption of the older and wilder folk game in English elite schools to its regulation and institutionalization in clubs and federations through its development as a worldwide game. Concomitantly, we will investigate the conditions that made it possible for football to become the "people's game" and conversely also ask what functions the game fulfilled in the popular culture of the late nineteenth and twentieth centuries after it had achieved this position. The fourth chapter concerns the commercialization of the game from payment of modest compensation to players from the working class and the beginning of entry fees in the last quarter of the nineteenth century to the transformation of football clubs into thoroughly commercialized entertainment companies that thrive through the marketing of television rights and are traded on stock markets at the beginning of the third millennium. The fifth chapter is focused on the emotional side of football through the prism of selected football personalities. Following upon this, the next four chapters investigate the extent to which the emotional side of football played a role in political contexts whether through the more or less incidental interplay of political and sporting event, to the conscious use of football for propagandistic purposes. The tenth chapter focuses, finally, on the question of why football up to the present largely remains the domain of the male half of humanity.

2 | *A Game for the Elite*

Modern football is a child of the nineteenth century. Its development is closely connected with various social and cultural historical processes that took hold first in Great Britain during the industrial revolution, and then were replicated, after some delay, in western and central Europe. This temporal delay can also be observed in the various steps in the development of modern football, including the introduction of the game into elite boarding schools, and the foundation of the first clubs along with the controversy about whether football would remain purely a leisure activity for amateurs or would become a profession for the best players. The French sociologist and ethnologist Pierre Bourdieu identified the fundamental difference between modern sports and traditional popular and elite-cultural games of the pre-modern period as purposeful leisure.[1] While games of the premodern period were always imbedded within a ritual context,[2] sport in the nineteenth century was conceived

1. Pierre Bourdieu, "Historische und soziale Voraussetzungen des modernen Sports," in *Sportphilosophie*, ed. Volker Caysa (Leipzig: Reclam, 1997), 101–27.

2. For the playing of ball games in early America, China, and Japan, see Theo Stemmler, *Kleine Geschichte des Fussballspiels* (Frankfurt-Leipzig: Insel Verlag, 1998), 11–22; Ulrich Köhler, "Das Ballspiel," in *Das alte Mexiko: Geschichte und Kultur der Völker Mesoamerikas*, eds. Hans J. Penn and Ursula Dyckerhoff (Munich: Bertelsmann, 1986), 273–81; Nigel Davies, *Die versunkenen Königreiche Mexikos* (Frankfurt: Ullstein, 1985), 157–59; Helmut Brinker, *Laozi flankt, Konfuzius dribbelt: China scheinbar im abseits: Vom Fussball und seiner heimlichen Wiege* (Frankfurt: Lang, 2006); and F. M. Trautz, "Kemari, das klassische altjapanische Fussballspiel," in *Fussball: Soziologie und Sozialgeschichte einer populären Sportart*, ed. Wilhelm Hopf (Bensheim: Päd.extra, 1979), 37–40. With regard to late medieval and early modern "Calcio," which served as a means of self-representation by the Florentine leadership, see Horst Bredekamp, *Florentiner Fussball: Die Renaissance der Spiele: Calcio als Fest der Medici* (Frankfurt: Campus, 1993); and Antonio Scaino, "Abhandlung vom Ballspiel [1555]," in *Fussball: Soziologie und Sozialgeschichte einer populären Sportart*, ed. Wilhelm Hopf (Bensheim: Päd.extra, 1979), 29–32. Concerning premodern football in England, see Eric Dunning, "'Volksfussball' und Fussballsport," in *Fussball: Soziologie*

as "art for the sake of art" of the body. Sport maintained certain patterns of movement from the traditional games but separated them from their traditional social and religious functions and rationalized them with a set of rules.

In light of this background, the development of modern football can be understood as exemplary of all of modern sport. This transformation essentially took place in four steps.[3] At the beginning there was the older, wild folk football, which can be traced back to the high medieval period on the British isles (as well as in northern France, with the name *soule*).[4] It is sometimes argued that this folk football is based upon the Roman ballgame *harpastum* (which was itself borrowed from the Greeks) that was supposedly brought to Britain by legionaries. However, this kind of continuity cannot be proved. The old form of football had very little in common with modern football. There were no codified rules, and there was no limitation on the playing field, the number of players, or the length of the game. Playing fields sometimes comprised the entire city (with the city gates serving as goals) or fields, meadows, and woods between two villages. In Ashbourne, in the county of Derbyshire, two millstones, located many kilometers apart, had to be touched by the ball, which was an air-filled animal bladder.[5] The competitors in these games often included entire villages, city neighborhoods, or parishes, who used the games to conduct their neighborly rivalries. As a rule, the competitors in the games were men from the lower classes, such as farmers and craft apprentices. The games were often played during festivals and church holidays. Between 500 and 1000, players from the parishes of All Saints and St. Peter's in Derby traditionally faced each other on Shrove Tuesday. The same day, two city teams faced off in Ashbourne.

There is a legend that in Derby the game dates back to antiquity.

---

und Sozialgeschichte einer populären Sportart, 12–18; Dunning and Norbert Elias, "Volkstümliche Fussballspiele im mittelalterlichen und frühneuzeitlichen England," in *Sport im Zivilisationsprozess: Studien zur Figurationssoziologie,* ed. Wilhelm Hopf (Münster: Lit, 1982), 85–104; and Fabian Brändle, "'Great Inconvenience': Zum traditionellen britischen Volksfussball und dessen Varianten," *Sportzeiten* 8, no. 3 (2008): 57–77.

3. The periodization is adapted from Eric Dunning, "The Development of Modern Football," in *The Sociology of Sport: A Selection of Readings,* ed. Eric Dunning (London: Cass, 1976), 133–51.

4. See Stemmler, *Kleine Geschichte,* 28–31. The oldest source for this game dates from 1137.

5. Desmond Morris, *Das Spiel: Faszination und Ritual des Fussballs* (Munich-Zurich: Droemer Knaur, 1981), 100.

According to the legend, the game has its origins in a victory of the inhabitants of Derventio over a Roman military unit in 217 A.D.[6] In Cornwall, people played the game of hurling, which is related to football, during weddings, with the guests on one side and the locals on the other.[7] Because of its rough nature, the game continually led to injuries, and in some cases to fatalities as well. As a consequence, football was banned, for the first time, by King Edward II in 1314. The fact that a new ban was issued every few years into the seventeenth century demonstrates that folk football continued to be played up through the beginning of the modern period.[8] However, by the mid-nineteenth century, the game was largely nonexistent. The multistage process of enclosure, the fencing in of waste and common land,[9] industrialization and urbanization, as well as regulatory repression almost caused the rural folk football to disappear. It is only in the context of folkloric gatherings that the traditional game has been kept alive in a few preserves. An example of this is Shrovetide football which is played annually under the name of De Olde Game on Shrove Tuesday and Ash Wednesday in Ashbourne between the Up'ards and the Down'ards representing those who were born north and south of the river Henmore, which is part of the playing field. Other examples include the Wall and Field game in Eton and Bottle Kicking in Hallaton where the locals are accustomed to measure themselves against outsiders.[10]

From about 1750, forms of folk football were adopted by the elite public schools and practiced in a more or less civilized manner. Between 1840 and 1860, the game received fixed rules, which were written down, in part, in the various schools. Finally two different sports emerged because of conflicts about the different sets of rules: Association Football and Rugby Union Football. Football then spread between 1850 and 1890. The game swept out of the gates of the elite schools back to the "people"

6. Philipp Heinecken, *Das Fussballspiel: Association und Rugby* (Hannover, 1898, reprinted Hannover: Schäfer, 1993), 11.

7. Elias, *Fussballspiele*, 94–100.

8. Ibid., 87.

9. These factors are stressed by Christiane Eisenberg, *"English sports" und deutsche Bürger: Eine Gesellschaftsgeschichte 1800–1939* (Paderborn: Schöningh, 1999), 39.

10. See Hugh Hornby, *Uppies and Downies: The Extraordinary Football Games of Britain* (Berkshire: English Heritage, 2008).

in a changed form. It developed clubs and leagues. Football became a mass spectacle that was turned into a profession by the top players from the 1880s onward. In parallel with the spread of football to all classes of the population, and particularly among the working classes, the elites turned away from football and became increasingly enthusiastic about more exclusive sports.

In this chapter we will follow the elite phase of football from its introduction into the public schools until the departure of the gentlemen, taking into account its social and cultural historical background. This chapter will not focus exclusively on Great Britain. Rather, we will also show how the academic and mercantile elites on the continent (and overseas) adopted football and thereby laid the foundation for its worldwide diffusion. As is so often the case, the transfer of culture utilized the mechanism of an elite practice serving as an admired example that prompted emulation.

A Healthy Mind in a Healthy Body: Football in the Public Schools

A fundamental prerequisite for the development of modern sports was a changed relationship between man and his body.[11] A bundle of factors influenced the approach to the human body in nineteenth-century Great Britain.[12] Victorian society was marked by a major preoccupation with the problems of physical and mental health. More than eight thousand physicians were trained in English universities in the first half of the century. More than seventy new hospitals were opened between 1800 and 1860. The rapid growth of industrial cities brought with it fear of filth and epidemics. As a consequence, hygiene became an important topic. In consonance with the classical motto *mens sana in corpore sano* (a healthy mind in a healthy body), the educated classes became increasingly convinced that illnesses had their origins in bodily defects. As a consequence, the members of the elite strove to keep their bodies healthy through appropriate activities. In the 1860s, the natural scien-

---

11. With regard to the history of the body during the long nineteenth century see, for example, Philipp Sarasin, *Reizbare Maschinen: Eine Geschichte des Körpers 1765–1914* (Frankfurt: Suhrkamp, 2001).

12. The following material is largely derived from Holt, *Sport and the British*, 86–98.

tist Francis Galton (1822–1911) began to study the inheritance of intellectual capacities. Convinced that intelligence was just as inheritable as any physical traits, he hoped to establish a strategy for improving mankind, to which he gave the name eugenics. By using the laws of natural selection, humans could achieve control over their own evolution. In particular, the intellectual elite of Great Britain were to be encouraged to have as many children as possible. However, it was not Great Britain, but rather Germany and the United States that became centers of eugenics at the turn of the century.

The development of elite football also led to a new conception of masculinity. A "real" man had to be moral, healthy, and of sound character. He always had to keep his feelings and his body under control. These pillars of masculine identity separated the members of the bourgeois and aristocratic elite, in their own self-conception, from sickly and emotional women, as well as from members of the lower classes, homosexuals, men of colonized societies, and the Jews. These latter groups were seen as emotional, of doubtful morality and, from a physical perspective, either as sickly or characterized by an overdeveloped sex drive. As a consequence, the elite schools were a place to develop both the characters and the bodies of the pupils. Sport seemed to be the appropriate means for achieving both goals.

The theories of Herbert Spencer and Charles Darwin had an important influence on these issues. The liberal thinker Herbert Spencer (1820–1903), who was influenced by the sociology of progress of the French social theorist Auguste Comte (1798–1858), viewed society as a developing organism and, like the philosophers Jeremy Bentham (1748–1832) and John Stuart Mill (1806–73), employed the principles of empiricism and utilitarianism.[13] As a consequence, Spencer attributed all phenomena to a comprehensive law of natural selection that led an organism to an ever closer adaptation to its natural environment, or, as in the case of humans, to their social environment. This process of adaptation took place through the inheritance of functional changes and the extinction

---

13. See the following books by Herbert Spencer—*Education: Intellectual. Moral and Physical* (London, 1861); *The Principles of Biology* (2 vols.) (London, 1864–67); *The Principles of Psychology* (2 vols.) (London, 1870–72); *The Study of Sociology* (London, 1874); *First Principles* (London, 1875); *The Principles of Sociology* (3 vols.) (London: 1876–96); *The Data of Ethics* (2 vols.) (London, 1879); and *The Principles of Ethics* (London, 1892–93).

of those that were maladapted. The role of the state, in this conceptual model, was limited to supporting and securing the process of development through appropriate laws. The "greatest good for the greatest number" could be achieved through liberal reforms and a policy of *laissez-faire* as Adam Smith (1723–90) had called for in 1776 in his classic work on the national economy, *An Inquiry into the Nature and Causes of the Wealth of Nations*.[14] In his work *On the Origin of Species,* published in 1859, the natural scientist Charles Darwin (1809–82) advanced the so-called theory of evolution, according to which the principles of evolution played a role in the types of variation, heredity, and surplus production of progeny.[15] This led from "the struggle for existence" to "survival of the fittest," that is, to the selection of stronger and more viable individuals and types. This model was quickly translated to human societies (social Darwinism). Here too, the idea developed that there was a war of survival among individuals, nations, and "races," in which only the strongest would survive.

The spirit of competition that was taking hold among the elite as a result of these theories strongly encouraged the development of modern sports, in general, and of football, in particular. The game seemed to embody regulated competition within human society, and therefore an ideal means of preparing students in boarding schools for life "outside." For example, one could read in 1893 in the journal *The Nineteenth Century*:

Surely, whatever tends to quicken the circulation, to raise the spirits, and to purify the blood is, *ipso facto*, a moral agent. This is so to all ages, but it is more especially the case during the age of boyhood. It is an incalculable blessing to this country that such a sport is so enthusiastically beloved by almost all part of our boyhood whom Nature has endowed with strong passions and overflowing energies. Its mere existence and the practical lessons which it preaches are worth all the books that have been written on youthful purity. I can say for myself that, under the circumstances of the luxurious and self-indulgent habits in which boys are increasingly brought up at home, the constant panic lest they should suffer any pain, the absence of apprehension lest their moral and physical fiber should become feeble by disuse, and the tendency of the examination system to make the development of character a secondary consideration, I would not care

---

14. Adam Smith, *An Inquiry into the Nature and Causes of the Wealth of Nations* [1776], eds. R. H. Campbell and A. S. Skinner (Indianapolis, Ind.: Liberty Fund, 1981).

15. Charles Darwin, *On the Origin of Species* [1859], eds. Paul H. Barret and R. B. Freeman (London: Freeman, 1988).

to face the responsibility of conducting a school were there not rooted in it, as I hope, an imperishable tradition, an enthusiastic love of football.[16]

Public schools, some of which had been founded during the medieval era, originally were established as private institutions to provide talented children from the bourgeoisie with a good education. Beginning in the eighteenth century, however, most of the students were the offspring of the higher and lower nobility. From around 1780, they were exclusively upper-class institutions. One result of this transition was that the authority of the faculty over their students was severely weakened. As a rule, the teachers were of substantially lower social status than their students, and were financially dependent on the tuition paid by the students and their parents. Between 1728 and 1832 there were no fewer than twenty-two student rebellions in the public schools. The school at Winchester, alone, witnessed six uprisings between 1770 and 1818. In 1797, it was even necessary to bring troops into the school at Rugby in order to compel the rebellious students to accept reason.[17]

In parallel with the hierarchy of students and teachers, there was an often countervailing system of student self-administration, in which the older and stronger students exercised domination over the younger and weaker students, largely through physical violence. In the second half of the eighteenth century, it was the dominant students who introduced the game of football, often against the will of the teachers. The game played an important role in establishing and reinforcing the pecking order among the students. The younger students often played on defense while the prestigious offensive role remained the preserve of the older students.[18] Around 1800, there were a number of similar games in the public schools, though they were a long way from being standardized.

The advance of industrialization brought with it a conflict for power between the old aristocracy and the upwardly mobile, industrial bourgeoisie. One of the ways in which this conflict manifested itself was in the struggle to control important social institutions, which included

16. Hely Hutchinson Almond, "Football as a Moral Agent," *The Nineteenth Century* 34 (1893): 902.

17. According to Dunning, *Development*, 135. Also see James Walvin, *The People's Game: A Social History of British Football* (London: Allen Lane, 1975), 32.

18. Dunning, *Development*, 136.

the public schools. It is within this context that the first half of the nineteenth century saw a series of reforms in the public schools that strengthened the authority of the teachers and weakened the ability of the students to govern themselves.[19] This process began in the period 1828 to 1842 at Rugby School under the leadership of the theologian, pedagogue, and historian Thomas Arnold (1795–1842), and resulted in a comparative decline in the number of students from the aristocracy. The function of football consequently changed. Rather than a sphere in which the dominant students manifested their independence, football was transformed into an instrument of social control and discipline in the hands of the teachers, as well as a means of building character.

A whole series of schools now set down the rules of the game in writing. Rugby, which generally served as a pedagogical model, again took a leading role, publishing a rulebook in 1846, *The Law of Football as Played in Rugby School*. In 1848 Cambridge published a very different set of rules. In 1849 Eton followed with a set of rules that had been used for football since 1747. At first, school leaders supported football in order to impart a sense of responsibility to the older students, who were now responsible for the organization of games that had to follow a specific set of rules and that also required a high degree of discipline.

Above all, however, the game was seen as a means by which students could be shaped according to the Victorian concepts of masculinity, noted above. In light of the close connection between body and mind that was fundamental to nineteenth-century thinking, it was a natural step to see physical training as inherent to the development of character. And it was the development of character that was the primary goal of the reformed public schools. For members of the upper classes in the nineteenth century, the lengthy period between the end of childhood and entry into "true" adulthood was a time in which students should learn to accept leadership roles but also to be able to subordinate themselves to others. They were to learn how to accept danger and defeat with honor, and to fight with every ounce of their being for their cause, though with-

19. In this context, see T. W. Bamford, "Public Schools and Social Class, 1801–1850," *British Journal of Sociology* 12 (1961): 224–35, as well as Eric Dunning and Kenneth Sheard, *Barbarians, Gentlemen and Players: A Sociological Study of the Development of Rugby Football* (Oxford: Martin Robertson, 1979), 65–78.

out stepping over the boundaries of what was permitted. Students were supposed to seek out "manly" contests, but at the same time internalize the difference between legitimate and illegitimate force. In the second half of the nineteenth century, the game was seen as the cause for the rise of the (second) British empire as a world power on every continent. In 1882, the rector of the Ripon School said in a speech:

> Wellington said that the playing fields of Eton won the battle of Waterloo, and there was no doubt that the training of the English boys in the cricket and football field enabled them to go to India, and find their way from island to island in the Pacific, or to undergo fatiguing marches in Egypt. Their football and cricket experiences taught them how to stand up and work, and how to take and give a blow.[20]

In addition, the game offered a means of ameliorating the "problem" of puberty. The lengthening of the time before the beginning of adult life came together with an earlier entry into sexual maturity in the nineteenth century.[21] The result was that the public schools, which were entirely male societies, were confronted with a number of homoerotic practices. These, along with onanism, were strongly combatted by the school leadership, since they stood in direct opposition to the Victorian ideal of the self-disciplined and responsible gentleman who suppressed his own sexuality until he was in a position to provide for a family. Football and other sporting activities served as a proven means of directing the energies of the youth along nonsexual paths, and thereby to raise these students as gentlemen.

Regulation and Institutionalization

The rules that were set down in the 1840s all had the common goal of limiting the violence of the game. Since every school had its own set of rules, competitions between the schools were, at first, virtually impossible. The most important difference was between the rules of those, such as Rugby, which permitted use of the hands, and of those, such as Eton and Cambridge, which prescribed a pure "kicking game." This problem first was noted by former students, who wished to continue playing the sport

20. Cited in Collin Veitch, "Play Up! Play Up! And Win the War!": Football, the Nation and the First World War 1914–15," *Journal of Contemporary History* 20 (1985): 366.
21. Holt, *Sports*, 89–91.

that they had learned in the public schools. It is not known what rules were employed by the oldest known football club, the "Foot-Ball Club," that existed in Edinburgh from 1824 to 1841. The oldest still-surviving football club, Sheffield FC, which was founded in October 1857, used the rules from Harrow. By contrast, the Blackheath club, which was established in southeast London in 1858, adopted the rules from Rugby. Many of the other early football clubs used the rules issued by Cambridge in 1848. It was certainly not accidental that the different sets of rules mirrored the rivalry for status between the individual schools, and particularly between the progressive school at Rugby and aristocratic Eton.

The first football clubs were thoroughly elite associations. Among the first 29 founding members of Sheffield FC, there were no fewer than eleven factory owners, three lawyers, two physicians, a surgeon, a dentist, a surveyor, a brewer, a veterinarian, a broker, an architect, a dealer in spirits, and a minister.[22] A majority of them were alumni of the Sheffield Collegiate School. Similar to the cricket clubs, the first football clubs were a place for elite social gatherings. Membership for those in the upper and middle classes generally entailed an expansion of their social and business networks. Making these types of connections was not limited to one's own club. Games against other clubs, which were accompanied by social gatherings, often were used for this purpose as well. However, there also soon were clubs that recruited members from outside the circle of school boys. In regions where only a few alumni of the public schools resided, the school boys had to work hard to find other players, and drew some of them from the lower classes.

On October 26, 1863, representatives of eleven London clubs established the Football Association (FA) in the Freemason's Tavern, a pub. After this beginning, they held numerous meetings in order to gain a consensus about a uniform set of rules. The public schools, each of which wished to keep its own set of rules, took very little part at this initial stage. When, on December 8, the representatives of the clubs agreed upon a set of rules that was strongly influenced by those from Harrow and Eton and that permitted only a minimal use of the hands, the Blackheath club and others that were oriented toward Rugby departed

---

22. Tony Mason, *Association Football and English Society, 1863–1915* (Brighton: The Harvester Press, 1980), 23.

the gathering in protest. However, it was not until eight years later that they established their own association, Rugby Football Union (RFU).[23] The eight members of the first RFU executive council were all, with one exception, alumni of the public school of Rugby. Five of them worked as lawyers, one was a civil servant, and another was a lecturer at the Military College of Richmond.[24] The departure of the representatives of the "handling game" from the FA sealed the division between the two disciplines, namely Association Football (or "soccer," for short), and Rugby Union Football (or "rugger," for short).

For a period, other associations existed alongside FA and the RFU The main competitor of the FA, whose influence at first was largely limited to London, was the union of Sheffield clubs, which was established in 1868 and played according to their own set of rules. Other associations were established in Birmingham (1875–76), Lancashire (1878), Norfolk, Oxfordshire, Essex, Sussex (1882), Berkshire, Buckingham, Walsall, Kent, Nottinghamshire, Middlesex, Liverpool, Cheshire, Staffordshire, Derbyshire, and Scarborough (1883).[25] The London and Sheffield associations merged in 1877. From this point on, the FA became the sole authority for the "kicking game" across the country. The other associations modeled their rules on those of the FA and gradually became part of the latter. In the 1880s, what had been an association of London clubs became a national umbrella organization for regional associations. In 1867, the FA had only ten member clubs. There were fifty by 1871, one thousand by 1888, and ten thousand by 1905.[26]

In spite of this, however, the Rugby-inspired "handling game" was far more widespread at first in both the public schools and in the clubs than the "kicking game" of the FA. Even in Lancashire, where professional football had its origins in the 1880s, there were more rugby than soccer clubs. In Scotland, the game of rugby enjoyed a near monopoly. This only began to change in 1880s as a series of rugby clubs converted over to the rules of the FA. An important reason for this was that the FA, in contrast to the rugby union, organized attractive competitions from an early date. The most important of these was the FA cup, which was first

---

23. See Dunning, *Barbarians*, 100–129.   24. Ibid., 123.

25. Mason, *Association Football*, 15.

26. Dietrich Schulze-Marmeling, *Fussball: Zur Geschichte eines globalen Sports* (Göttingen: Werkstatt, 2000), 26.

contested in the 1871–72 season. In the first cup final, on March 16, 1872, the Wanderers defeated the Royal Engineers (1–0) in front of two thousand spectators. The ranks of the victors included four alumni from Harrow, three old Etonians, and one "old boy" each from Westminster and Charterhouse schools, Oxford, and Cambridge. Playing the FA cup led to a substantial increase in the number of spectators, and the number of participating clubs also increased at a rapid rate. Only fifteen clubs participated in the first competition, all of which, with one exception, came from the greater London region. By comparison, more than 100 teams participated in the 1883–84 season, with the Midlands and Lancashire heavily represented.[27]

The Golden Age of the Gentleman Amateur

The philosophy of life that developed out of a combination of the changing understanding of the body in the Victorian period; the competitively oriented social theories of Adam Smith, Herbert Spencer, and Charles Darwin; and the new conception of masculinity based on the pillars of morality as well as a soundness of character and health, can be expressed by the slogan "fair play."[28] The manner in which "you played the game" became the central issue in Victorian sport. The standard bearers of the concept of "fair play" and the "gentleman amateur" from the middle and upper classes not only required of themselves a strict adherence to the rules of their respective sporting disciplines, they also avoided seeking any advantage from their opponents that could not also be sought from themselves. They were supposed to follow this rule not only in sport but in the rest of their social relations as well—in business, politics, and (ideally) in the conduct of war. The idea of "fair play" was even raised on occasion during the First World War, a conflict that required the main actors in the conflict to mobilize all possible resources.[29] In particular, the question was raised whether and to what extent non-white soldiers from the colonies should be brought into the European theater given that the other side did not have access to forces of this type. Writing on

27. Compare with the maps in Mason, *Association Football*, 60–62.

28. Holt, *Sport*, 98.

29. See also Aribert Reimann, *Der grosse Krieg der Sprachen: Untersuchungen zur historischen Semantik in Deutschland und England zur Zeit des Ersten Weltkrieges* (Essen: Klartext, 2000), 145–51.

this topic in 1915, the *Times* observed: "We British are constitutionally the last people in the world to take unfair advantage in sport, commerce or war of our opponents. The instinct which made us such sticklers for propriety in all our dealings made us more reluctant than other nations would feel, to employ coloured troops against a white enemy."[30]

The ideal of the gentleman amateur also included the avoiding of emotions. Even after the greatest exertion, one was not to notice the effort that was involved. Celebrating after a goal was just as inappropriate as protesting loudly against what appeared to be a bad call by the referee. The defeated should not quarrel with fate, but rather congratulate the victor. The latter was obliged to put aside the humbling gestures of the defeated. The high art of emotional control, that is the ability to keep a "stiff upper lip" at all times and in every situation, was something that the elites believed only they were capable of maintaining, and that this was not possible for the members of the lower social classes, whom they perceived as emotional and violent workers. Consequently, the members of the elite sought to keep people from the lower classes as far as possible from their own sporting activities.

Another central point of the ideology of fair play was the policy that one was not paid for sporting performances. As early as the middle of the century, the term professional appeared as an evil spirit in the sporting heaven. Then, in the 1880s, the term amateur, which had first been used to denote a lover of the sport, developed its modern meaning as a non-professional athlete.[31] In the eighteenth century, it was common for cricket to be played for money. This practice, however, was vehemently rejected by the gentlemen amateurs of the nineteenth century. The main objection to a commercialization of sport was the fear that winning would become more important than simple participation as soon as money entered the game. Athletes would no longer match each other in peaceful competition, but would rather become slaves to the investors and spectators. Fair play would be sacrificed to filthy lucre. In practice, amateurism was often a means of excluding the lower classes from sporting activities, and of avoiding contact with working-class people.

30. *The Times History of the War* (London, 1915), 1:155.
31. Holt, *Sport*, 103.

In 1886, the Amateur Athletic Association adopted a "gentlemen clause" that excluded from competition anyone "who is a mechanic, artisan or labourer, or engaged in menial activity."[32] The academic elite looked with contempt on those who, because they were not paid, stood to lose financially from participating in sports. For example, in 1863, the Amateur Athletic Club explicitly banned workers from membership since the latter could not afford to give up work and pay in order to participate in sporting competitions.

Both of the football associations, the FA and the RFU, took this position. In their first decades, both were confronted with the issue of creeping professionalism, "shamateurism," which they understood as a fundamental challenge to their existence. They developed two different strategies to confront this phenomenon. The FA gave up its repressive approach in favor of a paternalistic effort to control professional sport by establishing the professional Football League in 1888. By contrast, the RFU remained adamant and had to endure the splitting off of the Northern Rugby Football Union in 1895.[33] The main factor in the division was the question of the so-called broken-time payments, given to workers for the income that they lost by playing in a game. The newly established Rugby League altered in some respects the rules of the RFU. In addition to the broken-time payments, it also authorized actual payments to professional players. By 1904, Rugby League football had become a fully professionalized sport.[34] Richard Holt has suggested that the different approaches of the two associations toward the issue of professionalism may be related to the social roots of the FA and the RFU. The FA's champions came from the oldest and most prestigious public schools and had nothing to fear from aspiring players from the petty bourgeoisie and upper working classes and could afford to take a paternalistic approach. By contrast, the RFU's origin lay with the less prestigious Rugby School, so they may have found that professional players posed a threat to the status of their members, not only in the realm of sport, but in social respects as well.[35] No matter what the cause, the re-

32. Cited in Michael Krüger, "Zur Geschichte und Bedeutung des Amateurismus," *Sozial- und Zeitgeschichte des Sports* 2 (1988): 86.

33. See Dunning, *Barbarians*, 165–74.   34. Ibid., 205.

35. Holt, *Sport*, 106. Also see Dunning, *Barbarians*, 188, as well as Julian Doherty, "Dr. Ar-

pressive approach of the RFU and the consequent schism within rugby caused a reverse from which it never fully recovered.

The rise of FA rule football to a position as the premier team sport which increasingly attracted all classes of the population as players and spectators was accompanied by a retreat of the elites from the game in favor of other sports. Ironically, this included, among others, rugby, which had lost the battle with football as a result of the approach of its association to the question of professionalism, and which because of its rough nature would normally have appealed more to the working classes than to aristocratic gentlemen. The fact that football permitted professional play as early as the 1880s can only partially explain the withdrawal of "gentlemen amateurs" since there had been professional cricket players for an even longer period without this leading to an exodus by the elites. Rather, the decisive factor was the transformation of football into a "people's game" that no longer facilitated the gentleman's search for distinction and separation from the common people.

In his lengthy essay *La Distinction*, the sociologist Pierre Bourdieu formulated the thesis that taste is never a matter of individual preference but rather must always be considered from a societal perspective.[36] Bourdieu distinguished among three different dimensions of taste: the so-called legitimate taste of the upper classes, the middle taste, and the popular taste of the lower classes. These dimensions of taste cross into all areas of life. Bourdieu investigated music, theater, film, furnishings, eating and drinking, clothing, sport, and habits of newspaper reading. Legitimate taste is marked by numerous distinctive features that are supposed to prove the cultural competence and sophistication of those who possess it. The possessors of legitimate taste use the lower classes simply to draw contrasts in order to clarify their own superior position. At the same time, "legitimate" taste constantly renews societal differences in that children of the upper classes receive it, so to speak, from the cradle—Bourdieu deploys the idea of cultural capital in this context—while those rising up from the lower classes must work diligently to appropriate legitimate taste for

---

nolds Erben: Der Aufstieg und Fall des Amateurrugbys in Grossbritannien," *Sozial- und Zeitgeschichte des Sports* 4, no. 3 (1990): 46–55.

36. Pierre Bourdieu, *Distinction: A Social Critique of the Judgment of Taste* (Cambridge, Mass.: Harvard University Press, 1987).

themselves. Legitimate taste, however, is not fixed but rather changes constantly. In particular, those elements of culture that are adopted by social climbers, and those who would like to be climbers, move toward the position of middle or even popular taste, and gradually are sifted out from the realm of legitimate taste. These elements of culture have lost their distinctive function, and no longer are the exclusive preserve of the upper classes. They are then replaced by new cultural practices.

Football experienced exactly this fate. In a period in which the lower classes did not have any opportunity to participate in sporting activities because of their limited leisure time, football served the desire of the upper classes for exclusivity and differentiation. However, as the shortening of the working day made the game accessible to the lower classes, and professionalization made it possible for the best players from the lower classes to rise to the pinnacle of the sport—in short, as football became not only an element but rather the epitome of popular taste—gentlemen seeking distinction had no other choice but to clear the field and seek out new sports. In particular, they sought out those sports that were too expensive for the common man, or that were very unlikely to become popular because of their exceptionally complicated set of rules. Christiane Eisenberg used the reference work *Burke's Who's Who in Sport and Sporting Record* to show the sporting preferences of the aristocracy and bourgeoisie after the First World War. In this poll that allowed multiple answers, hunting dominated among the nobility with 48.4 percent, followed by equestrian activities at 32 percent, and yachting at 26.2 percent. Cricket was in fifth place with 12.3 percent and the two varieties of football, that is soccer and rugby, were at ninth place on the list with a combined 2.5 percent. Only track and field came below them on the list. Among the bourgeoisie the situation was very different. The two varieties of football commanded 54.9 percent, just before cricket with 50.5 percent. The "aristocratic" sports of hunting (6.5 percent), equestrian activities (4.9 percent), yachting (3.3 percent), and polo (1.1 percent) followed far behind.[37] A comparable analysis of the working classes would have shown an even greater domination by football (and here it would clearly be football of the FA variety).

37. Eisenberg, *English Sports*, 72.

International Expansion and National Obstacles

Football owes its contemporary diffusion across most of the modern world to the fact that the newly industrialized elites at the *fin de siècle* saw in the sport the highly admired "English way of life." Until shortly before the end of the progressive nineteenth century, Great Britain indisputably was the premier industrial power. The British were also the leaders in the colonial-imperialist expansion in Asia and Africa. Finally (and for our purposes most important), Britain was seen by continental liberals as the champion of free markets and parliamentary governmental reform. For the striving technical-mercantile youth on the continent, the universal rules and open competition of football embodied cosmopolitanism and competition as well as a modernity that was oriented toward the principles of free trade.

Its diffusion generally followed the same schema that has been identified in scholarship treating British-German cultural transfers of the nineteenth century: (1) the defining of two opposing forces, that is the distinction between those who belong and those who do not belong; (2) the development of a desire to appropriate; (3) the selection of those things that are worthy of being learned; (4) primary appropriation; (5) secondary appropriation, that is the assimilation of the appropriated material into the structures and customs of one's own country; and (6) contemplation of the other country's view of itself.[38] In general, the introduction of football onto the European continent and in Latin America followed steps 1 through 5, without usually reaching step 6.

In light of the previous discussion, it is certainly not surprising that football first gained a foothold on the European continent in those states that were the most industrially advanced. As Pierre Lanfranchi has shown, it was in Switzerland, Denmark (where the first national football association on the continent was established in 1889), and Belgium, the three states that had the highest per capita gross national product, that football expanded the most quickly.[39] Liberal democratic Switzerland ac-

38. Rudolf Muhs et al., "Brücken über den Kanal? Interkultureller Transfer zwischen Deutschland und Grossbritannien im 19. Jahrhundert," in *Aneignung und Abwehr: Interkultureller Transfer zwischen Deutschland und Grossbritannien im 19. Jahrhundert*, ed. Rudolf Muhs (Bodenheim: Philo Verlagsgesellschaft, 1998), 18.

39. Pierre Lanfranchi, "Football et modernité: La Suisse et la pénétration du football sur le continent," *Traverse* 5 (1998): 84.

tually played the role of a football bridgehead on the continent. The introduction of football here was connected to the newly developing avenues
for the education of the economic elite. The first evidence for the game of
football can be found in Geneva as early as the first half of the nineteenth
century. A ball game with uncertain rules was then played, under British
influence, during the very early days of the Institut du Château de Lancy,
which was founded in Geneva in 1853.

Beginning in the 1860s, British boarding school students, merchants, and Anglo-Saxon inspired pedagogues spread the games of football and rugby more broadly in the Lake Geneva region, although not
always in a gentlemanly manner. In 1866, a match and banquet in Lausanne led to a riot at the train station that was so large that the police had
to become involved.[40] In 1869, the game of football entered the Institut
de la Châtelaine at Geneva, and probably followed the rules from Rugby.
Other private schools located along Lake Geneva also adopted the game
in the following years, and the British colony in Geneva recruited players
from among the students.[41] In the 1870s, one could even purchase real
footballs in Calvin's city.[42] No later than the 1870s, football was adopted
in German-speaking Switzerland at the elite Institut Wiget auf Schön-
berg in Rorschach. In addition to Swiss students, this school also had
British, Spanish, Italian, and South American pupils. During the 1880s
and 1890s, the game with the round leather ball found its way into the
athletic activities of the Obere Realschule in Basel and into the secondary schools in Zurich, Trogen, Frauenfeld, and Schaffhausen.[43]

The establishment of clubs was already in train during the 1870s.
From 1871 on, the press was discussing football and rugby matches between British clubs of Geneva, Lausanne, and Châtelaine, which already
had formal team structures.[44] These clubs were quite as old as La Havre
AC, founded by Britons in 1872. This is often seen as the first continen-

40. *Gazette de Lausanne*, November 2, 1866.

41. See *Journal de Genève*, October 14, 1871, and November 14, 1871.

42. See *Journal de Genève*, May 12, 1878.

43. *Jubiläumsschrift 50 Jahre Schweizer Fussball- und Athletik Verband 1895–1945* (Basel: Schweizer Fussball- und Athletik Verband, 1945), 21.

44. See *Journal de Genève*, November 14, 1873; February 5, 1875; February 20, 1875; November 27, 1875; November 11, 1876; January 6, 1877; November 16, 1878; November 20, 1878;
December 3, 1878; and March 1, 1879; *Gazette de Lausanne*, December 2, 1871; February 4, 1876;
and October 1, 1878; *Manchester Times*, February 28, 1874; and *Wrexham Advertiser*, February 28, 1874.

tal football club. In 1879, FC St. Gall was founded, which is usually been considered as the oldest football club in Switzerland, and one of the first in continental Europe.[45] The founders were former students at Institut Wiget, and the first balls came direct from England. Around 1880, the Lausanne Football and Cricket Club was raised from the baptismal font, and its membership was largely composed of Britons.

The founding of the Grasshopper Club at Zurich in 1886 similarly owed a great deal to the British biology student Tom E. Griffith.[46] In complete consonance with the Victorian model, the purpose of this club, according to its statutes, was "the development of the body."[47] A donation of 20 francs by Colonel Nabholz made possible the importation of a leather ball as well as blue and white jerseys and caps from England. Analogously to the broader sporting preferences of the gentleman amateur in Great Britain, the Grasshoppers established a tennis section in 1890 and a rowing section in 1904.[48] It was not coincidental that the first game was organized against a side from the Federal Polytechnic Institute at Zurich. The founders of the Genevan Servette FC in 1890 were students at the Ecole professionelle. They first played with an oval ball, which one of the students had received from his father, who had brought it back with him from England. It was only after the turn of the century that the club turned from rugby to football using the rules of the English Football Association.

FC Basel was established by students and merchants, who previously had pursued sporting activities at the Basel rowing club. The academics saw football as providing an ideal balance for the one-sided upper body work in rowing. As was true everywhere on the continent, in the Swiss metropolitan centers it was students in the technical and natural scientific fields who were most engaged in the English game. The more conservative jurists and humanities students held fast to the sports that were characterized by a stronger national tradition. In Switzerland, the

---

45. See Martin Furgler, *1879–1979—Ein Jahrhundert FC St. Gallen: Offizielles Jubiläumsbuch zum 100. Geburtstag des ältesten Fussballclubs der Schweiz* (Herisau: Fussballclub St. Gallen, 1979), 23.

46. See Yves Eggenberger, *100 Jahre Grasshopper-Club Zürich* (Zurich: Grasshopper-Club, 1986), 35–39.

47. Ibid., 32.

48. Ibid., 7 and 19.

most important of these were gymnastics and shooting, which traditionally were closely related to military service.[49] Thus, football was not simply a matter for the elite, but rather for that faction of the elite that because of their belief in progress and internationalism were oriented toward England. Those members of the elite who stressed the nation, and cast concerned eyes northward toward their militarily powerful neighbors,[50] tended to reject the British import as "un-Swiss."

The establishment of the Swiss Football Association in 1895 marked an important step in the institutionalization of football in Switzerland. The founding members were FC St. Gall; the three Zurich clubs, namely the Grasshoppers, the Anglo-American Club, and Excelsior; FC Basel; Rovers Neuchâtel; FC Yverdon; La Villa Longchamp Ouchy; the Geneva Institute clubs, namely La Châtelaine and Château de Lancy; and the Lausanne Football and Cricket Club.[51] At the beginning, four of the five members of the leadership of the association were British citizens.[52] The first unofficial championship, which took place in the 1897–98 season, was won by the Grasshoppers who defeated La Villa Longchamp and La Châtelaine in the final round. The following season, the Anglo-American Club of Zurich won the first official championship. The 1899–1900 season saw the introduction of Series A as the top playing class with at first two, and then three regional groups after the 1901–2 season. This system remained in place until the 1930s when the increasing professionalization of the sport led to a transformation of the championship.

The names of a majority of the clubs betrayed their anglophilic origins for a long time. Before the First World War, the teams that played in Series A football included, along with the Grasshoppers and the Anglo-American Club, the Old Boys from Basel, the Blue Stars in St. Gall and their namesakes from Zurich, the Young Boys at Bern, as well as the Zurich clubs, namely the Anglo-American Wanderers, Kickers, Young Fel-

49. With regard to the tradition of these disciplines, see Walter Schaufelberger, *Der Wettkampf in der alten Eidgenossenschaft: Zur Kulturgeschichte des Sports vom 13. bis ins 18. Jahrhundert* (2 vols.) (Bern: Haupt, 1972).

50. In this context, see Rudolf Jaun, *Preussen vor Augen: Das schweizerische Offizierskorps im militärischen und gesellschaftlichen Wandel des Fin de siècle* (Zurich: Chronos, 1999).

51. *50 Jahre National-Liga* (Geneva: Ed. Sport Pub Bornadelly, 1983), 10; *Jubiläumsschrift 50 Jahre Schweizer Fussball- und Athletik Verband*, 17.

52. Markus Giuliani, *"Starke Jugend—freies Volk": Bundestaatliche Körpererziehung und gesellschaftliche Funktion von Sport in der Schweiz (1918–1947)* (Bern: Lang, 2001), 117.

lows, and Fire Flies.[53] The association itself did not Germanize its name as the *Schweizerischer Fussballverband* until 1913 in an effort to avoid criticism as being a British import, and to establish its status as an organization that had a right to state subsidies. Initially, it did not achieve the second of these objectives.[54]

Switzerland played an important role in the *fin de siècle* in promoting the diffusion of football on the European continent. A great many German, French, and Italian football pioneers learned to love the game with the round leather in Swiss schools. In addition, Swiss sporting pioneers, primarily merchants and academics, established and directed clubs in numerous continental European countries.[55]

Vittorio Pozzo, who was a two-time football world champion in 1934 and 1938 and an Olympic champion as the coach of the Italian national team in 1936, studied language and business at Zurich and Winterthur between 1906 and 1908. It was during this period that he learned football at the Grasshopper Club. After another year abroad at Manchester, he returned to his home city of Turin where he acted in turn as a player, referee, and sports journalist until he accepted the position of coach in 1929 for the Squadra Azzurra (Italian national team). The brothers Michele and Paolo Scarfoglio, who were among the founders of the first football club in Naples, learned the game a short time before during a training course in Switzerland. The French banker, Henry Monnier, who always wrote his first name with a "y" out of Anglophilia, introduced football to Nîmes in 1898. Also a mountain climber, Monnier had discovered the game while studying at Geneva. The French football pioneers Falgueirettes and Julien also studied in Switzerland. The German football pioneer Walter Bensemann attended schools in western Switzerland and later studied, among other places, at the university of Lausanne. He founded his first football club, Montreux FC, in 1887, before establishing numerous clubs in Germany, serving as one of the founders of the Deutsche Fussballbund

53. See Paul Ruoff, *Das goldene Buch des Schweizer Fussballs* (Basel: Verlag Domprobstei, 1953), 237–39.

54. Giuliani, *Jugend*, 122.

55. For the following, see Lanfranchi, *Football*, as well as Christian Koller, "Prolog: "Little England": Die avantgardistische Rolle der Schweiz in der Pionierphase des Fussballs," in *Die Nati: Die Geschichte der Schweizer Fussball-Nationalmannschaft*, ed. Beat Jung (Göttingen: Werkstatt, 2006), 11–22.

(German Football Union), organizing numerous international matches, as well as founding and acting as chief editor of the periodical *Kicker*.

Swiss also were involved in founding numerous clubs in southern and western Europe. The most famous of them is Hans "Joan" Gamper, who was born in Winterthur in 1877. Acquainted with football and other British sports as a student, he was among the founders of FC Zurich. As an official in the textile industry in Lyon he then played for FC Lyon. A short time later he settled in Catalonia and founded FC Barcelona in 1899, which numbered many Swiss, Britons, Germans, and Austrians among its members. Until 1925, Gamper held office as president of Barça.[56] One of the most successful teams in the pioneering phase of French football was called Stade Helvétique de Marseille. The gymnastic and sporting club, which was founded by the Swiss colony in the southern French commercial city of Marseilles in 1884 with the name La Suisse Marseille, added a football section in 1904. In 1909, this team, which comprised ten Swiss and one Briton, won the French championship and repeated this success in 1911 and 1913.

Swiss also played a role in establishing football in Italy. FC Bari was brought forth from the baptismal font in 1908 by the grain merchant Gustav Kuhn along with his German, French, Swiss, Spanish, and Italian friends. Internazionale Milano was established that same year, and the majority of its founding members were Swiss. A year later, the Swiss dentist Louis Rauch became the first president of FC Bologna. The Winterthur native Walter Aemissegger introduced football to Venice in 1912. Swiss also were among the founders of football clubs in Palermo and Bergamo. In 1906, there were four players from St. Gall on the championship team from Milan as well as a former player from Grasshopper. Third place Genoa had a player from Lausanne, and the previous year's champion, Juventus Turin, had both a Swiss president and two players from Basel. When the Turin eleven traveled to Winterthur for a friendly match in 1910, their ranks included no fewer than five former players from FC Winterthur.[57]

56. See Christian Eberle, "Protestant-Katalane-Ikone: Joan Gamper. Gründervater des FC Barcelona," in *Memorialkultur im Fußballsport: Medien, Rituale und Praktiken des Erinnerns, Gedenkens und Vergessens*, ed. Markwart Herzog (Stuttgart: Kohlhammer, 2010), 113–32.

57. See *Neues Winterthurer Tagblatt*, May 14, 1910.

Swiss sporting pioneers also introduced football into various regions of eastern Europe. At the turn of the century, a number of Swiss
merchants played leading roles in the most prominent athletic club in
the Russian capital of St. Petersburg, the multi-sport S.-Peterburgskij
Kružok Ljubitelej Sporta (St. Petersburg Circle of Amateur Athletes),
which was founded in 1888. The wealthy clothier Eduard Vollenweider,
who was personally involved in a wide variety of sports, served as secretary in 1896, and then later as treasurer, and finally as chairman of the
club from 1905 onward. His brother-in-law, Konrad Schinz, who played
football for the club for many years, followed Vollenweider as treasurer and then as president of the club. In contrast to the football teams
founded by British engineers and merchants in the metropolitan centers of the Czarist empire, which excluded participation by the locals, in
Kružok Swiss, German, and other foreigners interacted with Russians
from the upper classes around the round leather.[58] In the 1890s, Swiss
gymnastic instructors introduced football into Bulgaria.[59] In 1901, the
Jewish student Hugo Buli, who had learned the game with the round
leather in Germany, brought a real football—apparently just the second
one in Serbian sporting history—as well as a full set of football equip-
ment from Switzerland to Belgrade, thereby causing quite a stir.[60]

Naturally, in addition to the Swiss, Britons founded football clubs.
The Le Havre Athletic Club, noted above, was founded by English employees of textile and armaments factories. The first president was an
Anglican minister.[61] At first, Le Havre AC played football according to
both sets of rules. At a meeting of the club in 1882, the question was
raised whether in the future they should follow the rules of the FA, the
RFU, or a mixture of the two. A bare majority decided against adopting
the rules of the FA and voted for a combination of the two. However,
this in-house system of rules was not maintained for long.

58. See Ekaterina Emeliantseva, "Sport und urbane Lebenswelten im spätzarischen St. Petersburg (1860–1914)," in *Sport als städtisches Ereignis*, ed. Christian Koller (Ostfildern: Thorbecke,
2008), 31–76.

59. See Gergana Ghanbarian-Baleva, "Ein 'englischer Sport' aus der Schweiz: Der bulgarische
Fussball von seiner Entstehung bis zum Beginn der 1970er Jahre," in *Überall ist der Ball rund: Zur
Geschichte und Gegenwart des Fussballs in Ost- und Südosteuropa*, eds. Ditmar Dahlmann et al.
(Essen: Klartext, 2006), 155–82.

60. Danilo Stojanović, *Čika Dačine uspomene* (Belgrade, 1953), 5.

61. Alfred Wahl, *Les archives du football: Sport et société en France, 1880–1980* (Paris: Gallimard, 1989), 27–31.

A Game for the Elite

During the mid-1860s, Ferdinand Hueppe, later to become professor of health in Prague, played football in Germany with English students who were attending the Neuwied school. Britons largely introduced the game in Germany in commercial centers, bedroom communities, and in spas. British students at universities and technical schools, as well as British merchants played an important role. As early as 1875, a football side from Oxford went on a tour through Germany.[62]

The nucleus of native German football was provided by the grammar schools (*Gymnasien*) and institutes of higher education.[63] A pioneer was Konrad Koch, an instructor at a Braunschweig *Gymnasium*, who introduced the game (following the rules from Rugby) at the Martino-Katharineum-Gymnasium in 1874. The game then was introduced at the Johanneum, a *Gymnasium* in Hamburg, in 1876.[64] Koch's intention was to provide a counter balance to the drinking rituals that had become very popular among the high-school student associations, following the model of the university student fraternities. The game was intended to inculcate independence and self-discipline among the students. At this time Koch was a member of the Zentralausschuss für Volks- und Jugendspiele (Central Committee for Popular and Youth Sports) (ZA), an organization that was closely connected with the National Liberal Party and the Pan-German League, whose goal was to defeat Social Democracy through the establishment of a mass athletic movement. In additional to gymnastics, the ZA also supported British sports, such as football.[65] By 1882, the Prussian education ministry approved the introduction of the game into the schools.[66]

However, football did face considerable opposition from the ranks of the German gymnastic associations. The German gymnastic movement was founded under the leadership of Friedrich Ludwig Jahn during the period of Napoleonic "foreign rule" (1806–13), and had a nationalistic

62. Schulze-Marmeling, *Fussball*, 65–68. For the following also see Wilhelm Hopf, "Wie konnte Fussball ein deutsches Spiel werden?," in *Fussball: Soziologie und Sozialgeschichte einer populären Sportart*, ed. Wilhelm Hopf (Bensheim: Päd.extra, 1979), 54–80.

63. For the pedagogical background of gymnastics and athletics in German schools in the nineteenth century, see Jürgen Oelkers, "Physiologie, Pädagogik und Schulreform im 19. Jahrhundert," in *Physiologie und industrielle Gesellschaft: Studien zur Verwissenschaftlichung des Körpers im 19. und 20. Jahrhundert*, eds. Philipp Sarasin and Jakob Tanner (Frankfurt: Suhrkamp, 1998), 245–85.

64. Eisenberg, *English Sports*, 179; Arthur Heinrich, *Der Deutsche Fussballbund: Eine politische Geschichte* (Cologne: PapyRossa-Verlag, 2000), 21.

65. Ibid., 30.   66. Ibid., 22.

character from the very beginning.[67] Gymnastics was supposed to prepare German men for a rebellion against French occupiers, and thus had a military purpose. During the age of restoration (1815–48), the gymnastics movement was forbidden for a lengthy period in Prussia because it was seen as being related to the student fraternities, which were understood to be subversive. It was not until 1842 that the prohibitions against gymnastics were lifted. During the year of revolution in 1848, when there were already three hundred gymnastics clubs with around ninety thousand members,[68] the participants at the Hanau gymnastics tournament decided, after a heated discussion, that they would fight for the unity of Germany rather than for the establishment of a republic. The first German gymnastics festival took place in 1863 at Leipzig, with about twenty thousand gymnasts participating.[69] The Deutsche Turnerschaft (German Gymnastics Association; DT), which was founded in 1869, became one of the most important venues for the propagation of German nationalism.[70] Liberal (or even democratic) ideas quickly disappeared from their ranks.

When the memorial to the Battle of the Nations was unveiled at Leipzig in October 1913, in memory of the 1813 victory over Napoleon, the gymnasts organized so-called Eilbotenläufe, relay races, which came together at Leipzig from nine different directions.[71] Forty-three thousand gymnasts from all parts of the empire participated in the runs, as

67. See Hans Kohn, "Father Jahn's Nationalism," *Review of Politics* 11 (1949): 419–32; Thomas Stamm-Kuhlmann, "Humanitätsidee und Überwertigkeitswahn in der Entstehungsphase des deutschen Nationalismus: Auffällige Gemeinsamkeiten bei Johann Gottlieb Fichte, Ernst Moritz Arndt und Friedrich Ludwig Jahn," *Historische Mitteilungen* 4 (1991): 161–71.

68. Hagen Schulze, *Der Weg zum Nationalstaat: Die deutsche Nationalbewegung vom 18. Jahrhundert bis zur Reichsgründung* (Munich: Deutscher Taschenbuch-Verlag, 1985), 83.

69. Ibid., 105.

70. See Dieter Düding, *Organisierter gesellschaftlicher Nationalismus in Deutschland (1808–1847): Bedeutung und Funktion der Turner und Sängervereine für die deutsche Nationalbewegung* (Munich: Oldenbourg, 1984); Dieter Langewiesche, "'. . . für Volk und Vaterland kräftig zu würken . . .': Zur politischen und gesellschaftlichen Rolle der Turner zwischen 1811 und 1871," in *Kulturgut oder Körperkult? Sport und Sportwissenschaft im Wandel*, ed. Ommo Grupe (Tübingen: Attempto-Verlag, 1990), 22–61; Svenja Goltermann, *Körper der Nation: Habitusformierung und die Politik des Turnens 1860–1890* (Göttingen: Vandenhoeck & Ruprecht, 1998); Arndt Krüger, "Deutschland, Deutschland über alles? National Integration through Turnen und Sport in Germany 1870–1914," *Stadion* 25 (1999): 109–29; Michael Krüger, *Einführung in die Geschichte der Leibeserziehung und des Sports, Bd. 2: Leibeserziehung im 19. Jahrhundert: Turnen fürs Vaterland* (Schorndorf: Hofmann, 1993); and (also by Krüger) *Körperkultur und Nationsbildung: Die Geschichte des Turnens in der Reichsgründungsära* (Schorndorf: Hofmann, 1996).

71. See Wolfram Siemann, "Krieg und Frieden in historischen Gedenkfeiern des Jahre

did an even greater number of spectators. This was a national production that had a powerful mobilizing effect. A similar event took place in August 1934 when one hundred and fifty thousand gymnasts and athletes participated in a Saarland-Treuestaffel (Saarland-Loyalty Relay) and brought demonstrations of their loyalty to the Führer at Coblenz. This race served to prepare public opinion for the return of Saarland, which was under the administration of the League of Nations, to Germany in January 1935.[72]

Overall, during the last year of peace (1913), the Gymnastics Association included more than 11,100 clubs in 9,200 locations with more than 1.1 million members. When the "dedication of the German stadium" took place in Berlin's Grunewald in June 1913, fifty thousand gymnasts took part alongside Kaiser Wilhelm II.[73] In July of that same year, the twelfth German gymnastics festival took place in Leipzig, attracting seventeen thousand participating gymnasts, seventy-two thousand official festival participants, and a total of two hundred thousand spectators. The following description by an eye-witness captures the character of this event: "An indescribable picture: 104 rows, each around 165 men deep, awaiting the signal to begin the exercises. And what a success, no one made a mistake; and when the exercises ended and *Deutschland Deutschland über alles* rang out, it was not only the amazing display of gymnastics that filled the soul, no, everyone felt with joyful pride, *Civis Germanus sum* (I am a German citizen)!"[74] The official proclamation of the gymnastics festival of the German higher educational institutes, which was held at Gotha in May 1913, included the prophetic claim that: "history is circular; it appears that it wishes to replay the great game of the last 100 years. In the last few years we have felt on more than one occasion that we stand on the eve of a world war, just as was true a century ago, a war in which we once again will have to fight for our existence."[75] Gymnastics was supposed to prepare the Germans for precisely this "war for existence."

1913," in *Öffentliche Festkultur: Politische Feste in Deutschland von der Aufklärung bis zum Ersten Weltkrieg*, ed. Peter Düding (Reinbeck: Rowohlt, 1988), 304–7.

72. See Klaus Cachay, *"Echte Sportler"—"Gute Soldaten": Die Sportsozialisation des Nationalsozialismus im Spiegel von Feldpostbriefen* (Weinheim-Munich: Juventa, 2000), 182.

73. "Die Weihe des Stadions Grunewald," *Gartenlaube* 60 (1913): 536.

74. *Akademische Turnzeitung*, August 1, 1913, cited in Siemann, *Krieg*, 307. Also see "Das XII. Deutsche Turnfest in Leipzig," *Gartenlaube* 60 (1913): 647.

75. *Akademische Turnzeitung*, June 1, 1913, cited in Siemann, *Krieg*, 307.

Football faced a difficult road in face of this powerful organization. The gymnasts, who would understand this confrontation as a conflict between systems,[76] struggled with all of their might to brand this new game, which represented a possible source of competition, as foreign and to present it as ridiculous. The prominent gymnastics leader, Professor Karl Planck, published a pamphlet in 1898 with the title *Fusslümmelei: Über Stauchballspiel und englische Krankheit* (*Crudeness on Foot: Regarding the Rowdy Ball Game and the English Sickness*), which included, among other passages: "What does a kick mean everywhere in the world? It means that there is a person toward whom it is not worthwhile to lift a hand. It is a sign of dismissal, contempt, disdain, disgust, abomination.... Simply in terms of its form, this movement is hateful. The sinking of the leg at the knee, the bending of the hunched back, the thrusting of the chin lowers a man to the status of the apes."[77] The opponents of football happily pointed to the horrific injury statistics in Great Britain and the United States, although they consciously did not distinguish among football played according the FA rules, rugby, and American football—the latter of which was murderous, in the truest sense of the word, until a change in the rules that took place in 1905.[78]

The football pioneer Konrad Koch countered these charges by making the point that football was not a specifically English game, but rather had been played in many countries during the medieval period, including in Germany. He also worked to translate English terminology into German.[79] However, his efforts to establish a football tradition were not successful.[80] Football continued to face challenges in Wilhelmine Germany. It was forbidden in Bavarian schools until 1913. At first, its main area of success was in technical, scientific, and modern-language *Gymnasien* and higher educational institutes.[81] The first football clubs

76. E. Witte, "Wettkampf und Kampfspiel," *Deutsche Turn-Zeitung* 42 (1897): 757, cited in Heinrich, *Fussballbund*, 20.

77. Karl Planck, *Fusslümmelei: Über Stauchballspiel und englische Krankheit* (Stuttgart, 1898, reprinted Münster: Lit., 2004), 5.

78. Heinrich, *Fussballbund*, 22.

79. Ibid., 33–35.

80. Groundbreaking for the construction of traditions in the nineteenth century was the essay collection *The Invention of Tradition*, eds. Eric J. Hobsbawm and Terence Ranger (Cambridge: Cambridge University Press, 1983).

81. Schulze-Marmeling, *Fussball*, 68.

were often comprised of student teams where rugby football predated the FA variety. The first pure rugby club, the Heidelberger Flaggen-Club, was founded in 1870. It was not until the 1880s and 1890s that there were more clubs playing by the FA rules, and these were often established with the help of Britons.[82] The social milieu of these clubs consisted of the cosmopolitan circles of the educated bourgeoisie.[83] As late as 1912, an observer of the scene complained: "In a great many of the clubs, whose members include students, bureaucrats, merchants, and similar types of professionals, workers are basically excluded. The gentlemen think themselves too precious to run about in the games with 'common' workers. They are losing out."[84] Until 1918, the Berlin cricket and football club Britannia only accepted members with an advanced education.

The Deutsche Fussball- und Cricket-Bund (German Football and Cricket Union) was established as an umbrella organization in 1891. The first independent football periodical appeared in 1894. The Deutsche Fussball-Bund (German Football Union) (DFB) was established on January 28, 1900, in Leipzig with eighty-six founding clubs. It is noteworthy that two clubs from Prague, DFC Prague and DFC Germania, participated. The founders of the DFB understood the "D" in their abbreviation as representing the German people rather than the state.[85] The first German championship took place during the 1902–3 season, which ended in a victory for VfL Leipzig. In 1908, the German national football team played its first official international game, which they lost to the Swiss at Basel (3–5).

The DFB very quickly developed two rival currents. The first current saw football as a cosmopolitan means of creating understanding between peoples and of overcoming national prejudices. The second stream was nationalistic and drew heavily on the ideology of the gymnasts. In the years just before the beginning of the war, the latter gained the upper hand. The Association official Carl Diem encapsulated their creed in 1912 in the following words: "This sport stands on the ground of the German

---

82. Ibid., 70–72.

83. See Christiane Eisenberg, "Football in Germany: Beginnings 1890–1914," *International Journal of the History of Sport* 8 (1991): 205–20; and "Fussball in Deutschland 1890–1914: Ein Gesellschaftsspiel für bürgerliche Mittelschichten," *Geschichte und Gesellschaft* 20 (1994): 20–45.

84. Wilhelm Bommes, "Sport und Arbeiterschaft," *Fussball und Leichtathletik* 13, no. 29 (1912): 624, cited in Heinrich, *Fussballbund*, 26.

85. Heinrich, *Fussballbund*, 25.

fatherland, where it should remain! What we have achieved is good German work, and consciously German work. We also sing German songs, and keep faith with German loyalty."[86] The entry by the DFB in 1911 into the paramilitary Jungdeutschlandbund (Young Germany Union), which had the goal of creating a youth that was prepared for war, entailed a major victory for the nationalists within the association and was an expression of the increasing societal acceptance that football had gained in Germany in the years immediately preceding the war.[87] Numerous male members of the imperial family now demonstrated an interest in the game. Crown prince Wilhelm even established a football competition, the Crown-Prince Cup.

In 1910, football even became an element in the training plans of the German army. The revolution in combat tactics of the late nineteenth century, which had been brought about by the transition from front-loading to rear-loading weapons and the general introduction of repeating and magazine arms, brought about an enormous increase in firepower and led to the end of closed lines and column formations.[88] The changes in the conduct of war led to concomitant developments in military training.[89] Football, which taught both individual initiative and playing together as a unit, seemed to fit better with these new demands than did gymnastics that taught the kind of discipline and precision that was required for the older fixed formations. Consequently, in the final years before the outbreak of war, Prussian militarism suddenly made the British import available on its own exercise fields. High military officers claimed that football was a "nursery of military service." The games were like "small-scale maneuvers,"[90] and football taught "self-sacrifice of the individual and the deferment of personal glory in the interest of gaining a common success."[91]

86. Carl Diem, "Friede zwischen Turnen und Sport," *Fussball und Leichtathletik* 13, no. 46 (1912): 905, cited in Heinrich, *Fussballbund*, 29.

87. Heinrich, *Fussballbund*, 39–42.

88. See Martin van Creveld, *Technology and War: From 2000 B.C. to the Present* (New York: Free Press, 1989), 172.

89. Martin Samuels, *Command or Control? Command, Training and Tactics in the British and German Armies, 1888–1918* (London: Taylor & Francis, 1995).

90. Dietrich von Hülsen, "Fussballsport und Wehrfähigkeit," in *Deutsches Fussball-Jahrbuch 1912* (Dortmund, 1912), 126, cited in Heinrich, *Fussballbund*, 38.

91. Dedication by the Prussian minister for war in *Deutsches Fussball-Jahrbuch 1913* (Dortmund, 1913), 14, cited in Heinrich, *Fussballbund*, 38.

Britons also helped to establish clubs in the Habsburg empire, clubs that quickly became leaders on the continent.[92] Football was played in the large British colony in Vienna as early as the 1880s. The first two clubs were founded in 1894—the First Vienna Football Club and the Vienna Cricket and Football Club. The founding fathers were British gardeners from the Rothschild gardens, and employees from a range of British concerns.[93] Football expanded very rapidly from this point. In Vienna, there were seven clubs in 1897, forty-five in 1900, and eighty in 1910. Forty-nine of these clubs were organized in the Österreichischer Fussballverband (Austrian Football Association) (ÖFV), which was founded in 1904. Because the clubs vehemently opposed establishing a league championship on the British model but rather wished to seek out their own opponents in a gentlemanly manner on a week-by-week basis, they resolved to divide the association into different playing classes. Membership in "first division" was, therefore, less a measure of playing strength as it was a sign of good relationships among the clubs. In 1910, the "first division" included the following clubs: First Vienna Football Club, Floridsdorfer Athletiksportklub, Germania, Rapid, Rudolfshügel, Cricketer, Viktoria, Wiener Athletic-Sportclub, Wiener Sportklub, and Deutscher Fussballklub Prag.[94]

British merchants and engineers introduced football into the Russian empire in the 1880s, although this was, at first, limited to St. Petersburg and Moscow.[95] The introduction of football into South Amer-

92. For the following, see Matthias Marschik, *Vom Herrenspiel zum Männersport: Die ersten Jahre des Fußballs in Wien.* (Vienna: Turia + Kant, 1997).

93. Schulze-Marmeling, *Fussball,* 50.

94. Matthias Marschik, *"Wir spielen nicht zum Vergnügen": Arbeiterfussball in der Ersten Republik* (Vienna: Verlag für Gesellschaftskritik, 1994), 44.

95. See Victor E. Peppard, "The Beginnings of Russian Soccer," *Stadion* 8, no. 9 (1982–83): 151–68; James Riordan, "Russland und die Sowjetunion," in *Fussball, soccer, calcio: Ein englischer Sport auf seinem Weg um die Welt,* ed. Christiane Eisenberg (Munich: DTV, 1997), 130–48; Peter A. Trykholm, "Soccer and Social Identity in Pre-Revolutionary Moscow," *Journal of Sport History* 24 (1997): 143–54; Dittmar Dahlmann, "Vom Pausenfüller zum Massensport: Der Fussballsport in Russland von den 1880er Jahren bis zum Ausbruch des Ersten Weltkrieges 1914," in *Überall ist der Ball rund: Zur Geschichte des Fussballs in Ost- und Südosteuropa,* eds. Dittmar Dahlmann et al. (Essen: Klartext, 2006), 5–39; Emeliantseva, *Sport und urbane Lebenswelten;* Emeliantseva, "'Ein Fussballmatch ist kein Symphoniekonzert!' Die Fussballspiele und ihr Publikum im spätzarischen Russland (1901–1913)," in *Überall ist der Ball rund—Die Zweite Halbzeit: Zur Geschichte und Gegenwart des Fussballs in Ost- und Südosteuropa,* eds. Dittmar Dahlmann et al. (Essen: Klartext, 2008), 13–43; and I. B. Chmel'nickaja, *Sportivnye obščestva i dosug v stoličnom gorode načala XX veka: Peterburg i Moskva* (Moscow: Novyj chronograf, 2011).

ica followed a similar pattern.[96] The first football club was established in 1867 in Buenos Aires, which had a large British colony. The founders of Buenos Aires FC were William Herald and the brothers Thomas and James Hogg. The driving force in Argentinian football was the Scot, Alexander Watson Hutton, head of the English High School in Buenos Aires. He founded the Argentine Association Football League in 1893. A few years later, this association joined with the English FA. Until 1906, English was the official language of the Argentinian association. Football first was played in Brazil in 1894–95, again by Britons. The football pioneers in South American's largest state also included Americans, Germans, French, and Portuguese. In 1890, Britons also introduced football into Uruguay, which later became the host and victor of the first football World Cup in 1930. These included William Poole, a teacher at the English High School, and engineers from a British-owned railroad company. When, in 1905, Argentina and Uruguay played against each other in an international tournament, it was named after the Scottish tea-baron and philanthropist, Sir Thomas Lipton.

It is noteworthy that the game spread the least in those areas of the world where the British were not only merchants and technicians, but also were present as colonial masters and missionaries. The primary reason for this was that the Europeans in the African and Asian colonies of the empire belonged to those elite classes that had abandoned football when it had become the people's game, and sought out more exclusive sports for themselves. It was on this basis that sports such as cricket, rugby, and field hockey became established in Asia and Africa, while finding very little support on the European continent or in Latin America. Interestingly, football enjoyed the greatest diffusion in those colonies where the fewest European colonists settled, and which came under indirect rule.

Nigeria (where the first football game is supposed to have been played in 1841) became a football nation, while Uganda, Kenya, and Rhodesia adopted the aristocratic sports of cricket and rugby. The first Africans played for leading English clubs at the end of the nineteenth century. However, it was not until around 1980, when the process of

96. Schulze-Marmeling, *Fussball*, 55–57.

decolonization largely had been completed, that the number of African players grew massively. In 1979, Viv Anderson became England's first black international player.[97] In Africa, it was not the British, but rather the other great colonial power, the French, who made football popular. Football was already being played by the colonial masters in North Africa in the 1890s. Following the First World War, the French government officially supported the spread of football in Africa. The fact that the game also soon was adopted by the colonized is demonstrated, for example, by the complaint made by a farmer from Worms in the French occupational zone in Western Germany in 1920 regarding a unit of Senegalese garrison troops, who were playing football on his already planted fields.[98] Concomitant with the French understanding of colonization, which in contrast to the British was far more centralized and focused on the assimilation of their subjects, football in the colonies quickly was linked to football in the motherland.[99] In 1938, a total of 147 Africans played in the top two divisions in France. The African football association, which was founded in 1957, gave itself a French rather than an English name.

By contrast, football was not able to succeed in India, "the pearl" of the British Empire.[100] The Indian Football Association (IFA) was established in 1888 under the influence of the British military, and the first two leagues were established in Calcutta and Bombay in 1898 and 1902, respectively. However, football could not seriously challenge cricket and field hockey, the favored outlets of the Anglo-Indian elite, in their position as the Indian national sports.[101]

In Ireland, it was predominantly the Protestants, who were loyal to Great Britain, who played football according the rules of the FA

97. See Rogan Taylor and Andreas Skrypietz, "'Pull the trigger—shoot the nigger': Fussball und Rassismus in England," in *Fussball und Rassismus* (Göttingen: Werkstatt, 1993), 73–106; as well as Phil Vasili, *Colouring Over the White Line: The History of Black Footballers in Britain* (Edinburgh: Mainstream Publishing, 2000).

98. Worms City Archives 13/2243: II; report from the police administration, March 15, 1920.

99. With regard to the colonial sports policy of France, see Bernadette Deville-Danthu, *Le Sport en noir et blanc: Du sport colonial au sport africain dans les anciens territoires français d'Afrique occidentale (1920–1965)* (Paris: Harmattan, 1997).

100. See Tony Mason, "Football on the Maidan: Cultural Imperialism in Calcutta," in *The Cultural Bond: Sport, Empire, Society*, ed. J. A. Mangan (London: Frank Cass, 1992), 142–53.

101. Concerning Indian cricket, see Ramachandra Guha, "Politik im Spiel: Cricket und Kolonialismus in Indien," *Historische Anthropologie* 4 (1996): 157–72.

Catholic-nationalist circles founded the Gaelic Athletic Association for the Preservation and Cultivation of National Pastimes (GAA) in 1884. Then, in 1885, among other initiatives, the GAA issued its own set of rules for football.[102] Gaelic football was played with a round ball, but did not entirely exclude the use of the hands. The GAA established the first All-Ireland Championships in 1887 for the sports of hurling and Gaelic football, although only 12 of the 32 counties participated. As a result of the anti-British Easter Uprising by the Sinn-Féin movement in 1916, the GAA was banned by the British government in July 1918. However, the game survived. On November 21, 1920, British troops shot twelve spectators and a player in Dublin's Croke Park on the occasion of a Gaelic football game between Dublin and Tipperary. This event, which has gone down as the first Bloody Sunday in Irish history, marked a high point in the low-intensity war between the Irish nationalists and British troops that ended in 1921 with the recognition of the Irish Free State with only loose ties to the British crown. As a result of Irish migration throughout the world, offshoots of the GAA have been established in England, Scotland, the United States, Australia, and continental Europe. Since 1974, there has also been a Ladies Gaelic Football Association.

The British colonial settlements in Australia, New Zealand, and Canada, which as "dominions" achieved ever increasing rights of self-administration over the course of the nineteenth and twentieth century, underlined their claims to independence by refusing to accept the rules of the FA. In a similar manner, the former British colonies along the east coast of North America, which had been independent since 1776, established the rules for American football in 1873–74. In Australia, a home-grown game developed out of a mixture of rugby and Gaelic football—Australian Rules Football, or footy for short. A set of rules for this game was codified by 1858. The founding of the Victorian Football Association followed in 1896, which expanded through the country and rendered footy the most important spectator sport in Australia.[103] Although this variety of football now has clubs in more than 40 countries, outside of Australia it has only a marginal existence. In New Zealand, the domi-

102. On this point, see Mike Cronin, *Sport and Nationalism in Ireland: Gaelic Games, Soccer and Irish Identity since 1884* (Dublin: Four Courts Press, 1999).

103. However, it was not renamed the Australian Football League until 1990.

nant sport is Rugby Union Football, which also has claimed an important position in Australia. In Canada, where the first organized football games took place in the 1860s, and where the Hamilton Foot Ball Club was founded as the first club in 1869, a new and independent sport grew out of Rugby Union Football, which also was separate from American football. A Rugby Football Union was founded in Ontario and Quebec in 1883, and the next year the Canadian Rugby Football Union was established. The latter set down a *Code of Rules for Canadian Football* that underwent numerous changes over the following years and decades, sometimes in connection with divisions or new foundations of the association. In 1909, Governor-General Lord Earl Grey established the Grey Cup as the highest prize in Canadian football. The Canadian Football League was created in 1958.

Football remained a game of the elite for about half a century. In Great Britain, this period extended from the school reforms of the 1830s and 1840s up through establishment of working-class clubs in the 1880s. On the continent and in Latin America, this period lasted from the introduction of the sport in the 1860s up through the First World War. In both Great Britain and in the countries that followed her, the elite phase of football is divided into two phases: the first half in the schools, and the second half that was characterized by the establishment of clubs and associations. During the second phase, there were already signs of unorganized football activities among the lower classes.[104]

This wave of foundations reached a high point with the establishment of the Fédération Internationale de Football Association (FIFA) in 1904.[105] In the beginning, the future world football association had only seven participating nations, France, the Netherlands, Belgium, Denmark, Spain, Sweden, and Switzerland. The FA did not even respond to the invitation to the organizational meeting.[106] The FA did recognize FIFA in the

---

104. See, for example, Richard Holt, "Working Class Football and the City: The Problem of Continuity," *International Journal of the History of Sport* 3 (1986): 5–17; Christiane Eisenberg et al., *FIFA 1904–2004: 100 Jahre Weltfußball.* (Göttingen: Werkstatt, 2004), 17; and Christian Koller, "Transnationalität und Popularisierung—Thesen und Fragen zur Frühgeschichte des Schweizer Fußballs," *Ludica* 17–18 (2011–12): 151–66.

105. See Alan Tomlinson, "Going Global: The FIFA Story," in his book *The Game's Up: Essays in the Cultural Analysis of Sport, Leisure and Popular Culture* (Aldershot: Ashgate, 1999), 99–102.

106. England boycotted the football World Cup until 1950.

following years. However, before the end of the 1920s, it withdrew two times from the world football association for a variety of reasons. The establishment of FIFA laid the foundation for the organization of international competitions. Indeed, as soon as FIFA was established, people were dreaming of an international tournament. A world championship for club teams was planned and the final round was supposed to take place in Switzerland in 1906. However, at the end of the invitation period, not a single application to participate in the competition had been received. In contrast to the Union Internationale Amateur de Football Association (UIAFA), which competed with FIFA for a short time and organized a European championship in 1911, FIFA hesitated, and then decided instead to recognize the victor of the Olympic football tournament as amateur world champion. The outbreak of war in 1914 forced the cancellation of any further planning.

The First World War, which divided the "bourgeois century" from the "age of the masses," also led to a major fissure in the history of football. Its motherland, although among the victorious nations, lost its dominant position in the world. The United States, which shortly before 1900 had become the leading industrialized nation, emerged for the first time as a great political power as well. Soon afterward, her *cultural* influence also began to increase in the old world. The Bolsheviks gained power in Russia in 1917 and began the first effort to create a classless society following the teachings of Marx. In central Europe, imperial power collapsed in 1918 and was inherited by ephemeral democracies. The "old and the rotted" had broken apart, as the Social Democrat Philipp Scheidemann shouted to the jubilant masses of workers from the balcony of the Reichstag building in November 1918.[107] A few years after the conclusion of peace, the first fascist dictators emerged, who survived largely on the basis of their demagogic appeals to the "masses." All of these factors had an important impact on the character of football. Across the world, it became what it had been in Great Britain since the *fin de siècle*, namely the people's game.

107. Philipp Scheidemann, *Memoiren eines Sozialdemokraten* (Dresden: Reissner-Verlag, 1928), 2:312.

3 | *The People's Game*

The rules of modern football, as shown above, were the creation of the elite public schools. The elite turned away indignantly from football at the very moment when urban workers and white-collar employees were caught up in football fever, and instead devoted their attention to disciplines like Alpinism and rugby. The task of this chapter is to show why the lower classes were so excited about the round leather. A few numbers serve to illustrate the triumphant advance of football during the late nineteenth century. In the 1888–89 season, 602,000 spectators attended the games of the first English professional league. Ten years later, there were more than five million fans in attendance. In particular, the cup finals, which since 1895 had been held at the Crystal Palace in London and marked the true high point of the season, mobilized the masses. Countless chartered trains were organized for the final games. In 1900, 69,000 spectators attended the match. Three years later, more than 120,000 fans pushed their way into the stadium.[1] There were about 12,000 clubs in the Football Association (FA) in 1914. Countless other athletes kicked the ball around during their free time in numerous company, school, and parish teams.[2]

A number of factors led to the triumph of football.[3] First, the industrialization of Great Britain led to a division between work and leisure. The female and male hourly workers at textile factories had regular time away from work, and also a certain amount of money to use for enter-

1. James Walvin, *The People's Game: The History of Football Revisited* (Edinburgh: Mainstream Publishing, 1994), 78.
2. Kaspar Maase, *Grenzenloses Vergnügen: Der Aufstieg der Massenkultur 1850–1970* (Frankfurt: Fischer Taschenbuch Verlag, 1997), 85.
3. See Schulze-Marmeling, *Fussball*, 30–43.

43

tainment. They had fought for Sunday afternoons and also Boxing Day as additional times for leisure. In addition, the unions had gained the nine-hour day for craftsmen and certain factory workers in 1874. Between 1873 and 1896, the cost of living shrank dramatically, so that substantially more money remained for leisure activities at the end of the week.

A commercialized leisure culture oriented to the interests of craftsmen and white-collar workers had already begun developing in Great Britain in the late eighteenth century. Some of these attractions, which now enjoyed increasing popularity, had their origins in the pre-modern society. These included taverns, fairs, religious feast days, boxing without gloves or time limits, and finally the bestial cock and dog fights. New attractions included the popular Victorian small theatres, the massive music halls, dime novels that largely attracted women, as well as short trips to the ocean, which were made possible by the growing network of railroads that were now affordable for the less well to do. However, once one reached the ocean, social distinctions were again obvious. The vacationers strolling along the various piers were divided by wealth and social reputation.[4]

Second, the fact that football became the most popular pasttime of all possible options is explained by the German football historian Dietrich Schulze-Marmeling as resulting from its affinity to industrial labor. Physical strength, toughness, good conditioning, and robustness were required in the mine as well as on the turf. Qualities such as intelligence and craftiness joined together with masculine "English hardiness" that could be used to outsmart the opposing defense as well as the suspicious foreman or the hated work inspector. Football is a team sport, but it also allows a player to "exercise his own will." One can dribble and not, as might be expected, pass. One can mock the opposing player and take joy in one's own accomplishment. In short, a person can display what

4. Regarding the "contemporaneous nature" of rural traditions and urban, commercialized, mass culture in the case of the large London annual fairs, see Mark Judd, "'The Oddest Combination of Town and Country': Popular Culture and the London Fairs, 1800–1860," in *Leisure in Britain, 1780–1939*, eds. John K. Walton and John Walvin (Manchester: Manchester University Press, 1983), 10–30. With regard to "penny-theatres" see, for example, Michael R. Booth, "East End and West End: Class and Audience in Victorian London," *Theatre Research International* 2 (1977): 98–103. For journeys to the sea, see, for example, James Walvin, *Beside the Seaside: A Social History of the Popular Seaside Holiday* (London: Viking, 1978); as well as J. Lowerson and J. Myerscough, *Time to Spare in Victorian England* (Brighton: The Harvester Press, 1977), 30–40.

the German historian Alf Lüdtke has conceptualized as *Eigen-Sinn* (independent thought).[5] Just as workers sought to exercise their own will and, in this way, struggle against the all-encompassing discipline that they endured, so too did the relatively open rules of football provide a place for creativity and "small" innovations. In addition, football was an inexpensive sport. It required only a modest infrastructure. In contrast to the comparatively more expensive cricket, it could be played on back lots and on the streets.

Third, philanthropic and paternalist entrepreneurs as well as the various confessions and denominations vigorously supported the founding of clubs. Workers should spend their free time usefully, and not loiter on the streets and get drunk on cheap whiskey. The intent, quite certainly, was to discipline a culture that was increasingly seen as threatening. This support by the elite contradicts the long-held and overly simplified view that football was a central element in an autonomous working-class culture. The offer from "above" was gladly accepted from "below." However, over time football developed its own dynamic that was very difficult to control.

British social history of the 1970s was devoted to the grand narrative of the linear development of the lower classes into a homogenous working class that was committed to socialism. A trailblazer of this purely teleological historiography was E. P. Thompson, a social historian who was also a political activist.[6] Under the impact of the spectacular success of the neo-liberal and nationalist politics of Margaret Thatcher in traditionally left-voting but socially conservative urban strongholds, younger historians beginning in the mid-1980s pointed to opposing developments and raised multiple objections. Their interest was focused now on the role of smaller communities in creating identities, particularly the street and the public house. They also considered popular patriotism that was inculcated with imperial ideas, as expressed, for example, in a chauvinist manner in the music halls (jingoism), as well as particular gender roles.[7] The consensus in this newer scholarship is that rituals

---

5. See Alf Lüdtke, "Eigen-Sinn: Lohn, Pausen, Neckereien: *Eigensinn* und Politik bei Fabrikarbeitern in Deutschland um 1900," in Alf Lüdtke, *Fabrikalltag, Arbeitserfahrungen und Politik vom Kaiserreich bis in den Faschismus* (Hamburg: Ergebnisse Verlag, 1993), 120–60, especially 136–43.

6. E. P. Thompson, *The Making of the English Working Class* (London: Victor Gollancz, 1963).

7. See the exceptional summary of the state of the question by Rohan McWilliam, *Popular*

played a key role in the creation of collective identities. These periodic, sensual, and collective manifestations served both to construct the social ties of a group and, at the same time, reduce social disharmonies.[8] According to recent cultural and micro-historical research, the identities of the workers can be understood as a patchwork of heterogeneous elements. In our view, football in many ways played an integral role in the creation of elements of these identities.

City and Identity

The beginning came with the growth of the cities. The urbanization of Great Britain in the nineteenth century was unprecedented. In addition to the steadily growing metropolis of London, the cities of Lancashire—including Liverpool and the entire Greater Merseyside area—as well as Tyneside in the northeast and the towns of south Wales grew into industrial centers. Birmingham, Manchester, and Glasgow also experienced unprecedented population growth. By 1850, more than half of the inhabitants of Great Britain lived in cities. Blackpool on the Irish Sea, one of the birthplaces of professional football, had 4,000 inhabitants in 1861. Fifty years later, in 1911, there were already 58,000 inhabitants, and in 1921 around 100,000 people lived there.[9] Middlesborough, a city "which had won a name without a history, an importance without antiquity,"[10] had a middling population of 7,431 inhabitants in 1851, only to reach 100,000 inhabitants by the turn of the century. In 1851, there were ten cities in Great Britain with populations over 100,000. In 1911, there were thirty-six. Most of the inhabitants of the new large cities were immigrants, or

---

Politics in Nineteenth-Century England (London: Routledge, 1998). Also see John Belchem, *Popular Radicalism in Nineteenth-Century Britain* (New York: St. Martin's Press, 1996). With regard to the issue of gender, see, for example, Karl Ittman, *Work, Gender and Family in Victorian England* (New York: New York University Press, 1995).

8. Ritual is one of the most discussed ethnographical concepts. A splendid overview of the enormous literature concerning this concept is offered by the Scottish historian Edward Muir, *Ritual in Early Modern England* (Cambridge: Cambridge University Press, 1997), 6: "Ritual then is basically a social activity that is repetitive, standardized, a model or a mirror, and its meaning is inherently ambiguous."

9. Phillip J. Waller, *Town, City, and Nation: England 1850–1914* (Oxford: Oxford University Press, 1983), 4.

10. Asa Briggs, *Victorian Cities* (Berkeley, Calif.: University of California Press, 1993), 247.

their children, from the rural, agricultural regions of England, Ireland, or Scotland. In 1881, 212,000 men and women who had been born in Ireland lived in Lancashire. An additional 81,000 lived in London, 60,000 in Yorkshire, and 78,000 in Merseyside.[11] The large immigrant families often settled in the new, faceless developments, living in endless rows of identical brick houses. Relatives and acquaintances joined them and formed small communities, as in the new world, in America or Australia. Nevertheless, there was considerable geographic mobility, with strangers moving in next door, and leaving a short time later looking for work and fortune. People were torn from their ancestral social ties, from their cherished parishes or guilds, where periodic festivals gave them the opportunity to take stock and, not least, to patch up holes in their social networks. In 1808, there were forty-four holidays, but only four remained by 1834. Moreover, entrepreneurs seeking to maximize their profits succeeded in eliminating "blue Mondays," which had been a tradition of the journeymen in the craft trades. The doctrine of punctuality and discipline put a brusque end to the midweek holidays. This was symbolized by the factory sirens that summoned the workers to their machines early in the morning without pity.[12] The factories became ever larger. Some of them grew into anonymous corporations, such as the Great Western Railway in Swindon, an enterprise that tripled its staff between 1855 and 1914 to about 14,000 workers. During the same period, Tyneside, the region around Newcastle-upon-Tyne in northeastern England, had twelve shipyards in 1860, each of which employed more than 1,500 workers.[13]

If we begin with the Aristotelian conception that man is a *zoon politikon* (political creature), that people seek out relationships with other people and can only achieve self-actualization with others, it is hardly surprising that the immigrants and their children sought to ensure

11. Phillip J. Waller, *Democracy and Sectarianism: A Political and Social History of Liverpool 1868–1939* (Liverpool: Liverpool University Press, 1981), 9.

12. For an example of a suppressed holiday, see Alaun Howkins, "The Taming of Whitsun: The Changing Face of a Nineteenth-Century Rural Holiday," in Eileen Yeo and Stephen Yeo, *Popular Culture and Class Conflict: Explorations in the History of Labour and Leisure* (Brighton: Harvester Press, 1981), 187–208. With regard to the general suppression of the older popular culture, the standard work is P. Bailey, *Leisure and Class in Victorian England: Rational Recreation and the Contest of Control* (London: Routledge, 1978).

13. Eric Hobsbawm, "Die Entstehung der Arbeiterklasse (1870–1914)," in his book *Ungewöhnliche Menschen: Über Widerstand, Rebellion und Jazz* (Munich-Vienna: Hanser, 2001), 83.

a certain sense of belonging for themselves. A focus of this search for social stability was the public houses, the countless taverns and bars, which were facing increasing levels of criticism at this time.[14] Men drank together in pubs, sometimes to excess. They indulged in social drinking, and communicated with each other both verbally and nonverbally with gestures, including occasionally with their fists. If someone wished to show off and demonstrate his status, he went to the pub where he was already known. But important information and news could also be learned there. Barkeepers played an exceptionally important role in the commercialization of the sport. Even in the early modern period, they had organized seemingly archaic boxing matches and dog fights, bowling, and even rowing races.[15]

In the twentieth century, it was customary to have traveling musicians in the tap room. Fred Veitch (born 1926), who grew up in a pub as the son of a barkeeper and was, himself, a barkeeper for decades at Five Lions in York in northern England, said about this period in an interview with the historian Mick Race:

You've got to remember that pubs in those days (pre–Second World War) were the centre of entertainment. I can remember acrobats coming in and doing their turns, handstands and cartwheels and all that. You always had accordions and banjoes in the Five Lion, oh yes, and every night. Nearly all the pubs of any size would have a pianist, and you would pay the pianist, but these accordions, ukuleles, violins, just went round with a hat. I can remember me dad buyin' a radiogram before the war, and you had eight records that used to drop down, and I used to have to put the records on.[16]

---

14. The standard work regarding the history of pubs is Peter Clark, *The English Alehouse: A Social History, 1200–1830* (Harlow: Longman, 1983). For the "longue durée" perspective of popular leisure time activies, see James Walvin, *Leisure and Society, 1830–1950* (London: Longman, 1963). A summary of the state of the research regarding taverns and tavern keepers is available in Fabian Brändle, "Toggenburger Wirtshäuser und Wirte im 17. und 18. Jahrhundert," in *Obrigkeit und Opposition: Drei Beiträge zur Kulturgeschichte des Toggenburgs aus dem 17./18. Jahrhundert*, eds. Brändle et al. (Wattwil: Toggenburger Vereinigung für Heimatkunde, 1997), 7–51.

15. The authoritative study regarding the commercialization of leisure time is Robert Malcolmson, *Popular Recreations in English Society, 1750–1850* (Cambridge: Cambridge University Press, 1973). A particularly strong overview of the topic of popular cultures in the early modern period, which had received extensive scholarly attention, is offered by Barry Reay, *Popular Cultures in England 1550–1750* (London: Routledge, 1998).

16. Mike Race, *Public Houses, Public Lives: An Oral History of Life in York Pubs in the Mid-20th Century* (York: Voyager Publications, 1999), 95.

Customary games in York and other places included dominoes, billiards, darts, and a game called tippit that involved tossing coins. Increasing numbers of women came to the pubs during the course of the twentieth century, and particularly to participate in gaming competitions for which they were organized into ladies teams. Of the 129 fully licensed pubs in York in 1929, twenty-seven were run by women and an additional ten women, mostly widows, ran beer houses, of which there were twenty-seven in the city. Without the help of their wives and daughters, the men would not have been able to meet the high demands of both their customers and the breweries. A barkeeper's workday lasted more than ten hours, and in many cases, more than fourteen.[17]

In considering the resourcefulness of the barkeepers, both men and women, it is hardly surprising that the enterprising "landlords" recognized early that football was a profitable institution, and how to make a profit from it. The barkeepers were the true middlemen between commerce and popular culture, since they always had to keep up to date with what their guests wanted. According to the social historian Tony Mason, the presidents of the forty-six professional clubs in the period 1885–1915 were largely barkeepers and shopkeepers.[18] The lease-holder of the White Hart pub in the London neighborhood of Tottenham provided a field for the local Hotspurs. The backbone of Manchester United was the Three Crowns in the north of the city.[19] Often more important, however, were the frequently short-lived teams that were established by the regular customers of a pub. In a detailed study, D. D. Molyneux demonstrated that between 1876 and 1884 no fewer than thirteen teams were founded in Birmingham alone that bore the name of pubs.[20] Of the thirteen clubs in Sheffield in 1865, eleven had a public house as their postal address.[21] In the mid-1880s, entrepreneurial barkeepers began to provide the score of games for their customers. The club secretaries were enlisted to send

---

17. See ibid., 64–75 and 93–101.

18. Tony Mason, *Association Football and English Society, 1863–1918* (Brighton: The Harvester Press, 1980), 38 and 42.

19. Richard Holt, "Working Class Football and the City. The Problem of Continuity," *International Journal of the History of Sport* 3 (1986): 5–17.

20. D. D. Molyneux, "The Development of Physical Recreation in the Birmingham District from 1871–1892," Appendix A and B, PhD diss., University of Birmingham, 1957, cited in Holt, *Working Class Football*, 9.

21. Mason, *Association Football*, 51.

the results as quickly as possible, using the recently invented telegraph. Later, specialized thin publications, the "green'un," were posted on the walls of pubs. As communications became more rapid, there was a concomitant increase in interest in football. It was now possible to learn the results of the favorite team's game in a more useful timeframe, which meant that the standings could be discussed with friends.

In addition, the rapidly known results also led to countless wagers.[22] As Alan Metcalf demonstrated in a pioneering work of micro-history regarding the miners of Northumberland in northeastern England, interest in the sport was never simply a matter of fun. It was always bound up with gambling, jackpots, and other smaller money prizes.[23] Bets rarely went higher than a penny, but a really good result could bring the lucky winner a very welcome boost to the always limited household and leisure budget. As Ross McKibbin has made clear, betting among the workers was marked by a high degree of honesty, and was transformed, as a consequence, into a form of workers' self-help. In 1920, there were perhaps five million regular betters, who wagered millions of pounds sterling. Admittedly, horse racing was, far and away, the most popular outlet for betting, but betting steadily increased on football as well.[24] Football soon became the main topic of conversation in the pubs and was, according to Eric Hobsbawm, a true *"lingua Franca* of social discourse among men, and a part of the environment for *every* worker."[25]

In addition to the "green 'un" there were soon specialized sporting journals, which led to an increase in interest in both football and betting. For example, the weekly *Athletic News,* which appeared in Manchester in 1875, reached an enormous circulation of fifty thousand by 1891. J. Bentley, who was the publisher of this paper, served as president of the Football League from 1893 to 1910, and thus had a vested interest in popularizing the sport. In the 1890s, the *Sporting News,* the *Sports-*

22. J. M. Golby and A. W. Purdue, *The Civilization of the Crowd: Popular Culture in England 1750–1900* (New York: Schocken Books, 1985), 170–72.

23. Alan Metcalfe, "Organized Sport in the Mining Communities of South Northumberland, 1800–1899," *Victorian Studies* 24 (1982): 477. See also, by the same author, "Potshare Bowling in the Mining Communities of East Northumberland," in *Sport and the Working Class in Modern Britain,* ed. Richard Holt (Manchester: Manchester University Press, 1990), 29–44.

24. Ross McKibbin, "Working-Class Gambling in Britain, 1880–1939," *Past and Present* 82 (1979): 147–78.

25. Hobsbawm, *Entstehung der Arbeiterklasse,* 95.

man, and the *Sporting Chronicle* all achieved impressive circulations.[26] As a result, many newspapers began to publish sporting news in their popular evening editions.[27]

The breweries also benefitted from the football boom. They did their best to generate further enthusiasm. Gathered in an umbrella organization, the Country Brewers' Society (CBS), the breweries were a powerful pressure group that exercised noteworthy influence on William Gladstone's Liberal Party.[28] The brewers utilized numerous well-staged, media-savvy campaigns in their struggle against the many bourgeois church and left-leaning temperance and abstinence movements.[29] The slogan "Hands off the Poor Man's Beer! Don't we know when we've had enough, why should we drink tee total stuff?"[30] could be read on one of the many billboards of the CBS. The organization acted against the infantilization of the "freeborn Englishman" who understood the difference between a well-deserved drink after work and the excessive consumption of whiskey.

The brewery owner John H. Davies saved the professional Manchester United team from ruin in 1902, and seven years later financed the construction of the legendary Old Trafford, a stadium that could accommodate tens of thousands of spectators. Two years earlier, Davies had transformed United into a joint-stock corporation, an example that the presidents of most of the British professional clubs soon followed. The main shareholders of the club, as might be expected, included a conspicuously large number of barkeepers and small shop keepers. The average price of a share was around one pound sterling. However, less expensive shares, costing ten or even five shillings made it possible for workers, at least symbolically, to own a share of the club, although their dividends

26. McKibbin, *Working-Class Gambling*, 166.

27. Ulrich Matheja, "Soziale Aspekte des englischen Fussballs im 19. Jahrhundert," *Elf* 7 (1987): 24.

28. See, for example, Peter Mathias, "The Brewing Industry. Temperance and Politics," *Historical Journal* 1 (1958): 97–114; and David W. Gutzke, *Protecting the Pub: Brewers and Publicans against Temperance* (Woodbridge: Boydell Press, 1989).

29. Concerning the advocates for temperance, see the classical work by Brian Harrison, *Drink and the Victorians: The Temperance Question in England, 1817–1872* (London: Faber and Faber, 1971). Also see the survey by Norman Longmate, *The Waterdrinkers: A History of Temperance* (Edinburgh: Hamilton, 1968).

30. Gutzke, *Protecting the Pub*, cover page.

were correspondingly lower.[31] Beginning in 1881, William Suddell, the owner of the Peel Cotton Mill, located in Preston in northern England, devoted his attention to the local club, Preston North End. Suddell began to pay his best players on a regular basis, and thereby transformed his club into one of the most successful teams during the late nineteenth century. When he brought the Londoner John Goodall, the best middle striker of the epoch whose nickname was "Johnny Allgood," to Preston, he found a man who would be responsible for the North End being undefeated in twenty-two championship games, and becoming the first English champion in the 1888–89 season.[32]

John Houlding (1833–1902) from Liverpool, like John H. Davies a major brewer and hotelier, was masterful at combining patronage with politics. Houlding was an alderman and later mayor of his home city (1897–98), chairman of the Conservative Association of Everton, a member of the strongly Protestant and unionist Orange Order, a freemason, as well as an important sponsor of Everton FC, which he transformed into one of the leading professional teams in England up through 1890.[33] Because he raised the rent for the stadium, half of which belonged to him, from £100 to £250 in the space of three years, and monopolized the food stalls and eateries around the stadium, sharp protests were raised against the high-handed actions of the patron during the meeting of the membership in 1891. Without further ado, John Houlding tore up the rental agreement for the location on Anfield Road, and Everton F.C. moved to Goodison on the other side of Stanley Park. The FL decided that Everton could keep its name and, in addition, could play in the First Division. Houlding then went to Scotland to scout out talented professionals with whom he substantially strengthened the Liverpool Football Club with the result that within two years, that club rose from the semi-professional Lancashire division into the First Division. Liverpool then earned the nickname Team of Macs because of the play of their skillful Scottish ball handlers.[34]

Houlding was the prototype of the Victorian patron, who wished to

31. Schulze-Marmeling, *Fussball*, 42.

32. Alfredo W. Pöge, "Der 'goldene Schuh'—postum (Europas erfolgreichste Liga-Torschützen 1888–1900)," *Elf* 4 (1986): 16.

33. Waller, *Democracy and Sectarianism*, 495.

34. Walvin, *The People's Game*, 88. Also see Matheja, *Soziale Aspekte*, 20.

make his status as a self-made man publicly visible through the sponsorship of a sports team, but then went along the unconventional path of allowing the fans to celebrate him in the stadium and thereby accumulate symbolic capital in the sense set out by Pierre Bourdieu. He therefore stood in the centuries-old tradition of festively staged election campaigns which included the provision of food and drink as well as the patronage of various revelries.[35] The gentry, the lower rural aristocracy in England, had tried to use both lease agreements and generosity to keep the voting-eligible freeholders from doing them any harm. With his decidedly anti-Irish and anti-Catholic prejudices, Houlding attempted to mobilize numerous Protestant workers, both English and those from Ulster, because the Catholic Irish, who often worked for lower wages, were hated by members of these groups.[36] In many ways, Houlding anticipated the populist, fame-seeking, headstrong, aggressive but also affable club presidents who still attract attention in smaller cities today.

The American Charles Korr demonstrated the ways in which this paternalistic style of leadership continued to function over several generations in his study of the London club West Ham United.[37] The club had its origins in the working-class club Thames Ironworks FC in the proletarian east end of the metropolis. West Ham was founded by the owner of the factory Arnold F. Hills in 1895 after the end of a strike. The year before, in 1894, Hills had introduced the eight-hour working day so that his company was not disturbed by the great London Engineers Strike three years later. This patron offered other "games" to his workers in addition to football, including, for example, theater and concerts. The doctrine of the club claimed that the executives, players, workers, and other supporters would form one large family. This appealed to Korr, who lived for

35. See, for example, Frank O'Gorman, "Campaign Rituals and Ceremonies: The Social Meaning of Elections in England 1780–1860," *Past and Present* 135 (1992): 79–115; James Epstein, "Rituals of Solidarity: Radical Dining, Toasting and Symbolic Expression," in his book *Radical Expression: Political Language, Ritual, and Symbol in England, 1790–1850* (Oxford: Oxford University Press, 1994), 147–65.

36. With regard to the complex and often hostile relationship of English radicals to immigrant Irish Catholics, see, for example, John Belchem, "English Working-Class Radicalism and the Irish, 1815–1850," in R. Swift and S. Gilley, *The Irish in the Victorian City* (London: Croom Helm, 1985), 85–97.

37. Charles Korr, *West Ham United: The Making of a Football Club* (London: Duckworth, 1986). Also see S. Tischler, *Footballers and Businessmen: The Origins of Professional Soccer in England* (London: Holmes & Meier Publishers, 1981).

a lengthy period in the East End and thoroughly adopted the strongly expressed claims of the London dockers that they formed an extended family: "East Londoners have maintained a strong sense of extended family, which is one of the reasons why the club was and is so important to people. West Ham United shows that this community is different and important."[38] The workers had no say on the board of directors, however, which was expanded through a process of internal selection. This fact led to Korr's most important thesis: "In the creation of West Ham United, as in so many other areas of English life, working-class participation was limited to work either as players or as supporters."[39] It certainly appeared at the end of the century as if the employers had recognized the social-disciplinary character of football and integrated it into their long-held strategy of divide-and-rule.

Another important source of patronage came from the various churches and denominations. The ideological basis for this engagement with football came from "muscular Christianity," which began to spread in the mid-nineteenth century.[40] The worker was supposed to learn that a healthy body was pleasing to God and protected him from moral decline and eternal damnation. Many clubs had their origins in a religious milieu. As late as 1885, 25 of the 112 clubs in Liverpool had a religious background.[41] It appears that the numerous free churches, which characterized and still characterize Great Britain, were courting the favor of the workers as they established football clubs. In Britain, even the market in religion was largely liberalized. Celtic Glasgow was founded by a member of a Catholic religious order, while the Bolton Wanderers played their first game as Christ Church FC. The anecdote spread quite widely that football players for this club emancipated themselves from the church when the vicar had demanded that they all attend services regularly. The Wanderers transferred their headquarters to a pub across the street from the church.[42] In one last example, Aston Villa, which

38. Ibid., 209.

39. Ibid., 16.

40. Bruce Haley, *The Healthy Body and Victorian Culture* (Cambridge, Mass.: Harvard University Press, 1978); George Lewis, "The Muscular Christianity Movement," *Journal of Health, Physical Education, and Recreation* 37 (1966): 27–42; and Schulze-Marmeling, *Fussball*, 39.

41. Walvin, *The People's Game*, 59.

42. Ibid., 40; and also see Golby, *Civilization of the Crowd*, 166.

dominated professional English football during the 1890s, grew out of a Methodist bible school in Birmingham.[43]

In addition to the pub and the parish, streets and neighborhoods formed important points of reference for city residents and immigrants. Richard Holt who, along with Tony Mason, James Walvin, and Nicholas Fishwick, was one of the pioneers in investigating football from a social historical perspective, used the expressive term "street corner society" to denote the urban society of the lower social classes in the nineteenth century. By this he meant a society in which social activity took place out in the open, with admired local original characters such as hard-nosed men standing on the corners and youth gangs in whose rough rituals one can see similarities to the early-modern fraternities. The author Alan Sillitoe, who was himself a working-class child from Nottingham, admirably described this street corner society in his autobiographical novel *Saturday Night and Sunday Morning*, which was published in 1958.[44] The street was the place where the youth were socialized, where they emulated the local bruisers, and it was often the street that gave its name to the local club.[45] Just like the public house, the street was the living expression of the community of the old style where large parts of the social lives of the inhabitants played out. Honor and shame, masculinity and reputation, to name just a few of the key values of working-class culture, were handled publicly. The trouble-seeking bands of youths faced off against the other neighborhoods just like the football teams of the various housing blocks. David Smith observed that the ball they used to play football on the back lots and in the streets "was a sack made up of sawdust and rags, see. Perhaps might have an inner leather doings."[46] And just as the gangs of youths had fought each other during church holidays following a recurring script, now the lads of the neighborhood competed against each other, in so far as they participated in sports, although sports and violence often did overlap with each other. Moreover, as a rule, a defeat in a ball game would be avenged with bruises and black eyes. Nevertheless, despite all of the brutality and violence, it should be kept in mind

43. Matheja, *Soziale Aspekte*, 14.
44. Alan Sillitoe, *Saturday Night and Sunday Morning* (London: W. H. Allen, 1958).
45. Holt, *Working Class Football*, 8.
46. Citation from Steven Humphries, *Hooligans or Rebels? An Oral History of Working Class Childhood and Youth, 1889–1939* (Oxford: Blackwell, 1981), 203.

that this was usually limited to fist fights and that deaths were very rare. The ritualized violence served to release aggression in rapidly growing cities that were characterized by substantial social tensions. There were no similar opportunities in the rapidly expanding American boomtowns of the nineteenth century, especially in the company towns of the frontier. Because men generally possessed firearms and the whites, in particular, could claim in court that they acted in self-defense, a very high percentage of these conflicts ended with a death.[47]

Fundamentally, the inhabitants of the newer and rapidly growing large cities made use of a pre-modern repertoire of social places and rituals to make their community perceptible and to renew it. Many football matches took place on traditional holidays. Christmas was used early on for football matches. It was also common to play on the morning after Christmas (Boxing Day) and also on New Year's Day, generally against local opponents. New Year's matches quickly developed into the most popular events, above all in Glasgow where the derby between the Catholic Celtic team and the Protestant Rangers regularly attracted more than 50,000 spectators in the years before the First World War.[48] The name "derby" derived from the Shrove Tuesday custom, noted above, in which hundreds of men from the city of the same name sought for hours, using considerable violence, to maneuver a ball through the gate of the opposite side of the city. The noble upper class participated as spectators and as well-wishing patrons of this unpretentious game by providing the competitors with drink and food, and offering prize money to the victors. After a strongly puritanical city administration banned the game in 1845, cavalry had to be deployed to keep the protesting citizens in check. In the following years, troops were always kept ready to disperse the sporting enthusiasts. A reader of the *Derby and Chesterfield Reporter* wrote on February 7, 1845: "It is all disappointment, no sports and no football. This is the way they always treat poor folks."[49] According to An-

47. See, for example, Claire V. McKanna, *Homicide, Race, and Justice in the American West, 1890–1920* (Tucson, Ariz.: University of Arizona Press, 1997), especially 78–116 and 156–58 (equipped with an extensive bibliography).

48. Holt, *Working Class Football*, 13.

49. Anthony Delves, "Popular Recreation and Social Conflict in Derby, 1800–1850," in *Popular Culture and Class Conflict 1590–1914*, eds. Eileen Yeo and Stephen Yeo (Brighton: Harvester Press, 1981), 94.

thony Delves, who is the author of the basic work on this spectacle and its suppression, as late as 1853 there were still serious efforts being made to guard against this unloved game. From this point onwards, the wild activities took place in the fields outside of the city gates. Horse racing took the place of the wild football game. Finally, according to the social historian James Walvin, shinney, a local variant of folk football in the Midlands city of Nottingham, was the origin of modern football.[50]

The struggle of the lower classes for an autonomous area within the thickly settled inner cities and their decades long struggle to obtain green spaces, with their intrinsic connotations of power, is evidenced in the popular claims to autonomous social sites.[51] During the nineteenth century, at least, it simply was not possible to utilize empty meadows or fields located outside the cities. Police and armed gamekeepers saw to it that the exclusive rights of the upper classes to hunt and fish, privileges that dated back to the *ancien régime*, remained undisturbed. The right to "rambling and roaming," which was the name for wandering in the moors and hilly country outside the city, was highly contested well into the twentieth century. As a contemporary recalled, it was often necessary to travel long distances on the train to be able to play football. Even so, there was always the threat that the police would bring an early end to the fun. The same man observed that when a group began singing the popular song "Nelly Dean" on the train, a conductor intervened and severely chastised the singers.[52]

When they finally gained free spaces, such spaces were used for political events, including speeches by the radical orator Hunt, or as places to listen to the demands of the Chartists for universal suffrage, but also for theatrical and sporting events. Groundbreaking micro-historical case studies illustrate the tenacious decades-long struggle in the cities of London, Newcastle, Norwich, and Bristol.[53] The free space for community-

50. Walvin, *The People's Game*, 65.

51. With regard to the concept of social sites where resistance can be practiced and handed on, see James C. Scott, *Domination and the Arts of Resistance: Hidden Transcripts* (New Haven, Conn.: Yale University Press, 1990), especially 120–23.

52. See Humphries, *Hooligans or Rebels*, 205; H. Hill, *Freedom to Roam: The Struggle for Access to Britain's Moors and Mountains* (Ashbourne: Mooreland, 1980); and Robert Storch, "The Plague of Blue Locusts: Police Reform and Popular Resistance in Northern England 1840–57," *International Review of Social History* 20 (1975): 61–90.

53. For London see Alan Taylor, "Common-Stealers, Land-Grabbers and Jerry Builders:

based radicalism was defended, when necessary, with violence against attacks by the authorities.[54] The model here was the pre-modern riot, a disciplined protest that is directed toward a goal that is felt to be just.[55] The regular, communal journey to the football stadium that, as a rule, stood in the middle of the working-class district, made visible the collective claim to a social space that was not controlled from above. The stadium, in contrast to the concurrently flourishing vaudeville theaters, such as the Nickelodeon or Lunapark, was a purely masculine refuge. It was a place where a man did not have to make allowances for the presence of women. Correspondingly, men could, if they wished, swear, drink, chew tobacco and then spit it on the ground.[56] Participation by the upper classes was not well received. In the stadium, the common man was king, and settled disputes according to his own rough lights.

Just as opera houses and monumental train stations symbolized the bourgeoisie, the new stately stadiums were the pride of the small man.[57] The rapidly growing network of streetcars meant that the arenas could be reached quickly from far off neighborhoods. These streetcars were an element of modern urbanism that marked off the city dwellers from the backwoods, agricultural population. This was a world to which their grandparents or parents had belonged just a short time before. Farmers and oxen desired to spend their lives working in the fields, and

---

Space, Popular Radicalism and the Politics of Public Access in London, 1848–1880," *International Review of Social History* 40 (1995): 383–407. For Newcastle see Alan Metcalfe, "Sport and Space: A Case Study of the Growth of Recreational Facilites in North East Northumberland, 1850–1914," *International Journal of the History of Sport* 7 (1990): 258–64. For Norwich see Neil McMaster, "The Battle for Mousehold Heath, 1857–1884: Popular Politics and the Victorian Public Park," *Past and Present* 127 (1990): 117–54. For Bristol see Steve Poole, "'Til our liberties be secure': Popular Sovereignty and Public Space in Bristol, 1780–1850," *Urban History* 26 (1999): 40–54.

54. McMaster, *The Battle of Mousehold Heath*, 153.

55. See John Bohstedt, "The Moral Economy of the Crowd and the Discipline of Historical Context," *Journal of Social History* 26 (1992–93): 265–84; and John Stevenson, *Popular Disturbances in England, 1700–1832* (London: Routledge, 1992).

56. This was also true of American baseball stadiums that were constructed at the same time. See David Nasaw, *Going Out: The Rise and the Fall of Public Amusements* (Cambridge, Mass.: Harvard University Press, 1999), 96–103.

57. With regard to the representative function of train stations and opera houses for the British bourgeoisie see, for example, Eric J. Hobsbawm, *The Age of Capital 1848–1875* (London: Weidenfeld and Nicolson, 1975), 288–90. For the representational character of early baseball stadiums in the U.S., which fulfilled similar functions as British football stadiums, see Lawrence S. Ritter, *Lost Ballparks: A Celebration of Baseball's Legendary Fields* (New York: Studio, 1992), especially 20.

thereby bored themselves to death. The city-dwellers, by contrast, went out and regularly enjoyed their free time. They enjoyed the freedom that had been made available to them, and sucked in the growing range of entertainments as a sort of elixir of life.

As the two Austrian urban historians Wolfgang Maderthaner and Lutz Musner have shown, the city is "not only a spatial and social form of the modern life, it is above all the bearer of a decidedly modern consciousness."[58] They distinguish in this context between the center and suburbs of Vienna. The immigrants from rural areas, who lived in the suburbs, had a thoroughly ambivalent view of the necessary modifications that took place in their manner of life. In the Vienna of the *belle époque*, according to Maderthaner and Musner, the inhabitants of the suburbs maintained their oral culture, their dialects, their obscenities and jokes, as well as their songs as a defense against assimilation by the center.[59] It was often the second generation that adopted modern culture, which led to generational conflicts. It would be worthy task to situate the place of football in this highly complex micro-historical process.

The analogies between the football year and the Christian calendar are obvious to the observer. Lent/Easter as the highpoint of the Christian liturgical year can, in our view, be compared with the escalating intensity at the end of a season when both relegated teams and champions are decided, and the eagerly awaited cup finals are finally approaching.[60] Eric Hobsbawm, one of the foremost historians of our age, correctly described football as a secular religion.[61] In addition to the similar structure in the organization of the year, there are other conspicuous parallels between football and religion. These include countless customary

58. Wolfgang Maderthaner and Lutz Musner, *Die Anarchie der Vorstadt: Das andere Wien um 1900* (Frankfurt: Campus, 2000), 45. A foundational study for understanding for the relationship between countryside and city is Raymond Williams, *The Country and the City* (London: Chatto & Windus, 1973). Also see Henri Lefebvre, *Die Revolution der Städte* (Frankfurt: Athenäum, 1990). David Nasaw, *Going Out*, 4, stresses these aspects in an American context.

59. Maderthaner und Musner, *Anarchie der Vorstadt*, 46.

60. Concerning the traditional cycle of festivals, see Ronald Hutton, *The Rise and Fall of Merry England: The Ritual Year 1400–1700* (Oxford: Oxford University Press, 1996). Regarding the influence of Protestantism on the festival calendar, see David Cressy, *Bonfires and Bells: National Memory and the Protestant Calendar in Elizabethan and Stuart England* (London: The History Press, 1980).

61. Eric J. Hobsbawm, *Worlds of Labour: Further Studies in the History of Labour* (London: Pantheon Books, 1984), 185.

rituals and ceremonies, clear and unambiguous distinctions between good and evil, and participation from the cradle to the grave.[62]

With all due respect to the culture of camaraderie of laborers and white-collar workers, we should not forget that it also suppressed serious conversations, and that more sensitive spirits were pushed into the corner. Beery conversations about sports helped to paper over contradictions in one's private life. When Arthur Seaton, the protagonist in Alan Sillitoe's novel *Saturday Night and Sunday Morning*, who was a true madcap, hard-drinking, streetwise roughneck and sly ladies' man got the clear signal in the pub from Jack, his true friend and rival for the beautiful lady, Brenda, that he wished to speak with him, Arthur soon found a means of getting out of trouble.

Instead, he drew him into a conversation about football, and over their third pint Jack was declaiming on how Notts would get into the second division next year. Everyone at the club put in their various pieces of knowledge, using imagination when knowledge failed. Arthur had little to say, and ordered more pints for himself and Jack.... "But you've got to think of last week's transfer from Hull," Jack said, arguing skillfully, taking the other pint that the barkeeper passed to his table.... Arthur listened in a dreamlike way, happy from the beer he had drunk, dimly remembering the cold earth of the dark wood where he had lain with Brenda, hours ago: he had heard all about football before.[63]

In his magnificent novel *Last Orders*, another author, Graham Swift, criticized the superficiality of pub culture that removed individuality, history, and depth from people.[64] The author had to employ some very unusual tricks to compel the protagonists, who were four old friends, to confront each other. First, a friend of many decades had to die in order for them to find their way out of their comfortable rut of beer and slogans, wipe the slate clean, and finally consider speaking with one another. When the enormously different life stories finally come out, it becomes clear to the reader how widely the inner and outer selves of the men diverged from one another.

62. The classic interpretation of football as ritual is Morris, *Spiel,* particularly 31–112.
63. Sillitoe, *Saturday Night*, 56–57.
64. See Graham Swift, *Last Orders* (London: Picador, 1986).

Boundaries against the Other and the First Idols

Collective identity is constructed through community rituals and the establishment of boundaries. The social historian Asa Briggs pointed to these factors in a study of the protracted rivalry between the authorities in Leeds and Bradford. This competition was expressed, among other means, through the construction of neoclassical city halls and the installation of the most comprehensive possible system of gas lights in the center of the city.[65] The lower classes hoped to utilize a successful football team in precisely this manner. Matches against city rivals or against the team from a neighboring city attracted masses of spectators, not only in Birmingham or Glasgow, but also in Lancashire where the triangle encompassing Bolton, Blackburn, and Darwen witnessed the birth of modern professional football. In their efforts to defeat their rivals, club presidents gave ever higher bounties to their own players, and then actual salaries. Finally, bowing to the inevitable, they brought in highly capable Scottish players from beyond the nearby border.[66] Middlesborough Ironopolis, a team from a city without "a history or tradition" (J. P. Waller), obtained an entirely new group of players in just three days in 1893, a move intended to make the club the equal of their hated rivals from Huddersfield and Preston. For politically ambitious patrons of the cut of a Houlding, victory in the derby was particularly well suited to increase their prestige and thereby their clientele. In northeastern England, both the teams and the supporters of Newcastle United and Sunderland FC soon were engaged in bitter contests. Intracity matches mobilized masses of spectators in Liverpool, Manchester, Nottingham, Birmingham, Sheffield, and naturally the metropolis of London, where a dozen teams were soon competing in the various professional leagues.[67] City championships, with their institutionalized Derbies, particularly in Glasgow and Edinburgh, were among the first regular competitions in the history of football.[68]

65. Briggs, *Victorian Cities*, 150–57.

66. See Robert W. Lewis, "The Genesis of Professional Football: Bolton-Blackburn-Darwen, the Centre of Innovation 1878–85," *International Journal of the History of Sport* 14 (1997): 21–54.

67. Holt, *Working Class Football and the City*, 13.

68. See, for example, Robert McCutcheon, "'Edinburgh Football Association Cup' (1875–1888) & 'East of Scotland Football Association Challenge Shield' (1888–1900)," *Elf* 4 (1986):

It was possible to make contacts with like-minded strangers in the standing-room sections and on the bleachers of the new stadiums in the larger cities, and to establish a new kind of community outside of the street or the pub. Joining together in singing songs (a common pub tradition), the ringing of small bells, the wearing of scarves, and carrying painted umbrellas and banners in the team colors met the need for conspicuous symbols for the developing group identity.[69] According to Ian Crump's micro-historical study of Leicester, from the very beginning most fans were exceptionally loyal supporters of their teams, who always came together, suffered together, were anxious together, and rejoiced together.[70] Thus, the stadium provided a new forum for sociability.[71]

One woman, Mandell Creighton, wrote the following about Leicester at the turn of the century: "The winter recreation of Leicester is football, and the Saturday half-holiday is spent by very many inhabitants either in playing or watching the game, whilst the great roar made by the cheers and shots of the interested crowd penetrates to every part of the town."[72] In particular, the songs that shook the stadiums down to their foundations, the so-called roars, became quite common before the First World War. The fans of Oxford City all hawked up spit in unison when someone from the opposing team tried to fool one of their own players. The annual game between Oxford City and the side from the renowned and elite local university enraged the fans to such an extent that the match was notorious for leading to numerous fistfights.[73] Violence and abuse were part of creating a boundary from "them." True gangs came to the games and attacked opposing players and fans. According to Henry Grimshaw, an informant for the historian Stephen Humphries, if someone grew up in the working class neighborhoods of Manchester, "you were born in[to] a gang if you lived in that area.... There was the Cogan Gang, the Kendall Street Gang. I was in the Willesden Street Gang. We did used to

---

90–92. Also see Forrest C. Robertson, "'The Glasgow Merchants' Charity Cup' (1877–1900)," *Elf* 4 (1986): 93–99.

69. Holt, *Working-Class Football and the City*, 13.

70. Ian Crump, "Amusements of the People: The Provision of Recreation in Leicester 1850–1914," PhD diss., University of Warwick, 1985, 392.

71. See Mason, *Association Football and English Society*, 257; and Holt, *Working Class Football*, 15.

72. Citation following Waller, *Town*, 105.

73. Nicholas Fishwick, *English Football and Society 1910–1950* (Manchester: Manchester University Press, 1989), 61.

fight each other."[74] The gangs, which occasionally were armed, were particularly fond of hurling stones at the windows of public buildings and attacking the police. They were also involved in the petty crime scene in the city. Unfortunately, bitter fights against the gangs of other ethnic groups or religious communities, such as the Irish or the Jews, were a regular occurrence. In times of economic uncertainty, these could even escalate into true pogroms. Football hooligans can be shown to have taken part in the antisemitic "race disturbances" in Liverpool in 1919, and the similarly antisemitic "race riots" in South Wales in 1911 and 1919.[75]

Although they were poor, the members of the gangs still found opportunities to get into the stadiums. Stan Clowes from Stoke-on-Trent recalled: "I'd be down on the football ground and we used to jump over the top of the corrugated sheets, seven or eight foot high. Used to dodge over the top. That went on. I think I've followed Stoke City since I was about six or eight, and for years and years we've never paid."[76]

Furious fans regularly stormed the playing field, as happened, for example, in January 1900, when the championship game between the Blackburn Rovers and Sheffield United had to be stopped because unhappy spectators were on the field demanding their money back. According to a newspaper report, in 1890 the seemingly invincible goalie from the Birmingham team West Bromwich Albion was almost lynched by militant Sunderland fans. One year later, a violent group of Liverpool supporters waited for the team from Aston Villa at the Liverpool train station to curse and mock them. Vandalism by groups of fans, such as the wanton destruction of public buildings, was well-nigh endemic.[77] In 1901 Sir John Gorst

74. Citation following Humphries, *Hooligans or Rebels*, 178.

75. See ibid., 264–66; George Alderman, "The Anti-Jewish Riots of August 1911 in South Wales," *Welsh History Review* 6 (1972): 190–200, especially 192 94. Also see Colin Holmes, *Anti-Semitism in British Society 1876–1939* (London: Edward Arnold, 1979), particularly 13–34, 128–38, and 188–92; G. Pearson, "'Paki Bashing' in a North East Lancashire Cotton Town: A Case Study and its History," in *Working Class Youth Culture*, eds. G. Mungham and G. Pearson (London: Routledge & Kegan Paul, 1976), 48–81; James D. Joung, "Imperialism, Racism and the English Workers: Significance of the Race Riots in 1919," *Internationale Tagung der Historiker der Arbeiterbewegung: 20. Linzer Konferenz (Linz, 11. bis 15. September 1984): Koloniale Frage und Arbeiterbewegung 1917–1939; Österreich und Frankreich im Februar 1934 und die internationale Arbeiterbewegung (Stand und Probleme der Forschung)*, ed. Hans Hautmann (Zurich: Europaverlag, 1989), 171–96.

76. Citation following Humphries, *Hooligans or Rebels*, 184.

77. See Eric Dunning et al., *The Roots of Football Hooliganism: An Historical and Sociological Study* (London: Routledge, 1988), 32–90. Also see Rogan Taylor, *Football and its Fans: Supporters and their Relations with the Game, 1885–1985* (Leicester: Continuum International Publishing, 1992).

reported to the government that "the class of lads and young men who spring up in every city have emancipated themselves from all home influences and restraints."[78] A report to the Inter Departmental Committee on Physical Deterioration in 1904 raised the criticism that young members of the working classes had rejected all forms of parental authority. "[They] get to congregating around the street corners at night ... become what we call 'corner boys,' and get drunken habits ... they have no idea of discipline or subordination."[79] The media stoked the rampant fears, the so-called moral panics, by painting the behavior and culture of the youth in the darkest possible colors. In particular, the reading of the dime novels, the murder mysteries and cheap horror stories, the so-called penny dreadfuls, was held responsible for leading the youth to disregard authority. These same arguments and seemingly apocalyptic fears were periodically revived as, for example, the elite criticism of gangster films, comic books, heavy metal, punk rock, video games, as well as rap and hip hop.[80]

The members of gangs and corner boys were often the victims of police violence since they were among the usual suspects whenever some-

78. Citation following ibid., 85.

79. Citation following ibid., 86. Also see Michael J. Childs, *Labour's Apprentices: Working-Class Lads in Late Victorian and Edwardian England* (London: Hambledon Press, 1992); Lionel Rose, *"Rogues and Vagabonds": Vagrant Underworld in Britain, 1815–1985* (London: Routledge, 1988); Jerry White, *The Worst Street in North London. Campbell Bunk, Islington, between the Wars* (London: Routledge & Kegan Paul, 1986); Humphries, *Hooligans or Rebels?*; D. Robins and P. Cohen, *Knuckle Sandwich: Growing Up in the Working-Class City* (London: Penguin Books, 1978); Rob Sindall, *Street Violence in the Nineteenth Century: Media Panic or Real Danger?* (Leicester: Leicester University Press, 1990). Concerning the gangs of Vienna around 1900, the so-called "Platten," who were involved in prostitution and crime, see Maderthaner und Musner, *Anarchie der Vorstadt*, 151–56. With regard to Berlin see, for example, Rolf Lindner, "Die wilden Cliquen zu Berlin: Ein Beitrag zur historischen Kulturanalyse," *Historische Anthropologie* 1 (1993): 451–67.

80. An overview of the moral panics of the last 150 years is provided by John Springhall, *Youth, Popular Culture and Moral Panics: Penny Gaffs to Gangsta-Rap, 1830–1996* (London: Palgrave Macmillan, 1998). Also see Eric Goode and Nachman Ben-Yehuda, *Moral Panics: The Social Construction of Deviance* (Oxford: Blackwell, 1994); and *Policing the Crisis: "Mugging", the State and Law and Order*, ed. Stuart Hall (London: Macmillan, 1978). For popular cinema of the 1930s see, for example, Stephen Ridgwell, "The People's Amusement: Cinema and Cinema-going in 1930s Britain," *The Historian* 52 (1996): 18–21. For comic books, see Lee Server, *Danger Is My Business: An Illustrated History of the Fabulous Pulp Magazines, 1896–1953* (San Francisco: Chronicle Books, 1993). For rockers, see Stan Cohen, *Folk Devils and Moral Panics: The Creation of the Mods and Rockers* (Oxford: Basil Blackwell, 1972). With regard to brutal videos see, for example, John Martin, *The Seduction of the Gullible: The Curious History of the Video "British Nasty" Phenomenon* (Nottingham: Fantasma Books, 1993); and Ray Surette, *Media, Crime, and Criminal Justice: Images and Realities* (Pacific Grove, Calif.: Cengage Learning, 1992).

thing happened. Bert Teague from Bristol, for example, recalled an occasion before the First World War when he was playing football on the street. After playing, he returned briefly to his parents' home to change his clothing, and then went back out into the neighborhood. A policeman then spoke to him, ranting that Bert Teague and his friends were always disturbing the public peace. Finally, the policeman struck Bert and brought him back to the station. The street rallied behind Bert by organizing a collection to pay his fine.[81] A man named David Smith reported that a particularly bad-tempered and hated cop named Old Bloodnut regularly cut up every ball that his group received from the workers at the port: "He pinched our ball, and he knifed it, pierced it."[82] The Victorian police saw themselves as the tamers of popular culture and missed no opportunity to regulate the world of the gangs.[83] The local gangs took their revenge by cutting any of the police hats, the so-called tarpaulin capes, that came into their possession: "He done our football, we done his cape" was the simple logic of the ongoing small-scale war between the gangs and the authorities.[84] Physical violence increased even further in importance as an element of the aggressive, hostile to authority, and xenophobic working-class culture of Great Britain in the period after the First World War. Consequently, hooliganism cannot be seen merely as a phenomenon of the second half of the twentieth century. Mutual assistance during physical confrontations bound these supporters even closer together.

Cursing also took place on and near the field. Players were often warned about their foul language, or even expelled from the field. The supporters of Stoke City shouted out the following disrespectful words in 1912: "Knock Fleming in the bloody river!"[85] Harold Fleming was a star player for Swindon, a railway town in the county of Wiltshire in southwestern England. As a player for this club in the Second Division Southern League from 1907 to 1924, he scored no fewer than 148 goals. Fleming was a hero to the sporting fans of Swindon, beloved not only

81. Humphries, *Rebels or Hooligans*, 204.

82. Cited following ibid., 205.

83. R. D. Storch, "The Policeman as Domestic Missionary: Urban Discipline and Popular Culture in Northern England 1850–1888," *Journal of Social History* 9 (1976): 479–95.

84. Cited by Humphries, *Rebels or Hooligans*, 205.

85. Tony Mason, "'Our Stephen and Our Harold.' Edwardian Footballers as Local Heroes," *European Heroes: Myth, Identity, Sport*, ed. Richard Holt (London: Cass, 1996), 95.

for his many beautiful goals, but also for his loyalty to the club, where he remained despite many lucrative offers from the First Division. He was the first and only international player from this club, playing in nine international matches and scoring the same number of goals. The local *Daily News* praised the local hero in the highest possible terms: "Harold Fleming is already a Knight of Football.... Already Fleming of Swindon is becoming Wiltshire's most illustrious figure of all time."[86]

Harold Fleming, the son of a pastor, was a dutiful, religious, and sober man. Consistent with the strong Victorian norms, he was a good family man who never played on Christmas Day or Good Friday. He avoided pubs like the devil avoids holy water, and served as a captain in the Wiltshire regiment during the First World War. Fleming was the very model of petty bourgeois respectability toward which many workers strived.[87] He might be compared with Wynton Rufer, the self-identified and unwavering Christian striker from New Zealand during the 1980s and 1990s.

Stephen Bloomer, the star of Derbyshire who played professional football until he was forty years old, was cut from a very different cloth. The legendary Bloomer played in 293 league matches, as well as 23 international matches in which he scored 28 goals; or better said, headed in 28 goals, since he was the best header of his generation. The son of a working-class family, he was beloved for his friendly manner and his proverbial love for the pubs, where he happily quenched his thirst with the fans. According to the legend, he drank a couple of pints of beer before important matches. Whatever the truth of this, he was fined on several occasions for undisciplined behavior.

Both Fleming and Bloomer, despite their differences, fascinated people, at least in their own cities and in the surrounding areas. They scored many spectacular and decisive goals, were match winners, and incorporated many of the overlapping ideals of working class culture: On the one hand was the respectable social climber, a Christian and an officer. On the other side stood the hard drinking, tough lad, the undisciplined ruffian who was hostile to authority. Recalling Fleming as a pillar of the community, a small statue at the main entrance to the Swindon football club has the following inscription: "To the inspiring memory of Harold Fleming, the great footballer and gentleman, who played for Swindon

86. Cited in ibid., 79.
87. McWilliam, *Popular Politics*, 63; Harrison, *Drink and the Victorians*.

Town between 1907–1924, and was capped nine times for England."[88] In addition, a street in Swindon is named in his honor. As Stephen Bloomer, in a manner befitting his life, died in a pub in 1938, there is nothing left to recall him other than his statistics, and an essay by Tony Mason, on which this part of our study relies.

Players generally remained active up through their mid-thirties, although some played even longer. They received, on average, £3 to £4 for the winter, and £2 to £3 for the summer. They also received performance and victory incentives, and the stars received additional allowances and guaranties. For example, in 1913, Sheffield United offered the striker George Utley from Barnsley a captain's armband, a lucrative charity match for his benefit, the profits from a sporting goods business, and a five-year contract, which was unusual for this business.[89] These kinds of arrangements made it possible to get around the maximum salary that was established by the conservative Football Association, that remained in force up through 1961. In addition, illegal bounties remained quite common, as numerous legal cases make clear. Even so, in 1940, only seven hundred of the three thousand professional football players earned the maximum of £12. Football players earned more than industrial workers and miners, but certainly did not become rich. The best and most popular players could continue working in the clubs following their active careers, become coaches, or even manage a pub. However, many of them had to return to the factories or mines to fill their wallets by the sweat of their brow. Many fell victim to alcoholism, which led one official in the Football Association to instruct clubs that they should only take under contract those players who had learned a "fallback" profession.[90] The fact that breweries frequently leased successful public houses to beloved football players again quite clearly demonstrates the very close relationship between football and pub culture.

The professionals, themselves, thought about their status in conflicting ways. The contract rules of the FA were tied to the interests of the clubs, so that the players were completely dependent on the all-powerful club managers. The first efforts to organize themselves as a union failed. William Rose, the goalie of the Wolverhampton Wanderers, and Robert

88. Mason, "Our Stephen and Our Harold," 82.
89. Fishwick, *English Football and Society*, 77.
90. Matheja, *Soziale Aspekte*, 22.

Holmes, a defenseman for Preston North End, could not count on the solidarity of their colleagues when things became difficult, and thus failed in their challenge to the all-powerful presidents.[91] Even stars like the Welsh right winger William "Billy" Meredith of Manchester City, who later changed over to the local rival United and was elected by the readers of *Empire* in Manchester as the most popular player in the league, complained about his lack of free time, since he always had to play on Saturdays and holidays. On the one hand, the strong-willed Meredith, who played from 1895 to 1924, until he was almost fifty years old, understood better than almost anyone else of his period how to direct the attention of the media to himself. He was one of the first media stars of the sport and bore the nickname the "Wizard." On the other hand, the right winger complained that a professional was simply a better type of clown, albeit one who was better paid than the rest of society.[92]

Nathaniel "Nat" Lofthouse, a striker and idol of the 1940s and 1950s, stated: "You could say I'd only been getting fourteen quid a week, but it wasn't really work. They were working damned hard for eight quid. I'd got easy money. I know; I've worked down the pit and I've played football."[93] The comparatively higher wages, the physically and psychologically easier work in comparison to the factory or the mine, as well as the prospect of fame and honor generally made it an easy decision for young workers to choose to become professionals. British toughness as a reflection of the social origins of the players marked the playing style of the teams from the island up through the 1990s.[94] The American social anthropologist Don Handelman correctly observed that a ritual maps out how a society is supposed to function, as if it were a model of that society.[95] Thus, the mentality of the spectator effected the interpretation of the game so that the prevailing view of British players outlasted the corresponding social structure of Britain by several decades. British robustness and tenacity are outwardly celebrated, and set on the scale against Italian calculation or South American "dream dancing." For a long time, the game served as

91. Ibid.

92. John Harding, *Football Wizard: The Story of Billy Meredith* (Derby: Breedon Books, 1985).

93. Cited following Schulze-Marmeling, *Fussball*, 38.

94. See David Downing, *Passovotchka: Moscow Dynamo in Britain 1945* (London: Bloomsbury Publishing, 1999), 260–62.

95. See Don Handelman, *Models and Mirrors: Towards an Anthropology of Public Events* (Cambridge: Berghahn, 1990).

an allegory for the outmoded socially conservative milieu of the working class. First, the opening of the island to foreign coaches and players, such as Eric Cantona, Denis Bergkamp, and Gianfranco Zola, changed the style of play, at least in the Premier League, while the kick-and-rush style along with aggressive sliding tackles continued to be revered in the lower professional leagues. In certain regions, even today, there are pubs where excessive beer drinking, foul language, violent masculinity, and a lifestyle focused on football are practiced and have enjoyed a renewed vitality in lifestyle magazines that denote this kind of life as "laddism."

The historian Richard Holt argued in his methodologically path-breaking study of early football idols that "Edwardian professional football was an urban phenomenon and the players were local heroes representing the local community against all comers."[96] The rapidly expanding city was a microcosm in which modern football could develop freely, and consequently become one of the most popular sources of entertainment. Paternalistic businessmen, of a type with the Victorian self-made man, served as transmission vectors between the new sport and white-collar employees as well as laborers. Brewers, barkeepers, but also the churches, as well as the various denominations saw the sport as means of influencing a popular culture that they saw as sinful and un-Christian. The rivalries among the numerous small and large churches meant that no one had any reservations about supporting the sport. Consequently, at least in the early years, football became a suitable medium for transmitting petty bourgeois respectability. Soon, however, businessmen came to understand the ways in which patronage of the working class could be turned to their own benefit.

The urban lower classes originated overwhelmingly from rural areas and were separated from their traditional culture. Accordingly, they searched for new and meaningful ways to make sense of their world. Many of them chose the new forms of dissent, often Methodism in particular. Others turned to the traditional venue of the pub, and transformed the street and therefore the city into a new version of the old trusted village. The need for binding rituals was met equally by religion, by both radical and imperialist politics (with the latter focused on the kingdom or the fleet), as well as by sport. The specific rituals and focus of football on the pub and street tied it to older cultural patterns. On the other hand, it of-

96. Mason, "Our Stephen and Our Harold," 84.

fered the possibility of establishing something new. It was urban, modern, organized on a national basis, and integrated into the popular transportation network. It thus opened wide horizons that separated urban dwellers from the despised countryside. It would appear that it was the second generation of immigrants who took advantage of this opportunity.

Just like the typical worker's hat, the "Andy Capp," fish-and-chips stalls, dance palaces, trade unions and the Labour Party, from 1900 onward football was a fixed element in the common pattern of life of the lower classes. After 1910, when sinking real wages led to unrest, support for football increased even further and led to class-based rejection of the sports and hobbies of the upper class, including motor racing and aviation.[97] Working-class neighborhoods proudly became the constitutive elements in the new large cities, celebrating their communities with common songs and united actions in order to demonstrate their presence to the outside. The first stars represented these local identities and justified the varying ideals of the workers as well as the ubiquitous desire for distinction and social advancement.

In sum, the violent and decidedly anti-authority gangs, which often were synonymous with the first fan clubs, provided the most important social ties for the sons of the immigrants. The gang was an institution that called into question the traditional ties such as the family and school, with the result that they were seen as a threat by those in power. They were presented by the authorities and the media as a counter-cultural subculture, and their members were always first in line when it came to beating a particularly hated policeman or breaking the shop windows of Irish merchants. The fact that these hooligans participated in pogroms against ethnic minorities points to the ambiguity in working class culture that was directed against authority, but also often mercilessly attacked outsiders and foreigners.

Thus, in our closing thesis, football can be interpreted as an invention of tradition from below.[98] Old values and mentalities were integrated successfully into a new and modern style of life.

97. Hobsbawm, *Entstehung der Arbeiterklasse*, 81 and 95.

98. According to Eric J. Hobsbawm, "Introduction: Inventing Traditions," in *The Invention of Tradition*, eds. Hobsbawm and Terence Ranger (Cambridge: Cambridge University Press, 1987), 1–3. Also see Anthony D. Smith, "The Nation: Invented, Imagined, Reconstructed?," *Millennium* 20 (1991): 353–68.

4 | *Football and Money*

When in 1999 the German journal *Horizont* selected its entrepreneur of the year, the choice was Uli Hoeness, former German national player and now the manager of FC Bayern München, which was the first time someone of the world of sport had been recognized with this honor. Fifteen years later, Hoeness would be sentenced to three-and-a-half years in prison for tax evasion amounting to nearly 30 million euros. Symptomatic of the situation in football at the end of the twentieth century is the fact that the honor awarded in 1999 was positively received throughout the sporting world. This chapter will demonstrate that this situation is hardly self-explanatory.

The commercialization of football has been a burning topic of discussion in sporting politics for more than a century. Its roots are to be traced to both commercialization and the discussion about commercialization in late Victorian Britain. As soon as the sport departed from the gates of the public schools and returned to the people, it became a public spectacle. Soon thereafter, entrepreneurial club officials sought to charge admission. From here, it was a relatively small step to begin paying players. Nevertheless, in the early stages of the process, the transition to professionalization at the highest levels of football met with stiff resistance from the gentlemen amateurs.[1] However, as we will see, these academic circles were not able to hinder the institutionalization of professional football in England and Scotland during the 1880s.

---

1. The term "professionalization" is used here in the sense of the social-historical concept of professionalization, which is usually understood in the academic sense of "professional experts" and utilized to discuss the genesis of a nonacademic profession. See, for example, Dietrich B. Rüschemeyer, "Professionalisierung: Theoretische Probleme für die vergleichende Geschichtsforschung," *Geschichte und Gesellschaft* 6 (1980): 311–25.

There were similar conflicts on the continent in the interwar period. The resistance to professional football is to be understood in the context of the intellectual currents that were spreading throughout Europe in precisely this period. Large sections of the elite were concerned about the expansion of mass culture and saw the cultural inheritance of the continent threatened by Americanism, which was manifested, in their view, through jazz, film, and professional sports. Concomitantly, they conceived apocalyptic visions of the inhabitants of the large cities becoming increasingly stultified and bestialized.[2] Even at this early stage, the commercialization of football was bound together with the expansion of media coverage of the sport. In addition to the specialized sporting press and the development of sports coverage in the daily newspapers, the interwar period also saw the rise of radio and film where football also quickly became a regular feature through live broadcasts and segments on weekly programs. This led to a decentralization of the consumption of football. The spread of television during the 1950s led to a further decisive expansion in the consumption of football.

In this chapter, we will try to demonstrate that highly varied interests and ideologies were bound up in discussions about professional football and its commercialization more generally. Consequently, this discussion can serve as a panopticon for observing the cultural currents, social and economic processes, and political conceptions for which the professionalization of football served as a foil. This is equally true of the late nineteenth century, the interwar and postwar periods, as well as for the late twentieth and early twenty-first centuries.

The Development and Rise of the "Football Industry"

The path to professional football in Great Britain and thereby in the world at large ran through Lancashire.[3] The number of football clubs be-

---

2. See the brief sketch in Kaspar Maase, *Grenzenloses Vergnügen. Der Aufstieg der Massenkultur 1850–1970* (Frankfurt: Fischer Taschenbuch Verlag, 1997), 115–38. With respect to the forms taken by criticism of mass culture see, for example, Umberto Eco, *Apokalyptiker und Integrierte: Zur kritischen Kritik der Massenkultur* (Frankfurt: S. Fischer, 1984).

3. See Robert W. Lewis, "The Genesis of Professional Football: Bolton-Blackburn-Darwen, the Centre of Innovation, 1878–85," *International Journal of the History of Sport* 14 (1997): 21–54.

gan to rise rapidly there during the 1870s. The efforts to obtain money by charging admission led during the 1880s to professionalism, albeit hidden at first. The FA soon recognized that there was no plausible explanation for the numerous Scottish players who were in Lancashire other than that they had come to play football for money. As a consequence, it was determined that it would be necessary to deal with the issue of professional athletes. In 1882, the FA issued a formal prohibition against professionalism, one that was strengthened even further in 1884. However, in 1882, the FA did permit the reimbursement of expenses. One consequence of these decisions was that defeated clubs frequently levied the accusation that their opponents utilized professionals. In 1884, the teams from Preston North End, Burnley, and Great Lever were disqualified from playing in the FA Cup because of their violation of the prohibition against employing professional players, and were banned from competition for a year.

It was at this point that the contest began between London and Lancashire, between the south and the north, between amateurs and professionals, for supremacy in football. The restrictive policies of the FA led to a threat by thirty-one clubs at the meeting in Blackburn, including the leading clubs from Lancashire as well as Aston Villa, Walsall Swifts, and Sunderland, that they would leave the association and found their own organization. Under the pressure of this threat, the prohibition on professionals was lifted in July 1885. However, it is obvious that the FA sought in this manner to gain control over the process of professionalization. At the same time that professional players were legalized in 1885, the FA introduced a maximum rate of pay for these same players. Professional football was further regulated in 1893 through the introduction of a system for trading players and compensating teams. Players who signed a contract with a club (at first these contracts were limited to a maximum of one year) were registered with the association and could not go to new teams after the end of their contracts without permission from their old teams.

The legalization of professional players led to a marked shift in the center of power in the FA Cup, which had been dominated by the elitist clubs of the south since its foundation in 1871. The victors in the first ten

---

For the professionalization of English football, Tischler, *Footballers and Businessmen*, is particularly important.

competitions were The Wanderers (1872, 1873, 1876, 1877, 1878), Oxford University (1874), Royal Engineers (1875), Old Etonians (1879), Clapham Rovers (1880), and Old Carthusians (1881). In 1882, the Blackburn Rovers were the first team from the north to make it to the final game. The next year, the Blackburn Olympics inflicted a historic defeat on the Old Etonians in the final game and brought the cup to the north for the first time. The victorious team included four textile workers, three metal workers, one white-collar worker, one master plumber, one barkeeper, and a dentist. In contrast to their opponents, the Olympics prepared for the final game in a one-week training camp that had been financed by the owner of a local iron works. Eric Hobsbawm describes this game as a "symbolic turning point" for the character of football that was "recognized as a class confrontation."[4]

The cup was won in three consecutive years by the Blackburn Rovers from 1884 to 1886. A commentator for the *Pall Mall Gazette* made clear in his discussion of the final game in 1884 that the advance of the teams from the north was understood by contemporaries as a disruptive force in the culture: "An incursion of Northern barbarians on Saturday—hot-blooded Lancastrians, sharp of tongue, rough and ready, of uncouth garb and speech. A tribe of Sudanese Arabs let loose in the Strand would not excite more amusement and curiosity."[5] Obviously, the players and supporters of the working-class clubs from the north were seen by the upper classes in the south as no less strange than the "uncivilized" subjects from some far off corner of the Empire.[6]

From this point on, amateur clubs largely disappeared in the south. Many of the university and public school teams transitioned away from football toward other sports in which gentlemen could play each other, such as rugby, or toward individual sports. The only amateur team that continued to play against the professionals was the Corinthians. This was a select team drawn from among the academics of various clubs who held adamantly to the ideals of the gentleman amateur and fair play.

---

4. Eric Hobsbawm, "Mass-Producing Traditions: Europe, 1870–1914," in *The Invention of Tradition*, eds. Hobsbawm and Terence Ranger (Cambridge: Cambridge University Press, 1987), 289.

5. *Pall Mall Gazette*, March 31, 1884.

6. For the designation of members of the lower classes as barbarians, see Jörg Fisch, "Zivilisation, Kultur," in *Geschichtliche Grundbegriffe: Historisches Lexikon zur politisch-sozialen Sprache in Deutschland*, ed. Otto Brunner (Stuttgart: Klett-Cotta, 1992), 7:743.

Thus, for example, they cultivated the practice of taking their goalie out of the net when a penalty shot was taken so that they would truly have to bear the consequences of having committed a foul.[7] The founder of this select team was N. Lane "PA" Jackson who had voiced his intense opposition to professionalization while serving as assistant secretary of the FA. In the following years, the Corinthians won a number of spectacular victories over professional teams, including an 8–1 triumph over the Blackburn Rovers in 1884, who nevertheless went on to win the FA Cup, and a 10–3 victory over Cup champion Bury in 1903. The Corinthians, however, did not participate in either the FA Cup or in other championships because they saw this as antithetical to their amateur philosophy.

The foundation of the Football League (FL) in 1888 provided professional football with its own organization, and led consequently to a continuously tense relationship with the FA.[8] While the FA continued to be dominated by supporters of the old status quo, the elitist participants from the south who remained hostile to professionalism, the FL was controlled by the new money of the rising middle class from northern England and the Midlands. The founding members of the FL came exclusively from those regions as the final standings for the first championship in the 1888–89 season demonstrate (see table 4-1). It was not

Table 4-1. Final Standings in the First Football League Championship, 1888–89

Rank	Team	Games	Won	Tied	Lost	Points
1	Preston North End	22	18	4	0	40
2	Aston Villa	22	12	5	5	29
3	Wolverhampton Wanderers	22	12	4	6	28
4	Blackburn Rovers	22	10	6	6	26
5	Bolton Wanderers	22	10	2	10	22
6	West Bromwich Albion	22	10	2	10	22
7	Accrington	22	6	8	8	20
8	Everton	22	9	2	11	20
9	Burnley	22	7	3	12	17
10	Derby County	22	7	2	13	16
11	Notts County	22	5	2	15	12
12	Stoke	22	4	4	14	12

7. Holt, *Sport and the British*, 99.   8. Also see Tomlinson, *North and South*.

until 1891 that the Woolwich Arsenal became the first professional club in southern England. As late as 1914, only six of the forty clubs in the FL came from southern England, and all but two of these were from London. Up through 1931, the league championship was won exclusively by teams from the north and the Midlands. Between 1883 and 1922, the FA Cup was won just two times by southern teams.[9]

The moving spirit in the establishment of the FL was William McGregor, a liberal landowner and Methodist. Other founding fathers of the FL also came from the petty bourgeoisie or even from among the skilled laborers. The establishment of a championship, which guaranteed the clubs a regular source of income from the games and eliminated the risk of being excluded from the FA Cup, was a logical consequence of the legalization of professional football. The success of the FL was facilitated above all by two technological factors. The railroad, which had become a mass transportation system in the middle of the nineteenth century, made it possible for working-class football fans to travel from the hinterland into the large cities, and also to get to away matches. The first chartered trains were organized in Scotland on the occasion of the cup final in 1881. In addition, thanks to the developing telegraph and postal system in Great Britain, the early modernization of the press had a concomitant effect on the popularization of football. Beginning in the 1880s, reporting about football was a fixture of the local press. Thanks to the telegraph, the results from the entire country could be hanging on the walls of the editorial offices that same evening.

The numbers of spectators grew steadily. During the first season of the FL an average of 4,600 spectators attended the games. This had risen to 7,900 in the 1895–96 season, 13,200 in the 1905–6 season, 15,800 in the 1908–9 season, and 23,100 in the 1913–14 season.[10] The average number of spectators attending the final games of the FA Cup grew even more spectacularly (see table 4-2).[11] Up until the end of the nineteenth century, the players in the FL, which was able to establish a Second Division in

9. Concerning the development of professionalism in the south, see J. P. Korr, "West Ham United Football Club and the Beginnings of Professional Football in East London," *Journal of Contemporary History* 13 (1978): 211–32.

10. Wray Vamplew, *Pay Up and Play the Game: Professional Sport in Britain 1875–1914* (Cambridge: Cambridge University Press, 1988), 63.

11. Ibid.

Table 4-2. Average Numbers of Spectators at FA Cup Final Games

Period	1875–84	1885–94	1895–1904	1905–14
Spectators	4,900	23,400	66,800	79,300

1892, and in the Scottish Football League (SFL), which was established in 1890, were only part-time professionals. However, after the turn of the century, they generally became full-time professionals. At first, their salaries were equivalent to those of foremen or specialized craftsmen. In 1901, the average annual salary of a professional football player was £144, while a foreman in the metal industry earned £134 and a foreman in the printing industry earned £127.[12] Craftsmen from trades that were threatened with extinction and also miners were heavily represented among the professional football players. For the latter, football was not only an attractive alternative to their ancestral profession, it also offered one of the few means of escaping the exceptionally difficult and dangerous work under ground.

The first football union was established in 1899, but had only limited success.[13] Then, in 1907, the Professional Footballer's Association (PFA) was founded in Manchester. The core of this union was the players from Manchester United and the star Billy Meredith, who came from a mining village in South Wales. The central demands of the union were the elimination of the upper limit on wages and the free choice of employer, which was made impossible by the current trading system. The PFA joined the General Federation of Trade Unions (GFTU), thereby demonstrating that the players who were organized in the union considered football as a branch of industry and saw themselves as workers. This view, as well as the possibility that membership in the union umbrella organization might lead to solidarity strikes among the professional football players in support of work actions in other economic sectors, led the FA to take energetic counteractions. The players from Manchester United had their pay docked by the association. Finally, the PFA decided to act on its own and not to become integrated into the wider union movement.

12. Schulze-Marmeling, *Fussball*, 116.
13. See ibid., 120–22.

What forces led to this first impetus toward professionalization and commercialization? Was the primary purpose in paying players to secure the best possible team and thereby purchase athletic success, or were the first professional clubs already commercially oriented enterprises whose main goal was to earn as much as possible to maximize a return on investment for their investors? The economic historian Wray Vamplew investigated this question with regard to the Scottish Football League.[14] Between 1897 and 1914, the clubs in this league became joint-stock companies. However, as Vamplew was able to demonstrate, these companies were not dominated by a small number of major investors. Rather, the largest number of shareholders were members of the working class, who sought to demonstrate their close ties with the club by purchasing shares, and did not see these primarily as financial investments. The clubs generally did not pay any dividends, but rather either held onto their profits or "reinvested them" by paying new players. This suggests that athletic success was, in fact, more important than economic success.

In order to support his thesis, Vamplew directed his attention to the league as a whole in addition to his investigation of individual clubs. Beginning with the hypothesis that maximizing the number of spectators (which must be the goal of a sporting enterprise that is interested purely in profit) would be achieved with the most balanced, and therefore most exciting, championship, Vamplew examined the extent to which efforts were made between 1890 and 1914 to establish the broadest possible field of equally strong teams. Because there were no constraints on salaries, or limits on the pool of talent from which the teams could recruit, the three richest clubs—Glasgow Rangers, Celtic Glasgow, and Heart of Midlothian—were always able to duplicate their athletic dominance through the recruitment of new talent. In the period investigated by Vamplew, at least two of these teams were among the top three in the final standings in all but three years. Neither Celtic nor the Rangers ever ranked lower than fifth. Seen in statistical perspective, during its first twenty-five years, the Scottish championship was always less balanced than the English, without any efforts being made to alter this situation. This observation led Vamplew to conclude that the SFL was by no means a profit-maximizing cartel,

14. Wray Vamplew, "The Economics of a Sports Industry: Scottish Gate-Money Football, 1890–1914," *Economic History Review* 35 (1982): 549–67.

but rather, each of the individual clubs was focused on athletic success, since they were not willing to sacrifice this success for a more evenly balanced and exciting championship in order to gain greater profits.[15]

The situation was less unequivocal with regard to the English FL. Here, the restrictions on players moving from team to team and the limits on pay meant that the richest teams could not perpetuate their athletic success. The result, as Vamplew showed, was that the FL had greater competitive balance than the SFL. Nevertheless, the FL did not have explicit mechanisms to create equality, such as the draft system, which are common in the unequivocally profit-oriented U.S. team sports.

The interwar period saw a further impetus toward commercialization and professionalization.[16] The shortening of the workday and increasing per capita income, despite increasing unemployment, led to an increasing demand for leisure goods. For millions of people in this period, the consumption of football was the premier leisure time activity. The game was an integral element in working-class culture. The stadiums were located in working-class neighborhoods. The players and coaches, and sometimes the club officials, came from the same social milieu as the spectators: petty bourgeois, shopkeepers, white-collar workers, and above all workers. In addition, football was a comparatively inexpensive leisure time activity. Thus, during the 1937–38 season, the average attendance at the games of the First Division of the Football League was 30,000 (it was 15,800 during the 1908–9 season). The Second Division had an average attendance of 20,000, and the two groups of the Third Division had 11,000 and 7,000 spectators, respectively. The numbers of spectators at the games during the FA Cup were generally much higher still. There were only 2,000 spectators at the first FA Cup final in 1872. There were 17,000 in attendance by 1888, 42,000 in 1895, and 120,000 in 1913. The legendary White Horse Cup final in 1923, where the playing field was completely overrun by spectators before the match began and had to be cleared by mounted police, had an estimated quarter of a million people in attendance.[17]

15. Ibid., 562.

16. On this point, see Stephen G. Jones, "The Economic Aspects of Association Football in England, 1918–39," *British Journal of Sports History* 1 (1984): 286–99.

17. See Morris, *Spiel*, 273. However, this number is not certain. Officially, the two hundred thousand spectators who watched the decisive game between Brazil and Uruguay in Rio in the 1950 World Cup are counted as the largest crowd ever to attend a football match.

At this point, professionalization was not limited to the players. Although assembling the team and preparing for games at first fell to the heads of the clubs, a new figure entered onto the stage of professional football—the coach.[18] From this point on, a professional was always involved in the recruiting of players, in the physical and psychological preparation of the team, and in their deployment and tactics on the field. In addition, in case of failures on the field, the heads of the clubs now had a scapegoat available who could serve as a focus for the emotions of the masses. The first coach in the history of British football to think and act as a professional was Herbert Chapman. He won the championship three years in a row with Huddersfield Town (1924–26) and was a two-time championship and Cup winner with Arsenal between 1930 and 1934. The son of a miner from Yorkshire, Chapman earned a degree in engineering at Sheffield and considered that, aside from the spirit of the team, the most important factors were methodical planning and complex tactics. Through his W-M system, which was organized on the principle of overlapping coverage, he transformed his team into a collective that was focused unconditionally on success.

However, in addition to the narrow circle of players and coaches, there were many other people who made their living from football. A true branch of the economy developed around the British national sport. An independent football press had its origins in the nineteenth century. It experienced an enormous boost in the interwar period. Countless newspapers and illustrated magazines circulated among the football consuming public. Radio also took on a role in the most popular sport. Football shoes and jerseys had to be produced. The construction of stadiums required materials and created work. The little pictures inside cigarette packs, which were highly prized and widely collected in the interwar period, often used football for their theme. Drinks were sold widely in and around stadiums, and many club presidents were active in the brewing industry. Above all, however, the betting industry flourished, and soon was earning enormous profits. Admittedly, in 1920, the British parliament banned betting on football at the request of the FA, though the ban was quickly ignored. An estimate from the 1930s placed the number of

18. See Schulze-Marmeling, *Fussball*, 106–8.

betters as sixteen times the number of spectators who streamed into the stadiums. A total of roughly £800,000 was wagered every week, and the gambling companies had approximately 30,000 employees.

The Long Path toward Professional Football in Continental Europe

In the interwar period several non-British countries established professional leagues, which became an important element in the leisure activities of working class men. The first professional championships on the European continent took place in the mid-1920s in the east-central European Calcio Danubiano. A professional football league was established in Vienna in 1924.[19] Soon afterward professional leagues were founded in Czechoslovakia[20] and Hungary.[21] A few years later, professional football came to Spain (1929),[22] France,[23] Switzerland,[24] and Romania[25] (all in 1932). Other countries saw the beginnings of at least underground

19. See Matthias Marschik, "Wiener Melange: Fußball in Österreich 1918–1939," in *Fußball zwischen den Kriegen. Europa 1918–1939*, eds. Christian Koller and Fabian Brändle (Münster: Lit, 2010), 245–63.

20. René Küpper, "Fußball im multinationalen Staat: Tschechoslowakei," in *Fußball zwischen den Kriegen: Europa 1918–1939*, 265–80; Stefan Zwicker, "Fußball in den böhmischen Ländern," in *Hakenkreuz und rundes Leder: Fußball im Nationalsozialismus*, eds. Lorenz Peiffer and Dietrich Schulze-Marmeling (Göttingen: Werkstatt, 2008), 223–33.

21. See G. Molnar, "Hungarian Football: A Socio-Historical Overview," *Sport in History 27* (2007): 293–317.

22. Jürg Ackermann, "Spanischer Fußball in der Zwischenkriegszeit," in *Fußball zwischen den Kriegen. Europa 1918–1939*, 127–44.

23. See Alfred Wahl, "Un professionalisme de résignation en France," *Sociétés et Représentations 7* (1998): 67–75; "Le footballeur français: De l'amateurisme au salariat," *Le mouvement social* 135 (1986): 7–30; and with Pierre Lanfranchi, *Les footballeurs professionels des années trente à nos jours* (Paris: Hachette, 1995).

24. See Christian Koller, "Schweizer Fußball zwischen Modernität und 'Geistiger Landesverteidigung,'" in *Fußball zwischen den Kriegen. Europa 1918–1939*, 203–20; and Philippe Vonnard and Grégory Quin, "Eléments pour une histoire de la mise en place du professionnalisme dans le football suisse durant l'entre-deux-guerres: Processus, résistances et ambiguïtés," *Schweizerische Zeitschrift für Geschichte 62* (2012): 70–85.

25. See Sebastian Balta, "'Die Goldenen Dreißiger': Das 'legendäre Jahrzehnt' des rumänischen Fußballs von 1930 bis 1940," in *Überall ist der Ball rund: Zur Geschichte und Gegenwart des Fußballs in Ost- und Südosteuropa*, eds. Dittmar Dahlmann et al. (Essen: Klartext, 2006), 251–74; and Bogdan Popa, "'Our Team'? Ethnic Prejudices and Football in Interwar Rumania," in *Sport zwischen Ost und West. Beiträge zur Sportgeschichte Osteuropas im 19. und 20. Jahrhundert*, eds. Arié Malz et al. (Osnabrück: Fibre, 2007), 191–203.

professional play. Following a brief experiment in 1894, professional football came to the United States in 1921 with the establishment of the American Soccer League (ASL), which lasted for twelve years.[26] In the early 1930s, professional football came to South America, in part as a re-
sult of the poaching of players by European teams. Professional leagues were established in Argentina (1931), Uruguay (1932), Brazil (first in Rio de Janeiro and São Paulo, both in 1933),[27] Chile (1933),[28] Paraguay (1935), Mexico (1943), Colombia (1948),[29] and Peru (1951). These developments were not the result of a simple transfer of culture from Great Britain to the rest of the world. Rather, they grew out of a complex combination of external sporting influences, internal processes of negotiation, and the transcendent rise of a mass culture that was strongly influenced through its interactions with the media.[30]

The establishment of professional football outside the British Isles necessitated a further transnationalization of the professional game.[31] This was achieved, for example, through the development of international competitions, particularly the two central European competitions that were organized by the leader of the Austrian association, Hugo Meisl, in 1927. These were the Mitropa Cup for club teams and the Coupe Internationale Européenne for national teams. The purpose of these competitions was to increase the number and regularity of international matches and thereby provide new streams of income for the professional clubs that frequently were not very profitable.[32] International competitions also created a transnational market for both players and coaches.[33] While the English professional leagues were largely sealed off from foreign players until the late twentieth century, the American

26. See Colin Jose, *The American Soccer League: The Golden Years of American Soccer 1921–1931* (Lanham, Md.: Scarecrow Press, 1998).

27. Alex Bellos, *Futebol: Fußball—Die brasilianische Kunst des Lebens* (Frankfurt: Fischer Taschenbuch Verlag, 2005), 40.

28. See *Historia del Fútbol Chileno*, 1:17–21.

29. See Eisenberg, *FIFA*, 81–89.

30. The basic work on this topic is Maase, *Grenzenloses Vergnügen: Der Aufstieg der Massenkultur 1850–1970*.

31. Christian Koller, "Transnationalität: Netzwerke, Wettbewerbe, Migration," in *Fußball zwischen den Kriegen: Europa 1918–1939*, 37–63.

32. See Andreas Hafer and Wolfgang Hafer, *Hugo Meisl oder die Erfindung des modernen Fußballs: Eine Biographie* (Göttingen: Werkstatt, 2007), 127.

33. Mathew Taylor and Pierre Lanfranchi, *Moving with the Ball: The Migration of Professional Footballers* (Oxford: Berg, 2001), 51 and 145–51; Koller, "Transnationalität," 56–63.

league was an important employer of football legionaries during the 1920s. There were, for example, professional football players from Great Britain, Sweden, Austria, Hungary, and Ireland in the ASL. The 150 or so British players comprised a third of the total in the entire league during the mid–1920s.[34] Following the economic collapse of the ASL during the Great Depression, the newly established French league provided an alternate source of employment. It largely employed football players from the Calcio Danubiano and Great Britain but also attracted players from other European countries as well as a few from South America and the French colonies in northern and western Africa. Up through the outbreak of the Second World War, almost four hundred foreign professionals played in the Grande Nation.[35] Beginning in the late 1930s, the professional leagues in South America provided an exile for players and coaches who left Europe for political reasons—typically, Spanish republicans and Jews.

Criticism of this tendency toward professionalization and commercialization came from a wide variety of sources.[36] In addition to aristocratic Olympians, nationalists were also in opposition. They argued that sport should only serve as a means of strengthening the feeling of a sense of national community, and preferred gymnastics as a means of training the body for military service. They rejected professional spectator sports as an element of the "Americanizing" decadence of the masses. Left-wing circles, and especially the workers sports movement and their competitors in communist "Red Sport," anticipating the criticism of the Frankfurt school regarding the "cultural industry," criticized professional sports as a manifestation of capitalist drive for profit and claimed that they were intended to manipulate the working masses and turn them away from class struggle.[37]

34. Taylor and Lanfranchi, *Moving with the Ball*, 51 and 145–51; Werner Skrentny, "Hakoahs Exodus: Importe in die US-Profiligen," in *Davidstern und Lederball: Die Geschichte der Juden im deutschen und internationalen Fußball*, ed. Dietrich Schulze-Marmeling (Göttingen: Werkstatt, 2003), 433–58.

35. Pierre Lanfranchi, "Fussball in Europa 1920–1938: Die Entwicklung eines internationalen Netzwerkes," in *Die Kanten des runden Leders: Beiträge zur europäischen Fussballkultur*, eds. Roman Horak and Wolfgang Reiter (Vienna: Promedia, 1991), 168; and Lanfranchi and Taylor, *Moving with the Ball*, 51–58 and 170–73.

36. See Eco, *Apokalyptiker und Integrierte*.

37. See Robert B. Edelman, *Serious Fun: A History of Spectator Sports in the USSR* (Oxford: Oxford University Press, 1993), 7–11.

Although football had only a limited popularity in the pioneering land of Austria in its early phases, it became a mass phenomenon in the immediate postwar period. A professional football league, concentrated in the region of Vienna, was established for the 1924–25 season with two divisions. It quickly became very popular and was able to stay in business after the establishment of the clerical-fascist regime in 1934. In the Vienna of the 1920s and 1930s, where literature, art, music, as well as business and politics made their home in coffee houses, the popularity of football was not limited to the working classes living in the suburbs. Football was also an established element in the coffee house culture of the intellectuals, the bohemians, and the greater part of the metropolitan bourgeoisie. The major clubs, Rapid, Austria, Hakoah, and Vienna had their own coffee houses where their supporters met to discuss the sporting news.[38] Football was thus closely connected with theater, journalism, and other cultural affairs. Football fans from these circles produced poems, essays, and intelligent *bon mots*. These included the author Friedrich Torberg, the opera star Leo Slezak, and the essayist Alfred Polgar.[39]

However, there was also criticism in Austria of the mass spectacle. Antisemitic voices were very forceful, asserting that they could not bear the occasional dominance in the professional league that was achieved by Jewish-run clubs. In 1925, the first professional champion was SK Hakoah Wien, established in 1909, which was dedicated to the idea of Zionism.[40] Hakoah had several top Hungarian players under contract, such as the play-maker Béla Guttmann (1899–1981), who moved to the United States in 1926, and from 1932 to the 1960s coached numerous championship teams in Europe and South America as well as the Portuguese

38. In this context, see Roman Horak and Wolfgang Maderthaner, "A Culture of Urban Cosmopolitanism: Uridil and Sindelar as Viennese Coffee-House Heroes," in *European Heroes: Myth, Identity, Sport*, 139–55; and by the same authors, "Vom Fussballspielen in Wien: Überlegungen zu einem popularkulturellen Phänomen der Zwischenkriegszeit," in *Philosophie, Psychoanalyse, Emigration: Festschrift für Kurt Rudolf Fischer*, ed. Wegeler Cornelia Wegeler (Vienna: WUV-Universitätsverlag, 1992), 99–118.

39. See Roman Horak and Wolfgang Maderthaner, *Mehr als ein Spiel: Fussball und populare Kulturen im Wien der Moderne* (Vienna: Löcker, 1997), 113–40.

40. On this point, see John Bunzl, *Hoppauf Hakoah: Jüdischer Sport in Österreich von den Anfängen bis in die Gegenwart* (Vienna: Junius, 1987); *Hakoah: Ein jüdischer Sportverein in Wien 1909–1995*, ed. Jüdisches Museum Wien (Vienna: Jüdisches Museum der Stadt Wien, 1995); and Arthur Baar, *Fussballgeschichten—Ernstes und Heiteres: Hakoah Wien* (Tel Aviv: Brith Hakoah 1909, 1974).

and Austrian national teams.[41] Under the influence of Max Nordau's ideology of the "muscular Jew," Hakoah (Hebrew for "the power") wanted to dispel on the playing field the antisemitic prejudice that Jews were physically inferior. The club went on tours to Palestine, Romania, Poland, Lithuania, Germany, and Great Britain as an ambassador of Jewish sport. In Great Britain, the team defeated West Ham 5–0. At home, the club was always the target of antisemitic jokes and slogans.

This was also the case for the liberal and upper class Austria Wien. The club was originally called Wiener Amateur-Sportverein (Vienna Amateur Sporting Club), and only accepted intellectuals as members. When it moved into professional football, the name was changed. During the second half of the 1920s, Austria had the second most expensive team in the Vienna professional league, after Hakoah. Most of the club's patrons as well as many of the players came from the Jewish upper class. Although Austria, in contrast to Hakoah, did not claim a specifically Jewish identity, it was always cursed as a "Jewish" club, particularly by supporters of its in-city rival Rapid. (Even today, in games against Austria, which has not had any active Jewish players for decades, supporters of Rapid chant out "smash the Jews.")[42] The *Wiener Sport-Tagblatt*, one of the largest sporting newspapers in the country, regularly published antisemitic columns in which two Viennese with Jewish names, Schatzinger and Schmonzides, vent about the supposed greed and wealth of the Jewish professional football players. The *Sport-Papagei* similarly published regular stories about the Yiddish-speaking "kleine Moritzl" (little Morris).[43]

The players and officials of Hakoah regularly suffered assaults, inspired by antisemitism, at the hands of the public and from players of op-

41. See Detlev Claussen, *Béla Guttmann: Weltgeschichte des Fussballs in einer Person* (Berlin: Berenberg, 2006); as well as Ludwig Tegelbeckers, "Béla Guttmann: Weltenwanderer ohne Kompromiss," in *Davidstern und Lederball: Die Geschichte der Juden im deutschen und internationalen Fussball*, ed. Dietrich Schulze-Marmeling (Göttingen: Werkstatt, 2003), 347–68.

42. Regarding continuity in antisemitism in Austrian football after 1945, see Gerhard Fischer and Ulrich Lindner, *Stürmer für Hitler: Vom Zusammenspiel zwischen Fussball und Nationalsozialismus* (Göttingen: Werkstatt, 1999), 147–49; and Michael John and Dietrich Schulze-Marmeling, "'Haut's den Juden!': Antisemitismus im europäischen Fussball," in *Fussball und Rassismus* (Göttingen: Werkstatt, 1993), 141–43.

43. See Fischer, *Stürmer*, 129, as well as Michael John, "Aggressiver Antisemitismus im österreichischen Sportgeschehen der Zwischenkriegszeit: Manifestationen und Reaktionen anhand ausgewählter Beispiele," *Zeitgeschichte* 26 (1999): 203–23; and with Schulze-Marmeling, "Antisemitismus," 135–37.

posing teams. For example, the *Wiener Morgenzeitung* reported in November 1923 that there was an encounter between Hakoah and Admira Wien:

> People, who in the normal course of their lives follow rules of decency and good customs, became brutal terrorists during the game against Hakoah.... It was an orgy of cursing, in which the phrase "Jew pig" appeared over and over, and one could hear wild threats coming from every side. There is hardly a single match in which the players of Hakoah are not cursed in the vilest possible manner, and threatened. Even on their own field in the Krieau, it is necessary to have a column of mounted security on hand to keep the hordes of spectators in their place.[44]

The early professionalization of Austrian football led to success on the international stage at the beginning of the 1930s. The Austrian national team, nicknamed the "wonder team," was undefeated in twelve matches in a row in 1931 and 1932. Among their other victories, they defeated Scotland 5–0, Switzerland 8–1, Hungary 8–2, and Germany 6–0 and 5–0. On December 7, 1932, the wonder team was defeated by the English national team (3–4), although the wonder team largely dominated the game. In the following years, the success curve flattened out somewhat. Austria came in fourth in the World Cup in 1934, and made it to the Olympic finals in 1936. Austrian club football also had considerable success on the international level. Rapid Wien won the Mitropa Cup in 1930, and Austria Wien won it in 1933 and 1936.[45]

The German Football Union (DFB) cast a skeptical eye on the professionalism in its own backyard. In 1925, the DFB issued a rules change that made it very difficult for German clubs to play in matches against foreign professional teams. This was directed primarily against professional football in Austria, Hungary, and Czechoslovakia. This was a major issue because lucrative matches against German teams were quite important for the professional clubs from Austria, which regularly faced financial difficulties. It was not until 1930 that this boycott policy was finally abandoned under pressure from FIFA.[46]

The German *Anschluss* of Austria in 1938 had immediate consequences for professional football. Even before the plebiscite on April 10, which was intended to give a democratic patina to the National Social-

---

44. *Wiener Morgenzeitung*, November 8, 1923, cited in John, "Aggressiver Antisemitismus," 204.

45. Following Fischer, *Stürmer*, 138.   46. Heinrich, *Fussballbund*, 84–86.

ist annexation, the structure of Austrian professional football was shattered.[47] Hakoah Wien was prohibited from playing on March 13, 1938. The Jewish club president of Austria Wien, Dr. Emmanuel Schwarz, was forced to resign, and the club was taken over by some former players who belonged to the previously illegal National Socialist Party of Austria and its name was changed to S.C. Ostmark Wien. However, following protests by supporters, the name was changed back to Austria in July 1938. On March 28, the Austrian association was dissolved. There was an *Anschluss* game between Altreich and Ostmark on April 3 in Vienna. The "Ostmark" (Austria) was incorporated into the Deutscher Reichsbund für Leibesübungen (German Reichs Union for Physical Exercise) as district XVII. From this point on, there was a district championship in the "Ostmark" whose winner would play the other district champions in a final round for the German championship.[48] On May 31, 1938, all of the clubs were required to release their professional players. In total, about 160 players were affected. Jewish players were forbidden to participate in championship games. Hakoah Wien was dissolved, and its property was confiscated. Its field was assigned to SS unit 90.[49] As a result, Austrian football was assimilated into the National Socialist German football system with its (at least superficial) commitment to amateurism. However, many of the former Austrian professionals had their renewed amateur status sweetened through a share in "aryanized" businesses and other privileges that provided them with better material conditions than they sometimes had enjoyed as professionals.[50]

Around the turn of the century, however, even the Germans had been charging admission for football matches. Following the First World War, the sport enjoyed a considerable upswing, and football along with boxing became the two most popular sports with the public.[51] Many

47. On this point also see Fischer, *Stürmer*, 138–42.

48. Concerning football in Vienna during the National-Socialist period, see Matthias Marschik, *Vom Nutzen der Unterhaltung: Der Wiener Fußball in der NS-Zeit: Zwischen Vereinnahmung und Resistenz* (Vienna: Turia + Kant, 1998); "'Am Spielfeld ist die Wahrheit gewesen': Die Wiener Fussballkultur in der Zeit des Nationalsozialismus: Zwischen Vereinnahmung und Widerstand," *Österreichische Zeitschrift für Volkskunde* 50 (1996): 181–205; and "Between Manipulation and Resistance: Viennese Football in the Nazi Era," *Journal of Contemporary History* 34 (1999): 215–31.

49. John, *Antisemitismus*, 139.

50. Marschik, *Vom Nutzen*, 300 and 306.

51. Christiane Eisenberg, "Massensport in der Weimarer Republik: Ein statistischer Über-

men first came into contact with football in the military. Looking back over this period, the famous publicist Sebastian Haffner wrote in 1939:

> In the years 1924, 1925, and 1926, Germany developed overnight as a sporting power. Germany had never before been a sporting country. Never before had there been creativity and imagination in sport, as is the case in England and America. The true spirit of sport, the self-abandoning and playful transition into a fantasy world with its own rules and laws, is entirely foreign to the German spiritual condition. However, all of a sudden, membership in sport clubs and the attendance at sport festivals increased tenfold.[52]

A substantial sporting press developed in Germany at this time. Live radio broadcasts of football matches also began with increasing regularity from the mid-1920s.[53]

The issue of professional football also became the main topic of conversation in political discussions about sport in the Weimar Republic. In 1922, the DFB made clear that it stood firmly behind the idea of amateurism, and stated its principal in the following manner: "Sport is not an end unto itself, but is rather the means of reaching an ideal goal, namely using the moral medium of the team, and particularly the sport of football, to train the youth to develop strong character, and to become useful people."[54] In the following years, professionalization was denounced as a sign of decline. German clubs were forbidden to play matches against foreign professional teams. Players who switched clubs were banned from playing for three months in order to make it difficult to recruit star players from other clubs. In 1930, the annual publication of the DFB included an article with the title, "The Struggle against Professional Sport," in which it was stressed that the DFB "had always maintained the view that only amateur sports should be supported.... The support of amateur sports required a struggle against professional sports. It is our duty to drive out those professional athletes whom we find among our ranks."[55]

---

blick," *Archiv für Sozialgeschichte* 33 (1993): 137–78; and Erik Eggers, "Fussball in der Weimarer Republik," *Stadion* 25 (1999): 153–75.

52. Sebastian Haffner, *Geschichte eines Deutschen: Die Erinnerungen 1914–1933* (Stuttgart: Deutsche Verlags-Anstalt, 2000), 72.

53. See Diller Ansgar, "Die erste Sportübertragung im deutschen Rundfunk," *Publizistik* 17 (1972): 315–25.

54. Cited in Fischer, *Stürmer*, 31.

55. Cited in Schulze-Marmeling, *Fussball*, 130.

The opposition to professional sports came from different direction.[56] Upper class and aristocratic Olympians indulged in the ideal of the amateur in the manner of Pierre de Coubertin, which emphasized the role that (elite) international competition could have in unifying diverse peoples. National-conservative and chauvinist circles wanted sport to serve the sole purposes of creating healthy bodies for military service, and developing a common feeling of national unity. They were opposed to both international competition and professional sports, which they saw as elements of a decadent and purely materialistic mass culture and the hated Americanism.[57] Radical voices from the right combined their criticism of materialism with an emphasis on the very different natures of sport and gymnastics. For example, in his 1927 essay *The Rule of the Inferior*, Edgar J. Jung wrote:

The most important thing for most sporting fans ... is not the sport, itself. A glance at the mass of spectators, for example at an important football match ... demonstrates the convincing truth of this claim.... The top performances of the gymnastics movement lead all gymnasts toward emulation; the top performances in the sporting movement have as their goal the whipping up of passions that have become listless, the collecting of higher admission charges, and the sharing out of large monetary prizes.... In place of a morally valuable effort toward physical self-discipline, the inferior man searches for cheap thrills.... Thus, the new German has reached a physical low point in the pursuit of materialism. Material money celebrates its marriage to the material body. The multimillionaire stands alongside the boxing world champion as a worthy ideal. Thus, the circle is complete, and the return to barbarism is set in motion.[58]

The workers' athletic movement, which had its origins in the 1890s, also opposed professional sports because they represented a manifestation of the capitalist quest for profit.[59] As was true of the Olympians, the ability of sport to bring peoples together was in the foreground. However,

---

56. See Fischer, *Stürmer*, 29.

57. The basic work is Frank Becker, *Amerikanismus in Weimar: Sportsymbole und politische Kultur 1918–1933* (Wiesbaden: Deutscher Universitäts-Verlag, 1993).

58. Edgar J. Jung, *Die Herrschaft der Minderwertigen: Ihr Zerfall und ihre Ablösung durch ein neues Reich* (Berlin: Verlag Deutsche Rundschau, 1927), 80. Also see Oswald Spengler, *Preussentum und Sozialismus* (Munich: Beck, 1920), 41.

59. Frank Filter, "Fussballsport in der Arbeiter-Turn- und Sportbewegung," *Sozial- und Zeitgeschichte des Sports* 2 (1988): 85–93; and Heinz Timmermann, *Geschichte und Struktur der Arbeitersportbewegung 1893–1933* (Ahrensburg bei Hamburg: Ingrid Czwalina, 1973).

the workers' sport movement criticized the Olympic movement for failing to serve this goal, but rather stoking national rivalries in their competitions. It was not the upper classes and aristocratic elites, but rather the representatives of the working classes, who were supposed to join in brotherhood in the context of athletic competitions.

In 1939, Sebastian Haffner offered retrospective ridicule of both the nationalist and working class conceptions of sport:

The "nationalists" foolish and plump as always, found that our healthy instinct had come upon a wonderful replacement for the now absent military service. As if any one of us had thought about "physical exercise"! The left, too clever by half, and, as a result almost more stupid than the "nationalists" (as always), considered it a great discovery that warlike instincts could now be redirected to the friendly green grass through running and calisthenics, and therefore believed that world peace had been saved. They did not seem to notice that the "German champions" without exception wore black, white, and red ribbons, although the national colors at that time were black, red, and gold. They did not realize that the allure of the game of war, the old concept of the great and exciting competition between nations, was being practiced and kept alive here, and that warlike instinct by no means had been redirected. They did not see the connection, and did not see the relapse.[60]

In addition to the circles that simply opposed professional sports, there were those voices who did not believe that professional football was economically viable in Germany, and feared the loss of public subsidies and tax privileges.

However, by 1930, it was clear that amateurism at the highest levels of German football was really shamateurism. On August 25, 1930, the legal office of the West German Playing Association issued the judgment that fourteen players from FC Schalke 04 were to be declared professionals and suspended. Several officials from the club also were suspended.[61] In addition, a fine of a thousand Reichsmarks was imposed on FC Schalke. In fact, it long had been an open secret that the best players of Schalke, who

---

60. Haffner, *Geschichte eines Deutschen*, 74.
61. For the following, see Siegfried Gehrmann, "Fussball in einer Industrieregion: Das Beispiel F.C. Schalke 04," in *Fabrik-Familie-Feierabend: Beiträge zur Sozialgeschichte des Alltags im Industriezeitalter*, eds. Jürgen Reulecke and Wolfhard Weber (Wuppertal: Hammer, 1978), 377–98; *Fussball-Vereine-Politik: Zur Sportgeschichte des Reviers* (Essen: Hobbing, 1988), 99–101; Schulze-Marmeling, *Fussball*, 130–35; and Fischer, *Stürmer*, 153–55.

officially worked for the mining corporation Consolidation, no longer had to work underground and were given only light tasks by the company, which was fully aware of the positive effect on their image that came with sporting success. In addition, it was common to pay higher wages and give higher expense reimbursements to the players than really could be justified.

The press in the Ruhr region reacted with enormous indignation at the judgment, using a variation on the infamous propaganda lie from the political right regarding the German defeat in the First World War, namely the "stab in the back." The suspension affected an entire region that was particularly heavily affected by the world-wide economic crisis. The unemployment rate in Schalke's home city of Gelsenkirchen reached 67 percent during the worst period of the Depression. Willi Nier, the treasurer of FC Schalke, committed suicide following the judgment by the legal office. The enormous pressure on the leadership of the Association forced it to lift the suspensions that it had imposed. On the evening of June 1, 1931, a workday, when the Schalker "Squires" finally were able to field their regular side, the Glückauf arena in Gelsenkirchen was bursting at the seams. More than seventy thousand spectators wanted to see the friendly match against Fortuna Düsseldorf.

At this point, a growing number of voices called for ending the farce and legalizing a professionalization of the game. A private initiative in southern Germany in 1932 led to the establishment of a professional playing organization, under its own direction that included, among others, 1. FC Wuppertal, FC Mönchengladbach/Rheydt, and FC Schalke 04. The West German Football Union then demanded that the DFB establish clear guidelines for the separation of professional and amateur football, with the hope of isolating the former. An initiative by journalists, also in that same year, to develop a nation-wide league drew in clubs from the west as well as Hamburger SV, 1. FC Nürnberg, FC Bayern München, Wacker München, Hertha BSC Berlin, and clubs from Stuttgart and Frankfurt. Now on the defensive, in October 1932 the DFB decided against its will to permit the introduction of professional football.[62] This decision was also influenced by the intervening introduction of a

---

62. Heinrich, *Fussballbund*, 87.

football world championship outside of the Olympics in which midlevel amateur teams had no conceivable chance of competing.

In 2006 there was a highly polemical debate dubbed the *Fußball-Historikerstreit* (football historians' quarrel), regarding the reasons why the German association held so tightly to the principle of amateurism. At the core of the dispute was the question of how "brown" the DFB was in 1933 when it quickly offered its support to the new regime. The long uncontested view that the DFB had a national-conservative stance that was expressed in an antimodernist hostility to professionalism, and which converged with National Socialist ideology,[63] was challenged by the argument that the rapid acquiescence of the DFB was purely opportunistic, and more precisely economically motivated. Thus, the hostility to professionalism, both before and after 1933, was based on the fear of club officers that they would lose government subventions and tax privileges.[64] In this context, there has been criticism of Nils Havemann's connection of the argument about taxes with the theme of antisemitism, whereby fear of disadvantages in their tax status led to "resentment against the Jews" in the DFB because of the important role that Jews allegedly played in the movement for having professional players.[65] Earlier arguments that had pointed to multiple motivations, both ideological

63. See, for example, Gehrmann, *Fußball*, 28; Heinrich, *Fußballbund*, 75–92; Schulze-Marmeling, *Fußball*, 128–40; Dirk Bitzer and Bernd Wilting, *Stürmen für Deutschland: Die Geschichte des deutschen Fußballs von 1933 bis 1954* (Frankfurt: Campus, 2003), 39–41; and Rudolf Oswald, "Ideologie, nicht Ökonomie: Der DFB im Kampf gegen die Professionalisierung des deutschen Fußballs," in *Hakenkreuz und rundes Leder: Fußball im Nationalsozialismus*, 107–26.

64. See, for example, Erik Eggers, "'Berufsspieler sind Schädlinge des Sports, sie sind auszumerzen ...': Crux und Beginn eines deutschen Sonderweges im europäischen Fußball: Die Amateurfrage im deutschen Fußball der Weimarer Republik," in *Der lange Weg zur Bundesliga: Zum Siegeszug des Fußballs in Deutschland,* ed. Wolfram Pyta (Münster: Lit, 2004), 91–112; Nils Havemann, *Fußball unterm Hakenkreuz: Der DFB zwischen Sport, Politik und Kommerz* (Frankfurt: Campus, 2005), 56–62 and 159–64; and Markwart Herzog, "'Eigenwelt' Fußball: Unterhaltung für die Massen," in *Fußball zur Zeit des Nationalsozialismus: Alltag, Medien, Künste, Stars,* eds. Markwart Herzog and Andreas Bode (Stuttgart: Kohlhammer, 2008), 11–35.

65. Havemann, *Fußball unterm Hakenkreuz,* 159–64. For criticism of this thesis, see Rudolf Oswald, "Rezension zu Havemann, Fußball unterm Hakenkreuz," *SportZeiten* 6, no. 1 (2006): 164; *Ideologie,* 119 and 121; Dietrich Schulze-Marmeling, "Juden und Antisemitismus im deutschen und europäischen Fußball," *SportZeiten* 7, no. 2 (2007): 98; "Von Neuberger bis Zwanziger: Der lange Marsch des DFB," in *Hakenkreuz und rundes Leder,* 590–92; and Lorenz Peiffer, *Sport im Nationalsozialismus: Zum aktuellen Stand der sporthistorischen Forschung: Eine kommentierte Bibliografie* (Göttingen: Werkstatt, 2009), 22.

and economic, for hostility to professionalism have been pushed to the margins by the hardening of viewpoints on this issue.

There is also considerable controversy regarding the circumstances under which the plans for the establishment of a professional league, first mooted in 1932, were subsequently buried in 1933. For a long time, this was seen as needing no other explanation than that it resulted from National Socialist athletic policy, which rejected professionalism as a western and decadent phenomenon. Rudolf Oswald challenged this view, pointing to the important role played by the leading football official Felix Linnemann, who had been chairman of the DFB since 1925, and also took a position as the leader of the newly established Office of Football in the Deutscher Reichsbund für Leibesübungen (German Reich Union for Physical Exercise) in 1934. Linnemann used the sweeping authority that he had gained through the newly introduced *Führerprinzip* (Leader Principle) to roll back the 1932 decisions, which he had opposed, and did so without receiving any orders from above.[66]

In fact, the National Socialist athletic leadership was inconsistent with regard to the question of professional sports. Professionalism in boxing and cycling was allowed to continue, and hostility to professionalization in football was not unanimous even with regard to football.[67] In the summer of 1933, Fritz Mildner, who worked for the Reich sport commissar Hans von Tschammer und Osten, was convinced by the arguments of the South German Association for Professional Football Matches, founded in 1932, regarding the employment and political advantages of a professional league. This was before Linnemann pulled the emergency brake, pointing to the Olympic games of 1936.[68] In addition, ideological reservations about professionalism were juxtaposed against

66. Rudolf Oswald, *"Fußball-Volksgemeinschaft": Ideologie, Politik und Fanatismus im deutschen Fußball 1919–1964* (Frankfurt: Campus, 2008), 155. For a similar view, see Per Leo, "'Bremsklötze des Fortschritts': Krisendiskurse und Dezisionismus im deutschen Verbandsfußball, 1919–1934," in *Die "Krise" der Weimarer Republik: Zur Kritik eines Deutungsmusters*, eds. Moritz Föllmer and Rüdiger Graf (Frankfurt: Campus, 2005), 107–37. Regarding Linnemann also see Hubert Dwertmann, "Sportler-Funktionäre-Beteiligte am Massenmord: Das Beispiel des DFB-Präsidenten Felix Linnemann," *SportZeiten* 5, no. 1 (2005): 7–46.

67. See, for example, Hajo Bernett, "Die nationalsozialistische Sportführung und der Berufssport," *Sozial und Zeitgeschichte des Sports* 4, no. 1 (1990): 7–33; and Havemann, *Fußball unterm Hakenkreuz*, 99.

68. Havemann, *Fußball unterm Hakenkreuz*, 100.

the use of football as an escapist spectacle for the mass audience. There was also the possibility of using football to serve the needs of propagandizing the outside world. Here, however, there was a difference between Germany and fascist Italy. The latter sought to win the World Cup in 1934, which was open to professionals, while Nazi Germany focused on the Olympic games in 1936, for which the best athletes were intended to preserve their amateur status.

Even if bonuses were paid under the table, professional football remained forbidden in the Third Reich. In 1937, the sports journalist Lutz Koch claimed that when it came in third at the World Cup held in Italy in 1934, Germany became the "amateur world champion."[69] In truth, however, a camouflaged professionalism continued during the National Socialist period. There was even some renewed consideration of establishing a Reich league in 1939, but the outbreak of war ended this project.[70] There were true exceptions to the prohibition on professionalization in the Third Reich with regard to some other sports. These included motor sports, which enjoyed the support of long-time ADAC member Adolf Hitler, and boxing, which Hitler had already described in *Mein Kampf* as providing an almost ideal representation of the National Socialist conception of mankind as a pure fighting sport.[71]

The polemic against professional football, tinged with antisemitism, which had been part of public discourse in both the Weimar Republic and in Austria before the *Anschluss*, only became an important issue in the National Socialist press in 1938. The integration of Austrian football following the *Anschluss* and the general radicalization of anti-Jewish persecution beginning in 1938 played a decisive role in this development, which Oswald describes as an "antisemitic turn in the debate about professional football."[72] Professional football remained a target of antisemitic attacks during the war as well. The high-ranking football official

69. Lutz Koch, *Hinein . . . Tor, Tor! Deutschlands Nationalelf in 135 Fussball-Schlachten* (Berlin: Deutscher Schriftenverlag, 1937), 137–46.

70. Erik Eggers, "Profifußball im Amateurverband: Der deutsche Sonderweg," in *Fußball zwischen den Kriegen: Europa 1918–1939*, 242.

71. Adolf Hitler, *Mein Kampf* (Munich: Zentralverlag der NSDAP, 1941), 454.

72. Rudolf Oswald, "'Ein Gift, mit echt jüdischer Geschicklichkeit ins Volk gespritzt': Die nationalsozialistische Judenverfolgung und das Ende des mitteleuropäischen Profifußballs, 1938–1941," *SportZeiten* 2, no. 2 (2002): 53–67.

and former national coach Dr. Otto Nerz published an article on June 4, 1943, in the Berlin *12 Uhr Blatt* with the title "Europe's Sport will become free of the Jews," in which he claimed, among other matters, that

Jews and their bondsmen continually made the lives of the leadership [of the football association] very difficult, particularly with regard to the issue of professional players. During the crisis before 1933, there was a great danger that football would also become Judaized. The major clubs were always deeply in debt, and the creditors frequently were Jews. The drive toward professional football was very strong, and the state at that time could not give the leadership of the sport any support because the state, itself, was dependent on the Jews.[73]

The reestablished DFB renewed its struggle against professionalization after the end of the war. Nevertheless, in 1949, a system of "contracted players" was introduced that legalized paying football players on the basis of their performance. However, the players under contract were required to have a separate profession and their monthly pay for football was limited to the wages that a craftsman could earn. In addition, the cost of transfer fees were not left to market forces. It was reckoned on the basis of the yearly earnings of a player in addition to a guest appearance with the new club.[74] Just had been true in the past, there was no nationwide upper division. The national championship continued to be played in five regional upper divisions, in which the final round comprised the winners of each of these regional groups.

It was not until July 28, 1962, that the national council of the DFB established the Bundesliga (Federal League) with professional players.[75] After winning the World Cup in 1954, Germany had to be content with a fourth place finish in 1958. During the World Cup finals in Chile in 1962, Germany was knocked out of the competition in the intermediate rounds. At the same time, German clubs participated in the newly established European club competitions. Following the establishment of the European Champion Clubs' Cup in the 1955–56 season, just one German club made it to the final round. This was Eintracht Frankfurt,

---

73. Citation in Jürgen Leinemann, *Sepp Herberger: Ein Leben, eine Legende* (Berlin: Heyne, 1997), 265.

74. According to Heinrich, *Fussballbund*, 182–92, and Schulze-Marmeling, *Fussball*, 135.

75. See Siegfried Gehrmann, "Ein Schritt nach Europa: Zur Gründungsgeschichte der Fussballbundesliga," *Sozial- und Zeitgeschichte des Sports* 6 (1992): 3–37.

which lost to Real Madrid (3–7) in 1960. There were no German clubs in the final round of the Cup Winners' Cup established in 1960–61. At the same time, there was a threat that the best German players would leave for the Romance language-speaking countries, where professionalism long had been established. Between 1960 and 1963, no fewer than nine members of the German national team left the Federal Republic, mostly for Italy.

Even the establishment of the Bundesliga, which began play in the 1963–64 season with 16 teams, did not entail a full acceptance of professionalism by the DFB.[76] The first set of statutes of the Bundesliga required the players to have a profession in addition to football, insisted that the players have a "good reputation," and forbade them from using their names for advertisements. Precise upper limits were set for wages, expenses, bonuses, and transfer payments. The total monthly income of the players could not exceed 1,200 German marks unless an expert confirmed the extraordinary qualifications of a player and the playing committee gave its approval. Because of these restrictions, during the first season of the Bundesliga, just thirty-four players listed football as their full-time occupation. The great majority of the players chose to pursue another occupation and to treat football as an additional source of income.

However, this careful professionalization soon collapsed in the face of success at the international level. In 1966, the German national team made it to the final game in the World Cup against England. That same year, Borussia Dortmund was the first German club to win the European Cup. The next year, FC Bayern München achieved this same triumph. In 1965 and 1968, TSV München 1860 and Hamburger SV, respectively, reached the final game as the German representative in the competition, although each left the field as the loser.

Over the course of the 1960s, it became increasingly clear that the limits imposed by the Bundesliga statute were too narrow. Competition for the best players meant that the clubs in the Bundesliga continually came into conflict with the regulations concerning professional players. Just before the beginning of the first rounds of the Bundesliga in August

---

76. The following is based upon Schulze-Marmeling, *Fussball*, 135–38.

1963, there was considerable controversy regarding the transfer of two players between Karlsruher SC and FC Schalke 04, in which the bundling of the two players together was widely seen as a means of getting around the maximum transfer fee of 50,000 German marks. At first, the DFB punished both clubs with point reductions, but subsequently withdrew the penalty. The major scandal in the 1970–71 season, in which matches were fixed in order to avoid relegation, ultimately involved almost a third of the clubs in the Bundesliga and finally led to a change in thinking.[77] The pay limit of 1,200 German marks, which made the players susceptible to bribery attempts, was set aside. Transfer fees, players' salaries, and bonuses were now left up to the market, with the result that they quickly became astronomically high. As a consequence, over the course of the 1970s and 1980s, the Bundesliga became one of top destinations in European professional football.[78]

Football as Entertainment in
a Globalized Age

When one considers the discussions that took place in the interwar period up through the 1960s from the perspective of the early twenty-first century, they seem to come from the distant past. While in the early years of the Bundesliga, there was controversy whether the transfer of player had illegally breached the 50,000 German mark transfer fee limit, and in the 1980s the best players in the world were "worth" just a few million, at the end of the 1990s, the market value of some individual players reached into the hundreds of millions. In 2013, Real Madrid paid an astonishing transfer fee of 100 million euros for the Welsh midfielder Gareth Bale.

Even better than numbers such as these, which could be interpreted as the result of a linear development, is the clarity brought to the structural and even more to the cultural divergence of the 1990s by the

---

77. Kay Schiller, "Bundesligakrise und Fussballweltmeisterschaft 1974," in *Geschichte des Fussballs in Deutschland und Europa seit 1954,* ed. Wolfram Pyta (Stuttgart: Kohlhammer, 2013), 139–55.

78. Heinrich Väth, *Profifussball: Zur Soziologie der Bundesliga* (Frankfurt: Päd. Extra Buchverlag, 1994).

establishment of a football research unit at the University of Liverpool, that includes an expensive postgraduate program of study with the title Master of Business Administration (Football Industries). The goal of this educational program, which includes the areas of marketing, strategic management, accounting, and auditing, is "to combine professional development in the field of the football industries with a critical awareness of the issues involved in football management, marketing and the administration."[79] This development demonstrates clearly that during the decades of globalization of the capitalist economy and the creation of a virtual lived experience by the media, football has become a constitutive element of the international entertainment industry, in which professional managers, agents, media people, and marketing experts dominate alongside professional players and coaches.

This development was brought about by a complex interweaving of internal and external factors. Football lost much of its attractiveness on the playing field during the course of the 1980s. Following the refreshing offensive style of football that the national teams of the Netherlands and Germany, for example, played in the early 1970s, the game became increasingly defensive and cautious, with the greatest attention given to avoiding goals by the other side. The last Brazilian national team of "ball wizards" suffered a shipwreck at the hands of the Italians in the 1982 World Cup because of its weak defense. From this point on, even the South Americans, onto whom the Europeans have projected their ideas of football exoticism since the 1950s, have played a more tactically disciplined and "European" style of football, albeit one that was less spectacular than in earlier years. The decrease in the attractiveness of the game on the field led to decreasing numbers of spectators. The Bundesliga had an average of 25,987 spectators at each game in the 1977–78 season. This sank to 20,524 in the 1981–82 season, and reached a nadir of 17,662 in the 1985–86 season. It was not until the 1990–91 season that the average number of spectators increased back to 20,508, and then to 31,112 in the 1997–98 season.[80] Similar developments took place in the other professional leagues. These statistics played a considerable role in the decision

79. Football Research Unit, University of Liverpool: MBA (Football Industries); http://fru.merseyside.org/mba.htm.

80. The numbers are taken from Schulze-Marmeling, *Fussball*, 218.

to make changes in the rules that were intended to center the game on offense again. This same goal led to a change in the point system that made it more attractive to seek victory than to play for a draw.

The crisis of the 1980s, however, was not due solely to the decreasing attractiveness of the play on the field. Rather, several catastrophic incidents also inflicted considerable damage on the image of the sport. Thirty-nine people were killed at the final game of the European Champion Clubs' Cup in 1985 held at Heysel stadium in Brussels when rowdy supporters of Liverpool FC started a panic that led to the collapse of a wall in the stadium. Just eighteen days earlier, fifty-seven people were killed when an old wooden stadium at Bradford caught fire. Finally, in April 1989, ninety-six supporters of Liverpool FC were crushed to death in an overcrowded standing terrace at Hillsborough stadium in Sheffield.

These catastrophes, all of which were traced back to an aged stadium infrastructure, led to a significant push for modernization. Under pressure from a threat by the British prime minister Margaret Thatcher to ban professional football, safety precautions were improved and general surveillance systems were installed to fight hooliganism. In particular, however, stadiums in both England and internationally introduced seats. The uncovered standing-room bleachers, which had always been a symbol of the roots of football in working class culture as well as the emotional bonds of the fans with their club for which they were prepared to endure the wind and weather, now largely disappeared. Following the catastrophe at Hillsborough, the clubs in the top two divisions were legally required to equip their stadiums exclusively with seats. This modernization of the infrastructure combined with an increase in the price of admission—the least expensive adult ticket for the top league in England was £2 in 1984, £8 in 1992, and £12 in 1994—led to a substantial change in the social composition of the spectators.[81] Football games were transformed from spectacles that were attended largely by male members of the lower classes to events that were consumed by middle class families in a manner analogous to the professional leagues of several North American team sports. In addition, more women now ventured into the stadiums. In 1997, 50 percent of the season-ticket holders

---

81. The numbers are taken from Schulze-Marmeling, *Fussball*, 209.

were white-collar workers (versus 27 percent of the general population) and 28 percent were independent business owners or managers (versus 19 percent of the general population), but just 11 percent of such tickets were in the hands of skilled tradesmen (in comparison to 23 percent of

the general population), and 11 percent were held by workers without an apprenticeship in the trades (in comparison to 31 percent of the general population).[82] These changes in the social structure of the audience did not simply mirror a general social change, but rather exaggerated it. Similar developments were also seen in other countries, even if they were not as dramatic as they were in England.

In addition to these factors that were internal to football, there were also a number of important external factors in the 1990s that were all related to the neoliberal groundswell that dominated the economic and sociopolitical debates of the 1980s and 1990s in the Anglo-Saxon countries, in several Latin American military dictatorships, and, in a milder form, among members of the political and economic elites in continental Europe. The Thatcherite revolution, which was reaching its height during the early 1980s and had succeeded in withdrawing the state from the economy and dismantling the welfare state, predicated on the redistribution of wealth, encouraged the leading clubs to resist the structure of the Football League, which sought to maintain balance between richer and poorer clubs. "The socialism I believe in is everyone working for each other, everyone having a share of the rewards. It's the way I see football, the way I see life." The words of Bill Shankly, the legendary manager of Liverpool FC, were no longer heeded in Great Britain during the 1980s, either in politics or in sport. In 1983 the "Big Five" (Liverpool, Everton, Manchester United, Tottenham, and Arsenal) demanded that income from attendance remain solely with the host, and no longer be divided, as it had been since the First World War, between the host and the visiting club. In addition, they demanded a reform of the redistribution mechanism that required all 92 professional clubs to pay 4 percent of their income from attendance into a common pot so that the money could be redistributed in equal shares. In 1986, the division of television revenues

---

82. *Fletcher Research: Net Profits: How to Make Money Out of Football*, cited in Schulze-Marmeling, *Fussball*, 210.

was changed to the benefit of the clubs in the top division, and the contribution to the general pot was reduced to 3 percent of revenues from attendance. In 1988, the leading clubs in the First Division, with the support of the television company ITV, threatened to leave the FL and establish a Super League. As a consequence, the percentage of the television revenues that flowed into the pockets of the first division clubs increased again, this time from 50 percent to 75 percent. Then in 1991, a financially independent Premier League was established under the management of the FA, which formerly had been the guardian of amateurism. The Premier League was loosely connected with the other professional leagues through the relegation and advancement mechanisms, but no longer shared television revenues or money from sponsorships. This marked the end of the traditional redistribution structure of the FL.[83]

The other professional leagues saw similar processes, albeit somewhat later. The main cause is to be found in the liberalization of the electronic media, which drove television income to astronomic levels. The result was an increasingly sharp fight over the division of these revenues between the top clubs, whose bargaining position had been strengthened immeasurably, and the remainder of the professional clubs. In addition, television gained ever greater influence over the organization of the season and kick-off times, often to the detriment of the fans, who were still streaming into the stadiums.

The so-called Bosman judgment delivered yet another blow to the traditional system. In 1990, the Belgian player Jean-Marc Bosman brought a complaint before the European Court because his transfer from RC Liège to the French club Dunkirk was quashed through financial demands made by Liège. In 1995, the European Court declared that transfer fees for players who were not under contract were illegal. At the same time the court ruled, on the basis of the principle of the free movement of people that held sway in the European Union, that the number of EU nationals who were permitted to play on a team had been set arbitrarily. As a consequence of these decisions, the players were no longer the objects of transfers, but rather became contractual partners of the clubs.[84] The salaries of

---

83. According to Schulze-Marmeling, *Fussball*, 225.

84. Also see Thomas Kistner, *Das Milliardenspiel: Fussball, Geld und Medien* (Frankfurt:

the star players subsequently rose at a dizzying rate. At the same time, the top European leagues lost their national character. The number of foreign players in the English top league grew from 11 in the 1992–93 season to 166 in the 1998–99 season.

Over the course of the 1990s, the top level of European football came to resemble ever more closely the model of the thoroughly commercialized professional sports in the United States. The leading clubs were transformed into true entertainment companies. For example, Manchester United, which took the development of commercialization to the most extreme levels, employed no fewer than thirty cooks who worked in the sixteen restaurants in the stadium. The number of club administrators and people involved in merchandising far outstripped the number of players and coaches. In the 1998–99 season, the club had revenues of $290 million and admission fees comprised just 38 percent of the club's income. The remainder came from new sources such as television, merchandising, and food service. In keeping with the strategic alliance of economic concerns, in February 2001, Manchester United established a trans-Atlantic partnership with the New York Yankees, the American baseball team with the most championships, whose sports empire also included the New York Nets basketball club and the New Jersey Devils ice hockey club. Among other items, the agreement included the mutual marketing of fan merchandise. By the end of the 1990s, the 92 English professional clubs earned an average of $80 million per year. The clubs in the Italian, Spanish, and German professional leagues averaged $50 million per year.

On the other side of the equation, as noted above, wages and transfer fees also rose immeasurably. The total bill for the wages of the 412 employees of Manchester United was more than $150 million in the 1998–99 season. Overall, however, just a few of the major clubs, who understood how to draw on the new sources of income, benefitted from these developments. These were the same clubs that gained the most from the transformation of the European Cup into the Champions League in 1992. In comparison with the single knock-out system of the old competition, the Champions League guaranteed the top clubs, with their exceptionally

Fischer, 1998); and *Sport und Kommerz*, eds. Franz Jaeger and Winfried Stier (Zurich: Rüegger, 2000).

expensive teams, a fixed number of games within their groups, with the concomitant income. By contrast, the majority of the professional clubs were forced deeply into debt by the rising salaries and transfer fees. The introduction of the Champions League resulted in the establishment of a two-class system in the national leagues.

This reality was mirrored by the very different experiences of the professional clubs when they entered the stock market. In 1983 Tottenham was the first professional club to dare to go public. In 2000, nineteen English football clubs were quoted in the stock market. The biggest investors were, as a rule, media companies. A number of clubs in other leagues also ventured into the market. In 2000, Borussia Dortmund was the first club in the Bundesliga to do so. While the shares of a few clubs, such as Manchester United, rose very quickly in price, the shares of most football clubs fell in value.

In some cases, the interconnection of commercialized football, private media, and financial capital also had a political component. The best-known example is AC Milan, which was purchased in 1986 by the media and construction entrepreneur Silvio Berlusconi. At the beginning of the 1990s, Berlusconi, who served as club president until 2004, and then again from 2006 to 2008, entered politics. He founded a political party with a name drawn from the traditional chant of the Italian football fans, Forza Italia. In all, the Milan president, who regularly was involved in scandals and judicial conflicts, served four terms as Italian prime minister (1994–95, 2001–5, 2005–6, and 2008–11). Berlusconi's system, sometimes denoted as "Calciocracy" (ruled through football),[85] was emulated in Ukraine where "oligarchs" with political ambitions established, and still do establish, their influence through the financial support of popular football clubs.[86]

This is not the place to ask whether the further development of exceptional commercialization at the highest level of football, with the enormous media attention it receives, and the numerous betting scandals that have rocked the sport, as well as the almost daily presentation

85. John Foot, *Calcio: A History of Italian Football* (London: Harper Perennial, 2007), 326.

86. See Stefan Wellgraf, "Die Millionengaben: Fußball und Oligarchen in der Ukraine," in *Überall ist der Ball rund: Zur Geschichte und Gegenwart des Fußballs in Ost- und Südosteuropa—Nachspielzeit*, eds. Dittmar Dahlmann et al. (Essen: Klartext, 2011), 97–105.

of the top players on various television channels, will lead to an oversaturation of the sport. Nevertheless, within just a few years, Champions League football culture was facing a certain level of grassroots opposition, which found its voice in the numerous independent newspapers, the so-called fanzines.[87] The rise of the critical fan movement, known as the Ultras, is tied to this hostility toward the Champions League. Typical points of criticism by the Ultras regarding modern entertainment football concern the setting of the time of the games with a focus on the needs of television, and without concern for the fans who have to travel home after the game, the transformation of the game into an "event" through the introduction of individual seats in the stadium and the provision of additional entertainment programming for the purpose of titillating the emotions, the expansion of merchandizing, and changing stadiums (which increasingly bear the names of sponsors). They also criticize the increasing propensity of the clubs to relinquish traditions such as the names of the clubs and stadiums and banners, as well as basic regulatory matters such as separating home and guest fans, the deployment of police before, during and after games, often in the context of setting off fireworks, as well as the installation of security cameras in the stadiums, and the banning of certain individual fans from entering the stadiums.

The fact that the local connection is still very important, even in an age of satellite television and the internet, is made clear by the example of Charlton Athletic FC and its stadium, The Valley. Charlton lost its stadium in the 1980s because a young owner, who had inherited a majority stake, drove the club into the red through an unwise transfer. The sporting arena and all of its associated property subsequently had to be sold. After this, Charlton (known to its fans as the Addicks) was forced to play for several years in Selhurst Park, the stadium of Charlton's rivals Crystal Palace, which was located outside of the area where the Addicks's supporters lived, albeit still in southeast London.[88] At the end of the 1980s, the club was able to buy back the property, which had not yet been used for construction, at a reasonable price. Plans to replace

87. Richard Haynes, *The Football Imagination: The Rise of Football Fanzine Culture* (Aldershot: Arena, 1995).

88. For the spheres of influence of the various London clubs, see Morris, *Spiel*, 239.

the old stadium, which had since fallen into ruin, with a new building that had covered bleachers with seats, failed because of resistance by the authorities with jurisdiction in the district of Greenwich. The supporters of Charlton Athletic FC, who no longer wished to wait for the return of their club to their neighborhood, and already had their own institutional voice in the fanzine *Voice of the Valley*, established the Valley Party and received 10 percent of the vote in the council elections. As a result of this impressive democratic result, The Valley suddenly became an important political player, and the relevant authorities gave their permission for the construction project without any further objections. On December 5, 1992, the players from Charlton were able to play in their own arena after years of "exile."

A similar situation occurred in Hamburg in the winter of 1988–89. Here, the leadership of FC St. Pauli and a group of investors from Canada planned to tear down the old Millerntor stadium and construct a gigantic state-of-the-art project called the Sport Dome on the site. In response, a local campaign was organized by supporters of St. Pauli, who did not wish to lose their beloved stadium, and by inhabitants of the neighborhood, who feared that their property values would decline. For two months there were protests against the major project, which included numerous activities such as demonstrations, open forums, minutes of silence at games, and pamphleteering, at which point the club backed down. One result of the local action was the establishment of the fanzine *Millerntor Roar!* in the summer of 1989 that took a decidedly antiracist line from the very beginning. During the 1990s, the supporters of St. Pauli were known internationally for their "leftist" views in contrast to the generally extreme rightwing views that were cultivated in German fanzines.[89]

These developments seem to have been expressions of the capability of football to serve as a symbol of the dialectic between lightness and weight that marks postmodern globalized society, a capability that the sociologist Niklas Luhmann attributed to football as early as 1990.[90] It is a fundamental characteristic of football that it is able to create loyalties and indeed serve to create identities in the atomized society of the

89. Sven Brux, "St. Pauli-Fans gegen rechts! Chronik einer Bewegung," in *Fussball und Rassismus* (Göttingen: Werkstatt, 1994), 233–43.

90. Niklas Luhmann, "Der Fussball," *Frankfurter Allgemeine Zeitung*, July 4, 1990.

modern world without, however, cutting off the relations of the fan to their "real" social, political, and economic interests. Thus, it is possible for the fan to maintain his football loyalties over the long-term without succumbing to the rarified air of the "global players." It is precisely because of globalization that he faces a greater need to hold on to his local anchor in order to pursue his increased desire for authenticity and traditions.

5 | *Football and Emotion*

In his bestseller *Fever Pitch,* the English writer Nick Hornby recalled the background noise of the North Bank, the since-redesigned standing-room area of the venerable Highbury Park in London, the home of Arsenal FC: "I loved the different *categories* of noise: the formal, ritual noise when the players emerged (each player's name called in turn, starting with the favourite, until he responded with a wave); the spontaneous shapeless roar when something exciting was happening on the pitch: the renewed vigour of the chanting after a goal or sustained period of attacking."[1] Rhythmic clapping and drumming, communal singing and jeering, drinking alcohol and playing trumpets, all of this made the entry into the stadium a happy experience. When one adds in the fine aroma of grilling bratwurst and sausages, the fireworks and smoke, the colorful banners and deafening sirens, the rituals of football come vibrantly to life: they appeal to all of the senses. There is a feeling of solidarity. There is a festive and almost euphoric atmosphere. Thus, Hornby addresses two themes at the same time. These are the auditive or acoustic turn and the emotional turn, which have received considerable attention recently from cultural historians.[2]

In this chapter, we wish to examine how the game and its protagonists influence the emotions of the fans in the stadium, or as they listen on the radio or watch on television, and create a typology of the feelings that they express during the course of a match. We all know about the third goal at Wembley, that ominously sharply kicked ball by Geoff

1. Nick Hornby, *Fever Pitch* (London: Penguin Books, 1996), 75.
2. See, for example, *Acoustic Turn*, ed. Petra Maria Meyer (Paderborn: Fink, 2008) and Barbara H. Rosenwein, "Worrying about Emotions in History," *American Historical Review* 107 (2002): 821–45.

Hurst during the overtime of the World Cup game toward the German net that was tended by Hans Tilkowski. The ball struck the underside of the crossbar, landing either behind or in front of the line, and then going back into the field from where the German defender Weber headed it over the bar. There were several minutes of hope and dread while the Swiss referee, Gottfried "Gotti" Dienst, had an extensive discussion with the Soviet linesman Bakhramov, and finally decided that it had been a goal. Hurst, the tall midfielder from West Ham United, shot another goal to make the final result 4–2, and England won its first—and so far only—World Cup. For decades afterward, people in the Federal Republic of Germany lamented the contested decision and wanted to present evidence that the ball was not behind the line. The Wembley Goal became a site of memory that was heavily debated, analyzed, and condemned. The range of emotions that the "third goal" aroused in Germany went from sadness to scorn to defiance. There were even conspiracy theories in which the referee and linesmen were implicated.

In the second section of this chapter we will consider various players who serve as ideal model types for both fans and opponents. The final section of the chapter is focused on those who have been forgotten and the mavericks, and considers a small selection of players and trainers who still have the power to arouse emotions in modern observers because they suffered tragedies in their lives—lives that only would have been possible in the twentieth century.

"I am going crazy": A Dramatic Game as a Spark for Emotion

There are a great many games that a football fan remembers for his entire life, whether it is a cup game for his favorite team that was won on penalty kicks, or an important World Cup match that went back and forth before being decided in extra time, or the loss of the final and decisive game to avoid relegation. Games of this type are discussed for years among circles of friends. Important goals are joyfully recalled, and there is a palpable sense of suffering when one remembers the day his team was relegated. The words "if," "if only," and "but" play a central role in these conversations. Everything is in the past, but somehow is always new as well.

The history of the World Cup is filled with a whole series of games that fans will remember all the days of their lives. On July 8, 1982, the French and German teams faced each other in the semifinals of the World Cup in Piz Juan stadium in Seville.[3] While the Germans had needed all the luck in the world to reach the second round after their sensational loss to Algeria in the first round and the subsequent "disgrace of Gijón," a game in which the Austrians and Germans apparently made an arrangement to eliminate the North African team and enraged the entire world, the French delighted everyone with their technically inspired football, playing with *élan* and *supplesse*. Four years earlier, the coach Michel Hidalgo had put together a team for the tournament in Argentina whose midfield was all about ingenuity, an infield that was filled with virtuosos, namely the manager Michel Platini, the tiny and almost fragile technician Alain Giresse, the black long-distance runner Jean Tigana, and the lanky Bernard Genghini from Sochaux. The sweeper for the *équipe tricolore* was the veteran Marius Trésor from Martinique. The elegant offensive defenseman Manuel Amoros whirled along the edge. Up front, the wingers changed among Bernard Lacombe, Dominique Rochetau, and Didier Six, all of whom were excellent technicians, but who were nevertheless inconsistent in their main task of taking shots on net and coming away with the intended result.

Sympathies were clearly divided before the match. The football world, at large, supported the French, and Germany supported the Germans. The game was a duel between finesse and fitness, elegance and energy, ingenuity and directness. Pierre Littbarski from 1. FC Köln gave the Germans the lead in the eighteenth minute, but just ten minutes later Michel Platini scored the equalizer on a penalty shot.

Shortly before the end, this excellent and intense match seemed to be decided when the defenseman Patrick Battiston, who had come in as a replacement, appeared alone in front of the goalie Toni Schumacher. But then Schumacher brutally cut down the attacking player. The ball rolled a few centimeters in front of the empty net. Battiston remained unconscious on the ground. As a result of the exceptionally rough foul by the German goalkeeper, Battiston lost several teeth and suffered a se-

---

3. Erich Baumann et al., *Fussball-WM 1982 Spanien* (Künzelsau: Sigloch, 1982), 182–98.

vere concussion as well. The stereotype of the reckless, and pathological-ly ambitious Germans seemed to be confirmed on all counts. Ultimately, Manuel Amoros was only able to hit the crossbar during the extra time, and the German winger Klaus Fischer, who had come in as a replace-ment, missed a direct shot on goal by just a hair's breadth.

The French dominated the extra period, and gained an apparently in-surmountable lead of 3–1 with goals by Marius Trésor and Alain Giresse, and tried to score yet a fourth goal before the indefatigable Germans got back into the game. Hans-Peter Briegel, the "Walz aus der Pfalz," a former decathlete who had tremendous conditioning, kept on driving his team forward. Only Jean Tigana, the runner from Girondins de Bordeaux, could keep up with this increased tempo, at least for a while. Midfielders Karl-Heinz Rummenigge and the veteran Klaus Fischer were able to even the score with spectacular bicycle kicks. Then, following 120 stirring min-utes, the game was decided on penalty kicks. Here too, the "Blue" seemed to be the certain winners. The defenseman Uli Stielike missed a penalty shot, and sank to the grass in sadness and shame. The cameras were still directed toward the crumpled up Stielike and his dramatic suffering when the German were able to rejoice once again. Didier Six, the long-haired legionary in the service of VfB Stuttgart, took his shot and Schumacher was able to block it. In this short span of time, Schumacher had gone from bogeyman to hero. Finally came the pale central defender, Maxime Bossis, who would become a tragic figure as he missed the decisive pen-alty kick. The winger Horst Hrubesch from Hamburger Sportsverein, who had come in as a replacement and two years earlier against Belgium had secured the European championship with a header in the last minute, now used his chance to seal the victory. Fatalistically, he kicked the ball as it had been placed by the referee, without adjusting it to his own liking.

The Germans were once again in a final where they were defeated clearly and convincingly by the clever (and in this tournament, bril-liant) Italians 1–3. The severely disappointed French played their second squad in the match for third place and promptly lost to the Poles who, in their resilient veterans Lato and Smolarek, and the young and fast Zbigniew Boniek, had three scoring threats among their wingers. The "*bleux*" reached the finals three times. They celebrated an aesthetically pleasing but inefficient style of football, and the dream came to a sudden end when confronted by robustness and conditioning. Half of the planet suffered alongside the French, who had gone down with their banners flying high. Many people cried along with the creative and popular team, as their defeat became reality shortly before midnight.

The 1982 World Cup had already seen a match with similar intensity during the second round. Italy had to defeat Brazil in order to reach the semifinals. This was a Brazilian team that with Zico, Sócrates, Falcão, Eder, and Junior had a group of absolute artists in their ranks recalling the creativity of the Brazilians of the 1960s, Pelé, Garrincha, Didi, Vava, Coutinho, Tostão, Rivelino, Jairzinho, and Nílton and Djalma Santos— the Selecão that won the World Cup three times between 1958 and 1970. By contrast, Italy had been fortunate to make it into the second round after three draws. The team from Cameroon, built around goalkeeper Thomas N'Kono and winger Roger Milla, were knocked out of the first round only because of a scandalous whistle by the referee and Italy's slightly better goal differential. The veteran goalkeeper Dino Zoff and the defense with the masterful sweeper Gaetano Scirea (who died far too young), the merciless Claudio Gentile, the offensively talented Antonio Cabrini (all of whom played for Juventus Turin), as well as the relentless Fulvio Collovati, were the only ones who reached the usual high standard. The coach, Enzo Bearzot, cast off the tactical fetters and the Squadra Azurra stormed ahead. Giancarlo Antognoni pulled the strings in the midfield. The long-haired Bruno Conti, who also was in the service of AS Roma, played a dominant game on the wings. The Juventus player Marco Tardelli also played a strong game, moving forward and supported by the industrious Graziani and Paolo Rossi, the center forward, a lurker with an unbelievable nose for the goal, who in the late 1970s was embroiled in one of the worst corruption scandals in the history of football, though he denied any involvement. The Brazilians almost immediately took away the Italian lead, utilizing their short passing game and a variety of feints. However, the more attentive Italians resolutely exploited the weakness of the Brazilian defense and the notoriously porous goalkeeper Valdir Perez. Paolo Rossi scored all three goals to secure the victory for the Italians, who had risen far above themselves. Italy then defeated Poland in the semifinal before soundly defeating the Germans 3–1 before the eyes of the graying Italian president Sandro Pertini, who did not restrain himself from dancing in the stands. Rossi, Tardelli, and the Inter Milan player Alessandro Altobelli, who had been substituted into the game, each scored for the clearly dominant Azzurri before the Munich player Paul Breitner was able to score a consolation goal. Tardelli's goal celebration remains fixed in the minds of football fans as he shouted out his joy past the center line. His face made clear in an almost platonic manner what total release and boundless joy mean at their core.

Four years later, during the World Cup in Mexico City, the dream-dancing Brazilians failed against the French in a similarly dramatic match on penalty shots. Sócrates, the left-wing pediatrician and midfielder, made the decisive penalty kick against another intellectual, the French goalie Joël Bats from Paris St. Germain, who enjoyed writing love poetry in his spare time. In one of the most technically proficient games of all time, the goal-scoring Careca gave the lead to the Selecão. The French tied the score on a goal from Platini following a cross pass from Amoros. In the midfield, where the French had previously been dominant, they gradually gained a slight advantage thanks to the combative Luis Fernandez. Both teams, however, failed to capitalize on their numerous chances to score. In the penalty kicks, the preeminent Platini missed his shot, while the striker Bruno Bellone from AS Monaco took advantage of tremendous luck as his sharp kick sprang back from the post, bounced off of the goalie's back, and then rolled like a billiard ball into the goal. This time fortune was with the French, as Sócrates failed in his penalty kick.

In the semifinals, the French *equipe tricolore* again had to pay tribute to the effort of the Germans. The caustic Hamburger Wolfgang Rolff kept his attention on the visibly exhausted Platini. Felix Magath, who was also from HSV, played with great vision. The hard-nosed defenders Guido Buchwald and Karl-Heinz Förster did their part to frustrate the technical game of the French. The Germans lost in Aztec stadium in Mexico City to the Argentinians 2–3 after having rallied from an apparently insurmountable two goal deficit just as quickly as they had done four years previously against the French. The fact that Toni Schumacher allowed the Argentinians to take the lead in this final game on a goal by the sweeper José Luis Brown because of a bad error, and that he did not so much as see another goal brought a sense of gratification to many observers. The villain of Seville finally had been punished!

It is striking that both Brazil and France only became world champions when they acquired solid defensive players and strong goalies, namely Claudio Taffarel in the case of Brazil and Fabien Barthez in the case of France.[4] This success, however, came at the cost of concessions in both tactics and athleticism. Dunga, Mauro Silva, and Marcio Santos, or comparatively, Marcel Desailly, Didier Deschamps, Lilian Thuram, Patric Viera, and Emmanuel Petit were generally athletic and immensely robust players, whose conditioning was superior to that of even the Germans and English, and who occasionally drove forward without mercy in order to cover the backs of the artists such as Zinedine Zidane or Rivaldo, Romario, and Bebeto.

It was precisely the technically most proficient teams and players who failed at the decisive moment: Hungary in 1954, Netherlands in 1974 and 1978 when they unfortunately lost against the hosts in the World Cup finals, and the Portuguese in 2000 when a contested handball opened a path for the French to reach the finals of the European championship. The only consolation that Luis Figo, Joaõ Pinto, Rui Costa and Nuno Gomes have is that they were on the best-playing team, and that sympathy is on their side.

Around the turn of the millennium epic games of the type described above became quite rare. The "Golden Goal" and "Silver Goal" rules in place between 1993 and 2004 made it difficult to have apparently impossible comebacks rewarded in the last minute when the tactical shackles are finally removed and a world that believes in miracles seems to be filled with magic. The combination of suffering and hope, triumph and tears, which is characteristic of cycling, was almost completely played out for more than a decade. Those mythical duels, as they are known from the Tour de France or Giro d'Italia, such as the duels between Kübler and Koblet, Bartali and Coppi, Anquetil and Poulidor, Hinault and Zoetemelk, Le Mond and Fignon, seemed to have no place in a time with closely calculated windows for advertising.[5] Only the recent return

4. In 1984, France became European champion on its own home ground with five goals by the exceptional Platini.

5. Regarding the mythical nature of the Tour de France, see Michael Gamper, "Mythos Tour de France: Wie die Tour ihr Publikum fasziniert," in *Tour de France: Auf den Spuren eines Mythos* (Zurich: AS Verlag, 1999), 7–14. Concerning the Swiss cycling heroes Ferdi Kübler and Hugo Koblet

of the penalty kicks would then result in a return of such duels, for instance in the 2006 World Cup finals.

We would consider ourselves lucky to experience a high-scoring game such as the 7–5 victory of the Austrians over the Swiss during the World Cup quarterfinals in Lausanne in 1954. In the broiling heat, the hosts in the Pontaise stadium had gained a 3–0 lead just eighteen minutes into the match following two goals by Seppe Hügi from FC Basel as well as a goal from Ballaman. Both goalies suffered sunstroke, and the defenseman Bocquet also had to play with health problems. It was later discovered that he had a brain tumor. At that time, substituting players was not permitted. The Swiss, who were required by their association to be pure amateurs, were not properly conditioned for the demands of playing in such heat. For their part, the Austrians, and particularly the hat-trick scorer Wagner as well as Ocwirk, cleverly used the weakness of the Swiss defense and took long-distance shots, thereby gaining a 5–3 lead and finally managing to gain the advantage against the Swiss, who refused to retreat as they possessed in the winger Jackie Fatton (Servette Geneva) one of the best left outside strikers in the world.[6] On their side, the Austrians had two great players Gerhard Hanappi and the runner Ernst Happel. The latter went on to have great success as a coach, and frequently won the German championship with HSV. Even after he had been diagnosed with cancer, he coached the Austrian national team in a game just a few weeks before his death.

"I am going crazy," the reporter Edi Finger from Austrian TV shouted into the microphone in 1978 after Hans Krankl, a player for Rapid Vienna, scored for the third time on the German goalie Sepp Maier in Córdoba, Argentina.[7] Finger went "crazy" because the Austrians around "Schneckerl" Herbert Prohaska, Walter Schachner, sweeper Bruno Pezzey, goalie Friedl Koncilia, and the scorer Hans Krankl finally defeated the "Piefkes." This game also had gone back and forth. The laws of tactics

and their multiple efforts to cash in, see Fabian Brändle and Christian Koller, "'Ferdi National' oder 'Hugo International'? Radsport und Zeitgeist in der Schweiz der fünfziger Jahre," *Sozial- und Zeitgeschichte des Sports* 14 (2000): 7–25. For similar phenomena in Italy, see Stefano Pivato, *Sia lodato Bartali: Idealogia, cultura e miti dello sport cattolico (1936–1948)* (Rome: Edizioni Lavoro, 1985).

6. Fritz Hack, *Spiele des Jahrhundert* (Bad Homburg: Limpert, 1980), 73–75.

7. Martin H. Schwarz, *5 Jahrzehnte Fussball im Originalton: Die Geschichte des Fussballs in Deutschland*, 5 CDs (Hamburg: Hörbuch, 2000), CD 3, title 15.

and calculation had become inoperative. In short, it was a carnivalesque, even "crazy" time when the whole world was turned on its head.[8]

The Germans, who had even suffered an own goal at the hands of their captain Berti Vogts, were treated mercilessly in their homeland. The pop star Udo Jürgens had sung "Buenos Dias, Argentina" before the World Cup. A scornful "Buenas Noches, Buenos Aires" was then heard from many fan sections. The famous German sports journalist Hanns Joachim Friedrichs stated that it was completely appropriate for the defending champions to be knocked out of the tournament: "It is no wonder that a team that attempts to defend its world championship title in such a half-hearted, foolish, and lily-livered way cannot get anywhere in a football crazy country such as Argentina."[9]

Games like this, when the obvious underdog trips up a highly favored team, always fascinate us. There is always an element of schadenfreude when a big shot goes out to the sticks and loses a cup game in the midst of improvised steel bleachers with wooden railings, or when a prohibitive favorite in a tournament loses to an African or Asian team. Ridicule was poured onto the English when they failed to make a World Cup for the first time in 1950, losing 0–1 in Brazil to the United States, where football was meaningless. The Germans were bathed in malice when they lost 2–1 to Algeria in 1982 on goals by Madjer and Belloumi. The striker Rabah Madjer was able to cement his reputation as a terror of the Germans when in 1987 he carried FC Porto to the triumph in the European Champion Clubs' Cup with his unbelievably audacious equalizer against Bayern München in the final game. The Austrians had to endure abuse for their 0–1 loss against the Faroe Islands in 1990, in the latter's first ever official match. The goalie from the Faroe Islands, Knud Knudsen, lost his wool cap twice during the game, but never lost his concentration. Finally, the Swiss faced disgrace in 1996 when they lost 0–1 to the modest Azeris in a qualifying match after they traveled to Baku in a luxury jet with newly installed leather seats.

---

8. Also see Michael Wassermair, *3 : 2 Österreich-Deutschland: 20 Jahre Córdoba* (Vienna: Döcker, 1998).

9. Hans Joachim Friedrichs, *XI. Fussball-Weltmeisterschaft 1978 Argentinien* (Gütersloh: Bertelsmann, 1978), 129.

Heroes

Whoever has seen the great teams of football history for himself will remember them for his entire life. He will remember the Uruguayans of the 1920s and 1930s and their tall, dark-haired manager José Leandro Andrade.[10] A few decades later, one dreams about the Hungarian team that had the misfortune of losing the World Cup final in Bern in 1954. Older fans revel in the memory of the legendary Real Madrid team of the 1950s that won a total of five European Cup championships. The writer Wolfgang Frank recalled (in 1971):

Canario—Del Sol—Di Stefano—Puskas—Gento. There would never again be an attack such as this. Ten super feet, 100 hyper toes. To make a comparison to another area of life, one would have to imagine that Bach, Mozart, Beethoven, Haydn, and Handel had all come together to compose for the prince-bishop of Salzburg, at the same time, working on the same concerto, on the same piano, with Brahms in reserve.[11]

Classical high culture may have been an appropriate point of comparison for a child of the 1970s. However, a contemporary observer might suggest a session with Bob Dylan, Steve Earle, Shane McGowan, Townes van Zandt, and Joe Strummer in order to give an adequate description of the legendary Madrileno attack. Another author, the Madrileno Javier Marías, who was able to attend the games in Santiago-Bernabeu stadium as a child, daydreamed about the ways in which the Whites at the height of their ability always played with restraint:

Marquitos, the right defenseman, was able to clear a very dangerous ball just one meter in front of the net with a heal-kick toward the corner. Today, the coach would fine him for that. This is true of all of the other hat-trick artists, Di Stéfano included. Puskas, despite the four goals that he scored in the European Cup championship game in Glasgow against Eintracht Frankfurt, which Real won 7 to 3, would have been fined because he did not run enough. Gento would have been fined because his artful lobbing of the ball, his nutmegging, and his kicking of the ball into the net with his back heel compromised the team's possession of the ball.[12]

10. Andrade was one of the first dark-haired sports stars. The French journalists who watched him during the 1924 Olympic games, called him the "black marvel." See Edoardo Galeano, *Der Ball ist rund* (Zurich: Unionsverlag, 2000), 65.

11. Wolfgang Frank, "Was ist real an Real Madrid?," *ZEITmagazin*, September 28, 1973.

12. Javier Marías, *Alle unsere frühen Schlachten: Fussball-Stücke* (Stuttgart: Klett-Cotta, 2000), 133.

Real, which played an epic duel for the Club World Championship (Intercontinental Cup) against Peñarol Montivideo, was then defeated in Europe by Benfica Lisbon and their strikers Eusébio and Torres, who then contested against the Brazilian Pelé and his FC Santos for the crown in club football. The Brazilians were long considered the best club team of all time. Pelé, who in his long career for the Seleção, FC Santos, and Cosmos New York scored more than a thousand goals in professional football, many of which were spectacular and unforgettable, is seen by many experts as the best football player ever.

During the so-called iron 1960s, the game was dominated by the tactics and defensive-style of football, the so-called *catenaccio* (chain), which was taught by Herrera, the Argentinian coach of Inter Milan. The World Cup in Chile in 1962 was marked by numerous brutal fouls and violent conduct. Four years later, there was again more defensive than offensive play. The Swiss team did play an offensive style, but were not even a factor in the first round, where they were completely stalled. The Zurich *Sport* reported: "A team like ours cannot afford to play an offensive style in the World Cup. It is necessary to play carefully in World Cup matches.... In today's style of play, it is necessary to have attacking forwards, who can also fall back on defense."[13]

It was the Dutch, and particularly Johan Cruyff, who along with the South Americans rediscovered the original point of the game, namely scoring goals. In 1978, the Argentinians won the World Cup in their own country under the aegis of their coach Menotti, the top scorer Mario Kempes, the defenders Passarella and Tarantini, and the playmaker Oswaldo Ardiles, along with Bertoni, Luque, and Ortiz. The French and Brazilians had a pair of spectacular teams before the Italians and then the Argentinians again came through as worthy world champions in the 1980s. But we also do not wish to forget the Danes, Poles, Peruvians, Portuguese, and African teams from Cameroon and from the Maghreb that played a fast-paced and mixed style of football without, however, achieving great success.

In considering club football, the athletic and combative style of Nottingham Forest and Liverpool sticks in the mind, particularly their practice of forechecking. Liverpool's Scots, Kenny Dalglish, Graeme Souness, and Alan Hansen, as well as their powerful and tough outside defenders

13. Citation according to *Fussball-Weltmeisterschaft 1966*, ed. Friedebert Becker (Munich: 1966), 228.

Mickey Mills and Phil Neal, taught the ensembles of stars from South America to fear Anfield Road.

At the end of the 1980s and early 1990s, it was AC Milan that perfected the pressing defense with their resourceful sweeper Franco Baresi, the defenders Paolo Maldini and Costacurta, the midfielder Demetrio Albertini, and particularly the three Hollanders Ruud Gullit, Frank Rijkaard, and Marco van Basten, supported by the Yugoslav Dejan Savicevic. They then seamlessly turned to the attack with the captured ball. Connoisseurs will always remember Dynamo Kiev under coach Valeriy Lobanovskyi that offered a style of football with an unheard of tempo and very few mistakes, with fast strikers such as Oleg Blokhin and Igor Belanov. We also want to mention briefly Ajax Amsterdam, a team with a perfected style of offensive play with three strikers. After its victory over AC Milan in the Champions' Cup, Ajax was forced to release abroad almost all of its players, who as a rule had come up the ranks of the club into the team. These were the strategist and goal scorer Bergkamp, the elusive Fin Litmanen, the de Boer twins, Witschge, the long-limbed goalie van der Sar, the fast outside striker Overmars, the defenders Bogarde and Reiziger, all of whom left Ajax. There is a certain tragedy in the fact that fans from small countries can only enjoy the great talents for a short time before they convert their skills into economic rewards in the leagues of Italy, Spain, Germany, and England.

The English cultural historian Peter Burke, a trailblazer in his field, made clear in his standard work on premodern popular culture that certain prototypes such as heroes, rogues, and fools provide a means of understanding the popular system of values because the heroes fulfill and surpass the normally expected behaviors, the rogues call them into question, and the fools cannot live up to them.[14] A hero, whose original type, according to Burke, following the model of Max Weber, is the warrior, affords the audience someone with whom to identify. People can define themselves in opposition to the rogue. Fools are praised for providing entertainment. As the two British social historians, Richard Holt and J. A. Mangan, have described the matter, heroes embody the values and aspirations of their admirers and reflect their hopes and secret desires.[15]

14. Peter Burke, *Popular Culture in Early Modern Europe* (London: Temple Smith, 1978).

15. Richard Holt and J. A. Mangan, "Prologue: Heroes of a European Past," in *European Heroes: Myth, Identity, Sport*, 1–13.

It is obvious that the truly great players who have had a decisive impact on international championships are immortal in the eyes of the fans. Men such as Pelé, Jackie Charlton, Diego Maradona, and Michel Platini are honored for their entire lives. However, we think that there are certain more interesting mental constellations that transform specific players into the symbolic representatives of a (sub)culture. We discussed above Stephen Bloomer, who represented the rough pub-culture of England around 1900, while his colleague Harold Fleming epitomized a pious and sober class that desired respectability and social advancement.

The two Austrian urban sociologists Roman Horak and Wolfgang Maderthaner address, in their exceptionally important essay, the question of what the immense popularity of the two football players Josef Uridil and Matthias Sindelar meant in the Vienna of the 1920s and 1930s.[16] As observed above, Vienna at this time was already a center of professional football. Matches between First Vienna, Rapid, Wacker, Admira, Hakoah, and Austria, and international contests for the Mitropa Cup against Sparta, Bohemians, and Slavia Prague, as well as the best Hungarian and Italian teams, drew in tens of thousands of spectators.

Josef Uridil, who wrote his biography in 1924 while still a young man,[17] was born the son of a tailor in the working class suburb of Ottakring in 1895, and quickly joined SK Rapid, the favored club of the inhabitants of this suburb. As a fighter, he represented the working class ideal. He scored numerous decisive goals, enjoyed singing, and had a role in the now lost film about the game called *Pflicht und Ehre (Duty and Honor)*. In 1928, after many great successes with Rapid, he left Austria and coached Bratislava, Bari, then the Romanian national team, as well as numerous teams in Yugoslavia, Switzerland, and Germany. By no means a National Socialist, Uridil returned to Vienna at the start of the war in order, as the title of the film *Duty and Honor* unintentionally anticipated, to accept his obligation to serve in the German army. As was true in other working class districts, Uridil was that beloved kind of player who never failed to get up after a foul and to keep on fighting. With these characteristics, he surely would have succeeded in the cities of northern England, in the Ruhr region, or in Silesia, with the club Gornik Zabrze.

16. Horak, "Culture of Urban Cosmopolitanism."

17. Josef Uridil, *Was ich bin und was ich wurde: Die Lebensgeschichte des berühmten Fussballers von ihm selbst erzählt* (Leipzig: R. Läwit, 1924).

By contrast, Matthias Sindelar embodied an entirely different Vienna specialty, namely the coffee house hero. We have already mentioned the coffee houses of Vienna, those famous centers of the thought and conviviality, cosmopolitanism and debate, chess and literature.[18] The club coffee house was noted above as a peculiarity of sports history. Supporters of Austria met in Café Holub, supporters of Rapid in Café Parsifal, fans of Wacker did themselves the honor of meeting in Café Resch, while football philosophers and experts were to be found in the even more distinguished Café Ring. Matthias Sindelar was exceptionally fragile. His telling nickname was the "Paper Man." He had amazing technique and was an artist on the field. Sindelar was the captain of Austria Wien and the Austrian Wonder Teams of the 1930s that played a finesse style of football that sometimes seemed almost weightless. The creative Sindelar spoke to the artistic bohemians in the city, who flocked together indulging in non-purposeful lives, asking about the now and not thinking about tomorrow.[19] The exceptionally gifted football player became the object of artistic expression: authors described his moves and his finesse. His vision of the game was compared to the strategy of a chess grandmaster.

The son of a worker, Sindelar kept aloof from the dominant Austrian fascist and racist currents of the period, and represented a remnant of "Red Vienna" from the 1920s. In 1938, he became the owner of a coffee house. He paid the dispossessed former Jewish owner a fair price for the coffee house, offering a sum of money that was appropriate for a café in the neighborhood of Favoriten. His tragic early death led to the development of a number of myths about the Paper Man. He was found dead alongside his half-Jewish lover on January 23, 1939. The police listed poisoning as the official cause of death. There were rumors that the National Socialists had murdered Sindelar and his girlfriend. The Paper Man had opposed the "Greater Germany" team, which had been established in 1938 after the *Anschluss*. In the last match by "Ostmark" against Germany, he insisted on wearing a red-and-white jersey, played a great game, and after a goal by his best friend Schasti Sesta, Sindelar danced in front

18. See Horak, "Culture of Urban Cosmopolitanism," 140–42.

19. Also see Wolfgang Maderthaner, "Ein Dokument wienerischen Schönheitssinns: Matthias Sindelar und das Wunderteam," *Beiträge zur historischen Sozialkunde* 3 (1992): 87–91; and "Der 'papierene' Tänzer: Matthias Sindelar, ein Wiener Fussballmythos," in *Die Kanten des runden Leders*, 294.

of the VIP stand, which was filled with high-ranking Nazi functionaries. It was claimed, at least by the remaining opponents of the regime, that the Nazis had taken their revenge on Sindelar for his hostility to the regime. In fact, feelings about the Nazis in Vienna changed very quickly after the *Anschluss*. The euphoria from Heroes' Square quickly turned into a general feeling of disillusionment. The Vienna National Socialists were replaced in their positions by newer, sometimes "old German" power brokers. Among the social-democratic working class, particularly among the city tram operators, there remained a hard core of anti-regime critics, who had already begun to work underground during the period of the clerical-fascist corporative state.[20] The new authorities reacted to the serious charges by organizing a state funeral at which about 15,000 people paid their last respects to Matthias Sindelar. On January 30, Hitler finally removed the unloved careerist Dr. Odilo Globocnik from his office as the Gauleiter of Vienna in order to curb the unrest among the population in the capital city. The events surrounding the mysterious death of the Paper Man certainly led to a change of feelings in Vienna, bringing about an anti-foreign and anti-German sentiment.

Sindelar and Uridil were both the sons of immigrants who had come to Vienna from Bohemia. The real name of Raymond Kopa, who was born in 1931 in the mountainous Noeux-les-Mines region of northern France, was Kopaczewski. His father had immigrated from Poland and worked, along with Raymond's older brothers, in the local mine. The immigrant's son achieved phenomenal success as an outside striker with Stade de Reims, Real Madrid, and the French national team. He was a key player in the great Real teams of the late 1950s, and won a bronze medal in the World Cup in Sweden in 1958. The sport made him rich.[21] Kopa, who wrote several autobiographies, thereby gaining an audience outside the world of football,[22] was not particularly interested in his

20. Evan Burr Bukey, *Hitlers Österreich: "Eine Bewegung und ein Volk"* (Hamburg: Europa-Verlag, 2001), particularly 103–5; "Popular Opinion in Vienna after the Anschluss," in *Conquering the Past: Austrian Nazism Yesterday and Today,* ed. Fred Parkinson (Detroit, Mich.: Wayne State University Press, 1989), 151–64; and Gerhard Botz, *Nationalsozialismus in Wien: Machtübernahme und Herrschaftssicherung 1938/39* (Vienna: Mandelbaum, 1988).

21. Alfred Wahl and Pierre Lanfranchi, "The Immigrant as Hero: Kopa, Mekloufi and French Football," in *European Heroes: Myth, Identity, Sport,* 114–27; and Alfred Wahl, "Raymond Kopa une vedette du football," *Sport Histoire* 2 (1988): 4–6.

22. See Raymond Kopa, *Mes matches et ma vie* (Paris: Pierre Horay, 1958); and Raymond Kopa and Pierre Katz, *Mon Football* (Paris: Calmann-Lévy, 1972).

roots, as his name attests, although his parents spoke Polish exclusively to each other at home. He gained French citizenship at the age of twenty-one and was very happy to do his military service in the army. Many photographs show the strapping soldier posing. Just like the American Elvis Presley, who famously served in Germany, Raymond Kopa in uniform was a ubiquitous presence in all forms of media. Pierre Lanfranchi and Alfred Wahl argue in their assessment of Kopa that his impressive career demonstrates the success that can come from hard work if one abides by the cultural expectations of one's adopted country. During the 1960s, Kopa showed his other, political face. He campaigned against the growing power of the clubs and against contracts that bound players to their clubs until they were thirty-five years old.

Rachid Mekloufi, who was born in the town of Sétif in Algeria in 1937, was cut from an entirely different cloth than Kopa, who had sought to assimilate. In his youth, Mekloufi was playing for Union Franco-Musulmanne de Sétif when a talent scout for AS St. Etienne found him and brought him to France in 1954. Although football was a means of bridging divides in Algeria where French and North Africans played on the same teams, until 1956 Algerian teams were not permitted to play in French cup championships or in the professional championship. Mekloufi played so well that he became a French national player and won the world military championship in Buenos Aires in 1957. The media coopted his great talent by presenting him as a peaceful mediator between cultures. However, in April 1958, journalists were shocked to learn that Mekloufi refused an invitation to play in the World Cup for the ambitious French team in order to join together with nine other professionals the team of the Front de Libération Nationale (FLN), which was training in exile in Tunisia. Between 1958 and 1962 he played in numerous matches in Tunisia, Morocco, Libya, Iraq, Jordan, as well as in eastern bloc countries, China, and North Vietnam. Because he was the best and most prominent player on this team, he soon became a hero of the Algerian resistance and symbol of the revolution. In 1962, after independence had been achieved, Mekloufi went back to France and again played for money. In May 1968, he received the trophy he had won with his home club AS St. Etienne from the hands of the French president Charles de Gaulle. Back in Algeria, he criticized the government there because it had forbidden young domestic players from going to France. Other popular players, such as Mustapha Zitouni, who also had gone into exile, did not return. However, this "treason" did not damage Mekloufi's reputation. During the 1970s and early 1980s, he was several times coach of the Algerian national team as well as of the African continental selection, and in 1988 he became the president of the Algerian football association for a short period.

In view of the claim by the extreme right-wing politician Jean-Marie Le Pen that he could not identify with a French team composed of black players, it must be noted that the best players from the (former) colonies and other countries had long played in France. Budzinski, like Kopa, had roots in Poland. Ahmed Ben Bella, a successful striker for Olympique Marseille, was Algerian by birth and in 1962 became the first president of independent Algeria. Michel Platini's ancestors came from Italy to Joeuf in Lorraine to work in a mine. Luis Fernandez had Spanish ancestors. Marius Trésor came from the Antilles. The *equipe tricolore* that won the World Cup in 1998 and the European Championship two years later thus marks a high point in a long tradition. Zinedine Zidane, the preeminent player in both tournaments, is the son of Algerian immigrants. Other players had roots in Chad, Senegal, Mali, New Caledonia, and Guadeloupe. The French media celebrated these victories as triumphs of multiculturalism and the worldwide Francophone community. Whether things therefore improved for the countless undocumented aliens in Marseilles, Lyon, or Toulouse is another question.

Other European "motherlands" have also successfully integrated foreign players. The Netherlands would never have been able to achieve its legendary strength on the field without the Surinamese Ruud Gullit, Frank Rijkaard, or Aaron Winter. Black players such as Andy Cole, Des Walker, and Ian Wright have played a central role in British football for a very long time. Portugal relied on Eusebio, and also had players from Angola, Mozambique, Brazil, and Cape Verde, who combine athleticism with Lusitanian technique and love for the game (Vidigal, Abel Xavier). On the other hand, states without (former) colonies build on the sons of immigrants, as is the case in the Scandinavian lands (Osmanovski), Austria (Vastic, Akagündüz), and particularly Switzerland: Ciriaco Sforza, Marco Pascolo, Davide Sesa, Tranquillo Barnetta (Italy), David Pallas, Ramon Vega, Philippe Senderos (Spain), Kubilay Türkyilmaz, and the brothers Murat and Hakan Yakin (Turkey), to mention just a few. These players, who have been among the best in the nation for years and from the 1990s on have brought the Swiss national team back to the international stage after nearly three decades of absence from any major international tournament, are all second-generation Swiss. Almost every professional club has several so-called *Secondos* in their ranks, including Serbs, Albanians, Croats, Congolese, and others. In both of the top two amateur leagues, particularly in densely populated urban areas, these *Secondos* form a clear majority.[23]

By contrast, the Germans have a hard time integrating their immigrants. The winger for Schalke, Gerald Asamoah, was just the third black player, following the two children of the occupation Erwin Kostedde and Jimmy Hartwig, to wear the eagle on his chest. During the 1974–75 season, Kostedde suffered so much abuse from the racist fans of his own club in Dortmund that he would only play away matches for a time. Before this difficult period he had enjoyed so much success in Belgium with Standard Liege that he became the top goal scorer. He returned to this form in 1980 with the French provincial club AS Laval. Like the Germans, the Italians have finally realized the quality of their black players. In 2001, Fabio Liverani, from AS Perugia, was the first black player to participate in an international match. In a period when the president of Hellas Verona made clear that he would never bring in a black player because of the racism of the fans in the stands, this was certainly an important sign of change.[24]

Naturally, there are also mundane reasons why one from the great multitude of players sticks in the memory so strongly. There are goalies who on a good day stop everything, and cannot be beaten, bringing the strikers to despair. For example, in 1986, when Steaua Bucharest played against Barcelona in the European Cup Final in Seville, the Romanian Helmut Ducadam stopped all of the penalty shots taken by the Spanish. Keepers like the Soviet Lev Yashin always seemed to make the laws of gravity irrelevant. Goalkeepers are often like melodies one hears in childhood that continue to play in the ears for a lifetime. They are simi-

23. See Christian Koller, "Fussball und Immigration in der Schweiz: Identitätswahrung, Assimilation oder Transkulturalität?" *Stadion* 34 (2008): 261–84.

24. *Guardian*, May 30, 2001.

lar to evergreens that thanks to their almost biblical lifespans take on the guise of old acquaintances about whom one can marvel year after year in the final rounds of major championships. Yashin, Dino Zoff, Peter Shilton, Ronnie Hellström, Peter Schmeichel, and Pat Jennings were present for decades, and played at the highest level until they were forty or even older.

In general, we tend to note players because of their great age or tender youth. Roger Milla, the striker for Cameroon, was forty when he participated in his last World Cup finals in the United States in 1994, and promptly scored a goal. Stanley Matthews, the great dribbler of English football, was over fifty before he hung up his cleats, which he had laced on for decades for Stoke City. By contrast, Pelé was just seventeen when he won the World Cup for the first time with Brazil in 1958. Northern Ireland international Norman Whiteside was just a few months younger when he played in the World Cup in Spain in 1982. He was, nevertheless, one of the best players on the surprisingly strong Northern Ireland team. Other players fascinate us because of their small (Rui Barros) or very large (Jan Koller) size. Many athletes possess an almost supernatural beauty, such as the Italian outside defender Paolo Maldini. In Italy, where the concept of *fare bella figura* still has significant force, although it has come to be seen as somewhat conceited in recent times, there have been votes for years about who is the most attractive footballer in the country. During the European Championships in Belgium and the Netherlands in 2000, the Azurri set the esthetic bar as they wore particularly form-fitting jerseys that emphasized their figures. Roberto Bettega from Juventus Turin, the "white feather," was striking because of his snow-white hair. The Swiss Alain Sutter, the Argentinian Caniggia, and the Italian Beppe Signori besotted women with their flowing blond hair. Other players are present in our memories simply because they counter the quickly globalizing standards of beauty. Attilio Lombardo, who had his best years as a winger with Sampdoria Genoa, was almost bald by his mid-twenties. Jim Leighton, the Scottish goalie during the 1980s and 1990s, had a fearsome gap in his teeth that he happily flashed for the cameras.

Myth has surrounded the number 10 since Pelé's day, the number of the captain. This talk has surrounded Michel Platini, Diego Maradona,

Zico, and Günter Netzer. Alongside them stand Italy's playmaker Roberto Baggio, Bernd Schuster, Dirceu, Rivellino, and the Uruguayan Enzo Francescoli. In those smaller countries that only produce a top player once every few decades people are particularly prone to recall wistfully spectacular goals from free kicks, or the passes that made even the most refined defensive scheme obsolete. The Irish had Liam Brady, the Danes Michael Laudrup, the Belgians Enzo Scifo, the Austrians Herbert "Schneckerl" Prohaska, and finally the Romanians particularly revere Gheorge Hagi, the "Carpathian Maradona." The Swiss, for their part, remember with ecstasy the free throws and tactics of Georges Bregy. During the late 1960s and 1970s little Switzerland experienced the one-time constellation of factors that led to two top players competing for the crown as *patron*. They were Karli Odermatt from FC Basel and Köbi Kuhn from FC Zurich who fought grandiose duels on breathtaking stages in their struggle for mastery and a cup. The Joggeli in Basel and Letzigrund in Zurich were filled to capacity when these two antagonists faced each other. Odermatt recalled in an interview that Köbi was something of a rascal. "When FCZ won the cup yet again, he held out the trophy to me and called: 'so-long until the next time.' But Köbi played for our strongest competitor, and everyone wanted to win on the field. But we were also true friends."[25]

The heroic figure includes within it the sub-type of the tragic hero. The reliable goalkeeper who has a terrible lapse in a decisive game, the striker who, like the outstanding Netherlander Rob Rensenbrink hit the post rather than the net from a short distance in the final seconds just before the whistle blows in the World Cup finals of 1978. It is often the very best players who lose their nerve when taking the eleven-meter shots. Roberto Baggio, for example, who was the best player in the World Cups in 1990 and 1994, missed the decisive penalty kick against the Brazilians in the final in Los Angeles, and has never since been the brilliant player that he was before.

Then naturally, the goal scorers, the game deciders, also fascinate us. Frequently, they were non-descript figures, virtual opportunists, who simply were standing at the right place at the right time. Gerd Müller from FC Bayern München scored sixty-eight goals in sixty-two interna-

25. *SonntagsZeitung*, July 15, 2001.

tional matches. An excellent Brazilian striker took his name: Muller. Gerd Müller's legendary instinct for the goal also has entered the lexicon of sports coverage. A striker "müllers" the ball two meters across the goal line. Here is a list of great goal scorers without any claim of completeness: the Italian Paolo Rossi, the Englishmen Jimmy Greaves, Kevin Keegan, and Gary Lineker,[26] the Scotsman Ally McCoist, the Austrians Hans Krankl, Andreas "Anderl" Ogris, and Toni Polster, the Germans Uwe Seeler and Ulf Kirsten, the Argentinian Gabriel Batistuta, the Bulgarian Hristo Stoitchkov, the two Swiss Stéphane Chapuisat and Adrian Knup, the two Spaniards Emilio Butragueño and Raúl, the Mexican Hugo Sanchez, and finally the Dutchman Marco van Basten, whose legendary volley from a narrow angle against the Soviets in the 1988 European Championship final brought a long-sought major title to the "Orange." Overall, one can say that there are specialists in creating spectacular goals. The Italian Paoli from Pro Vercelli, who was a two-time World Cup champion in the 1930s, was one of the first to perfect the overhead bicycle kick. Laio Amadò, who played for FC Lugano and Grasshoppers Zurich, mastered the sideways scissor kick. Klaus Fischer was an expert at striking from the upside-down position. His overhead bicycle kick against the Swiss goalie Erich Burgener was voted best goal of the century in Germany. The Dutch have always had great long-range scorers in their ranks, Arie Hahn and Ronald Koeman to name just two. The Brazilian Eder had such a hard shot that the frame around the goal sometimes threatened to burst if it got in the way.

The aforementioned strikers are memorable for their efficiency. However, the eternal dribblers and side-steppers, who stay out on the wings and look out for trouble, can bring the spectators in the stadium to applause and sometimes to rage. Garrincha, Francisco Gento, Reinhard "Stan" (after Stan Matthews) Libuda, Pierre Littbarski, Brian Laudrup, and Tony Woodcock, for example, made fools of entire defenses. These players knew how to humiliate a defender with a ball through his legs, and to sow panic with their capers. At the 1998 World Cup we were delighted by the antics of the Mexican winger Cauthemoc Blanco who, among other ploys, mastered the legendary trick of locking the ball be-

---

26. Regarding the character of the English goalscorer see Tony Pawson, *The Goalscorers: From Bloomer to Keegan* (London: Cassell & Co, 1978).

tween his feet to jump past the opposing player and thereby outmaneu-
ver him.

Alongside these artists there are also the tireless, the fearless, the
battlers, and the rascals who have earned our lasting respect. For example, the short, red-haired Scot, Gordon Strachan, fought for literally every ball, as did the English World Cup champion from 1966 Nobby Stiles.
Once in a while the luster of fame shone upon those workers who otherwise remained in the shadows. For example, the modest Katsche Schwarzenbeck, who otherwise was known simply as the sweeper for "Kaiser"
Franz Beckenbauer, scored the equalizer on a brilliant long-range shot
in the additional time of the European Cup finals in 1974 in Brussels
against Atlético Madrid in the 120th minute, thereby forcing a rematch,
which the Bavarians won decisively 4–0. The defensive midfielder Walter
Iselin from FC Aarau scored a similar goal from 27 meters right into the
net that decided the 1985 Swiss Cup final. In British football, battlers are
particularly revered. Woe to a player who does not want to run after or
get control of a sharply passed ball, and stands still, letting the game go
by. Those players who do not give up despite injuries earn eternal glory
in Britain. The center defender Terry Butcher played despite a severe injury, wearing a bandage that became so soaked with blood that it had to
be replaced. The Scot Murdo McLeod, a total Highlander, ended a game
against Borussia Dortmund with such a severe concussion that he could
not remember how it had happened. In Scotland, they venerate the
coach Jock Stein, who suffered a heart attack while sitting on the coach's
bench as Scotland defeated Wales 1–0 on September 10, 1985, to qualify
for the World Cup in Mexico. Completely in keeping with our definition,
the players named here fulfilled, and even went beyond, the norms of
British working class culture to fight until they drop dead. The former
German prisoner of war, Bernd Trautmann, who played as a goalie for
Manchester City after 1945, finished a cup final with a broken neck. Together with his gallant and fair manner of play, this heroic deed helped
to relieve the massive anti-German sentiment of the time: there truly
were "good Germans."[27]

27. The memory of Trautmann remains unbroken up to the present. A fan magazine in
Manchester, for example, is called *Bernd Trautmann's Head*.

Villains

At the same time, Otto Fritz Harder, nicknamed "Tull," embodied the "bad German." Tall and blond, Harder was one of the best strikers in Germany during the 1920s and scored many goals for the Hamburger SV. The angular striker played in fifteen international matches between 1914 and 1926. His fans sang, "when Harder plays the score is three to nothing."[28] Harder was a popular hero, known as the "Kicker."[29] He never made a secret of his antisemitic feelings, joining the Nazi Party on September 1, 1932, and the SS on May 1, 1935. In 1939, he was mobilized for service in the Waffen-SS, and began his career in this criminal organization as a guard in the concentration camp at Sachsenhausen, ending up as camp commandant at the Neuengamme satellite camp of Hannover-Ahlem. A British military court sentenced the commandant to fifteen years in prison for the many gruesome crimes for which he was responsible. Even a plea by DFB president Dr. Peco Bauwens was not able to change this judgment. After four-and-a-half years, Harder received a pardon. After he was set free, Harder was an honored guest of the DFB at international matches held in Hamburg. During his burial in 1956, his coffin was draped with an HSV flag. It is not certain that Tull Harder personally sought out and plagued his former teammate, the Norwegian Asbjørn Halvorsen, in the concentration camp. As manager of the Norwegian team, Halvorsen had inflicted a severe defeat on the Germans in Berlin when, in 1940, he had participated in the country-wide strike against the cooption of football by the National Socialist conquerors and their domestic accomplices. In 1942, he was taken into custody in the concentration camp at Grini near Oslo. A year later, he was transferred to the Alsatian concentration camp at Natzweiler, before being deported, weighing a mere 40 kilograms, to Neuengamme. Halvorsen was an inmate at the same camp where Harder had been commandant, but it is unclear whether the two ever saw each other.[30]

Fortunately, not all of the biographies of the villains in football have

---

28. Citation following Fischer, *Stürmer*, 235.

29. Ibid.

30. See Arthur Heinrich, "Tull Harder: Eine Karriere in Deutschland: Versuch einer Dokumentation," in *Antifaschismus*, ed. F. Deppe (Heilbronn: Distel-Verlag, 1996), 83–95; and Fischer, *Stürmer*, 233–39.

taken such a dramatic turn. We are, however, disgusted by those who took bribes, such as Bernard Tapie and those who were responsible for the Bundesliga scandal of 1971, who systematically deceived the fans and trampled all over the idea of fairness. There is also a very negative sense about the agents for players, who sometimes act like slave traders, buying and selling, and wearing out young talent without any scruples.

Then there are also villainous players, the fakers and divers, the stompers, sore losers, the slick, and the provocateurs, who are seen by the fans of the opposing team as bogeymen. We are appalled when we think of the Italian defender Tassotti, who in the World Cup semifinal in 1994 smashed the nose of the Spaniard Luiz Enrique with his elbow while off to the side and behind the back of the referee, only to play the innocent afterwards. We have already discussed "Toni" Schumacher's ugly foul.[31] However, Jürgen Klinsmann was almost as bad when he cut down a Croatian player from behind in the middle of the playing field during the European Championship in England in 1996. He received just a yellow card for this, but was paid back with an assault by the Croatians, whom he had clearly provoked. Claudio Gentile, the Italian defender, fouled Diego Maradona more than twenty times in a single match. The merciless Spaniard Andoni Goicoechea broke the legs of both Dieguito and Bernd Schuster in the same season. The Argentinian Oscar Ruggieri received two red cards in two consecutive South American Cups. The Yugoslavian Sinisha Mihajlovic spit directly into the open mouth of the pitiful German Jens Jeremies, as television viewers were able to observe in dramatic fashion on a time loop.

We are appalled when we see that smaller teams, and particularly those from Africa, suffer from outrageous discrimination. The fast and youthful Moroccans, who were enchanting under the leadership of Hadji, were the victim of a questionable penalty whistle, which the Norwegians used to gain a victory over the Brazilians in 1998, and thereby reach the round of sixteen. Are not many games fixed in some way? Are the scandals that have been discovered merely the tip of the iceberg? Or is it rather the case that justice and order reign? Are we losing our way in notorious conspiracy theories if we suggest that the results of many matches

31. Schumacher enraged many German fans with his vulgar "revelations" in 1987. Harald Schumacher, *Anpfiff: Enthüllungen über den deutschen Fussball* (Munich: Droemer Knaur, 1987).

were the product of financial transactions? Scattered examples of match fixing were discovered in Italy in the context of the *totonero* (match fixing scandal), in which the winners took home millions. Bruce Grobelaar, the goalie for Liverpool FC, and others have sold matches over the years. In Oldham, a criminal wagerer manipulated the security deposits, taking advantage of a loophole in the regulations according to which the lines for games were set at a specific time. In this case, at least, higher authorities shone a spotlight on this deceitful practice.

It is not only the fans of Borussia Mönchengladbach who still curse Roberto Boninsegna, who acted like a dying swan and wallowed on the ground on October 20, 1971, after being struck by an empty can. Hennes Weissweiler's "foals," and above all the unbelievable Günter Netzer, humiliated Inter Milan, the master of the "chain," 7–1 in the round of sixteen of the European Cup. The Italians lodged a protest that the can that struck Boninsegna was full. In the rematch in Berlin, Boninsegna broke the leg of one of the Borussia players, and the heart of the foals. Inter, with superstars such as Sandro Mazzola and Giacinto Facchinetti and a strong lobby, continued on, while the "little" Germans were knocked out in a truly scandalous manner.

By contrast, the tragic story of the Brazilian goalie Moacyr Barbosa still touches the heart. Barbosa was the goalkeeper of the Brazilian eleven that sought with all their might to win a first World Cup in 1950 in their own country. After a rather embarrassing opening and a 2–2 result against Switzerland, the Brazilians swept all of their opponents from the field in the final round, led by the brilliant Ademir from Vasco da Gama. They defeated Sweden 7–1 and Spain 6–1. The warning shots by the Swiss Jackie Fatton were quickly forgotten. The country was bound up in a carnival-like euphoria. Since there was no true final game, all that the Selcção needed in the final game was a draw against Uruguay to claim the title. About 200,000 people were crammed into the circle of the gigantic Maracanã stadium. This was probably the largest number of spectators ever to attend a football match. Not more than three hundred of them dared to root for Uruguay. The Uruguayans were the obvious outsiders in this game. They had sparkled far less than the players from Rio and São Paulo. However, they battled doggedly, and successfully fought back. Schiaffino scored the equalizer after Friaça had scored the go-ahead goal for Brazil. With the score at 1–1, the striker Ghiggia received the ball in the middle of the field, dribbled, and shot toward the top right-hand corner. Barbosa, who had been voted the best goalie in the world, did not have a chance. The unreachable ball went in. The Uruguayans were world champions! In seconds, euphoria was transformed into abysmal sorrow. Several Brazilians took their own lives that same night. According to the historian Alex Bellos, this defeat set in train a collective trauma. Ghiggia's attack and his unusual goal received as much analysis as the recordings of John F. Kennedy's death. The dramaturge Nelson Rodrigues spoke in 1966 about the "Brazilian holocaust." The author Pedro Perdigão compared the defeat with Waterloo and the end of civilization, crippling Brazil for years.

The goalie Barbosa quickly became the scapegoat for this game. He was attacked mercilessly everywhere he went, and his career came to an end. His failed defense followed him to his death. Twenty years after the match, a woman pointed her finger at him and said this is the man who brought Brazil to tears. In 1993 he was expelled from the training center for the national team because he could only bring bad luck. In 1996, shortly before his death, he observed that the highest penalty in Brazilian law is thirty years, but that he had to do penance for about fifty. In 1963 he attempted to banish the curse with a ritual. At a barbeque one night, the flames flickered unusually high. Barbosa burned the goalposts that had been so merciless to him. In just a few seconds, Ghiggia's unusual goal had transformed the life of poor Barbosa, the best goalie of his time, into a hell.[32]

Another South American, the Columbian Andrés Escobar, paid for an own goal with his life. Although it is not entirely certain whether he was also involved in the drug trade, this own goal led to the exit from the 1994 World Cup of a Colombian team that had received extensive pre-tournament praise. It also brought a death sentence: a few days after the game Escobar was shot in a nightclub in Medellín by a group of three killers, possibly linked to the gambling syndicates that had bet on Colombia.

32. Galeano, *Ball*, 115.

Fools

A short while before, we mentioned the strikers who made fools out of an entire defensive scheme and clearly enjoyed entertaining the spectators with tricks and gags. Willy "Ente" Lippens, for example, dribbled, played tricks, and engaged in an ongoing patter. The Brazilian Garrincha had an "x" and an "o" leg, although after he had dribbled through his opponents, he certainly was no laughing matter for the opposing defenses. The Uruguayan author Edoardo Galeano described a legendary goal that Garrincha scored in a preparatory match in 1958 against the club Fiorentina:

Garrincha entered the penalty area, left a defender on the ground, played around a second defender, and then another. As he sized up the opposing goalie, he realized that another opposing player was on the goal line. Garrincha flirted, hesitated, and then acted as if he wanted to shoot the ball into the corner; the poor defender jumped with his head toward the post. Then the goalie started to move forward. Garrincha played the ball between his legs, and shot it into the goal.[33]

Goalkeepers were often absolute individualists who did not rely on spectacular saves alone to impress the spectators. Petar Radenkovic from TSV München 1860 happily made forays into the opposing side's half of the field, and his mangled "*Bin i Radi, bin i König*" (I am Radi, I am king) became a hit in the early 1970s.[34] Some goalies even went on the attack and scored goals. The Paraguayan José Luis Chilavert scored more than forty goals in his career, making goals on long-distance free kicks as well as on spectacular eleven-meter shots. Sepp Maier from Radi's local rival Bayern München always had a fitting comment ready, although his leather-pants humor probably fit best in Bavaria. In 1976, during the penalty shots at the European Cup finals in Belgrade, Maier attempted to irritate the exceptionally talented top player from Czechoslovakia, Antonin Panenka, with his shenanigans. He almost let his pants fall down. The lanky and canny Panenka, who had a massive mustache, did not allow himself to become irritated. Rather the opposite. He made a fool of the prankster Maier, making him look like a buffoon in the eyes of millions with a slow-motion curler toward the middle of the goal. Ma-

33. Galeano, *Ball*, 127.
34. Also see Petar Radenkovic, *Bin ich Radi . . .* (Munich: Moewig-Verlag, 1965).

ier had decided to go toward the left corner and had to watch as the ball almost stood still in the air before falling into the goal. The Italians call this type of shot "a spoon." The Roman striker Francesco Totti had the audacity to use it in the semifinal of the 2000 European Cup against the Netherlands.

Many fans think it is appropriate to call players such as the mustachioed Panenka, the Italian Franco Causio, the Portuguese Chalana, the Hungarian Laszlo Faszekas, or the Polish Andrzej Szarmach "smooth operators." This kind of player is now almost extinct. Players who calmly wait for the mistakes of their opponents, who play the ball tactically and with restraint, not flailing blindly for the ball but skillfully lobbing the ball over the goalie, or shooting so that he dives in despair, with his fingertips almost brushing it but nevertheless has to let it pass by into the goal. At times they are celebrated. Apparently abandoned, there only for the sake of their art, a bit of chamber music, seemingly conjuring their magic to no purpose at midfield, always preferring the simpler option to the more difficult one. Because they generally did not shoot the decisive goal, and as a rule were never World Cup champions, these "fools," who understood the relationship between the theater and the stadium, often retreated quickly into oblivion. Just as the great comedians of the silent films, such as Buster Keaton, Stan Laurel, Oliver Hardy, or Charlie Chaplin, no longer felt truly at home in the new medium of the talkies, modern athletic and fast football no longer has room for smooth operators, tricksters, and clowns.

The Austrian striker Toni Polster was one of the last of the dying breed of football fools. The goal scorer for Austria Wien often had a disinterested appearance on the field, almost apathetic, in order to be at the right place at the right time. His comments always seemed forthright and cheerful. He was always in a good mood, and lived this way after the game as well. Polster, who played for 1. FC Köln, soon became a popular cult figure in the cheerful Rhineland. The gas-station owner made audiences of the TV broadcast *Aktuelles Sportstudio* laugh with his song "Blaumann" ("Blue Man"). Then, with his song "Toni lass es polstern" he stormed onto the *Hit Parade* as "Radi" Radenkovic once had done.

Clearly there is a fine line between comedy and ridiculousness when engaging in these kinds of presentations. While the small tears shed by the big and tough England playmaker Paul Gascoigne after he received the yellow card that cost him a final chance to play in the World Cup in 1990 moved spectators around the planet, overly demonstrative displays are often rather repellent. The insightful observer Javier Marías recalled with regard to the small and theatrical striker for Real Madrid, Juanito Gómez: "Many years ago, Real Madrid lost a championship to Real Sociedad San Sebastían at the last moment, and the late Juanito Gómez rolled around on the grass like a *maenad* (also called a crybaby in school). It seemed far less that he was really suffering than it was important for us to see how much he was suffering."[35] Anyone who wishes to cut a good figure in the stadium has to reckon with the fact that he is dealing with perceptive spectators.

Outsiders

Steve Heighway, the Irish midfielder who played for Liverpool FC and had a major role in the success of the Reds in the 1970s, is one of the few professional football players with a university degree. The lack of interest among his colleagues in seeing the sights was shocking to him. During overseas trips, he went out alone to see the cities. His fellow players soon scorned Heighway as a pretentious intellectual. He finally gave in to peer pressure and henceforward played cards with them.[36]

Politically engaged football players are also the exception. Ewald Lienen, for example, went far out on a limb in support of disarmament and against the NATO Double-Track Decision. Alain Sutter's stand against the nuclear ambitions of the government of Jacques Chirac, which he expressed in the form of a banner before an important qualification match of the Swiss national team against Sweden in Stockholm, did not meet with much sympathy in football circles. The gifted football player Sutter went his own way in other areas as well. He refused to be treated with medications or injections and relied on homeopathic methods instead. Because of this, he never became the superstar that he could have been on the basis of his talent.

Clubs with politically active fan bases are also the exception. FC

---

35. Marías, *Alle unsere frühen Schlachten*, 46.
36. See Morris, *Spiel*, 183.

St. Pauli, for example, is the favorite club for the engaged Left, and Volker Finke, the coach of SC Freiburg from 1991 to 2007, has become a byword for "green" football. However, the majority of clubs do not participate in politics, and the boardrooms are decidedly apolitical. It is sometimes said that football and politics do not belong together. We will demonstrate below that this view actually does not correspond to reality.

Yet other football players fell victim to the multifarious political turmoil and excessive violence that characterized the last century. The German Jew Julius Hirsch, for example, who scored ten goals against Russia in an international match, thereby establishing an immortal record for international competitions, lost his membership in Karlsruhe FV in 1933. In 1937 and 1938 he worked as an auxiliary bookkeeper at a Jewish firm in Ettlingen-Maxau before being deported in 1943 to the concentration camp in Auschwitz, where he was murdered.[37]

Oscar Heisserer, born in 1914, played outside striker for Racing Strasbourg from 1934 to 1938. In 1938, he participated in the World Cup for his own country, where he scored France's only goal against Italy in the quarterfinals. Following the conquest of France by Hitler in 1940 and the Germanization of Alsace, Racing was renamed Rasensport. The club soon faced stiff competition from the team SS Strassburg, which put considerable pressure on Heisserer to play with them. Despite facing threats of being sent to the eastern front, Heisserer kept Rasensport at arm's length. Finally, in 1943, he fled to Switzerland where he was interned and compelled to do hard labor. Heisserer's wife was questioned under torture by the SS. In 1945, Heisserer returned to Alsace, but hard labor in the internment camp meant that he could no longer pursue his career as a professional football player.[38]

Oskar Rohr was a teammate of Heisserer at Racing during the 1930s. Up to 1933, Rohr was on the German national team on three separate occasions. The middle striker from Bayern München was accounted one of the most talented strikers in Germany. In 1933, he left Germany to become a professional player with the Grasshoppers in Zurich. This step had no political connotations. In 1934, Ossi Rohr went to Strasbourg where he won the goal-scoring crown several times in the French league.

37. Fischer, *Stürmer*, 201.
38. Ibid., 240–44.

In 1940, he fled to unoccupied Marseilles, but the Vichy regime arrested the football player, incarcerated him for a month, and then delivered him to Germany. The Nazis sent the "traitor to the fatherland" to the concentration camp at Kimslau near Karlsruhe, although he had been an apolitical man up to this point. After eight weeks, he was released from the prison camp and sent to the eastern front, where a light wound saved his life. But Rohr's path of suffering was not yet at an end. In 1945, after the end of the war, two French military police recognized him. Rohr once again had to face a court. The penalty that the Vichy government had imposed on him was supposed to run for three months. Rohr had only served a month. Finally, Ossi Rohr graciously was permitted to go free.[39]

The ways in which the joy of football can stabilize a life that was full of chicanery is made clear by the story of the St. Gall police captain Paul Grüninger (1891–1972).[40] As a winger with SC Brühl, the petty bourgeois football club in St. Gall, Grüninger became Swiss champion in 1915 and later served as president of the club. In 1926, he organized a celebratory publication in honor of the club's 25-year anniversary.[41] He soon joined the police force of the canton of St. Gall, making his career there, and eventually becoming the chief. According to the gendarme Fritz Kucker, Grüninger was always *thinking* about football and so let his body seriously deteriorate.[42] After the *Anschluss* of Austria, Grüninger illegally permitted many hundreds and perhaps even thousands of primarily Jewish refugees to flee into Switzerland. As a result, he was summarily dismissed from his position on April 3, 1939. At first, the thought was to have him seek psychiatric treatment. He was then convicted for abuse of office and forging documents. Different administrative authorities harassed Grüninger for the rest of his life, and he had to seek out odd jobs in order to keep afloat. However, he never complained about his tragic fate. In 1971, the central Israeli Holocaust memorial at Yad Vashem included Grüninger on the list of the "righteous among the nations." However, it was not until 1995, a good twenty years after his death, that Paul

39. Ibid., 244–49.
40. See Stefan Keller, *Grüningers Fall: Geschichten von Flucht und Hilfe* (Zurich: Rotpunkt-Verlag, 1998).
41. Paul Grüninger, *25 Jahre F.C. Brühl St. Gallen* (St. Gall: SC Brühl, 1926).
42. Keller, *Grüningers Fall*, 8.

Grüninger was rehabilitated in Switzerland. In 2006, SC Brühl's Krontal sports center was renamed the Paul-Grüninger stadium. Grüninger had played on the senior team with FC Au in Rheintal. The club thanked him for his commitment by giving him the presidency, the only honor for which Paul Grüninger was considered during his lifetime. We believe that football, which Grüninger always had on his mind, played a part in keeping him from having a hard heart like so many other high officials at that time. As he set in verse in his own celebratory volume: "We hold to each other strong and true. Hip hip hooray, hip hip hooray!"[43]

43. Citation following ibid., 41.

6 | *Football and the Nation*

According to the English historian Eric J. Hobsbawm, the twentieth century was an age of extremes.[1] The extremely large number of dead, who lost their lives on countless battlefields and in hails of bombs in countless wars, is a hallmark of the past century. The conflicts between competing ideologies, which saw themselves as the salvation for all mankind, were exceptionally virulent. By comparison, the history of football in this period was comparatively peaceful, so much so that one might have the impression that the leather ball brought understanding between the various peoples of our planet. However, despite all of the positive elements that we are inclined to attribute to the most popular pastime in the world, we should on no account forget that something which appears so apolitical is actually the entry point for nationalism, chauvinism, and regionalism. What liberal cosmopolitan, who is so proud of his own political enlightenment, has not caught himself cursing the opposing team in an international match, indulging in prejudices that are based on stereotypes dating back centuries? The occasionally "political" emotions that football brings to the fore, discussed in the previous chapters, create a sense of "us" and "them." This identification with players and teams has always meant that football can be made to serve as a tool, whether from above by politicians and captains of industry, or from below by populist right-wing radicals or other political fanatics.

A recent example is the abandoned Euro 2016 qualifying match between the national teams of Serbia and Albania in Belgrade on October 14, 2014. From the beginning of the game, Serbian fans chanted songs against Albanians and threw flares and other objects on the pitch. After forty-two

---

1. Eric J. Hobsbawm, *The Age of Extremes* (London: Michael Joseph, 1995).

minutes, a group of Albanians launched a drone quadcopter carrying an irredentist flag of Greater Albania. The Serbian player Stefan Mitrović brought down the flag from the drone, upon which he was attacked by Albanian players. This caused Serbian fans to storm the pitch, injuring four Albanian players. Afterwards, senior officials of both national federations blamed the other side for these incidents.

Specialists in cultural studies have been engaged for decades with the topic of national identities.[2] Most recent scholarship borrows the idea from George Herbert Mead that "identity" is constituted by defining "one's own" and distinguishing this from the "foreign," excluding difference.[3] In this context, the German social historian Christiane Eisenberg formulated the thesis that sport is a theater in which popular nationalism can produce itself, leading to self-confidence and also to a symbolic confrontation with "the other" and "the foreigner."[4] By using particularly

2. See, for example, *Nationales Bewusstsein und kollektive Identität: Studien zur Entwicklung des kollektiven Bewusstseins in der Neuzeit 2.*, ed. Helmut B. Berding (Frankfurt: Suhrkamp, 1994); *Mythos und Nation: Studien zur Entwicklung des kollektiven Bewusstseins in der Neuzeit 3.*, ed. Helmut B. Berding (Frankfurt: Suhrkamp, 1996); *Nation und Emotion: Deutschland und Frankreich im Vergleich—19. und 20. Jahrhundert*, eds. Etienne François et al. (Göttingen: Vandenhoeck & Ruprecht, 1995); Georg Elwert, "Nationalismus und Ethnizität: Über die Bildung von Wir-Gruppen," *Kölner Zeitschrift für Soziologie und Sozialpsychologie* 3 (1989): 440–64; *Nationale und kulturelle Identität: Studien zur Entwicklung des kollektiven Bewusstseins in der Neuzeit*, ed. Bernhard Giesen (Frankfurt: Suhrkamp, 1991); *Transformationen des Wir-Gefühls: Studien zum nationalen Habitus*, eds. Helmut Kuzmics et al. (Frankfurt: Suhrkamp, 1993); *Nationale Mythen und Symbole in der zweiten Hälfte des 19. Jahrhunderts: Strukturen und Funktionen von Konzepten nationaler Identität*, eds. Jürgen Link and Wulf Wülfing (Stuttgart: Klett-Cotta, 1991); Anthony D. Smith, *National Identity* (London: Penguin Books, 1991); Ruth Wodak et al., *Zur diskursiven Konstruktion nationaler Identität* (Frankfurt: Suhrkamp, 1998); Anne-Marie Thiesse, *La création des identités nationales: Europe XVIIIᵉ-XXᵉ siècle* (Paris: Seuil, 1999); Jaroslav Stritecky, "Identitäten, Identifikationen, Identifikatoren," in *Formen des nationalen Bewusstseins im Lichte zeitgenössischer Nationalismustheorien*, ed. Eva Schmidt-Hartmann (Munich: Oldenbourg, 1994), 53–66. For a critical history of the term "collective identity" see Lutz Niethammer, *Kollektive Identität: Heimliche Quellen einer unheimlichen Konjunktur* (Reinbek: Rowohlt, 2000).

3. For example, George Herbert Mead, *Die objektive Realität der Perspektiven* (1927), in his *Gesammelte Aufsätze*, ed. Joas von Hans (Frankfurt: Suhrkamp, 1983), 2:211–24; "The Problem of Society—How We Become Selves," in his *Movements of Thought in the Nineteenth Century*, ed. Merrit H. Moore (Chicago: University of Chicago Press, 1936, 360–85; and *Mind, Self, and Society: From the Standpoint of A Social Behaviorist*, ed. Charles W. Morris (Chicago: University of Chicago Press, 1972).

4. Christiane Eisenberg, "Sportgeschichte: Eine Dimension der modernen Kulturgeschichte," *Geschichte und Gesellschaft* 23 (1997): 296. Hobsbawm believed that he could recognize "a medium for national identification and factitious community" in sport (Hobsbawm, *Invention of Tradition*, 300). In 1971, the medievalist Marcel Beck placed football festivals in a line with me-

controversial matches, the this chapter will make clear how football and the construction of political identities can have the same catalyzing effects, and also that certain circles were aware of this fact and transformed athletic competitions into struggles for regional, ethnic, religious, or national superiority.

British Archrivals: England
versus Scotland

The first international match in football history, England against Scotland, took place on November 30, 1872, in front of a crowd of about three thousand spectators at the West of Scotland Cricket Ground in Glasgow and ended in a scoreless draw. The two national teams met each other frequently after this, though these first international matches did not draw very large crowds. The British Championship, which was founded in 1884, drew a lot more attention in the media and in the stadiums. More than 10,000 fans regularly attended these matches. After the English championship was professionalized in 1888 and the Scottish championship followed in 1890, with concomitantly larger stadiums available to them, the number of spectators at the international matches exploded. In 1895, about 45,000 fans came to Goodison Park in Liverpool. One year later, a crowd of 56,600 spectators filled the new Celtic Park in Glasgow in order to watch the international match being played there. After the turn of the century, crowds of this size became the rule. In 1937, a total of 149,515 spectators came to the modern Hampden Park in Glasgow, a number that was a world record at the time.[5]

These meetings became increasingly important for the creation of a sense of Scottish national feeling. During the first few decades of competition, the Scots were able to hold the English at bay, and even dominated their southern neighbors for a time. The Scots had a demonstrably superior feel for the ball, and possessed an exceptional technique for that time. Many of them sought employment in the better-paying English professional clubs, where they soon developed a distinct person-

---

dieval saints' feast days and modern national celebrations as an important factor in community-building (*Badener Tagblatt*, September 1, 1971).

5. See David Allen, "Länderspiele England (1872–1900)," *Elf* 4 (1986): 62–74.

ality. Sunderland FC, the English runners-up in the 1890–91 season, put forward an attacking formation that was composed exclusively of Scots, namely Johnny Harvie, Jimmy Millar, Johnny Campbell, David Hannah, and Jack Scott. For years, Campbell was the most fearsome goal scorer in the early period of English football. In 1897, he switched along with the inside right forward Harvie to Sunderland's most significant local rival, Newcastle United, for a record transfer fee of £40.[6] The dominance of Scottish football in the early decades is made clear by the fact that in the popular matches between the select teams from the two leagues, the English league usually came out on top, but it was Scottish players who usually scored the decisive goals against their countrymen.[7]

Scholarship on the topic indicates that the period between 1832 and 1914 was one of crisis for Scottish political nationalism. Broad sections of the Scottish elite began to think of themselves as Britons. They benefitted from the economic advantages of the steadily growing empire as well as from the new opportunities for profit that arose from the industrial revolution. In particular, entry into the free-trade zone of the empire strengthened the standing of Glasgow, which became a center of trade and the second largest city in the empire. Jacobitism, the hope for the restoration of a Stuart king, had unleashed a bloody revolt against England as late as 1745, but was now passing into oblivion.[8] Scots took on active roles as empire builders, as soldiers, officers, government officials, financiers, engineers, teachers, and merchants. In keeping with their economic interests, a majority of them voted for the Liberal Party of William Gladstone.[9] On the cultural level, a widely popular romantic image of the Highlands endowed the poets Robert Burns and Walter

6. Alfredo W. Pöge, "Der 'goldene Schuh'—postum," *Elf* 4 (1986): 14–40.

7. Mervyn D. Baker et al., "Großbritannien. 'Inter-League-Matches' (1892–1900)," *Elf* 4 (1986): 55–61.

8. Regarding Jacobitism, see, for example, Bruce P. Lenman, *The Jacobite Risings in Britain, 1689–1746* (London: Eyre Methuen, 1980); Murray G. H. Pittock, *Jacobitism* (London: Palgrave, 1982); *The Invention of Scotland: The Stuart Myth and the Scottish Identity, 1638 to the Present* (London: Macmillan, 1991); *The Myth of the Jacobite Clans* (Edinburgh: Edinburgh University Press, 1995); W. Donaldson, *The Jacobite Song: Policital Myth and National Identity* (Aberdeen: Aberdeen University Press, 1988); Christian Koller, "Glencoe 1692: Ein Massaker als komplexer Erinnerungsort," *Historische Zeitschrift* 296, no. 1 (2013): 1–28.

9. See, for example, Tom Nairn, *The Break-Up of Britain* (London: NLB, 1977); Richard J. Finlay, *A Partnership for Good? Scottish Politics and the Union since 1800* (Edinburgh: John Donald, 1997); and Linda Colley, *Britons: Forging the Nation 1707–1837* (London: Vintage, 1996).

Scott, as well as the legendary knight and terror of all Englishmen, William Wallace, "Braveheart," with the status of national heroes.[10]

Although members of the lower classes also on occasion harbored sympathies for the empire,[11] for most Scots the "we" feeling came predominantly from two sources that reinforced each other, namely an occasionally militant "anti-Englishness" and pride in their membership in the Reformed Presbyterian church, the Kirk.[12] The ever-present desire to establish boundaries against England was best served by the football matches during the British Championship. Thanks to the research of the British historian H. F. Moorhouse, we are well informed about a number of interesting aspects of this classic event.[13] During the interwar period, numerous chartered trains traveled from Edinburgh and Glasgow to London so that countless Scots could attend the prestigious contest at Wembley stadium. The travelers were accompanied by bagpipers dressed in traditional kilts, creating the impression of a wild invading army—the "tartan army," as they called themselves. When they arrived in London, the fans made themselves conspicuous with their instruments, occupying highly symbolic public spaces such as Trafalgar Square or Piccadilly Circus. When no fewer than 60,000 Scots made the trip to Wembley in 1938, the *Daily Record* reported that the events in the capital had become a regular institution of a burgeoning Scottishness. In general, wives and daughters accompanied their husbands and fathers to London in order to take advantage of the opportunity to visit one of the popular department stores, such as Harrods.

10. See Richard J. Finlay, "Heroes, Myths, and Anniversaries in Modern Scotland," *Scottish Affairs* 18 (1997), 152–78; M. Ash, "William Wallace and Robert the Bruce: the Life and Death of a National Myth," in *The Myths We Live By*, eds. R. Samuels and P. Thomson (London: Routledge, 1990), 83–94; Robert Clyde, *From Rebel to Hero: The Image of the Highlander, 1745–1830* (London: Tuckwell, 1995); Linas Eriksonas, *National Heroes and National Identities: Scotland, Norway and Lithuania* (Brussels: Lang, 2004); Graeme Morton, "The Most Efficacious Patriot: The Heritage of William Wallace in Nineteenth Century Scotland," *The Scottish Historical Review* 77, no. 2 (1998): 224–51; *William Wallace: Man and Myth* (Stroud: Sutton, 2001); Hugh Trevor-Roper, "The Invention of Tradition: The Highland Tradition of Scotland," in *The Invention of Tradition*, 15–41.

11. Also see Richard J. Finlay, "The Rise and Fall of Popular Imperialism in Scotland," *Scottish Geographic Magazine* 113 (1997): 98–114.

12. See, for example, T. M. Devine, *The Scottish Nation 1700–2000* (London: Allen Lane, 2000), 29.

13. H. F. Moorhouse, "Scotland against England: Football and Popular Culture," *International Journal of the History of Sport* 4 (1987): 189–202.

In 1977 enthusiastic Scottish fans stormed the playing field after England had finally been defeated again, following a long interval. Many of the Scots secured relics in the form of pieces of the goal posts or net. Some of them even dared to dig up some of the sacred sod from the field.

They met the outburst of anger in England with glee and T-shirts with the following legend: "ENGLAND 1, SCOTLAND 2. STOLE YER TURF AND YER GOALPOSTS TOO."[14] The decision by Margaret Thatcher's Conservative government to ban the Four Nations Cup following extensive rioting was met with disbelief by Scottish supporters.

High-ranking officials in the Scottish Football Association took a decidedly anti-English line. There was great suspicion regarding the steady departure of domestic talent who tried their luck in England to earn more money. The SFA reacted in 1949 by forbidding any player under the age of seventeen from joining an English club. It became increasingly difficult to obtain exemptions for players engaged beyond the Tweed, so-called Anglos, to play on the national team. In the nineteenth century, Anglos were excluded from being named to the national team. In 1929, just a year after the founding of the Scottish National Party (SNP), there was a conference to deal with this issue. In the interwar period, people generally accepted the view of the officials that the Anglos would undermine the combative Scottish style of play, and so-called all-tartan teams were recruited. The ironic result of this policy, however, was that precisely those players who gained a high profile for playing against the English soon after left their homeland to go south after the games had been played. No fewer than four of the top players from the 1925 all-tartan team were playing a year later in England. They included the goalie Harper, who moved from Hibernian in Edinburgh to Arsenal in London for £4,500, and the middle striker Gallacher (Airdrieonians), for whom Newcastle United was prepared to pay the whopping sum of £5,000. As late as 1983, Alec Ferguson, who was then a successful coach for Aberdeen FC and later the coach of the national team, said: "I'm against Anglos being in the Scots team.... Players go south and return with their llama coats and their discipline on and off the park isn't as good as that of the lads at home."[15] In 1986, Ferguson, the man with the principles, left Scot-

14. See Morris, *Spiel*, 285.
15. Ibid., 195.

land in order to coach Manchester United. He subsequently played a decisive role in making Manchester the dominant team in England and the richest club in the world. He was knighted by the Queen for his services to football, and the Scottish nationalist was transformed into Sir Alec!

Another successful Scottish coach, the crusty Alistair "Ally" McLeod, doggedly refused to allow the English media to describe him as the British coach. Scotland qualified for the World Cup final round in Argentina while the English again had to stay home. Players such as Archie Gemmill, the young Kenny Dalglish, and the captain McQueen were portrayed as bearers of Britain's hopes. McLeod, remaining true to his line, proclaimed that Scotland played exclusively for the Scots, and used the presence of the media to launch into anti-English tirades. Just like always, Scotland crashed miserably in the early rounds, and the returning players suffered scorn and derision. However, the surly nationalism of the coach made him an immortal in his homeland. One year later he participated in the campaign for an autonomous Scottish parliament.

Celtic versus Rangers: Football and Religion, Football and Regionalism

For most Scots, in additional to England there is another "alterity" that permits them to maintain and strengthen their national consciousness without a national state, namely the football team Celtic Glasgow. Beginning in the nineteenth century, and with increasing tempo after the great famine, many Irish sought their fortune overseas, whether in the new world, in Liverpool, or in the booming trade city of Glasgow.[16] The pressure to emigrate was so strong among the Irish that it almost had the force of a natural law. In 1901 there were no fewer than 205,000 people living in Scotland who had been born in Ireland. They were concentrated in large cities such as Glasgow and Dundee as well as in the mining region of Lothian.

16. Devine, *Scottish Nation*, 486–522; Bill Murray, *The Old Firm: Sectarianism, Sport and Society* (Edinburgh: John Donald, 1984); Tom Gallagher, *Glasgow: The Uneasy Peace* (Manchester: Manchester University Press, 1987); James E. Handley, *The Irish in Modern Scotland* (Cork: Cork University Press, 1947); Brenda Collins, "The Origins of Irish Immigration to Scotland in the Nineteenth and Twentieth Centuries," in *Irish Immigrants and Scottish Society in the Nineteenth and Twentieth Centuries*, ed. T. M. Devine (Edinburgh: John Donald Publishers, 1991), 1–25.

Most Presbyterian Scots did not thank the Catholic Irish for their substantial role in the economic "take-off" of the country, and held fast to their premodern stereotypes, according to which the pope was the anti-Christ (anti-popery), who would be only too happy to organize a broad-based conspiracy to destroy Protestantism and their beloved Kirk. During the first half of the nineteenth century, many Irish immigrants assimilated into the dominant Scottish culture, for example, by changing their names: O'Neil became McNeil, and McDade became Davidson. Until 1816, there was not a single Catholic school in western Scotland, and there was just a single priest for approximately 10,000 Catholics in Glasgow in 1836. The economic situation for the immigrants was also disadvantageous because they were denied entry into the more advanced schools because of discriminatory laws.

Sporadic violence, the so-called anti-Catholic riots, led most immigrant Irish to remain quiet and unobtrusive by keeping their nationality and religion invisible to those on the outside. The wave of so-called famine emigrants visibly strengthened the self-consciousness of the Irish after 1850. The number of Irish parishes steadily grew, and the Catholic church took the initiative to set up charitable agencies to care for the poor. The clergy concerned themselves increasingly with the immigrants, which led to the development of a social Catholicism that in Germany is associated with the name Kolping. The Catholic Church was the biggest community builder in Glasgow and other places as well.[17] It was primarily out of pastoral and charitable motives that Brother Walfrid, himself an immigrant from Sligo in County Donegal, established the Celtic club in the Glasgow slum known as the East End in 1888. With the revenues from admission to the games, which soon began to flow abundantly, he financed meals for the poor, and hoped to provide competition to the Protestant soup kitchens, which had successfully seduced believers from the Catholic parishes. Even in its early years, Glasgow Celtic practiced a political Catholicism in which the "Irish question" was dominant. President John Glass was a leading member of the Catholic Union and

17. Tom Gallagher, "The Catholic Irish in Scotland: In Search of Identity," in *Irish Immigrants and Scottish Society in the Nineteenth and Twentieth Centuries*, 27–50; Joseph M. Bradley, "Football in Scotland: A History of Political and Ethnic Identity," *International Journal of the History of Sport* 12 (1995): 81–98.

treasurer of the United Irish League, another institution that pushed for "home rule," meaning the establishment of an Irish parliament and thus political autonomy. Another countryman, William McKillop, sat as a committed home ruler for North Sligo in the British parliament, and Michael Davitt, a former popular revolutionary Fenian, planted the first strip of sod in Celtic Park in 1892, "the first sod of real Irish shamrocks." The shamrock, which is the symbol of Ireland, adorns the club's crest. Archbishop Eyre was another important patron of the club, whose colors were the green and white of Ireland. But Celtic was not the only Catholic team to cause a sensation. Hibernian Edinburgh was founded in 1875 and continues to play in the Scottish football league. Dundee Harp was also a strong professional team. There were also many Shamrocks, Harps, and Emeralds in the lower leagues.

During the early years of professional football in Scotland, Celtic dominated the competition, with the Green and White winning the league, the cup, the Glasgow Cup, and the Charity Cup in 1893. For those Protestant Scots, who saw their dominant position being threatened, this served as a call to action to pool their strength. The press demanded a powerful squad. In the end, it was the Glasgow Rangers, wearing royal blue, who met the call to respond to the hated Catholic immigrants. This led to the development of an intense religious and ethnic rivalry that was unique in Europe. The Rangers became the most popular anti-Catholic institution in the country. Both clubs built enormous stadiums. During the cup final in 1909 there were bloody riots that went on into the night. From this point on, these night-long brawls were an element of the Derbies.

Young Catholic talent went to Celtic, while the Rangers did not have a single Catholic player until 1989. That year, the striker Maurice Johnston, a nonpracticing Catholic transferred from FC Nantes to the Blues, which made quite an impression in both camps. For fanatic Celtic fans, Johnston was the epitome of a traitor, while the radical Protestants lodged strong accusations against their own leadership. But 1989 was not simply the year that the iron curtain fell. The Rangers, from then on, brought several Catholic players into the club, while Henrik Larsson, a Lutheran Swede, in 2001 helped their local rivals to achieve the glorious triple of winning the Championship, the Cup, and the League Cup by scoring more than fifty goals. However, this rivalry led to the pooling of resources that generally turned the other teams into mere statistics. Only Aberdeen FC succeeded during the 1980s in challenging the two Glasgow clubs on a regular basis. At best, the other smaller teams from Dundee, Edinburgh, Kilmarnock, and Motherwell compete with each other to reach a European competition. All too often they were outplayed and knocked out in Celtic Park or Ibrox. Only the bankruptcy of the 54-time Scottish champion Glasgow Rangers in 2012 brought the 120-year-old rivalry to a sudden end.

The battles between the immense and well-organized fan groups were fought with fists, but also on a symbolic level. After the SFA forbid the Irish tricolor to be waved above Celtic Park in 1950 there were sharp protests by Celtic fans, who triumphed in their bid to demonstrate their loyalty to their team. The Celtic supporters brandished the Irish flag, and many of them sympathized, at least in the stadium, with Sinn Fein, the party of radical separatism, and its military arm, the Irish Republican Army (IRA), while singing republican songs in the pubs. The Protestant fans, for their part, did not suffer from ambiguity in enunciating their views. After the British antiterrorism unit, the SAS, killed three IRA members in Gibraltar in 1988, the supporters of the Protestant Motherwell FC sang: "SAS 1, 2, 3 ... SAS 1, 2, 3 ...."[18] The riots between the two sides were among the worst in the world for decades. Nevertheless, Glasgow remains a football-crazy city. Scotland also has the highest per capita attendance at football matches of any country.

For many decades, Celtic Glasgow was the single most important factor in the development of a self-conscious Irishness in the diaspora. Political and social disadvantages were compensated for on the field and after the game. A victory over the Rangers repaid many supporters for their miserable wages. Victory in a street fight perhaps allowed them to forget their social disadvantages for a little while. For the Scots of Irish ancestry, Celtic Glasgow was the most important symbol of the fact that they could struggle for recognition and equality without being forced to give up their own identity in a foreign culture.

On a smaller scale, this was also true for the two clubs in Ulster,

18. Citation from Bradley, "Football in Scotland," 89.

namely Belfast Celtic and Derry City FC.[19] In 1949 Belfast Celtic, the leading Catholic club in Northern Ireland, withdrew from the professional First Northern Irish Division. The club's home and away matches were always accompanied by riots. Cliftonville, the only remaining professional Catholic club in Belfast, cannot play its home games against the flagship club of the Protestant unionists, Linfield FC, in its own stadium at Solitude. This stadium is located in the heart of the Catholic part of the city. The odyssey of Derry City FC seems just as grotesque. Founded in 1928 as Derry City Football and Athletic Club, the Catholic club from (London-)Derry played, until its withdrawal in October 1972, in the Northern Irish professional league. However, games in its stadium at Brandywell, in the Catholic part of the segregated city, were always moved to other stadiums. Its games against Linfield always led to politically and religiously tinged riots. In 1984 the club was finally refounded with the name Derry Football Club. After a great many discussions back and forth, the team finally was allowed to play the next year in the First Irish League, where it quickly became a magnet for spectators. For the fans, Derry has become a symbol for a united Ireland.[20] Just as was the case for the supporters of Celtic Glasgow, support for the Catholic club from Derry provides the opportunity to show on a regular basis their support for Irish republicanism, to show their colors, and to mark their presence. In a country where symbolic actions like the annual marches by the Orangemen notoriously lead to violence and counter-violence, the effectiveness of such demonstrations should not be underestimated.

There are a whole series of other clubs that give a voice to ethnic groups that are a minority in national states. The most famous example is FC Barcelona, as will be explained in detail below, which served as the most important symbol of anti-Castillian Catalonian identity during the Francoist dictatorship (1936–75). Negative excesses in the relationship between politics and football can also be seen in various periods in the Balkans. In communist Yugoslavia, the duels between Dynamo Zagreb and the two Belgrade clubs, Partisan and Red Star, provoked ethnically

---

19. See Dietrich Schulze-Marmeling, "Fussballspiele, Religion und Politik in Belfast," in *Sport als städtisches Ereignis*, ed. Christian Koller (Ostfildern: Thorbecke, 2008), 167–87.

20. Vic Duke and Liz Crolley, *Football, Nationality and the State* (Harlow: Longman, 1996), 70–76.

tinged riots in the early 1980s. On May 13, 1990, the Croat Zvonimir Boban, who played for Dynamo at the time, set in motion a massive brawl on the playing field because of his clear assault on another player, just months before the outbreak of the war. The brawl was continued by fans from both sides on the street, and set the stage for the nationalistic radicalization of the following decade. In 1992, Dynamo became Croatia, a team that was under the direct protection of the nationalist Croatian president Franjo Tudjman. The coach of Croatia, Miroslav Blazevic, was a friend of Tudjman, and also served as the coach of the Croatian national team that took a surprising third place in the World Cup in France in 1998 with players such as Boban, Robert Prosinecki, Robert Jarni, and Davor Suker, thereby setting off a new nationalist frenzy. Blazevic, who had been active in Switzerland during the 1970s and 1980s, sat next to Tudjman in the open state limousine while celebrating the "re-conquest" of Krajna.

A further example of the instrumentalization of football for nationalist purposes is provided by the Serbian super-fan Zeljko Raznatovic, who participated in several massacres under the name General Arkan. Raznatovic, who was himself finally assassinated, was under heavy suspicion for having participated in the murders of more than two thousand Bosnians and Croats in various theaters of the war with his death squad, the Tigers. As the fans' representative, Raznatovic unified the rival groups of militant Ultras of Red Star. He presented himself as a generous benefactor, inviting, for example, eighty supporters to an away match in Glasgow. In 1991, he appeared in Slovenia as the leader of a paramilitary unit, whose members were recruited largely from the ranks of football hooligans. The capture of Vukovar led to a wave of excitement in the Serbian sporting press. The newspaper *Zvedzivina Revija*, for example, reported: "All nicely groomed in their black military caps, they began to sing: 'The Serbian army, that is us, Arkan's tigers, volunteers in rank upon rank, we will never give up the land of Serbia.'"[21] In 1994, Raznatovic purchased the Belgrade club Obilic, whose name recalled the legendary prince Milos Obilic, who defeated an Ottoman army at the battle of Kosovo in 1389 and is still venerated today as a saint in some regions of Serbia. Obilic quickly achieved considerable success and be-

21. Ibid.

came champion in 1998. However, it returned just as quickly to insignificance following the death of its owner.

Football's role as a bearer of regional identity did not always, however, take a militant turn. In eastern Germany, FC Hansa Rostock became a symbol for an independent and resisting mentality while Energie Cottbus is important for the small ethnic minority of Sorbs. In the German Democratic Republic, Union Berlin stood for a resistance, even an iron resistance, to the communist regime. Finally, in France US Bastia is a symbol for the Corsican cause, while in Italy it was SSC Napoli, under the magisterial conductor Diego Maradona, that led to the growth of a southern self-consciousness directed against the arrogant Piedmontese. Winning the *scudetto* (little shield), which Naples first accomplished in 1987, set off what may have been one of the largest and longest parties in European history.

As these examples make clear, football stadiums are, in one respect, refuges for political autonomy, that is places where in periods of dictatorship and oppression people can engage in resistance with the protection of anonymity. On the other hand, the stands also regularly give a hearing to extreme forms of regionalism and nationalism, and therefore become threatening. The direct recruitment of hooligans for military actions, as documented in the example of Arkan and his Tigers, may be an exceptional case. However, it also shows that there is a fine line between battle songs and battles.

Switzerland versus "Greater Germany": June 9, 1938

The meeting between Switzerland and "Greater Germany" in the World Cup in France in the summer of 1938 provides a paradigmatic example of the mixing of sports and politics.[22] From the very beginning, the meeting between the two neighboring states was marked by political connotations. The prestigious *Neue Zürcher Zeitung* placed an article about sports on its front page for the first time in its history following the

---

22. For a detailed discussion of this matter, see Christian Koller and Fabian Brändle "'Man fühlte, dass die Eidgenossen eine Grosstat vollbracht hatten': Fussball und geistige Landesverteidigung in der Schweiz," *Stadion* 25 (1999): 177–214.

Swiss victory. Looking back from 1955, the chief editor, Fred Luchsinger, described the circumstances in this way: "In view of its effect on the national consciousness, the victory ... doubtlessly was political."[23] By the summer of 1938, Germany had found itself for some time on an aggressive expansionist course. In March 1935 Adolf Hitler had declared the "military sovereignty" of Germany, and the next year he remilitarized the Rhineland contrary to the obligations of the Versailles peace treaty. Two years later came the *Anschluss* of Austria. This led, as the Zurich *Tages-Anzeiger* observed at the end of May 1938, "to a situation in which the 'political sensitivities' of the Swiss grew quite acute. It was only with great unease that policies were pursued that might disrupt proper relations with the state to our north."[24] Shortly after the *Anschluss*, an issue of the *Schulungsbrief*, which had a circulation of more than three million and served as the main organ for transmitting educational materials for the NSDAP's evening classes, drew the attention of the Swiss authorities. The issue had a map in which Switzerland belonged to the "region of German peoples."[25] It is hardly surprising that an athletic meeting between the two states carried such importance in this charged atmosphere.

Even in the run-up to the World Cup, political events surrounding the game between Switzerland and Germany drew considerable attention. On March 28, 1938, the Austrian Football Association (ÖFB) was dissolved. Consequently, one of the sixteen teams that had qualified for the World Cup was eliminated from the tournament right at the start. The best football players from the "Ostmark" were supposed to strengthen the team of Greater Germany. The 22-man roster of the Greater Germany team included no fewer than nine Viennese, of whom five were selected to play in the first game against Switzerland. On the Swiss side, the eligibility of Génia Walacek from Servette Geneva to play remained unclear until two days before the match. As the son of a Czech piano player and a woman from Neuchâtel, Walacek only possessed a Nansen refugee card but had nevertheless played in nine international matches for Switzerland. He had already received federal approval for his request

---

23. Fred Luchsinger, *Die Neue Zürcher Zeitung im Zeitalter des Weltkrieges 1930–1955* (Zurich: Neue Zürcher Zeitung, 1955), 191.

24. *Tages-Anzeiger*, May 30, 1938.

25. Ibid.

for citizenship, but had not yet received citizenship in the city of Geneva, which was necessary to obtain Swiss citizenship. Consequently, he was prevented from participating in the World Cup. Then, on June 2, the FIFA board met to hear a Swiss request that the issue be reconsidered. After a heated debate, Walacek received permission to play on a 14–10 vote, after which the FIFA president Jules Rimet put on the record that this "was an extraordinary decision, and will not serve as a precedent."[26] The decision was greeted avidly by the Swiss press, which interpreted it through a political lens. The *Neue Zürcher Zeitung* stressed that "the delegates from the small states used the appeal from the Swiss association to help a player, who did not have his own political fatherland, find an athletic fatherland."[27]

The first meeting between Switzerland and Greater Germany stood at a 1–1 tie at ninety minutes following a hard-fought game. The "Swiss lock," a defensive formation that the Swiss had learned from their Austrian coach Karl Rappan, and whose main exponent and major support was Severino Minelli (the central defender of Italian extraction), remained solid so that a thirty-minute extension of the game did not serve to bring about a decision. The *Schalker Kreisel* (Schalke Spinning Top) around Fritz Szepan and Ernst Kuzorra did not work, as the integration of the technically stronger Viennese players did not go according to plan. Subsequently, the two teams faced each other again three days later. In the rematch, the Germans led 2–0 after twenty minutes. Then the Swiss, who played weakly in the first half, got back to within a goal before the intermission on a score by Walacek. Nevertheless, after 45 minutes, the game already seemed to be decided. However, the game was turned on its head in the second half. The German team fell apart. By contrast, under the magisterial conductor Fredy Bickel, and thanks to the nose for the net and the three goals by the prolific Trello Abegglen, the Swiss left the field as the sparkling victors after ninety minutes.

The victory over Greater Germany sent all of Switzerland into a spasm of joy. According to press reports, during the radio broadcast of the game "there was a striking silence . . . in all of the cities and localities

26. This is according to Walter Lutz, "Rudolf Mingers Dank und 175 Franken: 1938—Das Wunder von Paris," *Sport*, May 31, 1991.

27. *Neue Zürcher Zeitung*, June 4, 1938.

in Switzerland, and only a limited amount of movement to be seen."[28] It was only after the goals for Switzerland that the tense silence was broken by loud jubilation that could be heard out on the street. In some cases, the radio broadcast was played out in the open air, and heard by large groups of people.[29] After the final whistle, the national holiday was celebrated a few weeks early. "They gave expression to their joy with flags, lanterns, floats, and songs."[30] In Zurich, a huge throng of people gathered in front of the offices of the magazine *Sport*, celebrating the Swiss players as heroes and singing the Swiss national anthem in three languages.[31] The *Arbeiter-Zeitung* in Basel reported with regard to the mood in this border city: "Last night ... it was amazing in the streets of our city. All of the hatred toward the Third Reich was given full expression."[32] In the stadium, itself, the correspondent for the *Journal de Genève* reported of the Swiss spectators that "their eyes filled with tears when they saw the fourth goal, which definitively secured their victory."[33] The fact that this eruption of feelings among the "civilians on the home-front"[34] was based primarily on political grounds is made clear, for example, by the recollection of future president of the Social Democratic Party and long-time member of the national parliament Helmut Hubacher, who experienced the game in front of his grandparents' radio: "For my grandfather, it was a political match. It was Switzerland against Hitler's Germany, against the Nazis. The victory had enormous importance for him. He proudly said to neighbors and acquaintances, 'Switzerland beat the krauts.'"[35]

Reports in the press also make clear that the trial of strength in Paris was not seen simply as a sporting event. The *Neue Zürcher Zeitung* reported in an article about the first meeting between the teams that the game "clearly belongs to those that make clear that the idea of sport bringing peoples together is a mere platitude." In addition, the actions

28. *Tages-Anzeiger*, June 10, 1938; *Neue Zürcher Nachrichten*, June 10, 1938.

29. See Otto F. Walter, *Zeit des Fasans: Roman* (Reinbek: Rowohlt, 1988), 121–26, for a literary reworking of this account.

30. *Tages-Anzeiger*, June 10, 1938; *Neue Zürcher Nachrichten*, June 10, 1938.

31. *Sport*, June 13, 1938.   32. *Arbeiter-Zeitung*, June 10, 1938.

33. *Journal de Genève*, June 10, 1938.

34. Archive of the Swiss Football Association, box for the 1938 World Cup.

35. Helmut Hubacher, "Einwurf: Der legendäre Sieg in Paris," *Tages-Anzeiger*, June 12, 1998.

of the referee were those of someone who "seemed to understand that a special atmosphere had developed around the World Cup match between Switzerland and Germany" and "that it was not conducive to the normal handling of the game."[36] The *Tages-Anzeiger* complained that, of all things, bringing in the Viennese onto the German team "added a spiteful and even unsporting tone to the game."[37] Even the coverage in the official organ of the Swiss Football and Athletic Union regarding the singing of the national anthems before the game made clear that its importance transcended the realm of sport: "'Deutschland über Alles' and the 'Horst Wessel Song' were the musical selections, and the 2,000–3,000 Germans, who were present, ... sang along. They were answered by 10,000 throats singing 'Rufst Du mein Vaterland,' filling the entire stadium."[38]

There was very little difference among the individual newspapers in their characterization of the Swiss team. The *Neue Zürcher Zeitung* repeatedly mentioned "our brave eleven"[39] in their coverage of the game, who showed "what an iron will and a healthy spirit of comradeship can accomplish. They launched continuous attacks against the German fortress, until they capitulated."[40] In a similar manner, many of the daily newspapers in Zurich reported in their published accounts that the Swiss fought "like lions": "The Reds launched continuous attacks.... In the 35th minute, the Swiss took a 4 to 2 lead on a goal by Abegglen. The feeling was that the Confederates had accomplished a great deed.... They went onto the attack at a critical point with unfailing energy, and did a splendid job of turning the tide in their own favor."[41] The communist *Freiheit* rejoiced that the Swiss "had not succumbed to the regime of the German steamroller, but rather staunchly and bravely had achieved a victory."[42]

The *Journal de Genève* congratulated the Swiss team and their coach

36. *Neue Zürcher Zeitung*, June 7, 1938.

37. *Tages-Anzeiger*, June 7, 1938.

38. *Schweizerische Fussball- und Athletikzeitung*, June 9, 1938.

39. *Neue Zürcher Zeitung*, June 10, 1938.

40. *Neue Zürcher Zeitung*, June 10, 1938.

41. *Tages-Anzeiger*, June 10, 1938; *Neue Zürcher Nachrichten*, June 10, 1938; *Landbote*, June 10, 1938.

42. *Freiheit*, June 10, 1938.

"for the magnificent fashion in which they defended the white cross on the field of red,"[43] and the *Gazette de Lausanne* explicitly attributed an importance to the game that went far beyond the realm of sports:

This event goes far beyond sport. It is national. And all of us who are patriots have the right to be proud of our national team.... This team from a nation of just 4 million inhabitants was able to defeat ... a team from Greater Germany, that did not have enough, it would appear, from its 80 million. There it is, a step away from the ordinary. What is the importance of the eleven small Swiss who played Thursday evening, who played the match of their lives? They had what the others could not have: the will to conquer, faith in victory. Our side, wounded in the previous meeting, vilified by an arrogant and powerful adversary, serried their ranks and fought like they were at St. Jakob and achieved a victory that will live on.[44]

The reference to the battle near St. Jakob an der Birs points to the ideological context in which the event was conceptualized in Switzerland. The massacre on August 26, 1444, in which about 1,300 young Swiss lost their lives in battle against eight times as many French mercenaries led in the late sixteenth century to the development of myth about their sacrificial death, a myth that was further strengthened in the nineteenth century. This myth was particularly instrumentalized on the occasion of the five hundreth anniversary of the battle in 1944 to strengthen the spiritual national defense.[45] The Swiss football players were thus viewed as following in succession with the heroes of a Swiss national myth in consonance with the phrase "Hail to you Helvetia, Do you still have sons, such as those whom St. Jakob saw," from the contemporary Swiss national anthem. The *Patrie valaisanne* briefly and succinctly articulated what the overwhelming majority of Swiss population thought and felt on that day: "it doesn't matter that our eleven does not go any farther, they beat Germany, and one could say that is certainly something."[46] The *Arbeiter-Zeitung* of Basel pointed to the national team as a role model for the entire Swiss people. In a poem with the title "Thousands of Victors in the Family Register" a passage states: "If the people remained truly

43. *Journal de Genève*, June 10, 1938.

44. *Gazette de Lausanne*, June 10, 1938.

45. On this point, see *Ereignis-Mythos-Deutung: Die Schlacht bei St. Jakob an der Birs*, ed. Werner Meyer (Basel: Klingenthal, 1994).

46. *Patrie valaisanne*, June 10, 1938.

Swiss, and acted with such speed, then everything would be much easier and less of a burden!"[47]

There were interesting and clearly politically motivated differences in the image that was painted of the German team. The bourgeois press did not refrain from mentioning the toughness with which the German team played, particularly during the first half of the game.[48] The left-wing press presented the matter entirely differently. The Social Democratic *Arbeiter-Zeitung* from Basel wrote, playing on a line from the "Horst Wessel Song," that it was with great "satisfaction" that the Swiss team "stopped the crazed invincibility of the brown battalions."[49] The *Limmattaler Tagblatt*, the official publication of various working class neighborhoods and suburbs of Zurich, took pleasure, while casting a glance at the wars in Spain and China, in the fact that "between the battlefields where power politics glories in orgies of blood … the athletic representatives of four million democratic people defeated on the field the representatives of a major state controlled by a militarist ideology, doing so through their superior individuality and their ability to feel enthusiasm in their hearts."[50] The Social Democratic *Volksrecht* from Zurich and the communist *Freiheit* also made no secret of their political disgust for the "Nazi team," and emphasized in their reporting that the German team "began the World Cup match with their brutality … in an unpleasant manner" and "that they continued to play with increasing crudeness" that led to a "storm of indignation" among the public and to "a passionate chorus of cat-calls."[51] It was happily noted that the "normal opening of Hitler salute-gymnastics" by the German team before the game "received a chilly reception from the public," and that the German supporters of the team faced a chorus of hoots when they began to sing to the "Horst Wessel Song."[52]

The left-wing press offered even greater criticism of the German athletic officials than they did of the German players and their supporters in the stands. The fact that the German team did not remain in Paris

47. *Arbeiter-Zeitung*, June 11, 1938.
48. See, for example, *Neue Zürcher Zeitung*, June 7, 1938, and June 10, 1938.
49. *Arbeiter-Zeitung*, June 10, 1938.
50. *Limmattaler Tagblatt*, June 10, 1938.
51. *Volksrecht*, June 7, 1938, and June 10, 1938; and *Freiheit*, June 7, 1938.
52. Ibid.

between the two matches, but rather traveled back to Aachen—which was explained in the bourgeois press in Switzerland as resulting from the current lack of foreign currency in Germany—gave rise to major attacks in the left-wing press.[53] The *Arbeiter-Zeitung* from Basel and the *Volksrecht* scornfully observed that the German team "was surrounded by the touching concern of the upper, middle, and lower leaders of Nazi sports. Their greatest fear is that the German players might notice that France is a land of free and uncoerced life, that people in France can think, speak, have opinions, and laugh as they wish, and that it is not true that foreigners will be attacked by 'red mobs' on the Champs-Elysées." The unfair playing style of the Germans clearly was determined by their system:

> The Nazi sport leaders prefer exceptional fatigue brought on by these long journeys to a danger of "spiritual contamination." It is no surprise that these players—who are being held in cages like the animals that were set on gladiators in antiquity—go on to attack the gladiator, or in this case the other team, as soon as the cage is opened. Excesses of the kind that they inflicted on the Swiss are less the fault of the individual players than of the system under whose unhealthy pressure they have been set.[54]

The *Freiheit* went so far as to claim that the players on the German national team were being treated "like inmates in a concentration camp."[55] The Social Democratic *Berner Tagwacht* made clear it was pleased that the National Socialist regime would not be able to exploit the football world championship for propaganda purposes, "as happens with all athletic success in the Fascist states. And it is proper that small Switzerland made such a propaganda coup impossible. It is just that it was players from a democracy whose inhabitants have only 'filth under their skulls.'"[56]

These passages show the different conceptions of the media's approach to Nazi Germany. Left-wing coverage was on a clear course of confrontation with the northern neighbor. There was far less praise of the achievements of the Swiss, with a greater stress on the anti-Fascist tendencies of the French popular front. By contrast, the bourgeois press,

53. See *Neue Zürcher Nachrichten*, June 7, 1938.

54. *Arbeiter-Zeitung*, June 9, 1938; and *Volksrecht*, June 10, 1938.

55. *Freiheit*, June 10, 1938.

56. *Berner Tagwacht*, June 10, 1938. The insults quoted here are from a passage in a speech given by Goebbels in Freiburg im Breisgau.

concomitant with the idea of spiritual national defense, placed the putative virtues of "Swissness," bravery, force of will, willingness to make sacrifices, and comradeship, to the fore. In particular, the German Swiss avoided, as much as possible, making direct attacks against the Germans. While the left engaged in the diffusion of an image of the enemy, the bourgeois strove to strengthen and increase the national self-conception without explicitly renouncing an attitude of neutrality in foreign affairs. Seen in this light, the bourgeois reporting seems to be a prefiguration of the policies pursued toward the northern neighbor during the war, namely a demonstrated willingness to defend themselves combined with economic cooperation.

The day after their victory, the Swiss team's quarters were deluged with good wishes by telegraph, letter, and phone. One of the first to offer his congratulations was federal councilor Rudolf Minger, the head of the Swiss military department, who offered a "Swiss greeting for the brave Swiss national team ... that achieved a magnificent victory with exemplary dedication."[57] The Social Democratic national president Fritz Hauser, formally the "Highest Swiss" and former president of the Swiss Football and Athletic Union, made clear his joy about this "beautiful success" at a meeting of parliament on June 10, and ordered that the congratulations of the greater chamber be transmitted by telegraph to the Swiss team.[58] Further congratulations came from the Free Democratic faction in the federal assembly, from various athletic associations, clubs, and numerous private individuals.[59]

In the archive of the Swiss Football Association there is a box containing these congratulatory messages.[60] The letters and telegrams are interesting sources for the history of mentalities. The collection includes 456 texts by individuals, as well as 89 mailings by clubs, groups of pub regulars, and school classes. The missives are divided roughly in proportion to the populations in the various regions of the country. The number of congratulations sent by groups of regulars is striking, and points

57. *Neue Zürcher Zeitung*, June 10, 1938.

58. Concerning this point, see *Neue Zürcher Zeitung*, June 10, 1938; and *Arbeiter-Zeitung*, June 11, 1938.

59. *Neue Zürcher Zeitung*, June 11, 1938; and *Schweizerische Fussball- und Athletik-Zeitung*, June 15, 1938.

60. Archive of the Swiss Football Association, box for the 1938 World Cup.

to the practice of collective participation in listening to the radio. The reporting by Hans Sutter was praised on all sides. Another striking aspect is the high proportion of letters from young people, and particularly young women. It can be shown that 61 young men and 47 young women, as well as 18 school classes, acting collectively, sent congratulations. The self-identification with the victors may have been particularly strong among the youth. A class from the Collège de la Maladière in Neuchâtel signed off as "the future national team," a touching sign that the students identified with the players in Paris. By contrast, the desire of the students to have a ball sent back to them demonstrates a clear pragmatism. Requests for autographs attest to certain star cult in this period. At least 41 women also sent congratulations to the national team.[61]

The game between Switzerland and "Greater Germany" served as a true catalyzing force in the development of a Swiss identity in the sense of a "we" feeling differentiated from the northern neighbors. Just as had been true in the press, the congratulations stressed the bravery of the Swiss in their heroic victory.[62] A man from Lucerne was proud "because we can say of our national team that they not only know how to play, they know how to fight as well." The "heroic accomplishment" that a group of pub regulars from Zurich attributed to the team as a whole was particularly directed to Aebi, from Servette, who as a worker bee was given the nod over the more elegant Vernati and justified his selection by continuing to play despite suffering a severe injury to his face.[63] A man from Bern praised the perseverance of the runner with "Aebi, jaw out, jaw in."

Many of those sending congratulations recalled after the match the founding history of Switzerland, at the battle of Morgarten in 1315,[64] or the "liberator" and tyrant-slayer William Tell.[65] A man from Geneva praised "the courage that has made this country great across the cen-

61. Since many people only included the first letters of their names, it is not possible to give an exact number for the women. The large number of women does show that football was not a purely male domain.

62. All of the citations in the following section are drawn from the archive of the Swiss Football Association, box for the 1938 World Cup. Sixty-six mention brave, bravery, virtuous, fighting spirit, etc.

63. Three mentions (woman from Lausanne, man from Zurich, man from Locarno).

64. Two mentions (man from Basel, man from Dietikon).

65. One mention (regulars' table, Café Ernst, Zurich).

turies." Many of those sending congratulations showed their enthusiasm with a "Hopp Schwyz" in French or German.[66] The victory of the Swiss team became a "victory of our fatherland,"[67] the victory of an entire country. The members of FC Grandson sent special greetings to the German Swiss: "We are all red and white." A man from Zurich rhymed: "The self loses its charm—it is about something higher—it is about the honor of Switzerland." Borrowing from David and Goliath, little Switzerland had defeated the more powerful neighbor.[68] They "showed them over there who was the champion" according to class G4a of girls secondary school in Basel. Traugott Büechi, the president of the right-wing organization Schweizer Wehraktion claimed that the victory was proof that a small state could also be powerful. The regulars at Café Ernst in Zurich, clearly in a boisterous mood, wrote: "Switzerland knocked Germany out in football. They crushed the Germans despite shrieks of victory, and the baying of hail." Finally, Vereinigte FC Winterthur stated in a congratulatory telegram on the day after the victory over Greater Germany that they were glad that "our national team, through their superhuman achievement, promoted the sport of football to all levels of our population."[69]

The fact that a few days after their victory over Germany the Swiss team was defeated by the later finalist Hungary and thereby eliminated from the tournament did not dampen the excitement in Switzerland. As the team returned home on June 14, it received an enthusiastic reception. In Basel the players received a welcome home from the Social Democratic president of the cantonal government, Ebi, in front of a huge throng of people. In Zurich a delegation from the city government invited the team to have a snack during which the mayor Emil Klöti, who was also a Social Democrat, gave a speech "that came from the deep impression that the excitement of the last weeks had made on him."[70] The players from Geneva also were greeted by a delegation from the city

66. A total of twenty-six mentions. Today both German Swiss and Romance speakers continue to celebrate their team with a phrase that crosses the language boundary: "Hopp Schwyz/ Hop Suisse" (Go, Switzerland).

67. Hotel Touring Chiasso.

68. Fourteen mentions of small fatherland, etc.

69. F. C. Winterthur to the brave Swiss team in Paris, June 10, 1938.

70. *Neue Zürcher Zeitung*, June 14, 1938.

government. A member of the posh Zurich Grasshopper Club paid out the considerable sum of a 1,000 francs for the players. One week later, when the "heroes of Paris," as they soon came to be known, attended the rematch of the cup final between the Zurich Grasshoppers and Servette Geneva in Bern, the federal councilor Rudolf Minger brought them "the greetings of the government and the entire people" because "their achievements had unleashed a flood of happiness, jubilation, and satisfaction throughout the entire country."[71] Every player received a wristwatch paid for with the proceeds of a national fundraising campaign.[72] The inscription read: "Your magnificent success has filled each of us with pride, and we hope that you will frequently use your skills for the athletic honor of our beloved fatherland.... Sending our personal congratulations as well, we greet you with a three-fold 'Hopp Schwyz.'"[73]

The magazine *Sport* included an article on its front page a week after the game demanding that football be made an obligatory school subject.[74] This suggestion was supported by the claim that following the victory over "Greater Germany," football had finally lost the sense of being foreign in Switzerland and had become a means for strengthening the spiritual national defense:[75]

The citizen no longer sees in these football players a betrayal of Swiss tradition, no longer foreign representatives of an un-Swiss sport. Rather, the citizen sees in these football players a powerful sort of Swiss, who can show the others that we are still here, and that we are and always will be prepared to strive for and claim our place in the sun. Today, there is a great deal of conversation about the spiritual national defense. The achievements of our football eleven are part of this spiritual defense. The hundreds of thousands listening on the radio were not burning for a football victory, but rather for a Swiss victory. There is an enormous amount of patriotism in this excitement for football! Patriotism lives in the breast, not in the head, not in the brain. Love for the fatherland is a matter of the heart.... Seen from this point of view, the magnificent victories of our national team are an important element in the spiritual national defense. The Swiss man, whatever his class, is proud of the conduct of our men in France. Joy, overwhelming joy even, fills his heart! ... The appeal of the eleven brave Swiss

71. Following Walter Lutz, "Rudolf Mingers Dank und 175 Franken: 1938—Das Wunder von Paris," *Sport*, May 31, 1991.

72. See, for example, *Sport*, June 15, 1938.   73. Cited in *Sport*, June 20, 1938.

74. *Sport*, June 17, 1938.   75. Ibid.

to our hearts did not go unheard. The echoes have been powerful! Let us give a hearing to these voices! Let us give to football what it has richly earned!

A Second Fourth of July? Germany versus Hungary on July 4, 1954

For the Germans, the Third Reich ended in a complete defeat. The country was destroyed and divided. Large regions, such as East Prussia and Silesia, were lost forever. The horrors and deprivations that were bound up in the first years after the war soon led many Germans to feel that they were the victims, and no longer the culprits, who had begun the war and participated in genocide. Soon, a common view developed that it was the Nazis, Hitler, and the "party barons" who bore all of the guilt, and their own roles as participants or culprits were given very little consideration.[76] Their main concern was the reconstruction of the bombed out cities and the economic recovery that was quickly taking off thanks to American aid. Soon the "economic miracle" began and there was finally a little bit of extra money with which to indulge oneself. A Volkswagen commercial from 1954 echoed the positive atmosphere, "Ever more, ever better."[77] For the first time, a majority (60 percent) had positive expectations for the future.

The indignities that followed upon the national trance were countless. Germans were not welcome around the world. They had to struggle for the recognition that was and is so important to them. The goal was to find a place in the new world order. The solution was to look to the future. However, the West Germans did not really identify with the Bonn Republic. In 1954, a third of the citizens wished for a return of a king or emperor. One year later, just a third of the population was in favor of the Basic Law.[78] By contrast, football was an ideal bearer of identity. It

76. Ralph Giordano described this process of suppression, forgetting, and stylization as a victim of the "second guilt." Ralph Giordano, *Die zweite Schuld oder Von der Last Deutscher zu sein* (Hamburg: Rasch und Röhring, 1987).

77. Cited following Arthur Heinrich, *Tooor! Toor! Tor! 40 Jahre 3 : 2* (Hamburg: Rotbuch Verlag, 1994), 32. Also see Daniel Aeschlimann, "Der Tag, an dem das Wankdorf weltberühmt wurde," *Der Bund*, July 4, 2001; Siegfried Gehrmann, "Le sport comme moyen de réhabilitation nationale au début de la République Fédérale d'Allemagne: Les Jeux Olympiques de 1952 et la Coupe du Monde de Football de 1954," in *Sports et relations internationals,*, 231–43.

78. Heinrich, *Tooor! Toor! Tor!*, 18.

offered a certain freedom for a "loud" and otherwise taboo nationalism. The imperial eagle was displayed, as always, on the shirts of the national players. The German Football Union remained a refuge for conservative thought.[79]

In 1954 the Federal Republic was permitted to participate again in the World Cup. However, they did not seem to have any chance against the powerful teams from South America and above all against the Hungarians. The Hungarians, who had already become a leading team during the 1930s, were unbeaten in thirty-one straight games. In November 1953 they had defeated England at Wembley 6–3, thereby destroying the mystique of English indefatigability in their own country. During the return match in Budapest, the teacher was humiliated 7–1. The team around Puskás, Czibor, Boszík, Hidegkuti, and the prolific Koscís was the clear tournament favorite for the World Cup in 1954, which was to be hosted by Switzerland, a country that had emerged unscathed from the Second World War.

As expected, things did not go well for Germany at the start. After falling behind early, Turkey was defeated rather convincingly 4–1. Three days later, the team was defeated by the Hungarians 8–3. The coach Sepp Herberger, a sly fox and a cunning tactician, put in his reserve eleven, a trick that was not appreciated by either the press or the German fans, who had paid 57 German Marks for the journey and ticket. The blame went to the center defender, Werner Liebrich, who played an overly rough style. Liebrich's brutal foul against Puskás when the score was 1–5 hurt the exceptionally dangerous Hungarian playmaker so badly that he was unable to play again until the final match. The decisive game, which was now required against Turkey, ended in a clear and decisive 7–1 victory, and the critics quickly grew silent.

The quarterfinal was against the technically very capable Yugoslavians, who were favored by everyone to win. As a result, the way in which the Germans held their opponents in check 2–0 was even more astounding. The political scientist Arthur Heinrich demonstrated that the game against Yugoslavia strengthened the sense of national identity. The

---

79. In response to a internal demand for democratization of the DFB, president Peco Bauwens said in 1948: "Democracy does not belong to the high ideals that we maintain." Citation from Heinrich, *Fussballbund*, 166.

tabloid *Bild* wrote, for example, that Rahn achieved the "final victory"[80] against the Yugoslavs in the eighty-fourth minute—and thus the first bad relapse into jargon of the Third Reich, the Lingua Tertii Imperii (Viktor Klemperer) could be detected. The victory tasted even sweeter because the match had been moved to Geneva with the obvious purpose of limiting the number of German fans who could attend the game in Charmilles stadium. The semi-final was in the border city of Basel on June 30 against Austria, which had defeated Switzerland 7–5 in the highest scoring match in the history of the World Cup final round. The German team outclassed the Austrians 6–1. The Hungarians awaited them in Bern for the final. The Hungarians had played brilliantly up to this point, dominating the defending champion Uruguay in the semifinal.

Thus, on the fourth of July, David faced Goliath in the Bernese Wankdorf stadium. About half of the 60,000 spectators had traveled from Germany, and the drizzle gave them grounds for hope. This was "Fritz Walter weather,"[81] or so claimed the reporter Herbert Zimmermann, who greeted the nation gathered in front of their radios and even a few televisions.[82] The captain and playmaker Fritz Walter was one of five players from Kaiserslautern, who were supposed to achieve the impossible. Everything seemed like it would follow the course that people feared as the Hungarians took a 2–0 lead after just eight minutes with goals by Puskás and Czibor. The Nürnberger Maxl Morlock brought the Germans to within one in the 13th minute. Just five minutes later, the striker from Essen Helmut Rahn scored the equalizer. The game went back and forth although the clear advantage lay with the Hungarians, who again and again failed against the superb German goalkeeper Toni Turek (Fortuna Düsseldorf). He was a "football god"[83] according to the correspondent Herbert Zimmermann, whose reporting became increasingly euphoric. According to the *Frankfurter Allgemeine Zeitung*, "every man on the German national eleven fulfilled his duty to the utmost of his ability."[84] In the eighty-fourth minute, Rahn got the ball at the edge

80. Heinrich, *Tooor! Toor! Tor!*, 38.

81. Ibid., 46.

82. Also see Erik Eggers, *Die Stimme von Bern: Das Leben von Herbert Zimmermann, Reporterlegende bei der WM 1954* (Augsburg: Wißner Verlag, 2004).

83. Schwarz, *5 Jahrzehnte Fussball im Originalton*, CD 1, tracks 4–8.

84. *Frankfurter Allgemeine Zeitung*, July 5, 1954.

of the penalty area, dribbled around two opposing players, and shot. The ball, falling toward the wet grass, landed, unreachable for Grosics, the goalie, in the left corner. Herbert Zimmermann screamed into his microphone, "Rahn has to shoot from behind. Rahn shoots. Goaaal! Goal! Goal! Goal! Goal for Germany!"[85] Turek saved yet another unstoppable shot and the "miracle at Bern" became a reality. Germany was world champion for the first time.

Some sinister undertones, which recalled the very recent period of horrors, quickly mixed in with the understandable joy. In its reportage regarding the minutes after the end of the game, the *Frankfurter Allgemeine Zeitung* happily observed that "25,000 German spectators powerfully joined in singing the *Deutschlandlied*."[86] Indeed, the visiting fans sang the first stanza, although the more peaceful third stanza had become the text for the national anthem.[87] It is contested whether some individual spectators also raised their right arms in the Hitler salute. However, it was not only victory-besotted fans who sang "Deutschland, Deutschland, über alles" after the final whistle. This stanza was also played during the triumphal procession that the players enjoyed on their journey through Germany. The return trip on the chartered train, called "Red Lighting," turned into an unprecedented public event. More than 30,000 fans waited for the train at the border station at Singen. More than 500,000 people wanted to celebrate with the "heroes of Bern" in Munich. These were the first true mass events in nine years. Masses of German men and women also participated in the official tributes that were held for the world champions in Kaiserlautern, Essen, Düsseldorf, and Fürth.

Some players had qualities that made it particularly easy for fans to identify with them. In contrast to the other star players, the best player and their conductor, Fritz Walter, had been conscripted during the Second World War. His experiences as an infantryman, "a completely normal *Landser*" who simply carried out orders, matched the experiences of millions of German men, who had simply wanted to do their duty. During the war, Walter had played with other football players on the "Red

---

85. Schwarz, *5 Jahrzehnte Fussball im Originalton*, CD 1, track 8.
86. *Frankfurter Allgemeine Zeitung*, July 5, 1954.
87. Schwarz, *5 Jahrzehnte Fussball im Originalton*, CD 1, track 9.

Hunter" army team. At the same time, he put his life on the line during his tours of duty, and so did not have the same privileged existence as other elite athletes.[88] Five years after the game in Bern, Walter published a popular wartime memoir that corresponded exactly with these kinds of memories.[89] In addition, Walter was humble, or down-to-earth, as one says today. The literary critic Jörg Drews, who grew up in Kaiserslautern, remembered meeting his youthful idol in 1947 during a back lot game. Fritz Walter juggled a new leather ball, a luxury, on the sidewalk on Fischer street before offering comfort to the assembled boys: "You have it good, you boys. I was so poor, I never had a ball. My mother almost killed me because I wrecked my shoes playing with a bit of iron."[90]

Helmut Rahn, the "boss," came from the Ruhr region and was very friendly. He happily drank a beer, or two or three. He made his contemporaries laugh with his priceless parody of a market woman from Essen, which was also a play on the clever survival strategies of the immediate postwar period:

Top notch firm tomatoes people! The best grandma sucking berries for toothless grandmothers. Yes, red cabbage, white cabbage, savoy cabbage, spinach! If no one comes, then kiss my ... I am tired of life, today I am giving the merchandise away! Ah, here comes someone! Top notch firm tomatoes![91]

Just like the captain Fritz Walter, the happy-go-lucky Helmut Rahn spoke to many Germans, who did not want to hear any more about the World War, the Holocaust, or their associated historical guilt. In 1959, Fritz Walter cut to the chase when he wrote: "Let's not talk about the war, let's talk about football."[92] In the end, the legendary comradeship among the coaches and players in the continuously conjured up "spirit of Spiez" demonstrated to the Germans that it was possible to achieve anything as long as everyone held together and pulled on the same rope.[93]

However, the left-liberal press criticized this German chauvinism

---

88. See Fischer, *Stürmer*, 231.

89. Fritz Walter, *Elf rote Jäger: Nationalspieler im Kriege* (Munich: Copress-Verlag, 1959).

90. Citation from Jörg Drews, "Damals Moment siebenundvierzig jawohl: Sieben unwillkürliche Erinnerungen an eine Jugend am Fuss des Betzenberges," in *Netzer kam aus der Tiefe des Raumes: Notwendige Beiträge zur Fussballweltmeisterschaft*, eds. Ludwig Harig and Dieter Kühn (Munich: Hanser, 1974), 64.

91. Heinrich, *Tooor! Toor! Tor!*, 50.   92. Walter, *Elf rote Jäger*, 34.

93. Heinrich, *Tooor! Toor! Tor!*, 23.

harshly, highlighting the national dissonance. The *Süddeutsche Zeitung* reported, for example:[94]

Doubtlessly, there are many Germans who do not confuse a love for nation with arrogance. We understand quite clearly what they would like to achieve. But there is also a considerable number of Germans, who do not understand the difference between a willingness for an accommodation with other peoples, in the sense of a certain "international humility," and an exceptionally humiliating loss of national dignity.

An educated middle-class author of a letter to the editor at the *Frankfurter Allgemeine Zeitung* felt that the mass hysteria recalled the very recent German past:[95]

The fact that the eleven around Herberger unexpectedly found themselves the object of cult-like ovations demonstrates with terrible clarity how far the value system of the masses has again strayed on this side of the "zero point." After the values of veneration, which once had been reserved for the "throne and altar" in the sense of sacred entities, was transferred to a secularized "cult of the leader," today's triumphal procession of "king football" and its twelve apostles would seem to be the final step in an unbelievable process of forgetting the importance of those events. Football, a nullity that has been raised to a higher power, has usurped the "holiest" state given to mankind! An analysis of the pseudo-cultic expressions used in the sporting news on the radio and in the press (Turek as a football god), makes this fact very clear.... Once again ... the spirit triumphs over the soul, but what kind of "spirit."

The Hamburg weekly magazine *Der Spiegel*, by contrast, emphasized the positive side of this eruption of national feeling. The "little people" acted "in front of the entire world as if they had discovered the singular meaning and true purpose of their national existence at the end of June 1954, after the false path of the twentieth century":[96]

Never before ... had the collective feelings of the Germans churned so exclusively for anything, as they did for their football team. Earlier, national passions in Europe celebrated political triumphs. Today, national sentiments, which cannot yet be "assimilated," are flowing toward sport. These feelings ratchet up sports, and "make something out of them that they are not supposed to be" or so warn dozens of commentators. But the reverse is also true. Sport shapes emotions as well.

94. Ibid., 84.
95. *Frankfurter Allgemeine Zeitung*, July 12, 1954.
96. *Spiegel*, July 7, 1954.

The legitimacy of singing the first stanza led to a heated debate in which chauvinist voices from yesteryear also participated. It was said that other countries had much bloodier national anthems, and national symbols were used by every state. One letter to the editor to the *Spiegel* stated: "if someone does not want the first stanza, then we should get another national anthem. It is degrading to 'unlearn' the words of the national anthem. One could only come up with this sort of idea for the Germans."[97] However, the most disgusting nationalist tones did not come from the beery singers and euphoric people who went to the train platforms, but rather from "above" from sport officials and politicians. In particular, the president of the DFB, Dr. Peco Bauwens, did not refrain in his official speech, which unfortunately only survives in fragments, in the Munich Hofbräuhaus, from making references back to the "Third Reich." According to Bauwens, the German team "represented the best of Germany abroad," and was filled with the "spirit of the good Germans."[98] When Bauwens began to praise the "leader principle," Bavarian Radio Station turned off the broadcast.

Another academic, Dr. Joachim Beser, the chief reporter for the *Welt*, initially showed skepticism about the strength of the team from the Federal Republic and did not show any scruples about using the language of the last days of the Third Reich. "This sport of football, in all of its primitivism, possesses an uncanny symbolic power. Everyone felt it in Geneva [against Yugoslavia]. Here, they defended themselves vigorously and did not want to give in. Here, there were eleven who swore that they would not be smoked out of their fortress. Every one of them would have struck the ball with his tongue if that is what it took."[99] Bauwens and Beser received considerable criticism. The *Süddeutsche Zeitung*, for example, described this as a *"Sieg Heil"* speech.[100]

Abroad, the German reaction to the World Cup title was met with unease. In its reporting, the *Manchester Guardian* ambiguously compared the attack by the German team to the "old blitzkrieg."[101] In the *Daily Mirror*, the Labour parliamentarian Michael Foot warned that the Germans were already becoming arrogant.[102] The *Daily Express* had the headline

---

97. Heinrich, *Tooor! Toor! Tor!*, 85.
99. Heinrich, *Tooor! Toor! Tor!*, 94.
101. *Manchester Guardian*, July 5, 1954.
102. Citation from the *Frankfurter Allgemeine Zeitung*, July 7, 1954.

98. Ibid., 92. Also see *Spiegel*, July 14, 1954.
100. Ibid., 97.

"Der Tag—for Germans" and explained that "*Der Tag*" was a famous German term for the outbreak of the Second World War. The caption for this article was accompanied by the phrase, in German, *Deutschland über alles*.[103] The Copenhagen newspaper *Information* made the point that only the lack of an overt "hail victory" kept this from having the feeling of the 1936 Olympics. It went on to say, "the Germans sang *Deutschland, Deutschland über alles*, indeed there was a roar, and it seemed as if this victory cancelled out the one that they had failed to achieve from 1940 to 1945."[104] Finally, the correspondent for *Le Monde* cited an acquaintance who saw in Sepp Herberger's strategy of only playing the second team against Hungary in the early round, and then defeating them in the final, a basic characteristic of the Germans, and warned of the parallels with Adenauer's policy of integration with the West.[105]

The effect of the world championship on the self-confidence of German men and women remains contested until the present day. On the one hand, the triumph in Bern, even if it did come with an admixture of an ugly and invincible German chauvinism, did lead to a process of stabilization in the young Federal Republic and helped make it possible to avoid a basic rejection of the new system comparable with the views of the majority of the German people toward the Weimar Republic. By defeating the "golden" team from Hungary, the German squad demonstrated that "old" German values such as readiness for action, diligence, and comradeship, which had fallen into disrepute, also could be of great use in the new world order. By contrast, the politicians in the other German nation, the German Democratic Republic, had to experience the defeat of a "friendly" socialist country, an allegory for the superiority of the collectivist ideology, at the hands of the hated class enemy. The functionaries consoled themselves that, as *Vorwärts* wrote, "the ball that landed in the net behind Grosicz in the 82nd minute neither made the world fall down, nor did it improve the condition of West German imperialism."[106] The enemy Bonn government was charged with misusing the victory for political purposes. Nevertheless, many East German working men and women had the audacity to celebrate the victory of the Federal team as their own as well, and to celebrate it more or less openly just

---

103. Ibid.
105. Ibid.

104. *Spiegel*, July 14, 1954.
106. Heinrich, *Tooor! Toor! Tor!*, 127.

a year after the uprising on June 17. On the other hand, the German economic and social historian Franz-Josef Brüggemeier, taking account of the numerous dissonant voices in the press, warned against overestimating the importance of the football victory for the reawakening of a German national sentiment.[107]

And the "heroes of Bern"? Four years later, the now aged team was knocked out in the semifinal by the hosts in Sweden. They decisively lost the game for third place 3–6 against the strong French team that had two superior strikers in Raymond Kopa and the scoring champion Just Fontaine. The world champions also were not able to profit from their historic victory. Certainly, they received the silver laurel from the president of the Federal Republic as well as countless gifts from private individuals.[108] However, the first effort to earn money through endorsements was immediately blocked by the bigoted DFB enforcers of amateurism. The players received a modest bonus of a thousand marks for their title. A world champion who played in all of the games received just two thousand marks for a bonus. In recognition of Fritz Walter's service, decades later the Betzenberg stadium in Kaiserslautern was renamed the Fritz Walter stadium. Under pressure from the press and the association, the captain refused lucrative offers to play abroad. Helmut Rahn and Kohlmeyer drank too much, and the "boss" even had to spend some time in jail. Ottmar Walter finally fell so far into debt that he had to give up his filling station. None of the eleven had any success as a coach.

And the Hungarians? The trip home was a singular humiliation. The players got off the train before arriving at the main station in Budapest in order avoid the scorn of the "people." The experience in the capital was almost like an uprising. Businesses were plundered and photographs of the failures were publicly burned. Thousands of protestors marched in front of the editorial offices of the national sports newspaper, where they burned the most recent edition that dealt with the incomprehensible defeat. The main victim of the disappointment was the hated coach and theoretician Gusztav Sebes, whose immediate dismissal was demanded unanimously.[109]

---

107. Franz-Josef Brüggemeier, *Zurück auf dem Platz: Deutschland und die Fußballweltmeisterschaft 1954* (Munich: DVA, 2004).

108. *Frankfurter Allgemeine Zeitung*, July 5, 1954.

109. György Dalos, "Die ungarische Fussballkatastrophe von 1954," in his *Ungarn: Vom*

In a certain sense, these demonstrations prepared the way for the anti-Stalinist Hungarian popular uprising in 1956. Puskás, Czibor, Kocsis, and others emigrated in the course of the massive flight that took place after Soviet troops crushed Imre Nagy's reform communist state.

Major Ferenc Puskás, who had played for the army club Honved, became a top player in Francoist Spain for the most successful club team of the period, Real Madrid. Gold Head Koscis, who was the scoring champion in the World Cup in Switzerland with twelve goals, played for FC Barcelona. Like Czibor, both of them were naturalized as Spaniards, and played in the 1962 World Cup for Spain. Other emigrants, like the midfielders Lorant, Lantos, and Hidegkuti, had great success as coaches. Lorant, for example, coached for Bayern München and Schalke 04, and Puskás became a coach in Greece for Panathinaikos Athens. Much later, during the 1990s, he attempted in vain to bring the Hungarian national team back from its nadir. One consequence of the exodus of these stars was that Hungary never again achieved its former level of success. There were, admittedly, always great individual players. One can think of Florian Albert or Tibor Nyliasi, although their technical skill became lost in the increasingly physical game of world football. The success of Ferencvaros Budapest and Videoton Szekeszfehervar in the European Cup permitted the hope that there might be a renaissance in Hungarian football. Players such as the conductor Nyliasi, the mustachioed and lanky smooth operator Laszlo Faszekas, and the equally tricky Kiprich allowed the Hungarians to qualify for three World Cups in a row from 1978 to 1986, although in each case the early rounds were the final station. The country was one of the first socialist "people's republics" to open its borders, and after 1989, as was true in Poland, Romania, and Bulgaria as well, it became common for young and unrefined players to leave and play for a few more dollars in Austria or in the lower German leagues. A gifted player such as the midfield conductor Lajos Détari played in Italy, Switzerland, and Greece, but he lacked the ruggedness necessary for a long career. The era of Nyliasi ended at the World Cup in Mexico in 1986 with a 1–6 defeat against the Soviet Union. The athletic and fast Soviets relentlessly demonstrated that the skilled and crafty but slow Hungar-

---

Roten Stern zur Stephanskrone (Frankfurt: Suhrkamp, 1991), 17–30; as well as Tamas Aczel and Tibor Meray, *The Revolt of Mind: A Case History of Intellectual Resistance behind the Iron Curtain* (New York: Praeger, 1959), 242.

ian football was now thoroughly outmoded. During the 1990s, Hungary fell into the third class in national selections for the World Cup.

And Wankdorf?[110] Wankdorf stadium in Bern became a pilgrimage site for countless German football fans. During the late 1950s, it enjoyed its golden age as the modern home of the Bernese Young Boys. Between 1956 and 1960, the Young Boys won the Swiss championship four times. On April 15, 1959, sixty thousand spectators cheered the winning goal by Geni Meier in a home victory in the semifinal of the European Cup against Stade Reims. Although it was not otherwise spoiled for wins, the Swiss national team remained undefeated at Wankdorf from 1965 until 1975, and won a series of the their most beautiful victories here. The team was ready for the World Cup runner-up Sweden in 1961 and the up-and-coming team from the Netherlands in a World Cup qualifier in 1965. In both games, the goalie Elsener played like Toni Turek once had done. Finally, the team defeated Italy in 1993 on a goal by Marc Hottiger, setting the foundation for a qualification almost thirty years after the team's last participation in the World Cup final round. This stadium, packed with spectators, has witnessed many dramatic cup finals. Many Swiss football fans came to realize what a great setting Wankdorf offered. The distinctive twin clock towers with their large dials and minute hands have been imprinted upon tens of thousands of football fans.

The last European final to take place in Wankdorf was in 1989 when the FC Barcelona defeated Sampdoria Genoa 2–1 in the Cup Winners' Cup. The venerable stadium had noticeably begun to fall apart as no one wished to invest the money to modernize it. The stands were threatening to collapse, and it seemed more sensible to begin an entirely new construction rather than attempt a renovation that might save this important "site of memory" (Pierre Nora). While in London, serious thought was given to keeping the twin towers of the landmark Wembley stadium during the construction of the new building, in Bern a decision was made to go for a *tabula rasa*. The German chancellor Gerhard Schröder emphasized the memorial value of this stadium while celebrating the hundred-year anniversary of the German Football Association at Dresden. In a letter sent on June 29, 2001, he wrote:[111]

110. Regarding the history of Wankdorf stadium, see *Stadion Wankdorf: Geschichte und Geschichten*, eds. Charles Beuret and Mario Marti (Bern: Benteli, 2004).

111. Daniel Aeschlimann, "Der Tag, an dem das Wankdorf weltberühmt wurde," *Der Bund*, July 4, 2001.

There are places and buildings that have an exceptional importance in the history of a country, and which keep their symbolic meaning across many generations. We Germans are connected to the historical memories of Hambach castle, St. Paul's church in Frankfurt, the Berlin Wall, and Weimar. For us Germans, Wankdorf stadium in Bern certainly is included among these places, which remain unforgotten.... It may be unavoidable that Wankdorf is to be torn down, because something very different is demanded in a modern and up-to-date athletic complex. However, Wankdorf stadium will always have a place in the memory of the Germans.

There was a debate in German editorial pages whether Wankdorf stadium, as a site of memory, should be moved. Why not? There was a sense of wistfulness and melancholy when the demolition began in the summer of 2001. In an interview, Ottmar Walter said: "There will be some melancholy when I walk out today on the grass at Wankdorf and think that the days of this stadium are now numbered."[112] Football, which became part of popular culture despite all of the efforts of the elite to usurp control over it, stands in marked contrast to those in power who use official sites of memory to legitimize themselves. Football apparently makes no claim to a long-lasting official memory. Despite Sönke Wortmann's 2003 film *The Miracle of Bern*, regarding the mathematically measureable regularities of the fleeting "communicative memory," the "heroes of Bern" will be completely forgotten in a few decades.[113] Books and films can do little to alter this situation. A new state-of-the-art arena oriented toward consumption was built to replace Wankdorf stadium. Are there not enough of these? Is there no place any longer in our society for longer, deeper reflection, and for remembering one's self? Are people no longer prepared to sit on wooden benches knowing that in a setting like Wankdorf, Ferenc Puskás and Fritz Walter once held one of the greatest duels in football history?

112. Rudolf Burger, and Alexander Sury, "'Nach dem 2:2 waren wir obenauf': Interview mit Ottmar Walter," *Der Bund*, July 7, 2001.

113. According to the pertinent ethnological studies, "communicative memory," which is only transmitted orally, disappears in about eighty years. See, for example, J. Vansina, *Oral Tradition as History* (Madison, Wis.: University of Wisconsin Press, 1985); *Lebenserfahrung und Kollektives Gedächtnis: Die Praxis der "Oral History,"* ed. Lutz Niethammer (Frankfurt: Syndikat, 1985); and Assmann, *Das kulturelle Gedächtnis*, 50–52.

7 | *Football and Class Struggle*

As shown above, football was an integral element of working-class culture in Great Britain from the 1880s onward, and on the European continent after the First World War. Many of the best players were from proletarian backgrounds. For the most part, the spectators in the stands were workers, and football was eagerly played from childhood in the back lots of the working-class neighborhoods and factories. Many factory owners supported football in a paternalistic fashion, establishing company teams. Soon, there were company championships.[1] Top teams such as FC Schalke 04 operated as workers' clubs. However, this designation referred only to the players and the fans, and not to the members of the board and the owners of the club.[2]

The enthusiasm of the working class for sports, in general, and for football, in particular, was clear to leading circles of the labor movement. It was therefore a *desideratum* to utilize the sport to further the goals of the socialist class struggle. Football games were a common means of keeping striking workers busy during the interwar period, or of collecting money to support them.[3]

1. See, for example, Andreas Luh, *Betriebssport zwischen Arbeitgeberinteressen und Arbeitnehmerbedürfnissen: Eine historische Analyse vom Kaiserreich bis zur Gegenwart* (Aachen: Meyer & Meyer, 1998); *Chemie und Sport am Rhein: Sport als Bestandteil betrieblicher Sozialpolitik und unternehmerischer Marketingstrategie bei Bayer 1900–1985* (Bochum: N. Brockmeyer, 1992); Sebastian Fasbender, *Zwischen Arbeitersport und Arbeitssport: Werksport an Rhein und Ruhr 1921–1938* (Göttingen: Cuvillier, 1997); and Christian Koller, "Zur Entwicklung des schweizerischen Firmenfussballs 1920–1955," *Stadion* 28 (2002): 249–66.

2. Siegfried Gehrmann, "Schalke 04: Ein "bürgerlicher" Arbeiterverein," in *Illustrierte Geschichte des Arbeitersports*, eds. Hans-Joachim Teichler and Gerhard Hauk (Bonn: Dietz, 1987), 155–60.

3. See, for example, Sue B. Bruley, *The Women and Men of 1926: A Gender and Social History of the General Strike and Miners' Lockout in South Wales* (Cardiff: University of Wales Press, 2010),

In addition, there were efforts to transform sport from a cultural phenomenon of the working class "in itself"—drawing on the Marxist teaching (which borrowed the idea from the philosopher Hegel) describing the politically "immature" workers, who did not yet know their position—into an instrument in the service of the working class "for itself," of the proletariat as a class-conscious political subject. As a consequence, workers' sport movements, with their own clubs, associations, and championships in the various athletic disciplines, emerged in many European states.[4] However, the path toward workers' sports was very different in the various states, and had virtually no connection with the strength of the working-class parties in the respective countries. While around 1930 in Austria there were 44,000 worker athletes per million inhabitants, the number in Germany was 19,000, with 14,000 in Czechoslovakia, and 6,200 in Switzerland. By contrast, the number was just 260 in France, 200 in Hungary, and 100 in England, the motherland of the sport.[5]

In this chapter we will consider the development of football as part of the workers' sport movement in central Europe, Great Britain, and on the international stage until its general loss of importance at the end of the interwar period. Among the questions raised in this context is the extent to which "workers' football" was really working-class football. Did "workers' football" develop out of need by workers to have their own independent organization, or was its development the result of the efforts of elite functionaries who sought to instrumentalize the sport for their own goals? Furthermore, did workers' football really attract workers, or was it simply an ideologically tinged copy of "proper" football, which was

67–70; Christian Koller, *Streikkultur: Performanzen und Diskurse des Arbeitskampfes im schweizerisch-österreichischen Vergleich (1860–1950)* (Münster-Vienna: Lit, 2009), 165 and 357; "Kicken unter Hammer und Sichel—die vergessene Geschichte des Schweizerischen Arbeiterfussball-Verbandes (1930–1936)," in *Überall ist der Ball rund—Die Zweite Halbzeit: Zur Geschichte und Gegenwart des Fussballs in Ost- und Südosteuropa*, eds. Dittmar Dahlmann et al. (Essen: Klartext, 2008), 248.

4. With regard to this topic in general, see Robert F. B. Wheeler, "Organisierter Sport und organisierte Arbeit: Die Arbeitersportbewegung," in *Arbeiterkultur*, ed. Gerhard A. Ritter (Königstein: Verlagsgruppe Athenäum-Hain-Scriptor-Hanstein, 1979), 58–73.

5. Matthias Marschik, *"Wir spielen nicht zum Vergnügen": Arbeiterfussball in der Ersten Republik* (Vienna: Verlag für Gesellschaftskritik, 1994), 119; Markus Giuliani. *"Starke Jugend—freies Volk": Bundesstaatliche Körpererziehung und gesellschaftliche Funktion von Sport in der Schweiz (1918–1947)* (Bern: Lang, 2001), 128.

still able to capture the attention of the working masses? As we will see, there are no sweeping answers to these questions. Rather, there were significant geographical and temporal variations.

Workers' Football in Central Europe

The history of workers' football is closely connected with the development of the labor movement in Germany and Austria. German workers' athletics had its origins in the late nineteenth century.[6] The beginning came with the departure of workers from the Deutsche Turnerschaft (Association of German Gymnastics) (DT) in protest against its nationalist course. Around the turn of the century, workers' gymnastics clubs were founded in rural regions building outward from the center of the labor movement.[7] The Arbeiter-Turnbund (Workers Gymnastics Union; ATB) was founded in Gera in 1893. This gave rise to the Arbeiter Turn- und Sportbund (Workers Gymnastics and Athletics Union; ATSB) in 1919. In 1912, the various groups belonging to the workers' cultural movement joined together in an umbrella organization called the Central Commission for Workers Sports and Bodily Health. Working-class athletes comprised the strongest component in the union. In 1919, the ATSB had 106,000 members, and 652,000 in 1923. By 1930, there were 750,000 male and female workers' athletes.[8] The ATB and then the ATSB considered themselves as members of the socialist labor movement alongside the Social Democratic Party (SPD) and the Free Trade Unions.

The arrival of football brought with it similar conflicts within the workers' sport movement as it did in the "bourgeois" athletic world. Richard Koppisch wrote in 1901 in the *Arbeiter-Turn-Zeitung*: "If the English are held up as [an] example for us, it must be pointed out that the excesses in the sport and its play have spread in the most flagrant possible way there as well. The roughness and brutality, which are the hallmarks of the English national character ... are brought about to a great degree by

---

6. For an overview of this topic, see Heinz Timmermann, *Geschichte und Struktur der Arbeitersportbewegung 1893–1933* (Ahrensburg bei Hamburg: Ingrid Czwalina, 1973).

7. For a micro-study of rural workers' sports, see Klaus Schönberger, *Arbeitersportbewegung in Dorf und Kleinstadt: Zur Arbeiterbewegungskultur im Oberamt Marbach 1900–1933* (Tübingen: Tübinger Vereinigung für Volkskunde, 1995).

8. Gehrmann, *Fussball-Vereine-Politik*, 145.

the inordinate intensity of this type of activity."[9] As late as 1911, the ATB considered football damaging to the health of workers since the lengthy playing time put too high a burden on the heart and lungs.

However, during and immediately after the First World War, the number of working-class football players increased rapidly. In 1914 there were only 77 football teams in the ATB. By 1919 there were already 1,593,[10] with 8,000 by 1930.[11] The twelfth national meeting of the ATSB in Leipzig in 1919 endorsed the request by the working-class football players for an independent structure and leadership for their sport. This was established as a united football committee. At the thirteenth national meeting in Munich in 1921, football was recognized as an independent branch within the ATSB.[12] The membership in the ATSB-football division rose rapidly in the postwar period (see table 7-1).[13] Beginning in 1920, the working-class football players had their own championship.[14] The ATSB organized its own "national championship." This led to an international match in October 1924 against the former wartime enemy France, before the Locarno conference in 1925 led to a policy of easing tensions. The "bourgeois" Football Union (DFB) was not able to organize a similar match until 1931.[15] The political character of this game was clearly emphasized in

Table 7-1. Membership in the ATSB-Football Division

Year	Members	Year	Members
1919	26,053	1926	108,000
1920	48,130	1927	125,000
1921	88,794	1929	129,000
1922	100,893	1931	136,787

9. Cited in Frank Filter, "Fussballsport in der Arbeiter-Turn- und Sportbewegung," *Sozial- und Zeitgeschichte des Sports* 2 (1988): 56.

10. Filter, *Fussballsport*, 57n2.

11. Fischer, *Stürmer*, 71.

12. Gerhard Hauk, "Fussball: Eine 'proletarische Sportart' im Arbeiter-Turn- und Sportbund?," in *Illustrierte Geschichte des Arbeitersports*, 160–69.

13. Filter, *Fussballsport*, 58; and Gehrmann, *Fussball*, 146n2.

14. The victors were T.-u. Spv. Fürth (1920), Leipzig-Stötteritz (1921, 1922, 1923), DSV 1910 Dresden (1924, 1925, 1926, 1927), Adler 08 Berlin (1928), Lorbeer 1906 Hamburg (1929, 1931), and Nürnberg-Ost (1930, 1932).

15. Fischer, *Stürmer*, 74.

the working-class press: "The working-class athletes proudly stride over the barriers that the capitalist states erected in fear, the vanguard of a new age."[16]

However, there were some peculiarities in workers' football. The cult of the stars was taboo. The collective had to be in the forefront. Erwin Seeler, the father the future HSV star Uwe Seeler, scored seven goals for the German select team in their 9–0 victory over Hungary at the Workers Olympics in 1931 in Vienna in front of 60,000 spectators. Because the enthusiastic crowd put him on their shoulders after the game and carried him from the field, he was chastised by an ATSB functionary.[17] The names of the individual players were never given in news accounts. Rather, these discussed "midfielders," "halfbacks," or the "left defenseman" of a particular team. From 1924 onwards, the names of the team members were only made known during international matches or during important city games.[18] The introduction of different classes of competition was also opposed, at first because this was seen as the translation of the class system of the capitalist society onto working-class sports. Finally, however, the view prevailed that it was necessary "to match up the capabilities of the opponents with our own" and to take up the principle of merit to the benefit of the spectators and to be able to compete with the bourgeoisie.[19]

What importance did workers' football have in comparison with the football of the DFB, which saw itself as apolitical? A comparison of the numbers of members shows a relatively constant picture during the course of the 1920s. In 1920, the DFB had 480,000 members.[20] The number of working-class football players was a bit over 48,000, or just 10 percent of the DFB's total. The number of members in the DFB rose to 823,400 by 1925, while the number of ATSB football players climbed to 13 percent of the DFB's total. In 1931, the DFB had 1,025,000 members, and the ATSB Football Group had 136,000 members, which again equaled 13 percent of the DFB's total. The percentage growth of the working-class football

16. *Arbeiterfussball*, October 22, 1924, cited in Filter, *Fussballsport*, 61.

17. Fischer, *Stürmer*, 72.

18. Filter, *Fussballsport*, 69; and Horst Ueberhorst et al., *Arbeitersport- und Arbeiterkulturbewegung im Ruhrgebiet* (Opladen: Westdeutscher Verlag, 1989), 303.

19. Filter, *Fussballsport*, 70.

20. The membership numbers for the DFB are from Heinrich, *Fussballbund*, 62. For the membership of the ATSB see above.

players was 183 percent between 1920 and 1931, compared to 119 percent with the DFB. However, in considering the raw numbers, it is clear that the ATSB never succeeded in making a decisive breakthrough into the DFB's realm. During the 1920s, the DFB was able to greet 557,000 new members into its ranks, while the ATSB gained just 88,000 new football players. These numbers also show that the percentage of workers' football players in the total number of those playing organized football lagged far behind the percentage of voters supporting the left-wing parties. During the national elections in 1920, 41.6 percent voted for these parties in total (21.6 percent for the majority Social Democrats, 18 percent for the independent Social Democrats, and just 2 percent for the Communists). In 1930, the total left-wing vote came to 37.6 percent (24.5 percent Social Democrats, 13.1 percent Communists). If one assumes that the voting behavior of football players was not significantly different than that of the general population, one must conclude that just a quarter to a third of the left-wing voting football players belonged to ATSB clubs, and more than two-thirds played in the DFB. Siegfried Gehrmann's study of the Ruhr region, a stronghold of the labor movement and of football, paints a similar picture. In 1932, 88 percent of all organized football players in Hamborn, 72 percent in Gelsenkirchen, and 82 percent in Essen played in the DFB.[21] Even in the outspokenly "red" districts, whose inhabitants worked largely in the mines and voted overwhelmingly for the Communists in both national elections and on the workers' councils, only between 20 percent and 50 percent of the left-wing voting football players participated in the workers' sport movement.[22]

Siegfried Gehrmann sees four basic reasons underlying this bourgeois dominance.[23] First, the bourgeois clubs had a head start over the ATSB clubs. Until the November revolution of 1918, government officials were able to make use of legal means, drawing on the repressive law of associations to hinder the establishment of workers' athletic clubs. For example, an athletic club could be declared a political club because they sang certain songs and therefore be forbidden to accept youths as members. Before 1918, therefore, many workers joined bourgeois clubs, to which they remained loyal during the Weimer Republic.

21. Gehrmann, *Fussball*, 160.   22. Ibid., 162–78.
23. Gehrmann, *Fussball*, 183–97.

Second, the bourgeois clubs were strongly supported by industrial corporations. The German Institute for Technical Labor Education (DINTA), which was established in Düsseldorf in 1925 with the goal of overcoming the putative hostility of workers in the major companies toward ergonomic methods, expressly encouraged the support of athletics, and particularly football. The ideas expressed by DINTA were adopted by many factories in the Ruhr region. During the late 1920s and the 1930s there was a wave of foundations of athletic clubs that were connected to employment.

Third, Gehrmann suggests that the workers did not see sport as an expansion of their union and political activities but rather as an apolitical outlet. Membership in a workers' athletic club required an ever increasing participation in political action. By contrast, the DFB presented itself as apolitical. And if this claim does not bear closer scrutiny because the DFB maintained close ties to right-wing circles that were hostile to the Republic, there were, nevertheless, no efforts to enlist members to support a particular political party. In addition, the ideology of a *Volksgemeinschaft* (national community), which was supported by leading circles in the DFB, sought to overcome the issues of class and social background, and to reduce the importance of the political parties as much as possible.[24]

The fourth point raised by Gehrmann is the difference in the ways that "bourgeois" and working-class athletics presented themselves in public. The general effort to suppress the importance of the individual athlete took away much of the attractiveness of workers' football. The desire of the public to find someone with whom it could identify could not be met. Top players often were only mentioned by name in the working-class press when they "defected." When Erwin Seeler and one of his club comrades from SC Lorbeer 06 Hamburg switched over to Victoria Hamburg in 1932, the social democratic *Hamburger Echo* criticized them under the headline "Errant Proletarians!" "The proletariat should feel stained that they had to serve as parade horses for the coffers of the bourgeois movement!"[25] But transfers of the best players to the "bourgeois" clubs became increasingly frequent.

During the course of the 1920s, the ATSB also was caught up in the

24. See Heinrich, *Fussballbund*, 53–121.
25. Cited in Fischer, *Stürmer*, 73.

storm of contention between the Social Democrats and the Communists, which also did not help in attracting members. Leading functionaries of the ATSB were heavily criticized by the Communists during the national meeting in 1924 and were accused of having an insufficiently revolutionary attitude.[26] When, in the summer of 1925, several Saxon workers' clubs played against a Soviet team, against the expressed prohibition of such games by the ATSB, they were given suspensions by the association. The next year, the ATSB gave official permission to organize additional "Russian games," but these were to have an apolitical character. In early 1927, a select ATSB squad from Saxony went on a three-week return visit to the Soviet Union, which the Saxon workers' press covered in a very Soviet-friendly manner.[27] When a Soviet team began a series of games against ATSB teams in Leipzig, Hamburg, Bremen, Dresden, Chemnitz, Mannheim, Barmen, and Berlin in the summer of that same year, the Communists launched demonstrations at the matches and charged the leadership of the SPD and the ATSB with being traitors to the working class.[28] From this point on, the ATSB banned any further contacts with the Soviet Union.

In 1928 the Communists sharpened their confrontation with the Social Democrats, whom they called "social fascists." The new strategy was no longer simply to infiltrate the institutions of the workers' sport movement, but rather to split off all of the associations and organizations in which the Communists already enjoyed a strong position. The hope of this so-called "united front from below" was that the mass of workers would leave the Social Democratic associations and transfer over to the new Communist organizations. On the union level, they founded the Revolutionäre Gewerkschaftsopposition (Revolutionary Union Opposition; RGO). On the athletic front, they founded in the Kampfgemeinschaft für Rote Sporteinheit (Action Group for Red Sport Unity; KG) in 1929–30.[29] In 1932 and 1933, the KG held its own national championship

26. David Steinberg, "Die Arbeitersport-Internationalen 1920–1928," in *Arbeiterkultur*, 101.

27. Frank Heidenreich, *Arbeiterkulturbewegung und Sozialdemokratie in Sachsen vor 1933* (Weimar: Böhlau, 1995), 366–70.

28. Jürgen Fischer, "Die Russenspiele: Einheit(sfront) der Arbeitersportler für Demokratie und internationale Solidarität," in *Fussball: Soziologie und Sozialgeschichte einer populären Sportart*, 112.

29. Gehrmann, *Fussball*, 150.

in football, and the winners were DSV 1910 Dresden and FT Jessnitz.[30] The strengthening agitation of the Communists and the threatening rise of the National Socialists led the SPD to give up its formerly distant relationship with workers' sport, and to see in the ATSB an important vanguard organization. One thousand clubs and about 100,000 athletes decided to side with the Communists and thus were lost to the ATSB.[31] The relationship between the personnel of the ATSB and the SPD grew closer during the late 1920s. In 1932, the ATSB and the SPD joined together with the Free Trade Unions and the "National Banner Black-Red-Gold," a paramilitary center-left group dominated by Social Democrats, into an "Iron Front" against National Socialism.[32]

The ATSB was smashed just a few months after the National Socialists took power in January 1933. Following the ban on the workers' sport movement, the property of the ATSB clubs was raided.[33] The DFB watched the destruction of workers' football with delight. As early as March 1933, DFB issued a ruling that requests for membership by former ATSB clubs should receive "basically dismissive treatment" because up to this point, these clubs had only "played the sport in pursuit of political goals or for purposes of class conflict, while the DFB pursued athletics and the nurturing of the youth for the purpose of strengthening the people and the state."[34] Numerous workers' athletes managed to transfer individually to "bourgeois" clubs, where they sometimes formed conspiratorial groups. The National Socialist regime pursued these insurgents mercilessly. Many workers' athletes were sentenced to death in the Third Reich, given long prison sentences, or murdered without a trial.[35]

Austrian workers' sports also had its origins in the nineteenth century.[36] People were doing gymnastics in the working-class educational clubs in Vienna by 1892. This movement soon spread to Bohemia, Wie-

---

30. Filter, *Fussballsport*, 64.
31. Fischer, *Stürmer*, 73.
32. Gehrmann, *Fussball*, 152.

33. Fischer, *Stürmer*, 71; as well as Margit Unser, *Gelebte Geschichte: Alltagserfahrungen von Mannheimer Arbeitersportlern der Weimarer Zeit* (Mannheim: Landesmuseum für Technik und Arbeit, 1994).

34. Cited in Heinrich, *Fussballbund*, 134.

35. See Fischer, *Stürmer*, 76–78.

36. The basic work on Austrian workers' sports is Paul Nittnaus and Michael Zink, *Sport ist unser Leben: 100 Jahre Arbeitersport in Österreich* (Vienna: Mohl Verlag, 1992).

ner Neustadt, Mödling, and Linz.[37] At first, the Social Democratic Party was skeptical of this movement because gymnastics had a strong reputation as a national German phenomenon. Other branches of workers' athletics also organized alongside the gymnasts, including hikers and mountain climbers ("Friends of Nature") as well as cyclists.

The leaders of the Social Democratic Party viewed with suspicion both the establishment of the clubs and the associations, which seemed too apolitical to them, as well as the development of sport as a mass spectacle. Otto Bauer, one of the chief exponents of Austrian social democracy and an important theoretician of so-called Austro-Marxism,[38] complained in 1924 that "the mass of the working-class youth" use "the little bit more freedom and little bit more time" for which the labor movement had struggled in previous years and decades "just to go to see football matches." Bauer saw this as evidence that the class consciousness of the working-class youth was not yet sufficiently developed:

Because the better and more noble sources of entertainment are not available to the masses, either because they do not have enough money or lack sufficient education, they seek their pleasure in the cinema or at football games. It would be foolish to struggle against this. Instead, we wish to learn from this. What is the allure of football ... ? Football matches draw on the joy that youth take in struggle. So, let us seize on the joy that the young people find in struggle. We want to awake in them the joy that comes from a greater, more powerful competition. We want to arouse their interest in that which, in the end, is more interesting than whether Rapid defeats Amateure, that is whether the working classes defeat the capitalist classes for the cup in the match for history.[39]

The changed situation following the fall of the Austro-Hungarian Empire made it possible to establish an umbrella organization for Austrian workers' athletes. The head of state of the new Austrian republic, Karl Seitz, was close to the workers' cyclists, and the chancellor Karl Renner came from the ranks of the Friends of Nature movement. The Association of Workers and Soldiers Athletic Clubs (VAS) was founded in 1919.[40]

37. Marschik, *Arbeiterfussball*, 17.

38. On this point, also see Norbert B. Leser, *Zwischen Reformismus und Bolschewismus: Der Austromarxismus als Theorie und Praxis* (Vienna: Europaverlag, 1968).

39. Otto Bauer, "Die Arbeiterjugend und die Weltlage des Sozialismus," in his *Werkausgabe* (Vienna: Europaverlag, 1976), 2:882.

40. Marschik, "Arbeiterfussball," 20.

The workers' football players took a long time to create a unified body. They refused to give up playing against bourgeois clubs until 1926, thereby keeping the Austrian working-class athletes from joining the Socialist Workers Sports International (SASI) for quite a long time.[41] When the VAS became the Workers Union for Athletics and Physical Culture (ASKÖ) in 1924, the football players could only belong as guests. The workers' football players had a strong position in the Austrian Football Association (ÖFV) and its regional associations without, however, gaining complete control over the association. They formed a "free union" within the ÖFV while the "apolitical" clubs joined together as the Protection Association in 1921.

The de facto division of the association into two separate groups led to numerous conflicts. When Admira Wien, one of the clubs associated with workers' football, was relegated at the end of the 1919–20 season, the "free union" took action. After a great deal of negotiation, it was decided that the champion of the second league could move up, following the established rules, but that Admira could also remain in the first league.[42] The decisive breakup of the ÖFV came in 1926. The workers' footballers formed the Association of Amateur Football Clubs of Austria (VAFÖ), which legally replaced the ÖFV, and then was accepted as a member of the ASKÖ and the Socialist Workers' Sports International. The "apolitical" clubs, which included the clubs in the professional league that had been founded in 1924, established a new association, the Austrian Football Union (ÖFB).[43] VAFÖ established as a goal in its bylaws:

> To represent all of the common interests of workers football clubs that were established on social democratic foundations, and to support their efforts to nurture the working class physically and spiritually through their athletic activities. In addition to the holding of athletic events and the advancement of the athletic enterprise of the proletariat, their duties include educational work among the clubs that were part of the "free union," in order to make these clubs as well as their individual members useful to the social democratic movement.[44]

Aside from Carinthia and Vorarlberg, all of the federal states had their own championships and cup competitions for workers' football up through 1927.

41. Ibid., 12 and 22.
43. Ibid., 53.
42. Ibid., 64.
44. Ibid., 117.

The Austrian workers' sport movement reached its high point in the second half of the 1920s. The first Austrian workers gymnastics and athletics festival took place in 1926.[45] The second Workers Olympics took place in Vienna in 1931, and 100,000 athletes from 21 states participated.[46] Following the establishment of professional football, working-class athletics came to epitomize amateurism and weekend sports. The publication of the workers' football association bore the programmatic title of *Amateur Football* and included in its first edition: "We will spare no effort to make football again what it once was, namely the most beautiful game of the youth.... We no longer wish to look on as our youth sink into the state of submissive and reckless gladiators in the quest for the wretched money that is thrown at them for their athletic achievements."[47] The few remaining connections with bourgeois clubs were banned by the VÄFO, and the clubs were advised to move their headquarters from pubs to working men's clubs. The working-class football players were frequently involved in the propaganda activities of the party. For example, a "mass demonstration of working-class athletes" was organized during the national election campaign in 1927.[48] The number of working-class athletes appears to have plateaued between 1926 and 1931. In comparison with the international situation, however, their percentage of the overall population was quite high at 4.4 percent.

The greatest period of Austrian workers' sports had come to an end by 1931. The catastrophic state of the economy led to talented players moving over to clubs in the ÖFB where the players often received financial support, even on the amateur teams. No fewer than nine players from the wonder team of the 1930s originally came from working-class clubs. Moreover, the mass of workers did not refrain from going to see the more attractive games of the professional championship.[49] During the increasingly tense political situation in Austria in the period between 1930 and 1934, the Austrian workers' sport movement became

45. Ibid., 24.

46. See Reinhard Krammer, "Der ASKÖ und die Wiener Arbeiter-Olympiade 1931," *Illustrierte Geschichte des Arbeitersports*, 207–21.

47. Siegfried, Deutsch, in *Amateurfussball*, January 1927, cited in Marschik, *Arbeiterfussball*, 116.

48. Marschik, *Arbeiterfussball*, 116.

49. Ibid., 130.

much more militant. The "military gymnasts" and the Social Democratic Party had already joined forces by 1925. After the disturbances of 1927, the party, which was now on the defensive, mobilized all of its strength in defense of democracy. The workers' sport movement became increasingly bound together with the paramilitary Republican Protective Union.[50] The football clubs were also supposed to begin military sports. However, this directive was often followed reluctantly. Many workers' athletes were basically pacifist and rejected any form of armed violence. The close connection with the Protective Union had the consequence that the workers' athletes faced increasing pressure from the police and the right-wing Home Guard.

As soon as the democratic republic was transformed into a clerical-fascist corporative state under the direction of Engelbert Dollfuss's Fatherland Front in 1934, the workers' sports organizations were crushed alongside the political parties and the unions. Many former workers' athletes continued to operate illegally. The Fatherland Front was not able to convince the former workers' athletes to cooperate with the newly established Austrian Gymnastics and Athletic Front.[51]

Failure in the Motherland of Football

The workers' sport movement faced remarkable difficulties in Great Britain, which was not only the motherland of the sport, but also the first country to experience the development of a working class because of industrialization during the second half of the eighteenth century.[52] The organized labor movement in Great Britain experienced an enormous upswing during the First World War. The number of union members doubled between 1914 and 1920 to more than eight million. Because of their strengthened bargaining position, the laborers were able to gain improvements in working conditions, particularly a significant shortening of the working day. The interwar period saw a realignment of the two-party system that had reigned in Britain throughout the nineteenth

50. Ibid., 134.
51. Ibid., 27.
52. E. P. Thompson, *The Making of the English Working Class* (London: Victor Gollancz, 1963).

century, as the Labour Party replaced the Liberals as the opponents of the conservative Tories. Labour was able to form a government for the first time in 1924, but the workers' sport movement gained very little from this success. The social and economic historian Stephen G. Jones suggested that because English workers were much stronger than their colleagues on the continent, they were able to leave professional and bourgeois amateur sports to their own devices. As a consequence, workers' sports were not able to dislodge the numerous proletarian athletic activities that were not only played out in the clubs, but also frequently were tied to neighborhoods, worksites, or the pub.[53]

By the late nineteenth century, sport in general and football in particular had become the most important leisure time activities of working classes. However, it was not until the early 1920s that the local unions and party organizations began to interest themselves in the athletic activities of their members. The British Worker's Sports Federation (BWSF) was founded in April 1923 and joined the Socialist Workers Sports International.[54] Before this, politicized workers' clubs had only existed in cycling in the form of the Clarion Cycling Club, which was founded in the 1890s.[55] At first, the BWSF was able to make some headway. The Scottish subdivision soon had numerous sections, including football, cycling, swimming, track, gymnastics, and boxing, with about a thousand members. In London, the BWSF worked closely with several union groups as well as elements of the Labour Party and the Independent Labour Party.[56]

From the beginning, the British authorities viewed workers' sports with unease. As early as 1923, the intelligence section of Scotland Yard warned in a secret report "that the Young Communist League was organising sport sections throughout the country."[57] When the BWSF wanted to invite a Soviet football team in 1930, Ramsay MacDonald's Labour gov-

53. Stephen G. Jones, *Sports, Politics and the Working Class: Organised Labour and Sport in Inter-War Britain* (Manchester: Manchester University Press, 1988), 197.

54. Ibid., 74.

55. David Prynn, "The Clarion Clubs: Ramblings and Holiday Associations in Britain since the 1890s," *Journal of Contemporary History* 11 (1976): 65–77.

56. Jones, *Sports*, 76.

57. The National Archives, CAB 24/159, Report on Revolutionary Organisations in the United Kingdom, February 15, 1923.

ernment refused to issue entry visas, fearing that the tour would be focused more on communist propaganda than on athletics.[58]

As was true in other areas of the labor movement, there were conflicts within workers' sports between Social Democrats and Communists. In 1927 the London branch of the BWSF organized a tour for its select football team through the Soviet Union, with six games in Moscow, Leningrad, Kharkov, and Kiev. There were no fewer than 35,000 spectators at the game in Moscow. Subsequently, the Communists won a majority in the directorate during the national BWSF congress in April 1928. The Social Democratic forces then left the BWSF and founded a new organization in 1930, the National Workers' Sports Association (NWSA).[59] Neither the BWSF nor the NWSA was able to gain mass support among the workers in the following period. The BWSF dissolved in 1935 when Moscow came up with the plan of no longer fighting against the Social Democrats, but rather joining with them and the progressive bourgeois forces to prevent the further spread of fascism (the so-called popular front strategy). In 1931, the BWSF had six thousand members, while the NWSA had a membership of nine thousand in 1935. By contrast, at this time 750,000 football players were organized in the FA and the Cyclists Touring Club had more than 25,720 active members.[60]

Internationalism and Ideological Conflict

On the international level, the organization of the workers' sport movement had its first success with the establishment of the International Socialist Association for Physical Education (ASIEP) in 1913, whose original members included France, Belgium, England, and Austria.[61] Just as was true of the political organizations in the international labor movement, the ASIEP broke apart following the outbreak of the First World War. It

58. The Parliamentary Debates (Official Report), Fifth Series (London, 1930), 238:349; and Peter J. Beck, *Scoring for Britain: International Football and International Politics, 1900–1939* (London: F. Cass, 1999), 140.

59. Jones, *Sports*, 80.

60. Ibid., 197.

61. André Gounot, "Sport réformiste ou sport révolutionnaire: Les débuts des Internationales sportives ouvrières," in *Les origines du sport ouvrier en Europe*, ed. Pierre Arnaud (Paris: Harmattan, 1994), 219–45.

was resuscitated in 1920 with the founding of the International Workers' Association for Sport and Physical Culture, which was also called the Lucerne International (LSI) due to where it was founded. The founding members were Germany, Great Britain, France, Belgium, and Austria. In 1925 the organization was renamed as the Socialist Workers' Sport International (SASI). At first, this organization took a strictly neutral position with regard to the conflicts that broke out between the Social Democratic and Communist parties following the Russian revolution and the division in the international labor movement. A competing organization was established in July 1921 at the third congress of the Communist International in Moscow, called the Red Sport International (RSI), whose goals included the "conquest of the workers' athletic clubs on behalf of proletarian physical culture," "the organization of the working-class athletes, who were still in bourgeois organizations, to participate in workers' sport clubs," "the revolutionizing of the workers' sport clubs to become the physical vanguard of the proletariat," and the "struggle against the Menshevik Lucerne Sport International."[62] In pursuit of these goals, an effort was made to establish communist cells in workers' sports clubs and to gain leadership positions in the associations.

The first Workers' Olympics took place in Frankfurt in July 1925, organized by the LSI. No fewer than 1,100 male and female athletes participated in the games under the slogan "No More War." Both the opening ceremonies and the final football match, which was won by the German select team against Finland, were attended by 40,000 people. A parade through Frankfurt in which 100,000 people as well as 120 bands and 12,000 cyclists participated, attracted a further 300,000 spectators. The high point of the cultural program was the pageant "Struggle for the Earth," in which choruses presented sport as the means of building a new world. The Soviet Union was excluded from the event.

It was only in 1927 that the Workers' Sport International gave up its political neutrality and officially declared itself for social democracy.[63]

62. Gehrmann, *Fussball*, 147. The standard work on the RSI is André Gounot, *Die Rote Sportinternationale 1921–1937: Kommunistische Massenpolitik im europäischen Arbeitersport* (Münster: Lit, 1998).

63. See *Bericht über den IV. Kongress zu Helsingfors, 5.–8. August 1927*, s. l. 1927, 51; and International Institute of Social History, Labour and Socialist International Archives 2959/10 Exekutivsitzung der S. A. I., September 1927: Beziehungen zur Luzerner Sport-Internationale.

The second workers' Olympics took place in "Red Vienna" in 1931 with great participation by the public. Qualitatively and quantitatively, this marked the high point of the history of international workers' sports.[64] The games began with a "children's festival" in which about 30,000 children and youths participated. This marked a step in the creation of an athletic infrastructure. The national delegations, some of which numbered more than a thousand people, marched in the newly constructed Prater stadium during the opening ceremonies. Even fascist-ruled Italy was invited, although it did not send a delegation. Consequently, all of the flags were lowered in remembrance of the oppressed Italian workers. In total, 25,000 male and female athletes from 27 nations participated in the games despite the worldwide economic crisis, competing in 18 sports and 117 competitions. Sixteen teams participated in the football tournament. The football players also had an opportunity to participate in a three-event contest, which included a hundred-meter sprint, long-tossing a ball, and running with the ball followed by a shot on goal. The decisive match of the tournament, which the Austrian select team won against their German comrades, was watched by 65,000 spectators. There were also cultural events alongside the athletic competitions at the Vienna Workers' Olympics. The high point was a massive pageant, in which 3,000 female and male athletes participated, that told the story of the development of the labor movement and collapse of capitalism. At the end of the performance, the head of a capitalist, which had been set up in the middle of the stadium, was cracked in half. The closing ceremonies were marked by a festival of lights in which the opera, parliament, and the city hall on the Ringstrasse were lighted with thousands of incandescent bulbs. The parade, which had no fewer than 100,000 torch-carrying participants, lasted a full five hours, and was conducted under the slogan "For World Disarmament and Universal Peace."

In the following years, the political horizon grew more hazy. In 1933 the Nazis destroyed the workers' sport movement in Germany. Just one year later, the Austrian fascists did the same in their country. Thus, the two most important workers' sports associations no longer existed. The

---

64. Reinhard, "Der ASKÖ und die Wiener Arbeiter-Olympiade 1931," 207–21; and Matthias Marschik, "'... im Stadion dieses Jahrhunderts': Die 2. Arbeiterolympiade in Wien 1931," in *Sport als städtisches Ereignis*, 189–210.

Workers' Football European Championship of 1932–34, which the LSI organized in response to FIFA's 1930 World Cup and which began with the participation of both Germany and Austria, could only be partially completed. On the occasion of the hundred-year anniversary of English trade-unionism, an international sporting event was organized in Dorchester in the summer of 1934. The five nations football tournament that was planned in the context of this event shrank to just three teams because of the last minute cancellations. In addition, the original plan to use some of the games as a precursor for a second Workers' Football European Championship, or at least a West European championship, also failed.

For its part, Red Sport International organized the first international Spartacus Games in Moscow in 1928.[65] RSI invited working-class athletes from foreign countries to this Soviet sporting festival, while the LSI, at the same time, forbade its members to travel to Moscow. Dynamo stadium, which was constructed for the Spartacus Games, was built utilizing the most up-to-date standards. In total, 4,000 male and female athletes participated in the games, of whom about 600 came from abroad. The opening ceremonies in Red Square were attended by 30,000 flag and torch-bearing spectators. The eighty-year-old Frenchman Pierre Degeyter who had composed the melody forty years earlier directed the massed singing of the "Internationale." The sporting contests were dominated overwhelmingly by the Soviet athletes. The football tournament was at the same time an international competition (won by Ukraine against Uruguay in the final game) and the final round of the Soviet championship (won by Moscow).

The RSI organized a second international Spartacus Games to be held in Berlin in 1931. This was intended to compete with the Workers' Olympics that was to take place immediately afterwards in Vienna. Although police officials in Berlin prohibited the games from taking place, many delegations of Red Sport athletes traveled to the German capital. A number of athletic contests were held, including several football matches, under the code name "International Summer Festival of the Workers' Sports Cultural Cartel." Subsequently, an international delegation of Red Sport athletes traveled to Moscow and attended several

---

65. Lothar Skornig, "Vor 50 Jahren: Die Moskauer Spartakiade 1928," *Theorie und Praxis der Körperkultur* 27 (1978): 670–78.

sporting events there.[66] Additional Spartacus Games, including some matches of local football teams, were held in Chicago and Lyon in 1932 as counter-events to the Olympic games being held in Los Angeles.[67] RSI also planned to organize a large worldwide Spartacus Games in Moscow.[68] This was originally planned for August 1933, but then was delayed and finally scrapped.

The transition of the Communist International to the popular front strategy led to efforts to overcome the division of workers' sports into two international associations. The first major anti-fascist workers' sport event, in which both Social Democrats and Communists participated, took place in August 1934 in Paris. This was a multiday workers' sport gathering that included a large demonstration with 10,000 spectators.[69] In the context of this event, there was a tournament that was declared to be the workers' football world championship. This was presented explicitly as being distinct from the "bourgeois" world championship organized by FIFA, which had taken place a few weeks earlier in Italy, and had been used for propaganda purposes by the fascist authorities there. In addition to the national teams from the various RSI associations, a select team from a Norwegian workers' sport association, which was connected to the LSI, also took part in this football tournament. This Norwegian team was defeated in the final game by a select team from Moscow that was denoted as the "football team of the USSR."[70]

In 1936 SASI and RSI issued a joint appeal to the entire sporting world to boycott the summer Olympics in Berlin, which was being converted by the National Socialists into a vehicle for propaganda.[71] How-

66. *Die Rote Fahne*, June 20, 1931; June 21, 1931; June 23, 1931; June 25, 1931; June 26, 1931; June 27, 1931; June 28, 1931; July 1, 1931; July 2, 1931; July 3, 1931; July 4, 1931; July 5, 1931; July 7, 1931; and July 22, 1931.

67. W. S. Baker, "Muscular Marxism and the Chicago Counter-Olympics of 1932," *International Journal of the History of Sport* 9 (1992): 397–410.

68. André Gounot, "Sport und Inszenierung des sozialistischen Aufbaus: Das Projekt der Weltspartakiade in Moskau (1931–1934)," in *Sport zwischen Ost und West*, 75–91.

69. Horst Wetzel, "Paris 1934—Internationaler Sportleraufmarsch gegen imperialistischen Krieg und Faschismus," *Theorie und Praxis der Körperkultur* 18 (1969): 961–65; André Gounot, "Le rassemblement international des sportifs contre le fascisme et la guerre," in *Sports et relations internationales*, 257–72.

70. *Krasnyj sport*, August 12, 1934.

71. See, for example, Richard Mandell, *Hitlers Olympiade: Berlin 1936* (Munich: Heyne, 1980); Friedrich Bohlen, *Die XI. Olympischen Spiele: Berlin 1936: Instrument der innen- und aussenpolitischen*

ever, neither of the two organizations was responsible for the organization of the People's Olympics in Barcelona that was directed against Berlin.[72] The organizers came from the circles of the Catalonian left, who traditionally were drawn to left liberalism or anarcho-syndicalism rather than to Marxism. These games, which were organized in the course of just three months and had an expected participation of 6,000 athletes from 23 states and colonies, were supposed to include 17 sports, among which were football and rugby. In some states, such as France, athletes from "bourgeois" clubs and associations registered to participate. The French Popular Front government, a coalition of socialists and left-wing bourgeois radicals, which also was supported by the Communist Party, provided a government subsidy of 500,000 francs for the event.[73] However, two days before the planned opening of the games, General Franco began his coup with army units stationed in Spanish Morocco against the Popular Front government in Madrid and set off the Spanish civil war. "The starting shot, which was supposed to begin a peaceful testing of strength in the stadium, was taken away by the fascists and transformed into the rattle of machine guns, thunder of cannons, and the explosion of fighter bombers."[74] On the anticipated opening day, Barcelona was the scene of bloody street battles between rebellious army units and civilian security forces as well as quickly mobilized workers' militias. The People's Olympics, which were planned as a festival of peace and brotherhood, could not be held.

Propaganda und Systemsicherung des faschistischen Regimes (Cologne: Pahl-Rugenstein, 1979); Arndt Krüger, *Die Olympischen Spiele 1936 und die Weltmeinung: Ihre aussenpolitische Bedeutung unter besonderer Berücksichtigung der USA* (Berlin: Bartels & Wernitz, 1972); Krüger with William J. Murray, *The Nazi Olympics: Sport, Politics and Appeasement in the 1930s* (Urbana: University of Illinois Press, 2003); S. D. Bachrach, *The Nazi Olympics: Berlin 1936* (Boston: Little, Brown, 2000); Reinhard Rürup (ed.), *1936: Die Olympischen Spiele und der Nationalsozialismus: Eine Dokumentation* (Berlin: Argon-Verlag, 1996); and Guy Walters, *Berlin Games: How Hitler Stole the Olympic Dream* (London: Hodder & Stoughton, 2006).

72. Xavier Pujadas and Carles Santacana, "L'altra Olimpiada '36, Barcelona 1990"; "Le mythe des jeux populaires de Barcelone," in Arnaud, *Les origines du sport ouvrier en Europe*, 267–77; "The People's Olympiad, Barcelona 1936," *International Review for the Sociology of Sport* 27 (1992): 139–49; André Gounot, "Barcelona gegen Berlin: Das Projekt der Volksolympiade 1936," in *Der deutsche Sport auf dem Weg in die Moderne*, ed. Michael Krüger (Münster: Lit, 2009), 119–30.

73. "Volksolympiade gegen Hitlerolympiade: Die Volksolympiade von Barcelona," *Rundschau* 5 (1936): 1176.

74. "Arbeitersportler aus 20 Ländern marschieren in Antwerpen auf!," *Rundschau* 6 (1937): 1128.

In a sign of the popular front strategy, athletes from the Soviet Union took part in the third Workers' Olympics held in Antwerp in 1937. German and Italian emigrant teams wanted to demonstrate that "Hitler is not Germany and Mussolini is not Italy."[75] The Spanish delegation received great sympathy, and the members were greeted excitedly as active participants in the struggle against fascism.

A huge crowd of people filled the large train-station hall. Ten thousand people pressed in around the train station buildings and in the nearby streets.... When the Spaniards descended from the train, a huge celebration broke out. Singing the *Internationale* and led by the flag of republican Spain, the delegation made its way slowly through the masses of people.... The *Internationale* rose up again, and was continued by thousands crying out in chorus with fiery emotion "you shall not pass." The Spanish athletes ... raised their fists at this greeting and repeated, for their part, a solemn pledge of a youth who has demonstrated and daily continues to demonstrate that his word can be trusted, "you shall not pass."[76]

The Soviet athletes had excellent results in most of the sports. They set three world records and one European record, and also convincingly won the football tournament. Indeed, there were some among the Social Democratic workers' athletes who were skeptical whether the Soviet athletes could be considered amateurs, and thought it strange that two new additional Soviet players were flown in for the final football match against Norway. However, following the destruction of workers' sports in Germany and Austria, the Antwerp Workers' Olympics was just a shadow of the competitions from 1925 and 1931.[77]

The Antwerp Workers' Olympics was the last event of its kind. The Red Sport International was secretly dissolved in the run-up to the games. The Socialist Workers Sport International collapsed following the beginning of the Second World War. Its successor, which was founded in 1946, the International Labour Sport Federation (CSIT), remained relatively unimportant. Nevertheless, international workers' football games continued to take place under its umbrella until the 1970s. Following the Second World War, there were no noteworthy efforts to reestablish workers'

75. Ibid.

76. "Die Ankunft der spanischen Olympiade-Delegation in Antwerpen," *Rundschau* 6 (1937): 1170.

77. Jan Tolleneer et al., "Antwerpen 1937: Die dritte Arbeiter-Olympiade," in *Illustrierte Geschichte des Arbeitersports*, 223–25.

football associations in either Germany or Austria. Those workers' clubs that were reestablished tended to join associations that previously had been disdained as "bourgeois." On the international level, the Cold War also brought about changes. There was no longer any competition to the "capitalist" Olympics in the form of Social Democratic or Communist counterevents. A Soviet plan for a Workers Olympics immediately after the war came to nothing. Instead, the eastern superpower sought to become involved in "bourgeois" sport, and joined numerous international sport associations. The Olympic games, therefore, were elevated as a stage for global confrontations in which the athletes from east and west were supposed to demonstrate the superiority of their own systems. Only after the turn of the millennium would the International Labour Sport Federation start organizing CSIT World Sports Games that, including football tournaments, have so far taken place in 2008 (Rimini), 2010 (Talinn) and 2013 (Varna), but hardly attracted any media attention.

Conclusion

A comparative examination of the workers' sport movement in general and of workers' football in particular does not provide a uniform picture. In both Germany and Austria, the introduction of workers' sporting clubs before the First World War was the result of a demand "from below" and particularly a desire to be differentiated from the nationalist gymnastics movement. The workers' sport clubs were less a site of politicization than they were a means of stabilizing their own social milieu, particularly in light of the experience of being excluded from organizations devoted to bourgeois social relations.[78] Political parties and unions played no role in this foundational stage. Rather, at first, the leading socialist politicians had no understanding of workers' sports, and sometimes were even opposed to them. This only changed during the interwar period. In particular, pressure from the right as well as from the left led the Social Democratic parties increasingly to think of the workers' sport clubs as party organizations that could be put to political use. This was even more true of the communist sport clubs that frequently were founded for this very purpose.

78. This is also the view of Schönberger, *Arbeitersportbewegung*, 385.

The divergent spread of the workers' sport movement in the various states depended to a great extent on the societal structure and particularly the segmentation of the society into social milieus, by which we mean societal units that are marked by common characteristics such as religion, ideology, political affiliation, economic status, and cultural orientation.[79] Siegfried Gehrmann believes that the rather modest expansion of workers' football among workers who played organized football is an indication that the proletarian-socialist milieu in the Weimar Republic was not as internally cohesive as traditionally has been thought.[80] The four major social milieus in Germany, conservative-Protestant, bourgeois-liberal, Catholic, and proletarian-socialist, developed in the last third of the nineteenth century. Each one had its own political organization and developed its own network of clubs and associations that, to a great extent, determined the world that people experienced.[81] Different factors led to a loosening of this structure in the decade between 1914 and 1924. In addition to the experience of the war, one can include the hyperinflation of 1923 whose winners and losers were not neatly divided according to their membership in one of the social milieus,[82] the breakthrough of "mass culture," and the leveling effect of "Americanization."[83] The development of football as a mass phenomenon is to be understood as an element of this loosening process. In this circumstance, it should not be surprising that football exercised a great fascination among elements of society that were not part of the working-class milieu. The expansion of workers' football until its violent suppression in 1933 nevertheless shows that the traditional bonds of the social milieu still played at least some role.[84]

79. Following M. Rainer Lepsius, "Parteiensystem und Sozialstruktur: Zum Problem der Demokratisierung der deutschen Gesellschaft," in *Die deutschen Parteien vor 1918*, ed. Gerhard Ritter (Cologne: Kiepenheuer und Witsch, 1973), 68. Also see Klaus Tenfelde, "Historische Milieus—Erblichkeit und Konkurrenz," in *Nation und Gesellschaft in Deutschland: Historische Essays*, eds. Manfred Hettling and Paul Nolte (Munich: Beck, 1996), 247–68.

80. Gehrmann, *Fussball*, 195–97.

81. Detlev J. K. Peukert, *Die Weimarer Republik: Krisenjahre der Klassischen Moderne* (Frankfurt: Suhrkamp, 1987), 149.

82. These factors are emphasized, for example, by Martin H. Geyer, *Verkehrte Welt: Revolution, Inflation und Moderne, München 1914–1924* (Göttingen: Vandenhoeck & Ruprecht, 1998). Also see Gerald D. Feldman, "Die Inflation und die politische Kultur der Weimarer Republik," in *Nation und Gesellschaft in Deutschland: Historische Essays*, 269–81.

83. On this point, see Maase, *Vergnügen*, 79–114.

84. For the relationship between social milieus and political culture, see Dietmar Schirmer,

The situation was somewhat different in Great Britain. Here, football was already a mass phenomenon before the labor movement established itself as a political force independent from bourgeois reformism. The Labour Party did not emerge as an independent political party until 1900. Up until the First World War, workers followed the social reform wing of the Liberals. The decisive dividing line was between the "old status," the aristocracy, and the "new money" of the aspiring bourgeoisie to which the working classes were sometimes connected politically, that is the so-called Lib-Lab strategy. These two social groups also cooperated in the context of the establishment of a modern mass culture, where the British Isles were forerunners in Europe.[85] It is in this context that the introduction of professional football and the spread of football into working-class culture are to be seen. Thus, the starting conditions were very different than they were on the continent. The socialist workers' sport clubs (and soon the communist ones as well) did not develop from an initiative from below, but rather were the result of a retrospective effort to organize a central element of working-class culture to make it politically useful. This effort was destined from the very beginning to fail.

The fact that the workers' sport movement had its greatest successes in Austria was closely connected to the societal and political conditions there. Austria, much more so than Germany, was marked in the interwar period by a confrontation between hostile social milieus.[86] From the very beginning of the first republic, which was the undesired by-product of the disintegration of the Austro-Hungarian Empire, the socialist "reds" and the Catholic-conservative "blacks" viewed each other with suspicion. The remaining German nationalists, who represented the remnants of the once powerful Austrian liberalism, held the balance of power. This basic pattern proved to be quite enduring. It retained its significance under the dictatorship of the "blacks" in the period 1934–38, under National Socialism and during the Second World War, and into the second half of the twentieth century. Football could not get around this

"Politisch-kulturelle Deutungsmuster: Vorstellungen von der Welt der Politik in der Weimarer Republik," in *Politische Identität und nationale Gedenktage: Zur politischen Kultur in der Weimarer Republik*, eds. Detlev Lehnert and Klaus Megerle (Opladen: Westdeutscher Verlag, 1989), 31–60.

85. Maase, *Vergnügen*, 79–89.

86. Fundamental regarding Austrian workers' culture is Dieter Langewiesche, "Arbeiterkultur in Österreich: Aspekte, Tendenzen und Thesen," in *Arbeiterkultur*, 40–57.

deeply ingrained societal segmentation. Thus, Austria was the only state in which the workers' football players did not form a counter organization to the "official" association. Rather the reverse was the case as the "bourgeois" clubs left the association, which had become socialist, and had to found their own football union. The Viennese cultural scientist Matthias Marschik correctly stressed that even in "Red Vienna" it is possible to see two other lines of development alongside social democratic football. The first of these was the mass culture of professional sports, which was established with elements from among the bohemians, and led by bourgeois forces, but that also attracted the working classes. The second line of development existed below and athwart the dominant working-class culture and was marked by categories such as loyalty to one's club and ties to one's district in which workers did not shy away from contact with "bourgeois" football.[87]

87. Marschik, "Arbeiterfussball," 204.

8 | *Football and Dictatorship*

The headline of the American magazine *Foreign Affairs* in July 1936 was "The Dictators Discover Sports." The focus was on the use of the Olympic summer games in Berlin by the Nazis for propaganda purposes.[1] In fact, throughout the twentieth century, dictators of all stripes attempted to make sports in general and football in particular useful for their own purposes. However, football has always proved to be somewhat problematic in this regard. The relative transparency of the game did not always lead to the results for which one might hope from a propaganda perspective. Its appeal drew masses to the stadiums, but they could not be controlled easily, and games were, in a sense, in competition with the mass political events that were organized from above. The autonomous character of the game also threatened dictatorships, which sought organizationally and ideologically to monopolize the leisure time of the people as the game served to counteract the permanent mobilization of the masses.

This chapter will explore the relationship of the mass cultural phenomenon of football to various types of systems characterized as "totalitarian" or "authoritarian" with a focus on communist (Soviet Union and GDR), fascist (Italy, Germany, and Spain), and military (Brazil and Argentina) dictatorships. Thus, the discussion will turn on the nature of the game in the context of the three poles of modern mass culture, namely culture, politics, and economy, in conditions that are in stark contrast to the ideal type of the liberal-capitalist "west." In sum, did dictators see "king football" as a competitor for the favor of the (physically assembled) "masses," or as an aid in a strategy of providing bread and circuses?[2]

1. J. R. Tunis, "The Dictators Discover Sport," *Foreign Affairs* 14, no. 4 (1936): 606–17.
2. Also see Christian Koller, "Ein König und drei Diktatoren: Profifussball und 'Totalita-

Playing Football under the Hammer and Sickle

Soon after the October revolution in 1917, the new Bolshevik rulers considered how the cultural practices of sports and physical education should be
viewed within the parameters of the "dictatorship of the proletariat" and
how they should be organized. Various institutions competed for control
over sports in the early Soviet Union, namely the communist youth organization Komsomol, the unions, and the military organization Vsevobuč,
while the so-called hygenicists and the proletarian-culturalists rejected
athletic competitions as a bourgeois-capitalist residue.[3] A supreme council
for physical culture was established in 1920, and corresponding councils
on the regional level were established after 1923. A sign of further centralization came in 1930 with the founding of a supreme state athletic governing body, the All-Union Council for Physical Culture, which changed its
name frequently in the following period.

During the mid-1920s, "bourgeois" clubs were either forbidden or
had their names Sovietized. They were then connected with unions, the
army, or the police. In addition to the athletic associations of the secret
service and police (Dynamo, 1923), and the army (CSDKA, 1928), the 1930s
saw the establishment of corresponding institutions for numerous civic
organizations: trade, light industry, services (Spartak, 1935), civil administration (Burevestnik, 1936), arms industry (Zenit, 1936), railroads (Lokomotiv, 1936), water transportation (Vodnik, 1938), as well as technical
and professional schools (Trudovye Rezervy, 1943).[4] These organizations
established the first sports schools for the systematic acquisition of talent
during the 1930s and 1940s.

---

rismus' in der Zwischenkriegszeit," *Stadion* 37 (2011): 259–83; and James Riordan, "Sport under
Communism and Fascism: Reflections on Similarities and Differences," *Stadion* 28 (2002): 267–74.

3. See, for example, James Riordan, *Sport in Soviet Society: Development of Sport and Physical Education in Russia and the USSR* (Cambridge: Cambridge University Press, 1977), 68–123; Her-
mann Gross, *Körpererziehung und Sport in der Sowjetunion: Entscheidende Faktoren ihrer raschen
Entwicklung* (Graz: Institut und Wissenschaftlicher Kreis für Leibeserziehung der Universität
Graz, 1965), 25–37; Peter Sedlak, "Leibesübungen und Sport in der Sowjetunion," in *Geschichte
der Leibesübungen*, ed. Horst Ueberhorst (Berlin: Bartels & Wernitz, 1972), 4:92–99; and Stefan
Plaggenborg, *Revolutionskultur: Menschenbilder und kulturelle Praxis in Sowjetrussland zwischen
Oktoberrevolution und Stalinismus* (Cologne: Böhlau, 1996), 62–95.

4. Robert Edelman, *Spartak Moscow: A History of the People's Team in the Workers' State*
(Ithaca, N.Y.: Cornell University Press, 2009).

Football was an important element in this system. However, it still maintained its autonomous character and developed during the interwar period in a manner that demonstrated astoundingly close parallels to the rise of commercialized mass spectator football in western and central Europe and in Latin America.[5] During the period of the New Economic Policy (NEP) between 1921 and 1929, when elements of the new western mass culture seeped into the workers' and peasants' state under the cloak of the limited approval of private capitalist activities, the game with the round leather became the most appealing spectator sport, particularly in urban centers.[6] It also quickly became commercialized despite the official rejection of professional sports by the Communist Party. Although the competitions remained limited to regional championships, the top teams increasingly met in friendly matches with the goal of earning money from admission charges. Illegal betting on football also flourished underground.[7]

This was all a thorn in the side of the party and the authorities. The effort in 1926 to stop the creeping process of professionalization by requiring all clubs to be connected with factories, unions, the army, or the police had failed. The attacks in the press against professional football that began in this year also failed to stop the process of professionalization.[8] This process was actually encouraged in 1928 when the Moscow soviet issued an ordinance permitting the transfer of players between clubs without any restrictions.[9]

5. With regard to Soviet football under Stalin, see Robert Edelman, "Sowjetischer Fußball, 1917–1941," in *Fußball zwischen den Kriegen: Europa 1918–1939*, 299–326; "The Professionalization of Soviet Sport. The Case of the Soccer Union," *Journal of Sport History* 17 (1990): 44–54; *Spartak Moscow*, 61–194; *Serious Fun*, 45–72 and 81–110; "A Small Way of Saying 'No.' Moscow Working Men, Spartak Soccer, and the Communist Party, 1900–1945," *American Historical Review* 107 (2002): 1441–74; Thomas Heidbrink, "Das Lieblingsspiel der Massen: Fußball in der Sowjetunion vom Ende der 1920er Jahre bis zum Gewinn des Europacups der Nationen 1960," in *Überall ist der Ball rund: Zur Geschichte und Gegenwart des Fußballs in Ost- und Südosteuropa*, 44–50; and Barbara Keys, "Soviet Sport and Transnational Mass Culture in the 1930s," *Journal of Contemporary History* 38 (2003): 413–34.

6. Richard Stites, *Russian Popular Culture* (Cambridge: Cambridge University Press, 1992), 37–52; Anne Gorsuch, *Youth in Revolutionary Russia: Enthusiasts, Bohemians, Delinquents* (Bloomington: Indiana University Press 2000), 116; Frederick Starr, *Red and Hot: The Fate of Jazz in the Soviet Union* (Oxford: Oxford University Press, 1984), 58–60; Alan Ball, *Russia's Last Capitalists: The Nepmen, 1921–1929* (Berkeley: University of California Press, 1997).

7. Edelman, *Spartak Moscow*, 52–61, and "Sowjetischer Fußball," 303.

8. Edelman, *Serious Fun*, 52; *Spartak Moscow*, 66; "Sowjetischer Fußball," 303 and 307.

9. Edelman, *Spartak Moscow*, 67.

Even Stalin's decision to end the NEP and to make a transition to a planned economy at the end of the 1920s did not drastically change the situation. It was not until the 1931 regulation that all players on factory or union teams had to be employees of the factory or members of the union that there was a certain amount of disruption. During the period of the first five-year plan (1928–33), which was focused on the rapid development of the Soviet heavy industry with the concomitant enormous exploitation of the working classes through excessively long work days, football largely disappeared from the media.[10]

A further change occurred under the second five-year plan (1933–37) with the establishment of a national league in 1936.[11] The establishment of a championship for de facto professional teams—officially they were *pokazatel'nye komandy* (demonstration teams)—fit well in several respects with Stalin's policies during the late 1930s.[12] First, the idea of social equality was increasingly replaced in favor of privileging so-called specialists. The players, coaches, and functionaries of the national league became part of the new Soviet elite, which also included writers, scientists, ballet dancers, film stars, and pilots. Top players during the late 1930s earned eight times as much as industrial workers,[13] which marked an enormously privileged position in contrast with the corresponding situation in England.[14] In addition, the second five-year plan loosened the tight reins on the workers a little bit to permit more leisure time. The national league was a mass cultural form of entertainment that proved to be exceptionally popular, particularly among male urban workers. Third, the national league appeared to be an instrument for nation building.

However, it would be an oversimplification to describe the establishment of the national league as an element of a cultural master plan to distract the population during a period of accelerated industrial expansion and political cleansing. Rather, the initiative came from the football circles themselves. Their efforts in this regard achieved a breakthrough when a Moscow select team was narrowly defeated in a friendly match

10. Ibid., 69–72; "Sowjetischer Fußball," 308.

11. Edelman, *Serious Fun*, 59–72; *Spartak Moscow*, 84–93; "Professionalization."

12. Edelman, "Sowjetischer Fußball," 313.

13. Ibid., 315.

14. Matthew Taylor, "Beyond the Maximum Wage: The Earnings of Football Professionals in England, 1900–39," *Soccer and Society* 2 (2001): 101–18.

by the strong professional team Racing Paris on New Year's Day 1936.[15] After their return, Nikolaj Starostin, an official in the top team Spartak Moscow, and his sports colleagues successfully used this partial success to agitate for a reorganization of Soviet football along the lines of the professionalism practiced in France. They were able to secure the support of Aleksandr Kosarev, the head of the communist youth association Komsomol.

The interplay of the various interest groups in the institutionalization of the national league was made clear in the debates regarding its composition. At first, the league was a small competition concentrated largely in Moscow and Leningrad. In 1937, however, a number of leading politicians demanded a massive expansion of the league for the purposes of "nation building" in which all of the Soviet republics would be represented. Football officials countered that the best teams should be selected on the basis of their performance. The end result was an expansion of the league in a manner that did not satisfy the demands of either those advocating for nation building or those emphasizing sportive performance. Instead, the number of Moscow clubs from politically influential institutions was massively increased.[16]

Stalin himself was not particularly interested in football. However, in the first year of the national league, the Komsomol chief Kosarev suggested that a football demonstration match should be held in the context of the annual sports parade in Red Square.[17] Stalin watched the 45-minute match, which was held on a rolled carpet of sod, from Lenin's mausoleum. Kosarev stood behind him so that he could immediately give the signal to end the game in case the highest comrade grew bored despite the seven goals that, as agreed beforehand, were scored. The game was a success, and was repeated in subsequent years.[18]

15. Edelman, *Spartak Moscow*, 79–84; *Serious Fun*, 51; Victor Peppard and James Riordan, *Playing Politics: Soviet Sport Diplomacy to 1992*. Greenwich-London: JAI Press, 1992, 41; Heidbrink, "Das Lieblingsspiel der Massen," 48; Christian Koller, "Fussball und internationale Beziehungen 1918 bis 1950—Grossbritannien, Deutschland und die Sowjetunion im Vergleich," in *Sport zwischen Ost und West: Beiträge zur Sportgeschichte Osteuropas im 19. und 20. Jahrhundert*, 70.

16. Edelman, "Sowjetischer Fußball," 321.

17. On this point, see Malte Rolf, "Die schönen Körper des Kommunismus: Sportparaden in der Sowjetunion der dreißiger Jahre," in *Sport zwischen Ost und West: Beiträge zur Sportgeschichte Osteuropas im 19. und 20. Jahrhundert*, 310–25.

18. Edelman, *Spartak Moscow*, 101.

The institutionalization of Soviet professional football was thus the result of a confluence of interests between football circles, who initiated the venture, the broad cross-section of the male urban working class, and politically influential actors. The latter included Komsomol chief Kosarev, who sponsored the athletic association Spartak and the secret service chief Lavrenty Beria who was the *ex officio* head of the athletic association Dynamo and is supposed to have unceremoniously caused the dissolution in 1952 of the football section of CDSA Moscow, which was Dynamo Moscow's rival.[19]

The state and party leadership remained ambivalent, which was manifest in the repeated attacks on professionalism in the press as well as the arrest during the late 1930s and early 1940s of various top football players and officials. However, it was not the formal charges that were levied against them—these complaints ranged from the importation of "bourgeois" sport practices to "Trotskyite-fascist" plots against the life of Stalin—but rather their enormous popularity in a period of constant political cleansing that led to their doom.[20]

In addition to these developments, which were contingent upon internal factors, football also played a role in the foreign policy of the early Soviet state.[21] During an initial period lasting from 1917 to 1920, the primary foreign policy goal of the Bolshevik government was to secure the existence of the Soviet state. During this period, the government established its first foreign diplomatic relationships. The Communist International (Comintern) was founded in March 1919 to serve as an instrument for the hoped-for world revolution. The Soviet state cut itself off from the rest of the world with regard to the politics of sports. A second phase, which lasted from 1921 until 1933–34, was marked by the revival of diplomatic relations with the western great powers, and above

19. Ibid., 191.

20. Ibid., 110–13 and 125–35; Jim Riordan, "The strange story of Nikolai Starostin, football and Laverentii Beria," *Europe-Asia Studies* 46 (1994): 681–90.

21. Also see Peppard and Riordan, *Playing Politics*; Riordan, *Politique étrangère*; André Gounot, "Entre exigences révolutionnaires et nécessités diplomatiques. Les rapports du sport soviétique avec le sport ouvrier et le sport bourgeois en Europe 1920–1937," in *Sports et relations internationales. Actes du colloque de Metz-Verdun*, 241–76; "Vom „Rotsport" zur FIFA: Der sowjetische Fussball und seine internationalen Kontakte 1922–1946," in *Überall ist der Ball rund: Zur Geschichte und Gegenwart des Fussballs in Ost- und Südosteuropa—Die Zweite Halbzeit*, 269–85; and Koller, "Fussball und internationale Beziehungen," 65–73.

all by cooperation with Germany following the signing of the treaty of Rapallo in 1922. During this period, the world revolutionary perspective retreated from the forefront, giving way to the slogan "socialism in one country" during the 1920s. Correspondingly, the rejection of "bourgeois" sports was, at first, continued, and efforts were made to establish a revolutionary sports movement. To this end, Red Sport International (RSI), noted above, was brought to life in 1921. Until 1928, it followed a policy of infiltrating workers' sports associations and clubs in capitalist countries. Then, concomitant with the slogans "united front from below" and "social fascism," there was a transition to attempting to create divisions within these associations and clubs. In this context, RSI followed the tactics of the Comintern, which had set out a corresponding strategy in its fourth congress in 1928.

During the period when infiltration efforts were being undertaken, the Soviet Union sought to intensify contacts with European workers' sports organizations. There had already been a game between the Moscow sport club Zamoskvoretskij and a select team from the Finnish workers' sport association in 1922. Between 1923 and 1927, Soviet select squads played games against German, Swedish, Polish, Norwegian, Estonian, and English football teams. However, they were not able to participate in matches in Spain and Czechoslovakia in 1926 and 1927 because visas were denied. The same thing happened in Great Britain in 1930 and Bulgaria in 1932. In 1934 a game that was supposed to be played in Switzerland had to be moved to Saint-Louis in France.[22]

There was virtually no contact with "bourgeois" football teams during this phase of Soviet foreign policy. At the beginning of 1923, RSI banned any connections with bourgeois sports organizations. In 1926, however, new regulations were issued that permitted contacts with bourgeois organizations for propaganda purposes in those states that did not

22. See Heinz Machatscheck, *Sport—geboren im Feuer der Revolution: Körperkultur und Sport in der UdSSR* (East Berlin, 1966), 20–23; A.[leksej] O.[sipovič] Romanov, *Meždunarodnoe sportivnoe dviženie* (Moscow, 1973), 192; Lothar Skornig, "Chronik der deutsch-sowjetischen Sportbeziehungen bis 1937," *Theorie und Praxis der Körperkultur* 16 (1967): 888–90; Riordan, *Politique étrangère*, 138; *Sport in Soviet Society*, 352; Peppard and Riordan, *Playing Politics*, 29–41; Beck, *Scoring for Britain*, 140; Ghanbarian-Baleva, "Ein 'englischer Sport,'" 168; Heidbrink, "Lieblingsspiel," 47; Edelman, *Serious Fun*, 49; Christian Koller, "Proletarische Verbrüderung auf exterritorialem Gebiet: Schweiz—Sowjetunion 2:5 (22.8.1934)," *Sternstunden des Schweizer Fussballs*, ed. Christian Koller (Münster-Vienna: Lit, 2008), 51–61.

have a workers' sports movement. In the Orient, where the bourgeoisie allegedly still played a revolutionary role, these connections were to serve the cause of anti-imperialism. In those states that did have workers' sports movements, contacts were to be maintained exclusively with these movements. However, exceptions were made for Soviet teams because their victories against the capitalists could help to raise the prestige of the Soviet Union.[23]

In practice, however, there were meetings with "bourgeois" football teams from neighboring states. The most common of these were matches against teams from Turkey, which had belonged to FIFA since 1923. The Soviet Union had diplomatic contacts with this country from an early date. The Soviets had already made a treaty with the Kemalists regarding the frontier in 1921. The signing of a nonaggression pact followed in 1925.[24] Thus, there was a political background to the fact that the two states each hosted an international match against the other in 1924 and 1925. A phase of intensive football contacts began in in the early 1930s. Between 1931 and 1935, select teams from the two countries played each other thirteen times. The political importance of these games is made clear by the fact that the Turkish prime minister was present in the stadium during a match in 1932.[25] In fact, 1936 saw the beginning of Turkish efforts to negotiate a Balkan security pact with the Soviet Union.[26] In addition, there were 41 games between Soviet and Turkish clubs between 1924 and 1936.

Following the consolidation of the shah's regime in Persia there were also football contacts with this country, which had signed a neutrality agreement with Soviet Russia in 1921. In 1926 there were four games between the Persian national team and select teams from Baku and Azerbaijan. In 1927 and 1928, the Turkmen team Ashgabat played three games in Meshed, and in 1929 there were three additional meetings between

23. Gounot, *Sportinternationale*, 64 and 105; "Exigences," 253 and 255.

24. Stephen Joseph Stillwell, *Anglo-Turkish Relations in the Interwar Era* (Lewiston, N.Y.: Edwin Mellen Press, 2003), 44 and 114; William Hale, *Turkish Foreign Policy 1774–2000* (Lewiston, N.Y.: Edwin Mellen Press, 2000), 49–51.

25. *Der Kämpfer*, August 10, 1934; Romanov, *Meždunarodnoe sportivnoe dviženie*, 192; Beck, *Scoring for Britain*, 231; Gounot, *Sportinternationale*, 102; Heidbrink, "Lieblingsspiel," 48; and Riordan, *Politique étrangère*, 139.

26. Hale, *Turkish Foreign Policy*, 65.

teams from Baku and Tehran.[27] In fact, an eastern Spartacus Games was planned for the summer of 1926 in Baku, with participation expected from Turkey, Afghanistan, Persia, Palestine, Morocco, and China. However, the project failed for financial reasons.[28] By contrast, despite the treaty of Rapallo (1922), there were no games against "bourgeois" teams from Germany during the entire 1920s and 1930s since this conflicted with the efforts of the communists to take control over the German workers' sport movement.

Following the seizure of power by the National Socialists in Germany, the Soviet Union engaged in a policy of forging closer relations with the western democracies up through 1939. The declared goal was a system of collective security. The Soviet Union had already signed a nonaggression and neutrality treaty with France on November 29, 1932. Renewed diplomatic relations with the United States followed in November 1933, along with entry into the League of Nations in 1934. Treaties of mutual assistance were signed with Czechoslovakia and France in May 1935. In early 1934, the Comintern revised the social-fascism theory that designated Social Democrats as the main enemy of communism. In the summer of 1935, the sixth congress of the Comintern decided on a transition to the popular front strategy.[29]

Soviet international sports policies changed correspondingly, which was made manifest by the Soviet participation in the Parisian athletes' demonstration in 1934 and Workers' Olympics of 1937, noted above. At the same time there were increased efforts to work together with "bourgeois" sport. By 1934 Soviet teams had played against high-ranking "bourgeois" teams in France, Norway, and Sweden. These contacts were intensified in 1935.[30] The highpoint was the game, noted above, between the top French team Racing Paris and a Moscow select team in front of 60,000 spectators on New Year's Day 1936 in Paris.[31] In May 1934 Czechoslovakia gave diplomatic recognition to the Soviet Union. Shortly thereafter, a Soviet team visited Czechoslovakia at the initiative of the

27. Riordan, *Politique étrangère*, 140; Peppard and Riordan, *Playing Politics*, 101.

28. Gounot, "Exigences," 253.

29. Pierre Broué, *Histoire de l'Internationale Communiste 1919–1943* (Paris: Fayard, 1997), 649–73.

30. Gounot, "Exigences," 270; Peppard and Riordan, *Playing Politics*, 41.

31. Edelman, *Serious Fun*, 51.

Czech Communist Party and played against both Red Sport teams and teams that were members of the national association, which was itself a member of FIFA. Following the negotiation of the Soviet-Czech mutual aid pact in May 1935, a select team from Prague traveled to the Soviet Union.[32]

In 1935 the Soviet Union also established contacts with various international sports associations, including FIFA. However, the Soviet Union did not enter the world football association because, as an internal document stated, FIFA was led by "anti-Soviet fascists." The only objective was to gain permission to play matches against teams from the leading football nations.[33] When FIFA's hopes of finally bringing the Soviet Union into its ranks failed, the organization began to tighten the screws. In the context of the FIFA congress in Berlin in 1936, Turkey was informed that no further exceptions would be granted in the future for games against Soviet teams.[34] The world football association also took this action in other similar cases.

The conclusion of the German-Soviet nonaggression pact on August 21, 1939, which was given further precision on September 28 with a frontier and friendship agreement "that would provide a secure foundation for the continued development of friendly relations," brought Soviet foreign policy into a new phase.[35] This also had consequences for athletic matters. Parallel with the adjustment of propaganda in an antiwestern direction, with the elimination of anti-fascist tendencies and the valorization of Germany in Soviet cultural life, there was also a sudden discontinuation of contacts with western workers' sport organizations and with "bourgeois" sport in the western democracies.[36]

The German attack on the Soviet Union in the summer of 1941

32. Eisenberg, *FIFA*, 275; Riordan, *Politique étrangère*, 134 and 140; Peppard and Riordan, *Playing Politics*, 43; and Heidbrink, "Lieblingsspiel," 48.

33. Gounot, "Exigences," 272; Keys, "Soviet Sport," 424–27.

34. Beck, *Scoring for Britain*, 231.

35. *Akten zur Deutschen Auswärtigen Politik 1918–1945*, Serie D, vol. 8.1 (Frankfurt: Keppler-Verlag, 1961), 128.

36. Wolfgang Leonhard, *Der Schock des Hitler-Stalin-Paktes: Erinnerungen aus der Sowjetunion, Westeuropa und USA* (Freiburg: Herder, 1986), 69–74; Gustav Hilger, *Wir und der Kreml. Deutsch-sowjetische Beziehungen 1918–1941. Erinnerungen eines deutschen Diplomaten* (Bonn: Athenäum, 1964), 292; Bianka Pietrow, *Stalinismus-Sicherheit-Offensive: Das "Dritte Reich" in der Konzeption der sowjetischen Aussenpolitik 1933–1941* (Melsungen: Schwartz, 1983), 162–68.

brought an end to international sports contacts. Football was used solely to maintain morale. For example, during the German-Finnish blockade of Leningrad from September 1941 until January 1944, during which 1.2 million civilians starved and which is sometimes described in the most recent scholarship as a genocide,[37] there were games in the city that were attended by up to 8,000 spectators.[38] In addition, games were quickly organized in various cities after German sieges were lifted. This was the case, for example, at Stalingrad on May 2, 1943.[39] There were even games on Red Square in 1942 and 1943.[40]

The "great alliance" with the western powers in this phase of Soviet foreign policy also had consequences at the level of sport politics. In 1945, there were games between Soviet and western military teams in Germany. In the autumn of this same year, Dynamo Moscow went on a tour through Sweden, Norway, and Great Britain.[41] At the same time, the Soviet Union intensified football connections with those states that were in its sphere of influence. As early as 1944, Dynamo Tiflis played in Persia. In 1945 and 1946, Dynamo Moscow and Dynamo Tiflis played against Romanian, Yugoslavian, and Bulgarian teams.[42]

In 1946 the Soviet Union finally joined FIFA. Five years later, it became a member of the International Olympic Committee (IOC). The beginning of the Cold War dramatically changed the character of the sport contacts with the West, contacts which had become possible because of Soviet membership in these organizations. Soon, there was no longer a question of using sports to encourage friendly contacts. Rather, these competitions served to demonstrate the superiority of the two opposing systems. The Soviets were not able to accomplish this in football at the 1952 Summer Olympics.[43] Four years later, however, a gold medal

37. See Jörg Ganzenmüller, *Das belagerte Leningrad 1941 bis 1944: Die Stadt in den Strategien von Angreifern und Verteidigern* (Paderborn: Schöningh, 2007).

38. Alexander Chertov, "Fussball während der Blockade: Leningrad 1941–1944," in *Überall ist der Ball rund: Zur Geschichte und Gegenwart des Fussballs in Ost- und Südosteuropais—Die Zweite Halbzeit,* 45–64.

39. Peppard and Riordan, *Playing Politics,* 51; and Edelman, *Serious Fun,* 82.

40. Riordan, "Strange Story," 682.

41. Downing, *Passovotchka*; P. Sobolev, *Sport in der UdSSR* (Moscow: Foreign Languages Publishing House, 1958), 63; Riordan, "Sowjetischer Fussball," 247; *Sport in Soviet Society,* 366; with Peppard, *Playing Politics,* 53–58; Edelman, *Serious Fun,* 87–91; Heidbrink, "Lieblingsspiel," 50.

42. Edelman, *Serious Fun,* 51.

43. Concerning the political character of these games, see Nicholas C. Niggli, "Diplomatie

served as an impressive demonstration of the strength of Soviet football.[44] In 1960 the Soviet Union also became the first European football champion. In the following period, however, the Soviet Union did not have any success in the World Cup or in the European Championships, although the team was often seen as a dark horse favorite. It was only in the Olympic football tournament, where the Soviet "state amateurs," that is professional players with official amateur status, had an advantage over the western amateurs, that the Soviet Union regularly pushed into the ranks of the medalists.

During the Cold War, foreign sports and football relations continued to follow political cycles. Immediately following Stalin's death, athletic and cultural contacts with the west began to intensify as a sign of the ongoing thaw in relations. For example, in 1954 alone, forty Soviet delegations traveled to Great Britain, and nineteen British delegations traveled to the Soviet Union. In addition to scientists, artists, and union and youth organization officials, these delegations also included athletes and athletic officials.[45] For the first time since 1945, a Soviet football team, Spartak Moscow, made a tour in England.[46] Return trips were made by Arsenal and Wolverhampton to Moscow in 1954 and 1955, respectively.[47]

By contrast, in periods of political tension, there were repeated sports boycotts. Following the Soviet intervention in Czechoslovakia in 1968, Celtic Glasgow demanded that UEFA exclude Eastern Bloc states from participating in the European club competitions and threatened its own boycott of these competitions. The Eastern Bloc nations withdrew of their own accord.[48] Five years later, the Soviet Union refused to send its national team to a qualification game in Chile in a stadium that

---

sportive et relations internationales: Helsinki 1952, les 'Jeux Olympiques de la Guerre froide'?," *Relations Internationales* 112 (2002): 467–85.

44. Heidbrink, "Lieblingsspiel," 52–54.

45. *Times* (London), November 23, 1954.

46. *Times*, November 4, 1954, and November 19, 1954; *Manchester Guardian*, November 12, 1954; as well as Edelman, *Spartak Moscow*, 217.

47. The National Archives FO 371/111792, "Exchanges between the Soviet Union and the UK in the field of sport: Visit to Moscow by Arsenal Football Club"; as well as *Observer*, May 23, 1954, and October 10, 1954; *Times*, June 13, 1955; and *Manchester Guardian*, August 2, 1955; August 8, 1955; and February 15, 1956.

48. *Guardian*, August 24, 1968; August 27, 1968; September 5, 1968; September 17, 1968; and *Times*, September 17, 1968.

shortly before had been abused to incarcerate political prisoners in the aftermath of Augusto Pinochet's military coup. As a consequence, the Soviet Union lost its chance to participate in the 1974 World Cup.[49] In 1980 numerous states boycotted the Olympic summer games in Moscow in protest against the Soviet intervention in the civil war in Afghanistan. In a counter move, the Soviet Union and most of the Eastern Bloc states stayed away from the games in Los Angeles in 1984.[50]

The structure of Soviet athletic institutions during the Cold War did not change very much from the interwar period. The "volunteer sports associations" (*dobrovol'nye sportivnye obščestva*, DSO) in the civilian arena experienced considerable growth following the Second World War and had about 25 million members during the 1970s; notably, 29 of the 36 DSOs were tied to unions. Their basic units (which numbered around 114,000 at the beginning of the 1970s) comprised sports collectives in factories, administrative bodies, farm collectives, and educational institutions. Six of the DSOs were active across the Soviet Union. These were Spartak, which was reorganized in 1960 and counted about 6.2 million members in the 1970s, Trudovye Rezervy (2.7 million members), Burevestnik (which was a collegiate sports association beginning in 1957 that had 1.5 million members in the 1970s), Lokomotiv (1.3 million members), Vodnik (200,000 members), and Zenit. These sports associations were heavily involved in the organization of competitions (Spartacus Games) at a regional, republic, and union-wide basis. These organizations also participated in the system of sports schools, which was massively increased after the Second World War. Following the entry of the Soviet Union into the Olympic movement, this sport school system developed an elite branch in 1951 that was called the "schools for the Olympic reserve" (*specializirovannaja detsko-junošeskaja sportivnaja škola olimpijskogo rezerva*). At the beginning of the 1970s, there were more than 3,800 sports schools with 1.3 million students and 50,000 instructors.

Football continued to develop along the path of a hidden professionalism. At the same time, mass media attention had a similar effect on

49. Bernhard Hachleitner, "Das Stadion als Gefangnis," in *Das Stadion: Geschichte, Architektur, Politik, Ökonomie*, eds. Matthias Marschik et al. (Vienna: Turia & Kant, 2005), 267–70.

50. L. H. Derick, *The Political Olympics: Moscow, Afghanistan, and the 1980 U.S. Boycott* (New York: Praeger Frederick, 1990); Thomas Renkl, "Der Boykott der Olympischen Spiele 1980 und die öffentliche Meinung," PhD diss., FU Berlin, 1983.

fan culture in the Soviet Union as it did in the West. When the Ukrainian club Dynamo Kiev broke through the traditional phalanx of Moscow clubs in the 1960s and went on to win numerous Soviet championships and even twice won the European Cup Winners' Cup in 1975 and 1986, there was great joy in Ukraine. However, thanks to television broadcasts, the club developed fans throughout the entire union, and particularly in the non-Russian periphery.[51] The development of identities in which the autonomous world of football mixed with political, social, and cultural factors were just as complex in the fan culture that existed under the constraints of Soviet real socialism as they were in the west.

Beginning in the late 1940s, the states of the developing Eastern Bloc adopted many elements of the Soviet sport system. Just as had been true in the Soviet Union of the 1920s, "bourgeois" sport clubs were dissolved or had their names Sovietized, with the clubs subsequently placed under the authority of production centers or administrative units. Central sports organizations also developed, such as the army (CSKA, Vorwärts), and the internal security agencies (Dynamo). A distinctive element in the institutional development of the sport systems in the Eastern Bloc states was the development of both sports schools and mass participation in sports with a large number of corresponding competitions, and the systematic cultivation of talented players from the youngest possible age.

The German Democratic Republic, which struggled for international recognition, undertook the most intensive efforts of any of the Eastern Bloc states to promote sports. It soon became known as a "sport wonderland," taking third place in the Olympic medal count behind the two superpowers. The rigidity and totality of the sporting system in the GDR was exceptional.[52] The Soviet occupation authorities dissolved all sports clubs in their zone by 1945. The following years saw the reestablishment of athletic institutions under communist direction. In 1948, the Deutsche Sportausschuss (German Sports Committee, DS) was founded

---

51. Manfred Zeller, "Our Own Internationale, 1966: Dynamo Kiev Fans between Local Identity and Transnational Imagination," *Kritika—Explorations in Russian and Eurasian History* 12 (2011): 53–82.

52. On the GDR sports system see, for example, Grit Hartmann, *Goldkinder: Die DDR im Spiegel ihres Spitzensports. Leipzig: Forum-Verlag, 1998*; Andreas Ritter, *Wandlungen in der Steuerung des DDR-Hochleistungssports in den 1960er und 1970er Jahren* (Potsdam: Universitäts-Verlag, 2003); and *Schlüsseldokumente zum DDR-Sport*, ed. Giselher Spitzer et al. (Aachen: Meyer & Meyer Sport, 1998).

in the Soviet zone of occupation at the initiative of the Freier Deutscher Gewerkschaftsbund (Free German Federation of Trade Unions, FDGB) and the Freie Deutsche Jugend (Free German Youth, FDJ). A further centralization took place in 1957 with the establishment of the Deutscher Turn- und Sport-Bund (German Gymnastics and Sports Union, DTSB).

The DS organized sports in the GDR under the motto "reorganization on the basis of production." With the cooperation of the FDGB, Betriebssportgemeinschaften (corporation sport collectives, BSG) were founded in place of the former sports clubs. As a rule, these new sports organizations demanded a high degree of discipline and were financed from the union funds of the nationalized industries. In 1950, the DS decided to establish central sports associations on the basis of the trade union structure. The names of the individual BSGs were to reflect their superior sports association, thus "activist" for mining, "construction" for the construction industry, "tractor" for agriculture, or "turbine" for the power industry. Beginning in 1954, the sports associations chose the sports clubs in their branch of the economy that would receive the greatest amount of support and have to focus on competitive sports. The sports associations, Vorwärts of the National People's Army (NVA), and Dynamo of the internal security organizations (police and the Ministry for State Security), were outside of the BSG system.

The mass sport elements of the sport system in the GDR encompassed educational institutions alongside the major enterprises. The talent selection system encompassed almost all schools as well as the kindergartens in some cases. The numerous competitions at the school, district, regional, and national levels served to identify talented athletes. Children and youth who were identified for sports at the highest level were sent to BSGs that were focused on competitive sports, to training centers, or, from 1952 onwards, to child and youth-sport schools, where they often came into contact with doping at an early age.

During the late 1940s, "bourgeois" football clubs also were replaced by BSGs. There was political intervention from the very beginning. Many ambitious district officials or combine directors dreamed of endowing their own city with a top league team, and they acted very much in the same manner as club presidents in the capitalist West who were avid for glory. Politically orchestrated transfers of entire teams were not infre-

quent. In 1953, the players for ASK Vorwärts Leipzig, a team of the bar-
racked People's Police, received the order to move to Berlin. Just like the
men in uniform, the players also had to follow orders without a murmur.
For example, in 1954, the top Saxon sport club Empor Lauter was forcibly
removed to Rostock. As was true in the Soviet Union, the de facto professional top league was far removed from socialist ideals. At the same time,
it was subject to supervision and manipulation by the Stasi (secret police), which sought to benefit its own team BFC Dynamo Berlin. In fact,
Dynamo won ten GDR championships in a row from 1979 to 1988.[53]

Although football was exceptionally popular in the GDR, the sport
did not produce international success according to plan in the same
manner as other sports did. This was particularly painful for sport officials, given the strength of the German Federal Republic. According to
an article that appeared in 1983 in the paper of the Leipzig branch of the
Socialist Unity Party (SED), "as the most popular mass sport" football
should "play an appropriate role" in cementing "the position of the GDR
among the leading nations of the earth and its superiority, along with
the USSR, over the important imperialistic countries."[54]

However, the increasing demands placed on the youth beginning
in the late 1960s led to some success in the following decades. In 1973
Dynamo Dresden reached the semifinal of the European Cup Winners'
Cup. In the following year, 1. FC Magdeburg won the UEFA Cup Winners' Cup. In 1972 the GDR team won the bronze medal at the Olympic
games, and the gold medal four years later. In 1974 the GDR qualified for
a World Cup final round for the first time.

The World Cup in the Federal Republic led to the only inter-German
match in football history and to the greatest triumph of GDR football,
which took place on June 22, 1974.[55] Just a few weeks after West German

53. Dittmar Dahlmann, "Fußball als beschlossene Sache: Sport und Herrschaft in der
DDR," in *Überall ist der Ball rund. Zur Geschichte und Gegenwart des Fußballs in Ost- und Südosteuropa—Nachspielzeit*, 17–54.

54. Citation following Ingolf Pleil, *Mielke: Macht und Meisterschaft: Die "Bearbeitung" der
Sportgemeinschaft Dynamo Dresden 1978–1989* (Berlin: Links, 2001), 217. Also see *Sparwasser und
Mauerblümchen: Die Geschichte des Fussballs in der DDR 1949–1991*, ed. Horst Friedemann (Essen:
Klartext, 1996).

55. Thomas Blees, *90 Minuten Klassenkampf: Das Länderspiel BRD-DDR 1974* (Frankfurt:
Fischer, 1999).

Chancellor Willy Brandt, a great hope of the reformist left, had been forced to resign because of the scandal surrounding the East German spy Guillaume, two teams, which embodied two political and economic systems, met in the Hamburg People's Park stadium. Even as late as 1971, when East German fans traveled to see the team of the Federal Republic play an international match in Poland, they were not there to support their "own" side. No fewer than 204 citizens of the GDR, according to the Ministry for State Security, offered their loud support to the Federal Republic. Many of them even dared to wait for the team with banners stating "Chemnitz greets the German team and the Kaiser." Thus officials were very careful in handing out the 10,000 tickets that the GDR had ordered for the World Cup. Only principled citizens were permitted to travel to the games, people "who have earned particular distinction and recognition for their development and defense of the German Democratic Republic,"[56] as it stated in a directive issued by the secretariat of the central committee of the SED.

The Federal Republic was the odds-on favorite, which led the GDR to adopt a careful official tone before the game. What good would it do to present the game as a battle between systems if, as was expected, the East German team lost? Rudolf Hellmann, a member of the central committee of the SED, recalled twenty-five years later that "for us at that time it was actually a question of class."[57] There was no desire to put great weight on the match. Instead, the more aggressive tone came from certain players from the German Federal Republic. Captain and sweeper Franz Beckenbauer said that he would see to it that the communists would not get anywhere. Beckenbauer's club-mate Uli Hoeness stated that "many people were infected by the system" in the GDR, that is, they were sick.[58]

The complicated problem of using the terms "Germany" and "German," which was brought about by the Bonn government's Hallstein doctrine of stubborn diplomatic nonrecognition of the GDR, was discussed in detail by the reporter Werner Schneider, who provided commentary for the Second German Television Network (ZDF):[59]

56. Ibid., 42.   57. Ibid., 64.
58. Ibid., 22.   59. Ibid., 101.

Now, before we turn to the game, please allow me to say a few words about a particular matter. We all understand that we cannot please everyone in our choice of names for the two German teams in this game. Alfred Tetzlaff, the creep on television, you know his family history, would certainly only accept the word "zone." Others still write GDR inside quotation marks,[60] or would prefer to hear "East Germany" against "West Germany." Well, we have made inquiries of renowned scholars from German universities, including political scientists, Germanists, and so on, and they are almost unanimous in their view that one should abide by the official FIFA rules in this situation. That means plainly and simply, the GDR is playing against the Federal Republic of Germany this evening, just as it states on the stadium scoreboard.

For Heinz-Florian Oertel, a reporter from the GDR, the matter was much simpler. Officialdom in the GDR was pleased by being named on the stadium scoreboard, which was in itself a diplomatic success. Oertel pragmatically distinguished between the "team of the FRG" and the "GDR national eleven."

The game itself was evenly matched. The prolific scorer Gerd Müller for once struck only the posts. On the other side, Reinhard Lauck missed a great chance. The team from the GDR seemed to have better conditioning and eked out a slight advantage when, in the famous seventy-eighth minute, the substitute Erich Hamann from Vorwärts Frankfurt an der Oder took a throw from the goalie Croy, drove the ball to the right side of the penalty area, and passed it sharply to Jürgen Sparwasser, who dribbled around Horst-Dieter Höttges, from Bremen, and the central defender Berti Vogts before he fooled the goalie Sepp Maier and shot the ball halfway up into the right corner from six meters out.

The game was over, and the GDR "tourists," who were traveling home by train, mockingly held up copies of the tabloid *Bild*, with the headline: "Why we will win today."[61] The dining car of the Mitropa later sent a bill to the tour guide Helga Heinecke for just over 84,000 East German marks, which corresponds to 56 beers per fan. If this number seems to be too high, we can nevertheless conclude that the party officials had a rousing celebration. In total, the officials had to report five "fugitives from the republic," and three deserving old cadres died of heart attacks.

60. This is a reference to media outlets belonging to the Springer company, including the tabloid *Bild*.

61. Ibid., 111.

The leadership of the party, which had fearfully awaited the outcome of the game, was gleeful in its aftermath. *Neues Deutschland* mentioned the victory several times on its front page. The GDR then lost two games against the Netherlands and Brazil, and tied Argentina, which knocked the team out of the tournament.

"The defeat against the GDR was beneficial to us," recalled the captain Franz Beckbauer a quarter century later. "Today, we must thank our friends in Dresden and Leipzig that they gave us this shot across our bow in time."[62] As second in their group, the Federal Republic then moved on to what seemed to be an easier group. In the decisive "water fight in Frankfurt" the hard-running and powerful Polish team was defeated with a great deal of luck. In the final, the FRG again won with a great deal of luck against the strongest team in the tournament, namely the Netherlands. Their playmaker was the celebrated football player Johan Cruyff, whose fast style of play was carried on by the Van de Kerkhof twins from Eindhoven, René and Willy, as well as two other artists, the circumspect Johan Neeskens and the elegant defender Ruud Krool.

While the West German football players were properly compensated as world champions and were also successful in their later careers, things became calmer for the winners of the inter-German meeting following the end of the GDR. A West German mineral spring attempted to make money with the name of the goal scorer Jürgen Sparwasser, who said that overall the goal had been bad for him. The victory had been a poke in the eye of the opponents of the regime, and it was whispered behind closed doors that Sparwasser had been rewarded with a luxury car, a villa, and money for the deciding goal. In fact, it was money that encouraged some players to "flee the republic." In an interview with the journalist Thomas Blees in 1999, Sparwasser, a former member of the SED, explained that "we received, I believe, 2000 marks from the DTSB for the victory in the European Cup Winners' Cup with 1. FC Magdeburg in 1974, and a mark of appreciation from the city in the form of a cutlery holder made in 1956. During the celebration outside afterwards, we used them as targets for throwing knives."

The basic pay for players in the top league was 1,500 to 2,000 GDR marks. One player, who like many others acted as an informal agent for

62. Ibid., 130.

the Stasi, reported that after the members of the national team played a match in Iceland, they received $20 in pocket money and soda after dinner and complained about their low rate of pay. They had learned long before from television how much more their West German colleagues earned, and what kinds of goods they could purchase with their money. Beckenbauer, as the highest paid player, earned about 600,000 German marks a year, while some like Netzer earned only half this much with Borussia Mönchengladbach and promptly moved to Spain.[63]

Despite the intensive oversight and repression of team members, many GDR players managed to escape during foreign matches, including Norbert Nachtweih, Jörg Berger, the goalie Jürgen Pahl, Falko Götz, Dieter Schlegel, Frank Lippmann, and Lutz Eigendorf, whose death in a car accident in March 1983 gave rise to rumors. Heribert Schwan said that the Stasi had murdered Eigendorf, although he lacked proof for this. Nevertheless, Schwan was able to show just how thick the net of informers around Eigendorf was before his accidental death.[64]

In 1988, Sparwasser also defected, taking advantage of participating in a veterans tournament. In his farewell letter to his comrades, the goal scorer wrote the following: "We beg your pardon, that is Christa [his wife] and I, Christa is also here in the FRG. We have decided not to return to the GDR. We realize that you will not understand.... It is difficult and it is painful to separate from you, but there was no other choice for us.... Again, please forgive us. Jürgen."[65] A year before the iron curtain was raised, the player whose goal remains the best memory of many East Germans fled to the FRG. Sparwasser, who had made the triumph in Hamburg possible, fled and for a short time became an nonperson. He was subjected to a *damnatio memoriae*, expunged from official memory.

Shortly thereafter came the collapse of communism in eastern Europe, as well as the fall of the Soviet sport system along with the integration of the former East Bloc states into the top tier of commercialized football. As early as the 1988–89 season, the Ukrainian Sergij Baltača

---

63. Pleil, *Macht und Meisterschaft*, 140.

64. Heribert Schwan, *Tod dem Verräter! Der lange Arm der Stasi und der Fall Lutz Eigendorf* (Munich: Droemer Knaur, 2000).

65. Pleil, *Macht und Meisterschaft*, 144.

became the first Soviet football player to join the English professional league. During the early 1990s, the top clubs in the successor states of the Soviet Union and the former Eastern Bloc had to rapidly reorient themselves toward the practices of capitalist sports business.

King Football's Coexistence with Duce, Führer, and "Caudillo"

It was not only communist regimes that were confronted by the mass phenomenon of football. Their arch-enemies on the other side of the political spectrum, the fascists, also faced this issue. In Italy, which was the first country to fall victim to fascism in the early 1920s, the establishment of the Mussolini regime and the breakthrough of football as a mass spectator sport happened more or less contemporaneously. Top-tier Italian football underwent a creeping process of commercialization and professionalization during the politically and socially turbulent years following the First World War, which lured numerous players and coaches from Great Britain and from the east central European "Danubian football" to Italy.[66] These foreigners were obviously professional athletes, though they officially held to the principle of amateurism.

At first the fascist regime allowed this process to unfold and it only began to interfere during the mid-1920s.[67] In 1926 Lando Ferretti, a leading sports official who had aspired since the previous year to use his control over the Italian Olympic committee to transform this body into an auxiliary institution of the Fascist Party, dictated the authoritative rules for football in the port of Viareggio, the so-called Viareggio charter. This created a national league, the Divisione Nazionale, replaced the election of association officials with direct appointment, and put in place a compromise regarding the contested issue of professionalism, which divided the players between "amateurs" and "non-amateurs."[68] The creation of this fascist-inspired structure—a top-down process for

66. Marco Impiglia, "Fußball in Italien in der Zwischenkriegszeit," in *Fußball zwischen den Kriegen: Europa 1918–1939*, 168–72.

67. The basic work on the sports policies of Fascist Italy is Felice Fabrizio, *Sport e fascismo: La politica sportiva del regime 1924–1936* (Rimini: Guaraldi, 1976). For a particular focus on football, see Simon Martin, *Football and Fascism: The National Game Under Mussolini* (Oxford: Berg, 2004).

68. Impiglia, "Fußball," 151; and Martin, *Football and Fascism*, 51–78.

making decisions and a league organization that at least served the idea of nation building—was a pressing concern of the regime because of its ideological desire to eliminate an undesired move toward having professional players. In the beginning, however, the use of appointments was not universal and only affected the officials in the associations, while the leadership of the individual clubs continued to be chosen through secret ballots up until 1937.[69]

Subsequently, the stance of Mussolini's regime toward football remained diffuse. The sport policies of the fascists were marked by an ambivalence between the goal of developing top flight sports that were able to compete at the international level, which required at least a disguised professionalism, and the activation of the masses through the promotion of public health and particularly the capacity for military service, which suggested an official stress on the principle of amateurism.[70] Different leading officials, therefore, held divergent views. In the late 1920s, Augusto Turati, secretary of the Fascist Party from 1926 to 1930 and president of the Italian Olympic committee from 1928 to 1930, as well as other leading fascists frequently demanded efforts to "moralize" football, which was perceived as far too commercialized.[71] Turati even invented his own game called *volata*, which was supposed to be have been based on the old Roman ball game *harpastum*, and which was supposed to replace British football. However, this game could not even make headway in the fascist leisure-time organizations and disappeared after Turati's political fall in 1933.[72] On the other side was Leandro Arpinati, a personal friend of Mussolini from before the war and an original fascist, who, during his time as head of the Italian football association (1926–33) and of the Italian Olympic committee (1931–33), pushed for his vision of a sport system that was largely autonomous from the state as well as for an improvement in the financial position of the top clubs. He also carried through a reorganization of the national league that tended to promote its professionalization.[73]

69. Impiglia, "Fußball," 153.   70. Ibid.

71. Ibid., 152.

72. Marco Impiglia, "The Volata Game: When Fascism Forbade Italians to Play Football," in *La comune eredità dello sport in Europa: Atti del primo Seminario Europeo di Storia dello Sport,* eds. Arndt Krüger and Angela Teja (Rome: Coni, 1997), 420–26.

73. Impiglia, "Fußball," 153–55.

Il Duce himself was not interested at first in football. During the 1920s, he apparently attended just a single game, an international match between students. In 1928 he made dismissive comments about football and cycling stars in front of the directors of the most important Italian press outlets. It was not until 1930, that he deigned to attend his first match between national teams. Before it began, he ordered the captain of the Italian team to win the game.[74]

However, holding the World Cup in 1934 changed all of this radically. The world tournament was staged at great expense by the fascist regime as a propaganda event, which would show the world that Italy was a modern and capable nation, and would lead the people inside Italy to rally around Il Duce. This was the first World Cup during which football fans could hear many of the games directly on the radio. Coverage in European papers was also considerably greater than it had been four years earlier. The victory by the hosts was due to many questionable calls by the referees, who were whispered to have been influenced through the intervention of Mussolini. Recent research has questioned a direct involvement by Il Duce, but corroborated the thesis of cheating by Italian functionaries.[75] Following the final match, Mussolini, who demonstratively blocked the view of the FIFA president in the VIP stands, had himself celebrated as a great victor.[76]

Top level Italian football was marked by a type of professionalism during the 1930s that was covered by the mantle of "non-amateurism," which was accepted by the Viareggio charter. It was under this system that hidden payments to players and coaches, false accounts, and other financial irregularities were allowed. The fascist regime was de facto committed not to damage the interests of the football industry. In addition to the propaganda function of the national team, other, particularly financial considerations played a role because 15 percent of the income from admissions had to be paid to the government. In 1938, football paid 37 million lira to the state. Cycling, as the second most profitable professional sport, paid just two million.[77]

74. Ibid., 159.

75. Marco Impiglia, "1934 FIFA World Cup: Did Mussolini Rig the Game?", in *The FIFA World Cup 1930–2010: Politics, Commerce, Spectacle and* Identities, eds. Stefan Rinke and Kay Schiller (Göttingen: Wallstein, 2014), 66–84.

76. Jean-Yves Guillain, *L'œuvre de Jules Rimet* (Paris: Editions Amphora, 1998), 73; Martin, *Football and Fascism*, 183–89; and Impiglia, "Fußball," 174–78.

77. Impiglia, "Fußball," 155.

The de facto professional nature of football required several ideological adjustments. In 1927–28 teams were forbidden to field foreign players, whom leading fascists denoted as "barbarians."[78] As a replacement, the Italian clubs devoted substantial financial resources in the following years to recruiting the descendants of Italian emigrants to South America, particularly in Argentina, where the aggressive Italian recruitment efforts led to a professionalization of top-tier football there as well. Between 1929 and 1943, no fewer than 118 of these so-called *rimpatriati* played in the Italian leagues. The best of them also strengthened the national team.[79] The bringing home of these lost sons of the fatherland satisfied in an ideal manner the ideological ambitions of the fascist regime, and at the same time the need of the top clubs for imported stars, although this new practice was handled in exactly the same manner as the earlier acquisition of foreign professionals from Britain, Czechoslovakia, Austria, and Hungary.

Further restrictions on professionalism came in 1936 with the introduction of upper limits on pay and limits on transfers. In practice, however, these restrictions were regularly circumvented. Nevertheless, or perhaps because of this, there was no openly professional football up through the end of the fascist era. When the influential sports official Raffaele Manganiello, who was at this time also head of the Italian Olympic committee, suggested in 1941 that two professional leagues be established, he faced rejection on all sides and his plan was quickly buried.[80]

Overall, despite some interventions, the fascist regime made an accommodation with an undesired professional and mass spectator football because its propaganda and financial uses overrode ideological reservations. Thus, Marco Impiglia's metaphorical paraphrase of fascist sports policy is particularly apt with regard to professional football: "The fascist penetration of sports was not a matter of smothering everything with a layer of asphalt, but rather should be compared with the putting together of a puzzle."[81] In 1946 the structure of Italian top-tier football, which came into being under the fascists, was transformed relatively seamlessly into an openly professional league.

78. Ibid., 153.
79. Lanfranchi and Taylor, *Moving with the Ball*, 72–88; and Impiglia, "Fußball," 172–74.
80. Impiglia, "Fußball," 152.
81. Ibid., 153.

When the National Socialists came to power in Germany in 1933, football was for the most part well grounded but organizationally splintered, and its highly popular top echelon was marked by a hidden professionalism. Research on football under the swastika has experienced an explosion in the past two decades.[82] In this context, questions regarding the usurpation and autonomous character of football, the economic or opportunistic motivations for the rapid self-cooption of "bourgeois" football, as well as the grounds for the sustained, antiprofessionalism of football officials (which is difficult to reconcile with the prevailing reality), has led to heated debates among German historians of football.

Many characteristics of German football after 1933—the antiprofessionalism discussed above, as well as the successive exclusion of Jews, beginning in April 1933, first from leadership positions and then, depending on the club, from membership entirely[83]—appear to be a function of the mechanism described by the British expert on the National Socialist period Ian Kershaw as "working toward the Führer."[84] Without direct instructions from above, leading football officials followed a policy in their own interest, which they believed was aligned with the policy of the regime. However, there were also direct interventions of the regime, ranging from the bizarre struggle by the Bavarian sport leader Karl Oberhuber against the WM system[85] and the demand for parity on the national team for the 1938 World Cup between players from the "old Reich" and the "Ostmark" (Austria),[86] to the command by propaganda minister Joseph Goebbels that there must not be any defeats in international matches during the Second World War and the organizational incorporation of football into the German National Union for Physical Education, on account of which the basic functions of the DFB were taken

82. See, for example, Lorenz Peiffer, *Sport im Nationalsozialismus: Zum aktuellen Stand der sporthistorischen Forschung: Eine kommentierte Bibliografie* (Göttingen: Werkstatt, 2009).

83. Havemann, *Fußball unterm Hakenkreuz*, 158–72; Werner Skrentny, "Die Blütezeit des jüdischen Sports in Deutschland: Makkabi und Sportbund Schild, 1933 bis 1938," in *Davidstern und Lederball. Die Geschichte der Juden im deutschen und internationalen Fußball*, 170–201; and Fischer and Lindner, *Stürmer für Hitler*, 192–94.

84. Ian Kershaw, "Working towards the Führer: Reflections on the Nature of the Hitler Dictatorship," in *The Third Reich*, ed. Christian Leitz (London: Wiley-Blackwell, 1999), 231–52.

85. Markwart Herzog, *"Blitzkrieg" im Fußballstadion: Der Spielsystemstreit zwischen dem NS-Sportfunktionär Karl Oberhuber und Reichstrainer Sepp Herberger* (Stuttgart: Kohlhammer, 2012).

86. Hardy Grüne, "1933 bis 1945: Siege für den Führer," in *Die Geschichte der Fußball-Nationalmannschaft*, ed. Dietrich Schulze-Marmeling (Göttingen: Werkstatt, 2004), 99–106.

over by a government football office in 1934.[87] All of these interventions confirm the existence of multiple centers of power and the chaotic parallel and even contradictory structure of the various groups, offices, and persons that characterized the National Socialist system, whose Führer really had no interest in football.[88]

In 1936 the planning of international matches was transferred from the DFB to the Reich sport leader Hans von Tschammer und Osten.[89] Football could only serve propaganda purposes in a limited manner. Friendly matches could serve the needs of peace propaganda, but it was very difficult to plan a demonstration of strength toward either the outside world or for one's own population. In both the 1936 Olympic games and in the 1938 World Cup, the Germans were knocked out early by mid-level opponents. In 1936, the Germans were defeated by the Norwegians 0–2 in the quarterfinal. In 1938, Germany was defeated 2–4 by Switzerland in the round of sixteen. The fact that Adolf Hitler departed early from the imminent defeat against Norway, leaving a VIP stand that included Joseph Goebbels, Hermann Göhring, Rudolf Hess, and Hans von Tschammer und Osten, points to the ritual character of football according to which it was not opportune to be personally present at the moment when the German defeat was confirmed.[90]

The away international matches also made clear that the Nazi regime was not universally admired in Europe. This was clear, for instance, during a friendly match against Switzerland in Zurich on May 2, 1937. The day before, the city had been dominated by the red flags of the labor movement. However, on the day of the game, the 10,000 German away fans paraded through the Limmat city with swastikas. After the match, which the guests won 1–0, the Stuttgart Gestapo office complained in a

---

87. See Fischer and Lindner, *Stürmer für Hitler*, 119; Hans-Joachim Teichler, *Internationale Sportpolitik im Dritten Reich* (Schorndorf: Hofmann, 1991), 366; Grüne, "1933 bis 1945," 114 and 116.

88. See Peter Hüttenberger, "Nationalsozialistische Polykratie," *Geschichte und Gesellschaft* 2 (1976): 417–42; Klaus Hildebrand, "Monokratie oder Polykratie? Hitlers Herrschaft und das Dritte Reich," in *Der "Führerstaat": Mythos und Realität: Studien zu Struktur und Politik des Dritten Reiches*, eds. Gerhard Hirschfeld et al. (Stuttgart: Klett-Cotta, 1981), 73–97; Hans-Ulrich Thamer, "Monokratie—Polykratie: Historiographischer Überblick über eine kontroverse Debatte," in *Das organisierte Chaos: "Ämterdarwinismus" und "Gesinnungsethik": Determinanten nationalsozialistischer Besatzungsherrschaft*, eds. Gerhard Otto and Johannes Houwink ten Cate (Berlin: Metropol, 1999), 21–54.

89. Havemann, *Fußball unterm Hakenkreuz*, 226.

90. Grüne, "1933 bis 1945," 109–12.

report sent to Berlin that the international football match in Switzerland "was being misused for political purposes." The Germans were not "treated like guests, but rather were coldly handled as strangers almost everywhere. Swastikas were torn apart ostentatiously at the main train station. Women wore them on their buttocks."[91] In any case, the German away fans behaved themselves in a manner that was not conducive to creating friendship between peoples, either. According to a Swiss police report: "There was inappropriate behavior toward the Swiss public everywhere." It was reported that a passenger stuck out his tongue at the public, and another thumbed his nose. There were also calls such as "cow Swiss, [and] some Germans allegedly spit at the Swiss. In addition, there were continuous calls of yuck, and hail victory, etc., and they kept on loudly ringing the cow bells that they had brought along."[92]

At the same time, a civil war was raging in Spain that led in 1939 to the establishment of another fascist regime that remained in power until 1975. Shortly after the coup by the nationalist officers around Franco against the democratically elected left-wing government, football had its first victims to mourn. Francoist soldiers murdered Josep Suñol, the president of FC Barcelona, in August 1936. Suñol was a member of parliament for the left-wing nationalist party Esquerra Republicana de Catalunya (Republican Left of Catalonia), and his club was a thorn in the side of the men who staged the coup, as a symbol of Catalonian efforts to seek self-determination. In 1938 the Francoists bombarded the club headquarters.

Despite the war, football continued to be played.[93] In 1937 the Spanish Football Association moved from the endangered capital of Madrid to the more secure Barcelona. Shortly after this, Franco's supporters established a second association. Following efforts by Italy, FIFA recognized the Francoist association despite the rule in its bylaws that only one association from each country could be a member of FIFA. Within the context of the civil war, an all-Spain football championship naturally was out of the question. However, in 1936–37 there was a Catalonian as well as a "Le-

---

91. Leinemann, *Sepp Herberger*, 168.

92. City Archives Winterthur II B 29i 2:i Security and Political Police: Report on the interpellation by Mister E. Geilinger from May 4, 1937.

93. C. Fernández Santander, *El fútbol durante la guerra civil y el franquismo* (Madrid: San Martín, 1990); Christian Koller, "Kicken für die Republik—Sport im Spanischen Bürgerkrieg," *Die WochenZeitung*, August 25, 2005.

vantine" championship. The top teams in these competitions played in a "Mediterranean League," which was won by FC Barcelona. However, this was no longer feasible the next season. It was only possible to play games in Catalonia. In addition, there were demonstration games to entertain soldiers who were on leave.

Football not only played a role within the country during the civil war, but also abroad, where it served as a means of showing solidarity with the Spanish republic. In 1937, a British select team wanted to make a tour of the republican zone but this was forbidden by the Foreign Office. While Nazi Germany and fascist Italy, which were both members of the 1936 nonintervention pact, interpreted this very generously and provided both large numbers of troops and military supplies to Franco, the British government decided that it would not even permit a gesture of solidarity by left-wing football players.

Various Spanish sport delegations did, however, travel overseas. The Spanish athletes were the greatest heroes at the 1937 Workers' Olympics. Spanish football was also represented that same year in the World Exposition in Paris, where Picasso's monumental antiwar painting *Guernica*, which lamented the destruction of this Basque city by German bombers, hung in the Spanish pavilion. A select team from the republican zone defeated the Swiss workers' football champion Sportfreunde Basel 3–2.

A select team from the Basque country caused a sensation when it went on a tour of Europe and Latin America for the benefit of republican refugees.[94] The team, which was named Republik Euskadi (Basque Republic) was comprised of top players, particularly from Athletic Club Bilbao, the champion in 1930, 1931, 1934, and 1936. Under the influence of increasing Basque nationalism, the team had included only Basque players from 1919 onwards, and was a symbol of Basque independence. In 1937–38, the Euskadi team played numerous games in France, Czechoslovakia, Poland, the Soviet Union, Norway, Denmark, Mexico, Cuba, and Chile. In the Soviet Union, which was gaining increasing influence with the republican side because of the passivity of the western democracies, the Basques played nine games in six weeks in Moscow, Kiev, Tiflis, and Minsk, in some cases in front of 90,000 spectators.

94. Eisenberg, *FIFA*, 276; Riordan, *Politique étrangère*, 134; Peppard and Riordan, *Playing Politics*, 43; and Edelman, *Serious Fun*, 63.

Following the end of the civil war, numerous republicans, including a significant number of football players, went into exile in Mexico, which along with the Soviet Union was the only country to provide direct assistance to the Spanish republic. Some of them joined the top-ranked Asturias Club, which had been founded by Spaniards. The Basque team also remained in Mexico, and took part in the Mexican championship in 1939. In the following years, some of the players switched over to Argentinian professional clubs, while others remained in Mexico. About half of the players from FC Barcelona sought asylum in either Mexico or France.

In Spain, the new rulers sought to begin playing games again as soon as possible in order to illustrate the return to normality. In 1939 a "Copa del Generalísimo" was organized. The final game was between a club from the Generalissimo's Galician home town of Ferrol and Seville, which the former lost 2–6. The professional league began to play again in the 1939–40 season. The winner of the first two championships after the end of the civil war was the new club Atlético Aviación, favored by the military, which was formed by a fusion of Atlético Madrid and the air force club Aviación Nacional. In the 1940s, the authorities appointed Enrique Piñeyro y de Queralt, an aristocrat and Franco loyalist, as president of Barcelona. The club changed its name from the Catalan "Futbol Club" to the Spanish "Club de Fútbol," and banished the Catalonian national colors from its club emblem. In 1941 the regime banned non-Spanish club names, so that the club in the Basque metropolitan center had to change its name to Atlético de Bilbao.

International matches were renewed in 1941. Early that year, Spain played two matches against ideologically sympathetic Portugal. At the turn of 1941–42, the national team from neutral and democratic Switzerland traveled in the midst of the war to the Iberian peninsula to play friendly matches against Spain and Portugal. The 30,000 spectators for the match in Valencia included many dignitaries from the new regime.

After the Second World War, in which Spain had remained officially neutral but leaned toward the Axis powers, the openly fascist rhetoric and symbolism of the Franco regime was replaced by a much more diffuse Catholic-nationalist propaganda, as the fascists of the Falange Party were superseded by technocrats from the right-wing Catholic lay organization Opus Dei. In this context, football became an important element of a depoliticized "culture of distraction."[95] The five successive victories by Real Madrid, which increasingly took on the image of being "the regime's team" in the European Champion Clubs' Cup between 1956 and 1960, as well as the European championship by the Spanish national team in 1964, came at an opportune time for the regime.[96] However, in light of the very small scale of state support for athletics, the instrumentalization of these victories amounted to little more than jumping on the bandwagon and was marked by limited sustainability.

At the same time, despite Hispanicizing efforts at the end of the civil war, the leading Catalonian and Basque clubs remained crystallization points for regionalism, and also potentially for an anti-Francoist opposition. The games between Barcelona and Real Madrid became a forum for Catalonian demonstrations. The enormous concrete bowl of Nou Camp was an unpoliceable space for conversations and songs in Catalan. Real became a symbol for Castilian centralization, the referees acted as mercenaries for the dictator, and the Whites became hated figures.

The best known example of the sponsorship of Real by the Francoist regime is the case of di Stefano. In 1953 the club leadership of Barcelona signed the talented Argentinian Alfredo di Stefano, who actually belonged to River Plate Buenos Aires, but who had been loaned to the Colombian club Millionarios de Bogotá. The Spanish association used all possible legal avenues to block the already legally valid transfer. In the end, Real Madrid dealt directly with Millionarios and, in this unfair manner, signed the player who set the stage for the dominance of Real in Spanish and European football.

General Franco also quite consciously used the football card to provide an outlet for potentially dangerous regionalism. However, in the case of Barça, the Generalissimo made an error. As Carlos Rexach, a former player and coach of Barcelona, said in 1983: "As the Catalans had no political parties, or regional government, or any right to use their own language, they all put their cultural pride onto Barça. At a Barça match, the people could shout in Catalan and sing their traditional songs at a time when they couldn't do it anywhere else."[97]

95. See Jürg Ackermann, *Fussball und nationale Identität in Diktaturen: Spanien, Portugal, Brasilien und Argentinien* (Berlin: Lit, 2013), 69–144.

96. Duke, *Football, Nationalism, and the State*, 155.

97. Ibid., 44.

The experience of the two best-known Basque teams, Athletic de Bilbao and Real Sociedad San Sebastian, was similar to that of FC Barcelona. The club from Bilbao, which was founded in 1898, exclusively recruited native Basque players from 1919 onward, with a preference for those from the Biscaya, the region immediately around the city. The leading Basque republican politician during the 1930s, José Antonio Aguirre, was a former midfielder for the team. By contrast, Real Sociedad San Sebastian was open to foreign players and coaches, and pursued more of a pan-Basque line.

The increase in Basque political nationalism during the 1960s and 1970s brought about a rapprochement between the two rival clubs. The top echelons of the two clubs demonstrated sympathy for the program of the exiled Basque National Party and were rumored to have contacts with the terrorist Euzkadi ta Askatasuna (ETA). Bilbao's popular goalie, José Ángel Iribar, who also stood between the posts for the Spanish national team, openly supported political rights for his countrymen. Following the deaths of two ETA activists in September 1975, two months before the death of the dictator, Iribar even went so far as to wear a black ribbon, a symbolic gesture whose meaning could not be missed.

As had been true in Italy, the end of the dictatorship did not lead to major changes in football. Despite their relationship with the regime, the top Spanish clubs were integrated during the middle and late years of Franco's period into elite European professional football, and fought for the leading position in European club competitions. The political *transición* from 1975 to 1982 had little effect on the structure of Spanish football. However, the holding of the World Cup in Spain in 1982 meant that football played a significant role in creating a positive image for post-Franco Spain on the world stage.

Generals of the Junta as Football World Champions

When the Chilean military under General Augusto Pinochet launched a coup, with support from the CIA, against the democratically elected government of the Socialist president Salvador Allende on September 11, 1973, this was just one of dozens of coups d'état Latin America had experienced since gaining its independence from Spanish and Portuguese colonial rule in the early nineteenth century. For the first time, however, football played a sad and internationally noted role in such an event when the National Stadium in Santiago de Chile, which had hosted the final game of the 1962 World Cup, was temporarily transformed into an internment camp and execution center for up to seven thousand political prisoners.[98]

When Chile and the Soviet Union were to cross swords over the last remaining spot in the 1974 World Cup tournament in this same stadium, the eastern superpower refused to play the game. Despite this boycott, Pinochet arranged a "ghost game," without an opponent, which the Chileans won 1–0 on a goal by their captain Francisco Valdez. When the away game in Moscow ended in a 0–0 tie, the Chilean team thereby qualified "sportingly." A commission from FIFA had already concluded that the stadium was in good condition, and that the prisoners, who were all being held in locker rooms, would not cause a disturbance. Chile thus qualified through a bureaucratic decision.

Despite the massive police presence during the final round of the 1974 World Cup in Germany, there were still protests by Chilean exiles.[99] During the match against Australia, a number of the exiles, supported by European left-wing groups, stormed onto the field in Berlin's Olympic stadium. During the match against the GDR, there were numerous placards in the stands with slogans such as "Chile Yes, Junta No," "Socialism," or "Fascism No."

The two most powerful football nations in South America, Brazil and Argentina, also were not spared military regimes during the twentieth century, and several of the football triumphs of the two countries came in periods of dictatorial rule. The breakthrough of football as a mass phenomenon that went beyond class boundaries took place in Brazil in the 1920s. The next decade then saw the professionalization of the sport.[100] President Gétulio Vargas, who as the *Pai dos Pobres* (father of the poor) established an authoritarian regime (the Estado Novo) with the character

98. See Hachleitner, "Stadion als Gefängnis," 264–71.

99. Florian Mildenberger, "Die Angst des Diktators vor dem Elfmeter: Sport und Politik bei der Fussballweltmeisterschaft 1974," *Sozial- und Zeitgeschichte des Sports* 14 (2000): 57–65.

100. For the following, see Ackermann, *Fussball und nationale Identität*, 209–67.

of a modernizing dictatorship in 1930, realized from the beginning the importance of football for the image of the country abroad and also for internal national integration. Among other measures, he ordered that all football clubs Brazilianize their names, which in some cases were still in English. In 1938, for the first time, Brazil sent an ethnically mixed team to the World Cup, which won third place and generated considerable enthusiasm in the country.

Vargas was overthrown by the military in 1945. He then returned to power as the democratically elected president in 1951, a year after the traumatic defeat of Brazil in the finals of the World Cup in their own country at the hands of Uruguay. In 1954 Vargas, who had come under pressure from the army, the political right, and the United States, committed suicide. A spirit of economic and political optimism reigned during the late 1950s under the auspices of democracy. The presidency of the moderate left-wing politician Juscelino Kubitschek (1956–61) was marked by an economic boom, the rise of a domestic auto industry, large infrastructure projects, and the consecration of the new capital city of Brasilia, which was designed on the drawing board and whose construction had begun under Vargas. Parallel to these achievements, the Brazilian national football team, around the extraordinary Pelé, established itself definitively as a football superpower with World Cup championships in 1958 and 1962.

However, the sinking price of coffee led to an economic decline in the late 1950s that increasingly hindered the process of modernization. In 1964 the military staged another coup, supported by the political right, the Catholic church, and the American ambassador. Within a week of the coup, seven thousand politically undesirable people, including communists and members of the agrarian workers' movement, lost their political rights. The legitimization for this attack was the ideology of *Segurança Nacional* (national security). The generals Artur da Costa e Silva, Márcio de Souza Mello, Emílio Garrastazu Médici, Ernesto Geisel, and João Baptista de Oliveira Figueiredo, who took turns holding the top position in the state during the following two decades, combined a canon of military values with a belief in progress and an almost messianic sense of mission, and organized a government of officials and technocrats who were loyal to the regime.

Between 1969 and 1973, the country experienced an economic miracle with enormous rates of growth that, however, sharpened the extreme social contrasts. At the same time, the regime invested heavily in the sport in the run-up to the World Cup in 1970. Military specialists were commandeered for the development of the sport and coaching sciences. In addition, the transmission infrastructure was built up so that eventually 40 percent of the population could watch the games in Mexico live. The left-wing national coach João Saldanha posed a problem for the regime. He had friends in the underground opposition and in 1969 spoke freely in interviews with European newspapers about repression, torture, and disappeared members of the opposition in Brazil. Shortly before the World Cup he was sacked by João Havelange, the president of the football association, who had close ties to the dictatorship and a few years later became chairman of FIFA.

The regime thoroughly savored the third World Cup title that the team won in Mexico, which made Brazil the most successful football nation in the world and was treated as a symbol of the development and the golden future of the country. During the victory celebrations, the military dictator Médici presented himself to the masses as a Brazilian patriot who had kept his promise of winning a third world championship.

Even though the modernization process continued in the period immediately following the world championship—thirteen new stadiums with capacities of up to 100,000 spectators were constructed up through 1975, nine of them in the less developed north and northeast of the country—it soon became clear that the euphoria of 1970 was a flash in the pan.[101] The economic problems that came in the wake of the 1973 oil crisis eroded the power of the military dictatorship. In addition, the 1970s and 1980s did not see a continuation of success in football. Significantly, football played a political role in the period leading up to the transition to democracy in 1984–85. During the early 1980s, a group of politicized football players from the top club Corinthians São Paulo gathered around the left-wing physician Sócrates and called themselves "Corinthian Democracy." This group put into place rules in the club that signing players and disciplinary procedures on the team would be decid-

101. Tony Mason, *Passion of the People? Football in South America* (London: Verso, 1995), 64.

ed democratically. The team also put demands for free elections on their jerseys and became a model for social movements, which now began to express themselves.

Football had played an important role in the creation of a national identity in the immigrant society of Argentina since the early twentieth century. It was supported by the state and used for political purposes. At the same time, however, football clubs also were places for civic openness and democratic agreement. Although Argentinians in the interwar period thought of their "creole" playing style as particularly dominant, as their team came in second place behind Uruguay in the Olympic football tournament in 1928 and in the first World Cup in 1930, the following decades brought disillusionment in the form of long-lasting failure. On the political level, this period saw multiple transitions between democratic government, military regimes (with nine coups in the period between 1930 and 1970), and two presidencies of the charismatic nationalist Juan Perón (1946–55 and 1973–74).

In 1976, as the country suffered through a deep economic crisis and terrorist attacks from both left and right escalated, the Argentinian military staged yet another coup and established Jorge Rafael Videla as the head of a military junta. The following years were marked by political internment, torture, and the murder of between 15,000 and 30,000 members of the opposition. The economically liberal recovery plan did not have the hoped-for success, as Argentinian industrial production shrank about 20 percent between 1976 and 1983, and foreign debt exploded to $50 billion. The occupation of the British Falkland Islands and the subsequent military defeat led in 1983 to the collapse of the military dictatorship.

When it took power, the military junta was concerned with crushing the left-wing underground and stabilizing the economic situation but also with ending the phase of football failure. This was particularly important since the junta had inherited the hosting of the 1978 World Cup from the previous government.[102] The irreproachable organization of the games was supposed to make the outside world forget reports of torture and the murder of political opponents and give the impression

102. For the following, also see Ackermann, *Fussball und nationale Identität*, 280–332.

of Argentina as a country at peace. Following the recommendations of the American public relations firm Burson-Marsteller, the regime began a charm offensive in the run-up to the World Cup. Advertisements with positive information about Argentina were distributed across the world in an effort to appease doubts about the humanitarian situation in the World Cup host country. In addition, images of attractive officials were intended to give the country a positive and liberal image. The regime also made the propagandistic move of leaving the left-wing national coach César Luis Menotti in his position under the condition that he win the World Cup.[103] Parallel with these public relations efforts, the regime invested about $500 million in new stadiums, airports, highways, and the modernization of television and telephone lines. However, these expenditures proved to be counterproductive. Despite the expected 50,000 foreign fans, just 7,000 traveled to Argentina. The games ended with a substantial deficit and led to a greater Argentinian foreign debt.

Although River Plate stadium in Buenos Aires, where several games including the final match took place, was located next to the prison and torture center of Escuela de Mecánica de la Armada (the Naval Technical Training Center), the foreign voices criticizing the regime were limited to left-wing organizations and human rights groups. There was no plan at all to organize a broader boycott of the type that took place two years later under American leadership against the Olympic games in Moscow. Rather, FIFA president João Havelange declared after the military coup that Argentina was still able to host the World Cup. Hermann Neuberger, the vice president of FIFA, organizational head of the World Cup, and president of the German Football Union refused during the course of the tournament to receive a report in the quarters of the German team by the human rights organization Amnesty International about torture and abduction in Argentina. By contrast, he did not refuse the request by Hans-Ulrich Rudel, a right-wing extremist as well as a propagandist and adviser to many Latin American dictatorships, to make a visit.

Considered from a sports perspective, the tournament ran smoothly for the generals in the junta, although in one case it appears that it

---

103. See Beat Jung, "César Luis Menotti: Der Mythos vom 'linken Fussball,'" in *Strategen des Spiels: Die legendären Fussballtrainer*, ed. Dietrich Schulze-Marmeling (Göttingen: Werkstatt, 2005), 203–13.

was necessary for them to intervene in order to secure the world title for the hosts. In the final game of the intermediate stage, the Argentinians needed a victory of at least four goals over the already knocked out Peruvian team in order to move past the Brazilian team, which had the same number of points as the Argentinians, and thus make it into the final game. The 6–0 victory by the hosts as well as several irregularities led to speculation afterwards that the game had been fixed.[104] Apparently, the Argentinian junta had used middlemen and the large transfer of grain supplies to Lima to influence individual players and the Peruvian coach. General Videla also visited the Peruvian team in their dressing room before the game, and appealed for Peruvian solidarity with Argentina. In addition, the Peruvian coach placed several players on the reserve bench who had played well in earlier games.

While, after the final game, the coach Menotti as well as the Dutch players refused to shake hands with generals of the junta, the leaders of FIFA celebrated with the dictators what was, in their eyes, the High Mass of world football. The military regime thoroughly savored the triumph, which seemed to make plausible the rhetoric of Argentina as a "great nation" and its rebirth under the rule of the generals. However, the continuing economic collapse and the misguided Falklands adventure quickly eroded the foundation for these claims.

Conclusion

If we consider the diverse findings treated here, it is clear that "king football" was a chameleon that was able to take on a range of mass cultural forms in the most variable types of systems, whether in liberal capitalist democracies, communist one-party states, or right-wing dictatorships. Within the context of these differences, each dictatorship was confronted by the ambivalent situation that mass spectator football was exceptionally popular and offered alternative foci for identification (stars and clubs), but because of the relative transparency of the outcome of games offered only limited options for use in propaganda. The physical presence of the dictator in the stadium always brought with it the risk of a

104. Ricardo Gotta, *Fuimos Campeones: La dictadura, el Mundial 78 y el misterio del 6 a 0 a Perú* (Buenos Aires: Edhasa, 2008), 276.

fiasco. This is in contrast to the claims for power that come from the synchronized movement of trained bodies performing in symbolic sporting events, such as the German gymnastics festivals or the athletic parades on the Soviet Day of Physical Culture. In addition, spectator football created rare gatherings of unruly masses of people in public spaces in which oppositional views sometimes could be articulated. These areas of ambivalence led to a situation in which the form taken by mass spectator football was the result of an open-ended process of negotiation within specific contexts among various interest groups, which included the leadership of individual clubs and association officials as well as circles from the ruling powers that were interested in sport. These latter included ideological, economic, and propaganda interests, as well as the interests of well-connected individuals.

9 | *Football and War*

Inter armes silent musae—the muses are silent in times of war. This idea, which was widespread in antiquity, was no longer completely valid in the twentieth century, a "mass age" and an age of "total war." The "masses" continued to demand entertainment particularly in times of war, wishing a diversion from the experience of war while behind the lines. Thus, the arts could no longer remain silent, but they had to be subordinated to the needs of war and to proclaim what was desired by the leadership, and thus were instrumentalized for propagandistic purposes.

There is no doubt that football belonged to those arts that had a close affinity to war. Indeed, George Orwell's dictum that sport is "war minus the shooting" fits football particularly well.[1] Football jargon is filled with expressions that are borrowed from military language, such as a match that is fought, a ball that is shot, the other side that is defeated or capitulated, as well as strategy, battle, and loss. These analogies go back to the pioneers of football. For example, a treatise from 1882, which promoted the introduction of the English sport in Germany, had the following description:

Two teams, usually composed of eleven combatants, stand on the field of battle. The goal is to bring a large leather ball into enemy territory using the feet and, if possible, to bring it into the enemy's sanctuary, which is a "stand" marked out by two poles. If this happens in a proper manner, then the team wins a "stand." The number of "stands" that are won or lost determine victory and defeat. In order to understand the following rules we note that each team stands under the leadership of a "captain," who distributes his forces over the field. He will put one or two skilled, tireless, and offensively capable players in the first rank

---

1. George Orwell, "The Sporting Spirit," *Tribune of London*, December 1945.

near where the ball is expected. The remainder of his army remains behind. He should keep himself in the rear-guard so that in case of emergency, he can meet the threatening danger.[2]

The expression "war in the stadium" was used not only to denote events on the field, but also frequently for the violent behavior of the spectators.[3]

On the other side, Sebastian Haffner, who experienced the First World War as a child, recalled it in 1939 as a kind of enormous football game:

What counted was the spell of the military game, in which mysterious rules of numbers of prisoners, the conquest of territory, captured defenses, and sunken ships played the role of goals scored in football or "points" scored in boxing. I never grew tired of compiling tables of points in my mind.... It was a dark, mysterious game, with a never-ending and immoral excitement that obliterated everything that made real life dull, bringing one into a narcotic state, like roulette or smoking opium.[4]

The German minister of propaganda Joseph Goebbels also drew a comparison between football and war in a speech shortly before the German defeat at Stalingrad in the winter of 1942–43:[5]

It has never been the case that a defeat came from a *"pure"* victory, or that a victory came from a *"pure"* defeat—there is no such thing. The English say: Yes, we will win the *final* victory! It seems to me that this would be like having the Kitzbühel football club, which always loses in the local championships, being allowed to participate in the district championship out of pity, where the team is also always defeated. Then a fellow says: that doesn't matter. If we meet Schalke 04 in the stadium in Berlin, then everything will be fine. But then the response is: You are not coming to the stadium my man! The ones going to the stadium are those who have always been victors, not those who were defeated. You are not coming to the final match. What kind of nonsense are you talking! The team that wins the final battle is the team that has earned its place with previous victories.

---

2. F. W. Racquet, *Moderne englische Spiele: Zum Zweck der Einführung in Deutschland* (Göttingen, 1882), 50, cited in Heinrich, *Fussballbund*, 35.

3. See, for example, Morris, *Spiel*, 262; Thomas Gehrmann, *Fussballrandale: Hooligans in Deutschland* (Essen: Klartext, 1990), 200.

4. Haffner, *Geschichte eines Deutschen*, 20.

5. *Goebbels-Reden*, vol. 2: *1939–1945*, ed. Helmut Heiber (Düsseldorf: Droste, 1972), 145.

Indeed, a real military conflict has gone down in history as the "Football War." The meeting between El Salvador and Honduras in the context of a qualification match for the 1970 World Cup catalyzed the release of pent-up tensions between the two neighboring states in 1969. Immediately following El Salvador's 3–0 victory, both states set troops in motion, bombarded strategic locations in the neighboring country, and broke off diplomatic relations.[6] At the beginning of the 1930s, German football officials appear to have thought of the First World War as having been a "great experiment" that proved running a great deal was not damaging to the heart, a charge that always had been used to impugn football, but rather served to strengthen the heart.[7]

Soldiers always played football on and behind the front during the twentieth century. The examples from the First World War have become famous. During the period of trench warfare on the western front, British units sometimes kicked footballs during the deadly rush through no man's land to reach the enemy side.[8] Football proved itself to be an effective alternative to a brandished pistol, which officers otherwise used to drive their soldiers into the hail of enemy bullets. An anonymous patriot wrote about such an event in the following verse:

> On through the heat of slaughter
> Where gallant comrades fall
> Where blood is poured like water
> They drive the trickling ball
> The fear of death before them
> Is but an empty name
> True to the land that bore them
> The Surreys play the game.[9]

---

6. See William H. Durham, *Scarcity and Survival in Central America: Ecological Origins of the Soccer War* (Stanford, Calif.: Stanford University Press, 1979); Thomas P. Anderson, *The War of the Dispossessed: Honduras and El Salvador, 1969* (Lincoln: University of Nebraska Press, 1981); Ryszard Kapucinski, *Der Fussballkrieg: Berichte aus der Dritten Welt* (Frankfurt: Fischer Taschenbuch, 1990), 251–88; as well as *Fussball-Weltmeisterschaft 1970*, eds. Ernst Huberty and Willy B. Wange (Zurich: Lingen, 1970), 279.

7. Otto Nerz and Carl Koppehel, *Der Kampf um den Ball: Das Buch vom Fussball* (Berlin: Prismen Verlag, 1933), 172.

8. On this point, see J. G. Fuller, *Troops Morale and Popular Culture in the British and Dominion Armies 1914–1918* (Oxford: Clarendon Press, 1990), 137; Veitch, "Play Up," 363; Morris, *Spiel*, 160.

9. Cited in Paul Fussell, *The Great War and Modern Memory* (Oxford: Oxford University Press, 1975), 27.

There are also always those rumors about the fraternization that supposedly took place at various places on the front lines around the time of the first war-time Christmas in 1914. Supposedly, it was not only cigarettes, alcohol, and the bodies of fallen comrades that were exchanged, but also that there were football games between German and allied soldiers in no man's land.[10] Soldiers also played football behind the front lines, and this has been substantiated by firsthand accounts of participants in the war. The British general Jack noted in his journal that "no British Troops ever travel without footballs or the energy to kick them."[11] At first, British officers were skeptical of these athletic activities because they feared that the soldiers would become unnecessarily exhausted.[12] Soon, however, there were organized competitions both within and between army units as, for example, in the corps tournament in Gallipoli.[13] Important games were watched by 1,500 to 3,000 spectators. While the British brought the game from their homeland to the front, many French and German soldiers played football for the first time in the years 1914–18, and many of those who survived did not want to do without the sport after the war was over. At the end of 1918, the German War Ministry saw football as a proven means of keeping the German units, which no longer were under arms, from becoming involved in political activities during this period of revolutionary turmoil.[14]

In this chapter, we will focus largely on one aspect of the relationship between war and football, namely the possibilities of using football to strengthen morale. The economic historian Alan S. Milward used the term "strategic synthesis" to denote the interplay of political, economic, military, social, and psychological factors that were necessary for the successful conduct of war.[15] The economic sphere included issues such

---

10. See Michael Jürgs, *Der kleine Frieden im Großen Krieg: Westfront 1914: Als Deutsche, Franzosen und Briten gemeinsam Weihnachten feierten* (Munich: Bertelsmann, 2003); and Niels Van Echtelt, "The Forgotten Front: The Multicultural War of 1914–1918 in Eyewitness Accounts from Flanders," in *World War I: Five Continents in Flanders,* eds. Dominiek Dendooven and Piet Chielens (Tielt: Lannoo publishers, 2008), 169.

11. *General Jack's Diary*, ed. J. Terraine (London: Eyre & Spottiswoode, 1964), 227.

12. Ibid., 91.

13. R. R. Thompson, *The Fifty-Second (Lowland) Division 1914–1918* (Glasgow: Maclehose, Jackson & Co., 1923), 156.

14. Eggers, "Fussball," 159–61.

15. Alan S. Milward, *Der Zweite Weltkrieg: Krieg, Wirtschaft und Gesellschaft 1939–1945* (London: Lane, 1977), 38–78.

as the means by which limited resources were deployed under wartime conditions In order to optimize competing demands and goals—for example, the supply of the military versus the supply of civilian population, or deploying a workforce for the arms industry versus soldiers for the army. There are also conflicts regarding goals in the area of culture and sport. These include the questions that will be considered below, such as whether top athletes should fight in the war on the front or remain at home and strengthen morale on the athletic field. Government authorities and athletic associations are always confronted with these issues in times of war. Because the fate of "sporting aces" was not a matter of indifference to the population, it was always necessary to consider whether the value that would come from the deployment of athletes on the home front to raise morale would outweigh the discontent that is directed against the concomitant privileged treatment of the athletes or whether it would be better to deploy popular athletes on the front and derive the benefit that accrues to having them there as an example. In this chapter, we will consider these problems through a comparative examination of Great Britain, Germany, and neutral Switzerland in the context of both world wars.

"No Time for Football": Professionalism and Military Service in Great Britain

On September 1, 1914, the worker F. N. Charrington sent a telegram to King George V, the honorary chairman of the Football Association, demanding that football be banned during the war.[16] Charrington, and a great part of the public opinion in Great Britain, was disturbed that the English professional league continued to play championship matches despite the outbreak of war. The London *Times* published the following poem from their house poet, R. E. Vernède, two weeks after the war began:

> Lad, with the merry smile and the eyes
> Quick as hawk's and clear the day,
> You, who have counted the game the prize,
> Here is the game of games to play.

16. *Times* (London), September 8, 1914.

Never a goal—the captain say—
Matches the one that's needed now:
Put the old blazer and cap away—
England's colours await your brow.[17]

Shortly afterward, the *Evening News* published the following criticism: "This is no time for football. This nation has got to occupy itself with more serious business. The young men who play football and the young men who look on have better work to do. The Trumpet calls them, the heroes in the trenches call them. They are summoned to leave their sport, and to take part in the great game. That game is war, for life or death."[18] Particularly disturbing was the claim by the recruitment authorities that the argument that every man was needed on the front would be less believable if week after week hundreds of young men in the best physical condition had nothing to do other than run after a ball (a general military obligation was not introduced in Britain until the beginning of 1916). A recruitment officer complained to the *Times* in November 1914:

It has a moral effect. . . . These professional footballers of England are the pick of the country for fitness. Nobody has a right to say that any body of men are not doing their duty, and there may be excellent domestic reasons why every one of these thousands of players does not enlist. But when the young men week after week see the finest physical manhood of the country expending its efforts kicking a ball about, they can't possibly realize that there is a call for every fit man at the front.[19]

In order to combat the public ill humor regarding the continued holding of games, the FA placed its entire administrative structure at the disposal of the War Office. The playing fields of all of the league clubs were made available to the military for training purposes.[20] A placard was even placed in a London stadium with the following text: "Do you want to be a Chelsea Die-Hard? If so join the 17th Battalion Middlesex Regiment 'The Old Die-Hards' and follow the lead given by your favourite Football Players."[21] In the following months, two thousand of the five thousand professional football players answered the call of their country. Thus,

17. *Times*, August 19, 1914.
19. *Times*, November 24, 1914.
21. Walvin, *People's Game*, 89.

18. *Times*, September 3, 1914.
20. Veitch, "Play Up," 370.

football players were represented at a far higher percentage than men of their same age, of whom approximately 25 percent freely volunteered for military service between August 1914 and December 1915. Corresponding to the practice of organizing "mate battalions," in which groups of friends, neighbors, and professional colleagues were placed together, a football player battalion was organized.[22] There were only 600 bachelors among the remaining 3,000 players.[23] The FA put pressure on them to volunteer and also took measures to convince both amateur players and spectators to join the army. However, in September 1914, the management committee of the Football League still decided "that in the interests of the people of this country, football ought to be continued."[24]

Discomfort about the apparently unpatriotic behavior of the football players did not disappear until the FL ended play following the completion of the 1914–15 season and did not start again until 1919. Most league clubs continued to play in regional competitions, but football ceased to attract criticism. The FA Cup was not renewed until the 1919–20 season. After the final game in April 1915, which was called the Khaki Cup Final because of the many soldiers in the stands, ended with a 3–0 victory by Sheffield United against Chelsea, Lord Derby was able to hail the players in the following manner: "You have played with one another and against one another for the Cup; play with one another for England now."[25]

The conflict between the English national sport and the "needs of the war," which had caused tempers to flare, was settled. In Scotland, the first division of the professional league continued to play throughout the entire war. The second division was put on hiatus following the 1914–15 season. Here too, many football players freely volunteered for service on the front. The entire Hearts of Midlothian team, with the exception of one man, volunteered. In 1915 it became clear that the good patriot did not allow his man to remain on the green grass of Lancashire but rather made him stand trenches in Flanders. The argument about strengthening the morale of the home front was no longer valid. In this situation, a game that previously had been mocked, sidelined, and even partially

22. W. J. Reader, *At Duty's Call: A Study in Obsolete Patriotism* (Manchester: Manchester University Press, 1988), 100.

23. Mason, *Association Football*, 253.   24. *Times*, September 9, 1914.

25. Veitch, "Play Up," 374.

forbidden now attracted considerable attention—namely, women's football. Its rapid rise during the First World War and its subsequent suppression during the early 1920s will be dealt with in greater detail in a later chapter.

The responsible authorities learned from the negative response to the initial decision to continue holding championship games. When the Second World War began in September 1939, the English and Scottish professional leagues immediately cancelled normal league play, even though championship play had already begun for the 1939–40 season. The FA Cup was also cancelled. But the government quickly realized that mass spectator football could not stop completely. In conjunction with the Football Association and the Football League, the government organized in record time a provisional organization for the playing of games, which became known as wartime football.[26] Nearly all of the English professional clubs (82 of 88) participated in the new league, which began games on a regional basis on October 21, 1939. The creation of regional units was intended to increase the number of lucrative contests and to lower expensive transportation costs. The London league was particularly popular. The scramble to obtain a place in this league was therefore correspondingly intense. Scotland had an east and a west group.[27] There was also a War Cup, which attracted relatively large numbers of spectators. Overall, however, the numbers of spectators declined significantly. There were rarely more than two thousand spectators in attendance, and frequently fewer than one thousand. Most of the young single men, who in peacetime comprised the largest part of the audience, were doing

26. See John Ross Schleppi, "A History of Professional Association Football in England during the Second World War," PhD diss., University of Ohio, 1972; Anton Rippon, *Gas Masks for Goal Posts: Football in Britain During the Second World War* (Stroud: The History Press, 2007); Tim Purcell and Mike Gething, *Wartime Wanderers: A Football Team at War* (London: Mainstream Publishing, 2001); Simon Kuper, *Ajax, the Dutch, the War: Football in Europe during the Second World War* (London: Orion, 2003); Derek Birley, *Playing the Game: Sport and British Society, 1910–1945* (Manchester: Manchester University Press, 1995), 317–33; Pierre Lanfranchi and Matthew Taylor, "Professional Football in World War Two Britain," in *War Culture: Social Change and Changing Experiences in World War Two*, eds. P. Kirkham and D. Thoms (London: Lawrence & Wishart, 1995), 187–97; and Norman Baker, "A More Even Playing Field? Sport During and After the War," in *Millions Like Us? British Culture in the Second World War*, eds. Nick Hayes and Jeff Hill (Liverpool: Liverpool University Press, 1999), 125–55.

27. Matthew Taylor, *The Association Game: A History of British Football* (Harlow: Pearson Education, 2008), 186; and Rippon, *Gas Masks*, 20–23.

their military service. However, the fans were well informed about who was stationed where and who was playing. Clubs that were located near army camps often had the best teams, as was the case with Darlington, which was able to draw on the reliable strength of the Wolverhampton Wanderers.

Wailing sirens often interrupted games, particularly in the south of the country. As players and spectators had to seek out shelters, a match could last three hours. This was naturally a great deal of time for someone to take in light of the complex organization of a difficult work day.[28] Admittedly, air attacks were greatly reduced after the victory in the Battle of Britain. However, rocket attacks and general fear did spoil the fun for fans.[29] Many stadiums were destroyed by bombs, or at least damaged to such an extent that they could not be reopened. The grass was also frequently unplayable.[30]

Noteworthy games such as the War Cup Final in the Empire stadium in London or the games between England, Scotland, Wales, and Northern Ireland were staged for propaganda purposes and were carried live on the radio. These games were attended by members of the royal family, high nobility, politicians, and members of the military, such as the popular marshal Montgomery.[31] In October 1941, 70,000 spectators watched a scoreless match between Scotland and England. Spitfires watched the air over the stadium, whose occupants included the exiled kings George of Greece and Haakon of Norway.[32] The not insignificant sums taken in admission for such games were given, partly for public relations purposes, to the Red Cross.[33] In 1944 and 1945 some British select teams participated in benefit games on behalf of the Aid to Russia Fund, the president of which was Winston Churchill's wife, Clementine.[34]

A number of football players fought for Great Britain, including on the very front lines, and gained distinction for their bravery. Many did not return home, and others were badly wounded.[35] However, numerous football players also enjoyed privileges. Many volunteered to serve

28. Taylor, *The Association Game*, 186.   29. Schleppi, "History," 9.
30. Rippon, *Gas Masks*, 93–117.   31. Ibid., 170.
32. Ibid., 175.   33. Ibid., 25 and 90.
34. Tommy Lawton, *Football Is My Business*, ed. Roy Peskett (London: Sporting Handbook, 1946), 95, 105, 110–21, and 142–45.
35. See Rippon, *Gas Masks*, 127–68.

in industries that were critical for the war effort, such as munitions factories or mines. Many of the best players were promoted as physical training instructors (PTIs) in the Royal Army or Royal Air Force. In 1940 no fewer than 154 football players served as PTIs far from the shooting. Others, like Matt Busby, were staff officers with the task of supporting the troops and improving their morale. He was responsible for the selection, the choice of tactics, and the training of the men whom he had recruited.[36] Tom Finney gave the following account to the historian Simon Kuper:

When I was called up I thought, well, I'm not going to see much football. I knew we were going to a good climate but I didn't know where until we arrived. And of course it was Suez, Egypt. I was stationed at a base depot there, and playing an awful lot of football really. And athletics, and generally, you know, it was a real surprise to me. Because they had a very good side there, called the Wanderers, which was pretty well a semi-professional team really.[37]

Thus, even if the FA Cup was not played again until the 1945–46 season and the professional league did not start up play again until the summer of 1946, the Second World War was far from a football-free period in Great Britain. However, the extent to which wartime football actually served to strengthen morale and the will of the British population to persevere remains a contested question.

"Sport Prepared You for War": German Football in Two World Wars

In the period before the First World War, the German Football Union was completely in line with the nationalist position and did not differ at all in this regard from the gymnasts. The burning problem in England regarding the continuation of championship play did not arise in Germany for two reasons. First, Germany was not even close to having professional football. There was no national league. Instead, the championship was played out in regional groups that were very similar to what was introduced in England after 1915. The second reason was that Germany

36. Taylor, *The Association Game*, 187.
37. Kuper, *Ajax, the Dutch, the War*, 154.

had universal military conscription from the beginning of the war, and so did not have to concern itself with recruitment in a manner similar to Great Britain.

The position of the DFB with regard to "war" was clearly outlined in the *German Football Yearbook* for 1913:

The times march along with weapons clanging, crushing with a steel fist what has become rotten and old, and fertilizing the land to overflowing with blood and bone. Clarion calls greet the advance that forces the wheel of fate forward. The struggle that takes place on the battlefield, and in the same manner in the factory, and the mine, in the house and in the field, is a fact of life, that no one will resolve if he simply wishes to bind up the wild spirits. Development, life means struggle, mother nature shows this everywhere! History has seen peoples rise and fall, and it was always victory that brought them forward, and always cowardly fear before the match that brought the fall. Man can only improve his character in regular conflict with others, who are better and stronger. But the fools in our own land call out: war to the war! It would be dangerous if their calls were to find success among the people. If we went back on our iron decision for weapons, then we would certainly be destroyed. Or have recent events not taught us what threats await emasculated peoples, that the law of jungle is in effect, and that this is eternal, because it brings life? We will be happy in Germany if a strong desire for struggle returns, and we give our welcome to the greatest prophet of this new age, namely sport.[38]

When war broke out in August 1914, General Field Marshal Freiherr von der Goltz, the founder of the Young Germany Union to which the DFB had belonged since its foundation in 1911, wrote to the German youth: "Young Germany has long been accustomed to the idea that it would be summoned to the defense of the fatherland. Now it appears that this is to be fulfilled sooner than we thought. Young Germany takes pleasure in this, and employs all of its strength to show that it is worthy of this task!"[39] The DFB itself did not refrain from this emotionalism: "Year in and year out we have struggled during the more than two decades of German football history. Now comes the great, true struggle. Now is the time to show courage and will to the utmost. It may be that

38. Alfred Rahn, "Von völkischer Arbeit des Sports im deutschen Land," *Deutsches Fussball-Jahrbuch 1913*, cited in Heinrich, *Fussballbund*, 42.

39. Freiherr von der Goltz, "An die deutsche Jugend," *Der Jungdeutschland-Bund* 3 (1914): 241, cited in Heinrich, *Fussballbund*, 42.

many skirmishes are lost. It may be that thousands, and thousands upon thousands, remain on the battlefield. But there is only one thing: the final victory for our flags."[40] Less emotional, but no less enthusiastic for war, the Northern German Football Association issued the followed statement: "Sport prepared you for war, so go at the enemy, and do not tremble!"[41]

The DFB and its regional associations seized upon the war as a welcome opportunity to finally overcome the societal reservations about "un-German" football and to present themselves as hyper-patriots. Football players were commanded to hold themselves up as role models on the front and thereby act as advertisements for their own sport.[42] Arguments like those of the English professional players in the autumn of 1914 that the games must continue with the elite players for the benefit of the nation were unthinkable in Wilhelmine Germany. The conscripted players went to the front and were replaced by those who had not yet been conscripted.

Special representation games were sometimes played for propaganda purposes, such as those between Berlin and Vienna or between Berlin and Budapest.[43] In addition, football also played an important role in military sports. According to the historian Peter Tauber, who first addressed this topic in a comprehensive manner in his doctoral thesis, the numerous football games played by German soldiers in the First World War were not only for the purpose of providing a diversion, but also to strengthen the soldiers' morale.[44] Football games served as a stabilizing factor among German troops when, for example, high-ranking officers such as Walter von Reichenau used the sport to gain social recognition for themselves among the other ranks. The close interlocking of football with the military gradually led to the Germanization of the sport. Categories such as determination, bravery, fortitude, and discipline were attached to the already existing values of the "British sport." In this manner, the canon of values of the sporting movement were expanded and

---

40. Alfred Perls, *Mitteldeutscher Sport,* cited in Heinrich, *Fussballbund*, 44.

41. Ibid.   42. Ibid., 45.

43. Eisenberg, *English Sports*, 314.

44. Peter Tauber, *Vom Schützengraben auf den grünen Rasen: Der Erste Weltkrieg und die Entwicklung des Sports in Deutschland* (Münster: Lit, 2008).

altered.[45] DFB officials were still convinced after the "great war" that the military had profited from the athletic development of its members. At the same time, during the war they had come a decisive step closer to the most important goal that they had set, namely, the development of football as the most popular German sport.

Football achieved its breakthrough as a mass sport in Germany during the interwar period. When war broke out in 1939, it was no longer the case, as it had been in 1914, that football was the pastime of a relatively small elite. Rather, it quite clearly had become the top spectator sport. Correspondingly, it was a public matter whether the popular players, in contrast to the population, enjoyed special privileges in wartime. The Nazi regime was therefore concerned to avoid the development of any rumors that top players received beneficial treatment. Consequently, in 1939–40 most of the national football players were conscripted into the German army. The national sports official Christian Busch commented on the situation as follows: "Our men no longer step on the field for international competitions, no longer do they participate in great festivals ... rather they go where the Führer and the high command of the army summon them."[46]

The championship competition was stopped suddenly on September 1, 1939. Just a few weeks later—Poland had been conquered in the meantime—the ban on competitions was loosened so that city championships and regional cup matches could again be played. In November the national minister for sport, Hans von Tschammer und Osten, ordered that national championship play be restarted.[47] Following the successful *Blitzkrieg* against the eastern neighbor, the regime was determined to give the population a sense that normalcy was returning.

Up through 1942 the German national team played numerous friendly matches against neutral, allied, and defeated states. Just after the beginning of the war, the Berlin *12 Uhr Blatt* programmatically declared: "Certainly, in light of the current situation, many of the planned international matches have to be cancelled. But in the future, athletic meetings will still take place with those nations that have not been

---

45. Tauber, *Vom Schützengraben*, 273. Also see Eisenberg, *English Sports*, 321.

46. Fischer, *Stürmer*, 113.

47. Ibid., 215.

ensnared by Judah and the hate-filled British commercialism. For it is precisely in times such as these that the value of athletic contests for the creation of understanding between nations should not be underestimated."[48] The national coach Sepp Herberger attempted to use the internal contradictions in official doctrine, which rejected the privileging of top athletes but was also quite aware of the propaganda value of athletic events, by summoning his fosterlings as often as possible to training courses, and to obtain special treatment for them even from their military superiors. In well-informed circles, these efforts were denoted as "operation stealing heroes."[49] However, the authorities then made it a rule that players could only be utilized on the field if they had already served on the front. The population had no tolerance for giving privileges to top athletes. Helmut Schön, who was declared unfit because of a protracted knee injury, was met with catcalls at away games with his team Dresdner SC, including "Helmut Schön k.v." (that is, fit for military service). The national player Edward Conen, who was stationed in Germany for a time, was sent back to the front following protests.[50]

The wartime international matches served propaganda functions in two different ways. For the purposes of internal consumption, they distracted people from the ongoing war and gave the appearance of normality. From the perspective of foreign policy, these games were intended to improve relationships with those nations with whom one was not at war through the medium of sport contacts. The German national team was intended to emphasize the strength of the Third Reich for both internal and external consumption. However, there were several glitches in this plan. In early 1941 the Germans lost a friendly match to the Swiss in Bern 1–2.[51] This loss was particularly bitter because it took place on April 20, the Führer's birthday. Helmut Schön, who was playing for the German national team at the time, later recalled: "It bordered on a high treason and lese majesty."[52] The minister of propaganda Goebbels wrote to national sport leader von Tschammer und Osten that in the future "no athletic contest will be permitted about which there is the least doubt about the outcome."[53] The next year, Germany lost against Sweden, and

48. Cited in ibid., 113.
50. Ibid., 228.
52. Leinemann, *Sepp Herberger*, 200.

49. Ibid., 118.
51. *Fussball-Woche*, April 22, 1941.
53. Fischer, *Stürmer*, 119.

this was a home match in Berlin, regarding which the state secretary Luther wrote from the Foreign Ministry: "100,000 people left the stadium depressed. For these people, a win in the match was more important than the capture of some city in the east. For the sake of the atmosphere in the country, it is necessary to prevent these kinds of events."[54]

The final wartime international match took place in November 1942 in Bratislava against Slovakia and ended in a 5–2 victory for Germany. The Germans, who under the best of circumstances received a cool reception in away matches, but rather more often were treated with hostility, faced undisguised hatred in the Slovakian metropolitan center, and there were even riots, as was also earlier the case in Denmark.[55] After the defeat at Stalingrad on February 20, 1943, the Third Reich ended all international matches.

By contrast, championship play in the country continued until 1944. The final game of the championship in the 1941–42 season between Schalke 04 and First Vienna FC was watched by 100,000 spectators in Berlin's Olympic stadium. The motives for continuing play in the middle of a World War are obvious. In February 1942 the national sport leader von Tschammer und Osten wrote regarding this issue: "It is critical to the war to incorporate sport events and competitions into the overall conduct of the war. Sport events and competitions of a local and neighborly character up through the district level are to be continued for the maintenance of the will to work and to carry on."[56] But the number of available players continued to decrease. In 1940 there were still 14,000 teams that participated in competitions, which was down from 30,000 in 1937. However, beginning in 1942–43, the situation became increasingly precarious. The teams had to continually change the composition of their rosters.[57]

The sixteen district leagues were discontinued in the 1944–45 season because of limited opportunities for travel. The remaining six hundred clubs and wartime sport collectives were divided into a hundred regional echelons. The playing strength of the clubs became increasingly uneven and led to an exceptionally large number of double-digit differentials in the final scores.[58] The mobilization of the *Volkssturm* (home

---

54. Cited in Teichler, *Internationale Sportpolitik im Dritten Reich*, 366.

55. Fischer, *Stürmer*, 123.

56. Cited in ibid., 223.

57. Ibid., 220–23.

58. Ibid., 222 and 224.

guard), which comprised the entire male population between the ages of 16 and 60, in September 1944 did not yet lead to the definitive end of championship and cup play. However, because of air attacks and the capture of German territory by allied forces, ever more games had to be moved or simply cancelled.[59] As late as the beginning of January 1945 there were still representative games between select teams from the north, south, east, and west.[60] On March 31, 1945, the National Socialist Party organ, the *Völkischer Beobachter*, placed sport in the service of Goebbels's campaign for perseverance, claiming that the continued playing of sports should be interpreted in the following manner: "This is less a demonstration of joy in track and field, or football games, or sport in general, than it is a sign of the vitality of a fighting community. A people, however, that continues to seek and find strength, excitement, and impetus in sport, will and must stand its ground."[61] In mid-April, TSV München 1860 won the final game for the Munich Tschammer cup.[62] The last known football game of the Third Reich took place on April 23, 1945, a week before Hitler's suicide in the Führer bunker in Berlin. FC Bayern München defeated its city rival TSV 1860 in a friendly match, 3–2.[63] On April 27, just two weeks before Germany's unconditional surrender, the *Völkischer Beobachter* reported in its penultimate edition on the beginning of the Bavarian spring championship, which was to commence on April 29. This competition could no longer be held.[64]

Football and "Active Service" in the Neutral Island of Peace

In August 1917, Charles-Ferdinand Ramuz, one of the most important names in Swiss literature, and probably the best known Swiss author in French, wrote in an article in the *Gazette de Lausanne* dealing with life in time of war, and was very positive about the game of football and

---

59. See, for example, *Völkischer Beobachter* (Munich edition), January 4, 1945; January 16, 1945; March 19, 1945; March 21, 1945; March 28, 1945; March 31, 1945; and April 27, 1945.

60. *Völkischer Beobachter* (Berlin edition), January 6, 1945.

61. *Völkischer Beobachter* (Munich edition), March 31, 1945.

62. *Völkischer Beobachter* (Munich edition), April 14, 1945 and April 17, 1945.

63. See *Völkischer Beobachter* (Munich edition), April 21, 1945; as well as Fischer, *Stürmer*, 225.

64. *Völkischer Beobachter* (Munich edition), April 27, 1945.

other entertainments.[65] Neutral Switzerland was one of the few European countries that was spared direct experience with military events in both World Wars, and was able to continue to play football with almost no interruptions. But the question then arises about what role football played in the war years, which were marked by the mobilization of the army, the transition to a bureaucratically directed wartime economy, a difficult balancing act with regard to both the internal and external economic and political position of the country, and finally challenges to the traditional order.

Championship play for the 1914–15 season was only begun after a delay of several weeks, since mobilization at first almost completely paralyzed the activities of the Football Association. Series A began at a greatly reduced level in the autumn of 1914. There were twenty-three teams in the 1913–14 season, playing in three groups. Only sixteen clubs entered the 1914–15 season. Because the number of groups also was increased by one, each club now only played six games in the championship competition, instead of the twelve to fourteen played a year earlier. In the 1915–16 season, there were twenty-one clubs, so that it was possible to return to the older format.[66]

Shortly before the outbreak of the war, articles appeared in the press claimed that more than 90 percent of football players had heart disease. The Football Association countered these claims in the context of the general mobilization of 1914 with the evidence that 96 percent of the players in Series A were mustered as fit for service.[67] The military authorities, who at first had been skeptical of football, increasingly came to recognize the physical conditioning of the mobilized football players. When FC Cantonal Neuchâtel won the second wartime championship in 1916, it had to gain leave for no fewer than ten players from active military service for the final game. The team received the following good luck telegram from divisional commander Treytorrens de Lloys, who had learned the game of football in the 1870s as a student at King's College London: "I am happy about your success, and about the thought that

65. *Gazette de Lausanne*, August 6, 1917.

66. See Ruoff, *Buch*, 239; Willy Baumeister, *50 Jahre Fussballclub Zürich 1896–1946* (Zurich: 1946), 21–23.

67. Giuliani, *Jugend*, 115.

the physical nurturing of our soldiers had a role in it."[68] The question of giving the players leave to participate in championship competitions remained an issue, but it was normally not a major problem.[69]

A bigger issue was the problem of where to hold the matches. Of the 923,500 square meters of land owned by the football clubs in 1914, 420,000 had to be used for agricultural purposes for the entire year, and a further 430,000 had to be made available from early in the year until autumn. More than half of the clubs in the Football Association thus had no place to play.[70] In the autumn of 1914, the stadium of FC Old Boys Basel was even used as a makeshift transit point to help Italians, who had fled from the warring states, to continue their journeys.[71] The problems of space, and the mobilization of most active players for military service led to an interruption in football's successful trajectory. In the period before the war the number of members in the Football Association rose very rapidly. However their numbers decreased during the war, from 15,256 to 13,564.[72]

Within weeks of the outbreak of war, there were games between military teams and between military teams and clubs.[73] The Football Association, which included several officers in its leadership, actively supported the playing of football in the army by organizing benefit games to support the distribution of footballs to active duty units.[74] The association also organized games where money was collected for needy and out-of-work soldiers, for their families, for Swiss expatriates in emergency situations, and for the Red Cross. These games further improved the image of the sport with both the population and with the authorities.[75]

International matches also did not come to a complete end. There

---

68. Jürg Schmid, *Schweizer Cup und Länderspiele: Nationalismus im Schweizer Fussballsport* (MA thesis, University of Zurich, 1986), 42.

69. *Gazette de Lausanne*, November 12, 1915, and December 7, 1915.

70. Schmid, *Schweizer-Cup*, 45.

71. *Die Schweizerische Grenzbesetzung 1914*. Basel: Frobenius, 1916, 9.

72. Ruoff, *Das goldene Buch des Schweizer Fussballs*, 239; Baumeister, *50 Jahre Fussballclub Zürich 1896–1946*, 21–23; Giuliani, *Jugend*, 120.

73. See, for example, *Gazette de Lausanne*, November 6, 1914; October 9, 1914; December 10, 1914; January 25, 1915; February 12, 1915; July 7, 1915; August 16, 1915; May 3, 1916; May 13, 1916; May 18, 1916; and August 3, 1917.

74. *Gazette de Lausanne*, June 30, 1915; September 4, 1916; and May 26, 1918.

75. See, for example, *Gazette de Lausanne*, June 26, 1915, and April 26, 1917; *Journal de Genève*, June 26, 1915; April 6, 1916; April 10, 1916; April 20, 1916; April 23, 1916; and July 24, 1916.

were five international matches up through 1918, three of which took place outside the country. After a pause of about half a year, the Swiss were the guests in January 1915 in Italy, which was still neutral at this point. By contrast, the game against France, which was supposed to take place in Geneva in November 1917, was cancelled because of the closed frontier. That same year, the Swiss association issued an invitation to the German Football Union for a friendly match. However, the Germans declined, pointing to "difficulties with vacations and deployment schedules."[76] In December 1917 the Swiss played two home games within the space of four days against Austria. In light of the drop off in membership dues, the association was in urgent need of income from admission to competitive matches. However, with 3,500 and 3,000 spectators respectively, these games were rather disappointing from a financial perspective.[77] Finally, in May 1918, there was a tour through the moribund Danubian monarchy with games in Vienna and Budapest against the national teams from Austria and Hungary. These games received very little public attention in the media. Despite the opposing sympathies in the different regions of the country for the various warring powers, these games were played without any political overtones.[78]

The opposition between the different language groups—German Swiss sympathized largely with the central powers, and the western Swiss with the Entente—was, however, reflected in events surrounding football. Just before the war began, a game between German Swiss and west Swiss sides, which was organized in the context of the national exposition in Bern, was played in a hate-filled atmosphere. The game ended with a 6–0 victory for the French-speaking team, and was recapitulated in both 1915 and 1916.[79] The western Swiss football players regularly demonstrated their solidarity with the Entente. In 1915 a select team from Geneva traveled to Lyon to play in a game to benefit French military invalids.[80] A

76. Cited in Christian Koller, "1898 bis 1919: 'Uneben und oft zerfahren,'" in *Die Nati: Die Geschichte der Schweizer Fussball-Nationalmannschaft*, ed. Beat Jung (Göttingen: Werkstatt, 2006), 34.

77. See, for example, *Gazette de Lausanne*, December 24, 1917 and December 28, 1917.

78. Koller, "1898 bis 1919," 32–34.

79. *Gazette de Lausanne*, April 15, 1915; May 15, 1915; May 17, 1915; September 15, 1916; and September 18, 1916.

80. *Journal de Genève*, May 28, 1915.

Franco-Belgian select squad played in Geneva against a western Swiss select team and also against Servette Geneva for the benefit of the French Red Cross and to purchase balls for Entente soldiers who were prisoners of war in Germany.[81] In 1916, there was a benefit game between two west Swiss squads on behalf of hospitalized French and Belgian internees,[82] and a game between Servette Geneva and a Catholic select team from Geneva for the benefit of blinded French soldiers.[83] The integration of refugees and interned Entente soldiers into domestic football demonstrated these same tendencies. In 1914 a school in Vevey created a team that included five Belgian refugees as players.[84] Teams comprised of British, French, and Belgian internees were favorite opponents of west Swiss sides.[85]

The starting conditions in 1939 were far different. With the National League, there was now a professional football championship. This situation, however, was not uncontested, and football went through a process of re-amateurization during the late 1930s and early 1940s.[86] The sensational victory against "Greater Germany" in the 1938 World Cup, however, had made clear, even among the ranks of the critics, the potential of professional football to act as a mobilizing factor on behalf of the "spiritual national defense."[87]

The general mobilization for war in September 1939 brought the regular championship competition to a standstill. An improvised mobilization championship was organized in its place.[88] The organization of this competition took place, not least, thanks to the support of the commander of the Swiss army, General Henri Guisan, whose selection to the top position in the army was greeted with great joy in sporting circles, where he was known as "Fussball-Henri" because of his enthusiasm for

81. *Gazette de Lausanne*, March 12, 1915; May 3, 1915; May 19, 1915; May 22, 1915; May 24, 1915; and May 25, 1915; *Journal de Genève*, May 23, 1915; May 24, 1915; and May 25, 1915.

82. *Gazette de Lausanne*, May 6, 1916.

83. *Journal de Genève*, May 8, 1916.

84. *Gazette de Lausanne*, December 19, 1914.

85. *Gazette de Lausanne*, October 9, 1916; January 5, 1917; and April 9, 1918.

86. See Koller, *Schweizer Fussball*.

87. See, for example, *Sport*, June 17, 1938; as well as Koller and Brändle, *Eidgenossen*.

88. *Gazette de Lausanne*, September 8, 1939; September 15, 1939; October 2, 1939; October 11, 1939; and January 15, 1940; *Journal de Genève*, September 14, 1939; October 22, 1939; and July 24, 1940; as well as Fritz Pieth, *Sport in der Schweiz: Sein Weg in die Gegenwart*. Olten: Walter, 1979, 140; Andreas Schoch, "Die Schweizer Fussball-Nationalmannschaft 1904–1945: Fussball-Spitzensport und dessen politische Instrumentalisierung," MA thesis, University of Zurich, 2004, 79.

football.[89] A largely regular schedule of games was already being orga-nized for the 1940–41 season. No later than 1943, there were no longer any difficulties in obtaining leave for National League players in active service so that they could play in championship games.[90]

Football played an important role in maintaining the morale and will to persevere in both the army and the population. International football matches, as will be seen in greater detail below, were staged in a manner that fit neatly with national events. Just as had been true dur-ing the First World War, playing football in the army was important. This took place in public matches between larger army units in which top players participated and which were viewed by high-ranking military officers. Games also were organized between military select teams and top clubs.[91]

The value placed on football by leaders in the government and in the army is demonstrated by the subsidies provided by the federal De-partment of the Military. The Football Association had to bear dispro-portionate cuts as a consequence of cost-saving measures during the 1930s. By contrast in 1944, a time when the grant of federal money was increasingly tied to criteria such as military training and paramilitary sports, football was the only sports association to receive substantially higher subsidies than it had requested.[92] On the other side, the Football Association supported a call in 1940 for the introduction of mandatory gymnastic-military training of the male youth. However, the project

89. *Journal de Genève*, September 1, 1939.

90. Christian Koller, "Le Championnat et la Guerre," in *75 Ans Swiss Football League—Ligue Nationale ASF*, ed. Philippe Guggisberg (Köniz: Ast und Jakob, Vetsch AG, 2009), 37–54.

91. See, for example, *Sport*, June 3, 1941; *Gazette de Lausanne*, September 29, 1939; Novem-ber 4, 1939; November 6, 1939; December 5, 1939; December 13, 1939; December 15, 1939; Decem-ber 18, 1939; April 19, 1940; May 3, 1940; August 13, 1940; September 6, 1940; September 14, 1940; October 4, 1940; October 7, 1940; May 23, 1941; May 27, 1941; October 6, 1941; September 15, 1942; September 19, 1942; September 21, 1942; July 20, 1944; July 24, 1944; and February 1, 1945; *Jour-nal de Genève*, September 16, 1939; October 29, 1939; October 31, 1939; November 5, 1939; Novem-ber 6, 1939; December 16, 1939; December 18, 1939; July 27, 1940; July 30, 1940; August 7, 1940; August 23, 1940; August 24, 1940; September 4, 1940; September 20, 1941; September 24, 1941; September 28, 1941; October 2, 1941; October 3, 1941; October 4, 1941; September 16, 1942; Sep-tember 21, 1942; May 3, 1944; July 20, 1944; and July 25, 1944.

92. Christian Koller, "Sport, Parteipolitik und Landesverteidigung: Die Auseinanderset-zungen um die Subventionierung des schweizerischen Arbeitersports in der Zwischenkriegs-zeit," *SportZeiten* 3, no. 2 (2003): 52; and Giuliani, *Jugend*, 203.

from the Department of the Military was rejected in a plebiscite by 56 percent of those voting.[93]

The issue of having a place to play again became a problem.[94] Admittedly, the total surface area of all Swiss football fields taken together amounted to just 0.62 percent of the requisite 50,000 hectares of additional land that was required for the so-called "cultivation battle."[95] However, pictures of football fields transformed into acres of potatoes played a significant role in the propaganda for the effort (which proved to be only modestly successful) to achieve independence in food production. Although the Federal Office for Wartime Food Production showed itself to be cooperative in some cases, the consequences for broad-based football were necessarily grave.[96] The number of active football players in the Swiss Football and Athletic Association shrank from 76,254 to 61,767 during the first two years of the war, rising only to 74,132 by the end of the war.[97]

In contrast to the Swiss army, following the beginning of the war, the Swiss national football team did not retreat to its redoubt. The Swiss A-national team played in sixteen official international matches during the Second World War, of which eleven were against the Axis powers and their allies (Germany, Italy, Hungary, and Vichy France), and four against neutral states (Spain, Portugal, and Sweden). In addition, there were three unofficial games against Croatia and one against AS Saint-Etienne. Planned games against Belgium, Yugoslavia, Finland, Sweden, Portugal, Hungary, Bulgaria, and Slovakia had to be cancelled. The B-national team played twice against a select team from the "free zone" in France in 1940–41.[98] It was only following the change in the general military situa-

---

93. Giuliani, *Jugend*, 593–698.

94. See, for example, *Sport*, January 29, 1941; *Journal de Genève*, April 20, 1941 and April 28, 1942; *Gazette de Lausanne*, February 16, 1944, and March 22, 1944.

95. Giuliani, *Jugend*, 251.

96. *Gazette de Lausanne*, March 8, 1944.

97. Giuliani, *Jugend*, 120.

98. See Christian Koller, "1938 bis 1945: Landesverteidigung mit dem runden Leder," in *Die Nati: Die Geschichte der Schweizer Fussball-Nationalmannschaft*, 63–88. Regarding the issue of media coverage, see Christian Koller, "Elf Fussballsoldaten verteidigen die Eidgenossenschaft—Zur medialen Repräsentation der Schweizer Fussballnationalmannschaft im Zeitalter der 'Geistigen Landesverteidigung,'" in *Mediensport: Strategien der Grenzziehung*, eds. Felix Axster et al. (Munich: Fink, 2009), 147–65.

tion that the opponents began to change. In April 1945 there was a game against the now-free France with the French ambassador in attendance. This was the only game played by the A-national team against an allied power.[99]

All of these games were organized by the Football Association, but under the indirect oversight of the federal authorities. The Swiss federal government expressly endorsed sport contacts with the Third Reich in a circular letter sent to athletic associations in March 1941, "also in light of the prospective shaping of international relations," and lamented that these contacts had come to almost a complete halt since the outbreak of the war.[100] However, this position was revised in October 1942 as the government now urged restraint in regard to athletic contacts with Germany and claimed a right of veto. The authorities also granted the Football Association a free hand in choosing the players for the national team, including some rather controversial decisions. On the one hand, the German Jew Hans-Peter Friedländer had become a Swiss citizen in 1940 after living there for fifteen years and thus could make his debut on the national team in 1942. On the other hand, the Austrian Karl Rappan was reappointed to his position as national coach in 1942, although the federal prosecutor's office was aware of his membership in the Nazi Party.[101]

The home games of the national team were played in the presence of prominent politicians and military officers, and the players, most of whom traveled in uniform, were greeted personally at several games by General Guisan.[102] The high point from an athletic perspective, but also in the context of ongoing diplomatic affairs, was the game against Germany on April 20, 1941. The Swiss won a surprising 2–1 victory in the Bern Wankdorf stadium. Thirteen chartered trains brought about

99. *Tages-Anzeiger*, April 7, 1945; *Sport*, April 9, 1945; *Gazette de Lausanne*, April 9, 1945, and April 10, 1945; *Journal de Genève*, January 20, 1945, and April 9, 1945.

100. Swiss Federal Archives E27: 8559 circular letter from member of federal councillor K. Kobelt to the SLL, to the Swiss shooting federation, to the federal wrestling association and the committee for multisport race in the army, March 5, 1941.

101. Beat Jung, "Karl Rappan—ein 'Nazi' für die Nati," in *Die Nati: Die Geschichte der Schweizer Fussball-Nationalmannschaft*, 119.

102. *Gazette de Lausanne*, November 3, 1939; Severino Minelli, "Meine 14 Jahre bei der Schweizer Fussball-Nationalelf 1930–1943," *Küsnachter Jahresblätter* (1968): 60; Jacques Ducret, *Das Goldene Buch des Schweizer Fussballs* (Lausanne: L'Age d'homme, 1994), 109.

15,000 people to Bern, so that in the end 38,000 spectators watched the game. Officially, the friendly character of the game was stressed. In addition to the general, a member of the federal government, two members of the Bernese cantonal government, the mayor of Bern, and numerous high-ranking staff officers also attended the match. The representatives on the German side included a member of the embassy staff, a military attaché, and the mayor of Stuttgart.[103] The Swiss victory on the Führer's birthday not only sent the German propaganda minister Goebbels into a rage, it also led to delirious joy throughout Switzerland, which recalled the scene following the victory against the same opponent in the 1938 World Cup. In the lead-up to the match, media outlets were forbidden by the Federal Commission for Radio and Press to make any political comments. Because of violations of these conditions, the social democratic *Berner Tagwacht* and the west Swiss specialized journal *Le Sport Suisse* were temporarily banned.[104]

The games against Germany and Italy served as demonstrations of the friendly relations with the two states, with which extensive economic contacts were maintained during the war but which also posed a threat to Swiss independence and whose political systems were rejected by broad sections of the Swiss population. By contrast, the matches against neutral Sweden in November 1942 in Zurich and in June 1943 in Stockholm were actually friendly games against a country with which Switzerland felt strong political ties. Thus the *Neue Zürcher Zeitung* noted "the friendly demonstration of a neutral point of view," and the *Sport* mentioned alleged age-old Germanic "bonds of blood" that ostensibly persisted between the Swiss and the Swedes.[105] At the banquet after the game in Zurich, the Swedish representative Westrup stressed "the agreement between views that prevailed in Sweden and in Switzerland regarding war and peace" and said that "current events, which have been

103. *Sport*, April 18, 1941; April 21, 1941; April 23, 1941; and April 25, 1941; *Berner Tagwacht*, April 21, 1941; *Neue Zürcher Zeitung*, April 21, 1941; as well as Christian Koller, "Fussballerische Landesverteidigung an Führers Geburtstag: Schweiz—Deutschland 2:1 (20.4.1941)," *Sternstunden des Schweizer Fussballs*, ed. Christian Koller (Münster: Lit, 2008), 63–75.

104. *Berner Tagwacht*, April 23, 1941; *Sport*, April 21, 1941; Emile Birbaum, *Rencontres sportives et voyages, 1904–1954* (Lugano: Tipografia, 1954), 123–25; and Georg Kreis, *Zensur und Selbstzensur: Die schweizerische Pressepolitik im Zweiten Weltkrieg* (Stuttgart: Huber, 1973), 453.

105. *Neue Zürcher Zeitung*, November 16, 1942; *Sport*, November 13, 1942.

the cause of so much apprehension and unhappiness, at least have had the benefit of bringing Switzerland and Sweden closer together."[106]

After the war, football served as a means of reestablishing friendly relations with the northern neighbor. As early as 1946 and 1947, Swiss football teams broke through the isolation that had been imposed on Germany, including in the athletic sphere, and played the first friendly matches in the southern German region. In September 1948 FC Wiesloch was the first German team to travel outside the country after the war, for an international match in the Zurich suburb of Schlieren. During the reception for the German team, which included members of the district government, there were frequent references to football's mission to bring about reconciliation between peoples.[107] Three weeks later there were games in Stuttgart, Munich, and Karlsruhe between local teams, and select squads from Zurich, St. Gall, and Basel, respectively, which had a powerful effect in Germany.[108] The organizers of the games—which included both Swiss sports officials and the sports officer of the American military government—acted against the embargo that FIFA had imposed on Germany, and did so in the name of bringing about reconciliation between the peoples. The Swiss Football Association sanctioned these offenses with a more or less symbolic punishment of the Swiss organizers of the games, but at the same time demanded a lifting of the embargo against Germany, with the argument that "if Germany is to be healed" it must be brought back into contact with the democratic world. It was not until 1950 that the DFB was brought back into FIFA following energetic lobbying by Ernst B. Thommen, the central president of the Swiss Football Association. On November 22, the German national football team returned to the international stage with a 1–0 victory over Switzerland.[109]

106. *Neue Zürcher Zeitung*, December 17, 1942.

107. *Sport*, September 29, 1948, as well as Eugen Hochstrasser and Hans Stahel, *Jubiläumsschrift 75 Jahre FC Schlieren* (Schlieren: Fussball-Club Schlieren, 1996), 34–39.

108. See *Neue Zürcher Zeitung*, October 11, 1948; as well as Max Rüdlinger and Urs Frieden, "Vor 50 Jahren: Schweizer Fussballer missachten Verbot: 'Man spielt wieder mit uns,'" *Die WochenZeitung*, October 8, 1998.

109. The basic studies regarding the role played by sports in the reintegration of the Federal Republic into the international community of nations are Henry Wahlig, *Ein Tor zur Welt? Der deutsche Fussball und die FIFA 1945–1950* (Göttingen: Werkstatt, 2008); and Siegfried Gehrmann, "Le sport comme moyen de réhabilitation nationale au début de la République Fédérale

Conclusion

A comparison of the British, German, and Swiss experiences during the World Wars clearly shows that athletes were understood as role models in both official and popular perception, and that it was consequently expected that football would "put its men" into military service during times of war. In contrast to members of the political elite, athletes were not seen as indispensable. In all three of the cases considered here, because the population was opposed to special treatment for athletes, the authorities could take a hard line, knowing that a hoped-for propaganda effect from the ostentatious granting of special privileges for athletes would immediately fail. Thus they only organized special sporting events that could be accommodated, at least to some degree, within the "normal" demands of military service. However, the propaganda value of these sport events also was quite well known. Strikingly, these events could be organized somewhat better in states with universal military conscription than they could in Great Britain, where there was a fear that they would have a negative impact on recruitment efforts. In all three states considered here, the conflict in goals ultimately resulted in a compromise that tended more to one side or the other, depending on the actual military situation.

---

d'Allemagne: Les Jeux Olympiques de 1952 et la Coupe du Monde de Football de 1954," in *Sports et relations internationales*, 231–43.

10 | *Football and Gender*

For a long time, football was seen as the epitome of masculinity. In contrast to highly paid male stars, women's football, insofar as it existed, had a puny presence, and was mocked and belittled with sexist comments by "experts" sitting around local pubs, if they took any notice of it at all. Football-playing women only really came to the notice of these circles when the Matildas, the players on the Australian national women's team, put a naked calendar on the market in 2000.

Even the terminology points to an asymmetry with regard to the sexes. Football played by women is generally denoted as "women's football," while football played by men is simply "football." As a rule, boys are supported in their passion for football from childhood, while girls with the same interests frequently are encouraged to pursue other, "more feminine," less "hard" sports. But it is not only on the green turf that men dominate. Female faces long have been an infrequent occurrence among the ranks of spectators as well. Apparently, the prospect of being able to observe thoroughly trained male bodies in shorts for ninety minutes did not attract many women to the stadium, while numerous other men did not, under any circumstances, wish to miss this opportunity.

This image of an overwhelmingly male-dominated sport is almost completely reversed when one considers the situation in the United States. Here, soccer has long been a sport for elementary and high schools, played predominantly by girls and women, while a "real" man focused on the "harder" sports such as American football or baseball. Men who played soccer were long considered to be weaklings, and only recently have not had to justify themselves to their athletic comrades in the other sports. In addition, the masculine socialization of the true American did not take place, as for example in England or Scotland, at the father's side in the football stadium, but rather at a baseball game, as can be seen in the novels of Philip Roth or Don DeLillo.[1] The Super Bowl, which is the final game of the National Football League, is comparable in terms of masculine heroization and myth creation with the European Football Cup finals, while soccer does not have a similar fixed point in the annual calendar.

These observations indicate that the question of whether a particular sport is masculine, feminine, or gender neutral is not dependent in the first instance on its structure, rules, or conduct. The decisive factors are rather societal conventions. Girls are not supposed to play football because this does not belong to girls, because it is clear that girls do not play football, and so on. Certain sports, and here football has an exceptionally important place, are to a high degree gendered, to use a favorite expression of scholarship in the cultural sciences. The term "gender," in contrast to the biologically determined "sex," concerns the "nature" and "roles" of the sexes as these are determined by societally dominant and historically determined conceptions, relational categories regarding the interplay between men and women. It has become the dominant view in social and cultural history over the past few decades that descriptions of human societies in the past are only adequate if they include an investigation of the relationships between men and women alongside the categories of rich and poor, powerful and weak, as well as native and foreign.[2]

The social and cultural history of football is highly suitable for an investigation of the questions of gender history. First, it can be asked why football in Europe and Latin America is commonly accepted as typically masculine, which quickly leads to general observations regarding the gendered structure of the relevant societies.[3] One can also turn this question around and investigate the consequences that the conception

1. Philip Roth, *The Great American Novel* (New York: Holt Rinehart and Winston, 1973); and Don DeLillo, *Underworld* (New York: Scribner, 1997).

2. See, for example, the programmatic essays by Joan W. Scott, "Gender: A Useful Category of Historical Analysis," *American Historical Review* 91 (1986): 1053–75; and Gisela Bock, "Geschichte, Frauengeschichte, Geschlechtergeschichte," *Geschichte und Gesellschaft* 14 (1988): 364–91.

3. In the early days of Argentinian football, however, the players typified the youth rather than adult men. See, for example, Edoardo P. Archetti, "Playing Styles and Masculine Virtues in Argentine Football," in *Machos, Mistresses, Madonnas: Contesting the Power of Latin American Gender Imagery*, eds. Marit Melhuus and Anne Stølen (London: Verso, 1996), 34–55.

of football as typically masculine has for football itself and also for society as a whole. In this chapter we will analyze the "masculinity" of the
male sport of football. We will make use of a concept that has proven
itself useful in research regarding gender, the idea of *Maennerbund*, that
is, male societies characterized by specific rules, rituals, symbols, and internal hierarchies.[4] We will also investigate the difficulties that women
who played football confronted in the past and still face, to a certain extent, today. It will be shown that these difficulties are closely connected
with the character of football as a Maennerbund.

Football and *Maennerbund*

The gendered nature of football was already clear in the nineteenth century. As we have seen, football played an important role in its elite phase
in the establishment and reproduction of a very specific concept of masculinity, the ideal of the "gentleman." The transformation of football
into a mass sport changed, to a certain extent, the underlying ideals of
masculinity. However, the foundational fact that football was a locus of
masculine self-representation changed very little. Football remained a
starkly masculine sport.

Social and cultural scholarship presents Maennerbund as those formal and informal groupings of men that are characterized by the clear
drawing of boundaries against the outside, and the inward staging of
"masculine" behavioral patterns. Instruction in aggression and violence
as well as the practice of gender-specific behavior roles have an important function in "masculine" socialization in male societies. The need for
men to participate in groups of this kind is explained by psychology, in
part, as going back to the fact that boys, in contrast to girls, were raised

4. With regard to the concept of the Maennerbund see, for example, Thomas Schweizer,
"Männerbünde und ihr kultureller Kontext im weltweiten interkulturellen Vergleich," in *Männer-
bande—Männerbünde: Zur Rolle des Mannes im Kulturvergleich*, eds. Gisela Völger and Karin von
Welck (Cologne: Rautenstrauch-Joest-Museum für Völkerkunde, 1990), 1:23–30; Helmut Blazek,
Männerbünde: Eine Geschichte von Faszination und Macht (Berlin: Aufbau Taschenbuch Verlag,
2001); Jürgen Reulecke, *"Ich möchte einer werden, so wie die ...": Männerbünde im 20. Jahrhundert*
(Frankfurt: Campus, 2001; and Ulrik Brunotte, *Zwischen Eros und Krieg: Männerbund und Ritual
in der Moderne* (Berlin: Wagenbach, 2004). Regarding the genesis of this concept, see Claudia
Bruns, *Politik des Eros: Der Männerbund in Wissenschaft, Politik und Jugendkultur (1880–1934)* (Cologne: Böhlau, 2008).

by caregivers of the opposite sex, and thus required a separation into purely male company in order to find their own personality and develop a stable masculine identity. In sum, according to the relevant research, Maennerbund societies served above all to demonstrate masculine dominance and enforce patriarchal heterosexual hegemony.

As a result of his research into the early German gymnastics movement and an English rugby club, the psychologist Michael Klein developed the thesis that "sport clubs" were Maennerbund societies par excellence.[5] It was here that those male-centered values, which were highly prized by society, were represented. The factors that are attributed to sport as a "worthy educational tool" are revealed, under closer inspection, to be simply instruction in violence and aggression—exercises in sexist modeling in the devaluation of women up to the point of misogyny as well as the stylization of masculine dominance and conceptions of superiority. There are at least three areas in which examples of Maennerbund can be localized in the world of football: the official caste in associations and clubs, the teams, and finally the fan groups, which often come very close to the ideal type of the Maennerbund in both their behavior and in their orientation.

As a rule, the leadership echelons of the clubs and in the committees of the national and international societies are comprised almost entirely of the lords of creation. As was shown above, male sociability was always an important element of membership in the very first football clubs of the nineteenth century. This has hardly changed up to the present day. The behavioral scientist Desmond Morris, who has studied football clubs as "tribes" using cultural anthropological methods, describes the heads of the clubs as a "council of the tribal elders," and thus draws a powerful analogy with the patriarchal structure of traditional societies.[6] The situation is not usually any different in the associations. So it is hardly surprising that it is always men who stand at the top of the most important organizations of national and international football, and that both in their disposition and in their association policies truly embody the ideal type of the patriarch. In particular, the dealings of the associations with women's football, which will be treated in detail below, dem-

5. Michael Klein, "Sportbünde—Männerbünde?," in *Männerbande—Männerbünde*, 137–48.
6. Morris, *Spiel*, 216–21.

onstrate their Maennerbund character. Football-playing women were excluded from the associations until they threatened to present a source of competition through the foundation of their own institutions. At this point, an effort was made to control women's football in a paternalistic manner. The men did not want "their" sport to be taken away by the other gender.

The football teams represent a different type of Maennerbund than the clubs and associations. The observation that in football, in contrast to other sports, mixed teams are almost unheard of points to the male-centric formation of the football team (which in German is called *Mannschaft*, literally "crew of men"). The Maennerbund character of football teams is made particularly clear by the fact that the damaging effects of sexual activities before playing a game was a long-simmering topic of discussion in sports medicine. Despite opposing scientific findings, many coaches, until very recently, held the view that sex before a game impaired physical performance, and therefore forbade the wives of the players from coming to training camps.[7] The commonly used expression "barracking" to denote football players in training also points to the Maennerbund par excellence, namely the military. Both institutions share the same view that the presence of women is damaging to fighting strength.

This strong Maennerbund conception often had the consequence that within the official male societal "team," there was an informal Maennerbund that was directed against the authority of the coach that has strong parallels with a certain form of military comradeship. The stories of groups of football players visiting brothels are abundant. A somewhat unusual example of this kind of unofficial Maennerbund concerns George Best and his teammates in the 1960s. Best is reported to have had sexual relations with more than a thousand young women early in his career, including with seven girls within the span of twenty-four hours. Strikingly, the young star did not utilize his attractiveness to the world of women for himself alone. Instead, it soon became his practice to allow his teammates to hide in closets and behind curtains so that they could watch him as he engaged in the sexual act.[8] By making them public, Best fundamentally

---

7. See, for example, *Sport*, April 12, 1994.

8. M. Parkinson, *Best: An Intimate Biography* (London: Arrow Books, 1975), cited in Morris, *Spiel*, 184.

altered the nature of his affairs. What had the potential to threaten the Maennerbund when one individual had to answer for the intrusion of the other sex into the male preserve, became instead a means of strengthening the Maennerbund and at the same time a reinforcement of the collective experience of the internal hierarchy, that is, a demonstration of male potency and superiority as well as the degradation of the woman into a mere object of lust.

The widespread homophobia that is to be found even today among not only the fans but also among players and coaches is also closely connected with Maennerbund character of the football team. Occasional comments by prominent football players and coaches such as, for example, the idea that gay football players are not "real" men or that they cannot really play, are not infrequent even today. Most homosexual top players, therefore, recoil from "coming out."[9] The up-and-coming German talent Marcus Urban decided against a professional career in the early 1990s in order to avoid the pressure to hide the fact that he was homosexual.[10] The Englishman Justin Fashanu outed himself in 1990, the first professional player to do so. Eight years later, he committed suicide because of a never-proven charge of rape. The American professional Robbi Rogers in 2013 came out and announced his retirement from professional sports at the same time. A short time later, however, he announced his comeback and thereafter played as the first professed homosexual in Major League Soccer.

Fan groups represent yet another form of male society. As Peter Becker demonstrated in a stimulating essay, the activities of youth fan groups are oriented towards a "masculine grammar."[11] In large part, their conduct turns on the demand for and defense of power and masculine honor, which is mirrored in the forms of their physical presentation, in the text of their songs and conversations, in their behavior toward women, in their drinking behavior, and in the content of magazines and

9. See, for example, Andreas Erb and Dirk Leibfried, *Das Schweigen der Männer: Homosexualität im deutschen Fussball* (Göttingen: Werkstatt, 2011).

10. Ronnie Blaschke, *Versteckspieler: Die Geschichte des schwulen Fussballers Marcus Urban* (Göttingen: Werkstatt, 2008).

11. Peter Becker, "Fussballfans: Vormoderne Reservate zum Erwerb und zur Verteidigung männlicher Macht und Ehre," in *Männerbande—Männerbünde: Zur Rolle des Mannes im Kulturvergleich*, 149–56.

newspapers. Behaving like a "true" fan, requires, in the first instance, that one adhere to a strict code of conduct.

The most important challenge to the power of the fan group is the slanderous provocation by a rival group.[12] This could be verbal. In this context, the denigration of the opposing team and their supporters, which impugns their manhood, plays a central role. For example, there are chants that the players on the opposing team were cuckolded by their wives, or that they are homosexuals. One favorite suggestion is that the opposing players and their fans had to get their sexual satisfaction from masturbation. An analysis of the songs of the supporters of Oxford United has unearthed no fewer than seven different "masturbation chants" ("We all agree NN is a wanker," etc.).[13] Alongside this verbal abuse, there is an entire palette of nonverbal provocations, beginning with obscene gestures and the theft of the opposing teams' scarves and banners up to invading the opposing fan block during the game or the opposition's favorite pub after the game. Such border violations are understood as attacks on the collective honor of the group and must be answered with counter-provocations in order to restore this honor. As a consequence, there can be violent excesses, and even traditions of violence between arch-enemies. An attack on collective honor is at the same time a challenge to the honor of each member of the collective.[14] In extreme cases, if a fan wishes to reestablish his honor, he must give greater precedence to revenge than to his own physical well-being. Becker sees this as a parallel to the classical duels of the aristocratic and bourgeois elite.[15] Whoever refuses to accept this mechanism falls in the collective esteem of his own fan group.

There are two primary reasons why women are not welcome in these male societal groups. Because they are not in a position to respond on their own to dishonoring attacks in a "masculine" manner, they repre-

12. Basic for the role of honor in modern society is Ludgera Vogt, *Zur Logik der Ehre in der Gegenwartsgesellschaft: Differenzierung, Macht, Integration* (Frankfurt: Suhrkamp, 1997).

13. Morris, *Spiel*, 312.

14. Fundamental for the relationship between individual and collective honor is Georg Simmel, *Soziologie: Untersuchungen über die Formen der Vergesellschaftung* (Munich: Duncker & Humblot, 1923), 326.

15. Crucial on this point are Ute Frevert, *Ehrenmänner: Das Duell in der bürgerlichen Gesellschaft* (Munich: Beck, 1991); and Kevin McAleer, *Duelling: The Cult of Honor in Fin-de-Siècle Germany* (Princeton, N.J.: Princeton University Press, 1994).

sent an additional burden to the men in their group as a potential object of provocation. A fan who is not able to defend his girlfriend must
assume that he will lose his social position within the group. A second
threat for the fan comes from the potential that his girlfriend will be
unfaithful and will shame him in front of the group. These dangers can
be avoided if women are excluded from the activities of the group. If
women do, however, appear with the group, it is expected that they will
adhere to very traditional and stereotypical feminine roles. They should
be caring, willing to sacrifice themselves, and selfless, as well as give
warmth and security to the "heroes."

On the basis of this description, Becker characterizes the football
fan as having a generally anachronistic and pre-modern behavioral structure.[16] In an era in which individuals are required to maintain a high level
of control over their emotions and to possess the capacity for dissocia-
tion, and in which social positions overwhelmingly are distributed on the
basis of one's achievements, fan groups are a locus where the ability to
maintain and defend one's masculine honor is the one factor that counts.
It is a place where the hierarchy depends upon premodern mechanisms.[17]

This raises the question of the extent to which the phenomenon of
the violent fan group, the so-called issue of hooliganism, is related to this
diagnosis.[18] Soon after football left the gates of the elite public schools,
the problem arose that although the game was no longer a brawl between
violent masses, violence had by no means disappeared from the game.
The violence had simply moved from the turf into the stands. Admittedly,
William McGregor, one of the founding fathers of the Football League,
said in 1907 that football attracted the middle class and the "more respectable" levels of the working class.[19] The consumption of football was
seen as a means of fighting the alcoholism that was rampaging among
the working classes. But from the very foundation of the Football League
up to the First World War there was a large range of offenses that later

16. A similar point is made by Thomas Gehrmann, *Fussballrandale: Hooligans in Deutschland*
(Essen: Klartext, 1990), 169–72.

17. The classic work is Pierre Bourdieu, *Outline of a Theory of Practice* (Cambridge: Cambridge University Press, 1977).

18. For an impressive personal account of this issue, see Bill Buford, *Among the Thugs* (London: Vintage, 1990).

19. Eric Dunning et al., *The Roots of Football Hooliganism: An Historical and Sociological
Study* (London: Routledge, 1988), 39.

would be subsumed under the general term "hooliganism": invading the playing field, cursing, vandalism, and actual attacks against players, officials, and opposing fans.[20] In almost every year from 1895 to 1914, at least one club each year was called to account for such offenses.[21] The culprits were usually denoted as blackguards rather than hooligans.[22]

Violence did not disappear from the stands during the interwar period. However, it did diminish somewhat and was not seen by contemporaries as a problem. It was during this period that increasing numbers of men from the middle and upper classes, as well as some women, made their way into the stadium alongside workers. Thus, half of the passengers on the trains that carried supporters of the Bolton Wanderers and the team from Portsmouth to London for the cup finals in 1929 were women.[23] However, in the 1930s, the level of violence began to increase somewhat. The 1940s and early 1950s were again relatively quiet. At the end of the 1950s, the so-called Teddy Boys (or *Halbstarke* as they used to be called in German)[24] started to become a topic of discussion.[25] This public problematization of the violent behavior of the youth soon began to be directed against football fans. In the period leading up to the 1966 World Cup, hooliganism was treated in the public discourse in Great Britain as a distinct social problem.[26]

At the end of the 1960s, this problem developed a new dimension following the introduction of the skinhead subculture. As soon as they began appearing in football stadiums, the "skins" cultivated their "masculine" toughness through violence against non-whites, homosexuals, and hippies. They also played a significant role in the expansion of hooli-

20. See the tables in Dunning, *Roots*, 51.

21. Ibid., 52.

22. Ibid., 76. The use of the term "hooligans" for those who caused a ruckus seems to have appeared quite early and to have been used broadly on an international basis. It was already being used, for example, in St. Petersburg at the turn of the century. See, Joan Neuberger, *Hooliganism: Crime, Culture, and Power in St. Petersburg, 1900–1914* (Berkeley: University of California Press, 1993), 1. It was also used in a German book in 1919 to describe an aroused rabble during the Bolshevik revolution. See Hans Vorst, *Das bolschewistische Russland* (Leipzig: Der neue Geist, 1919), 112.

23. Schulze-Marmeling, *Fussball*, 93.

24. See Thomas Grotum, *Die Halbstarken: Zur Geschichte einer Jugendkultur der 50er Jahre* (Frankfurt: Campus, 1994).

25. On this point, see Dunning, *Roots*, 161–64.

26. Dunning, *Roots*, 141.

ganism outside of the stadiums. Acts of vandalism and violence were no longer limited to the standing room areas around the field. Train stations and entire inner cities now took center stage. This development peaked in the mid-1970s with the phenomenon of "super-hooliganism." The actions of the "hools" now were rarely spontaneous any longer. Rather, they tended to be planned, not least to counter an increasing police presence.[27] In the mid-1980s, this phenomenon reached its high point of visibility with the catastrophe at Heysel.[28] From this point onward, the questions about hooliganism increasingly took on political overtones, particularly in regard to its proximity to organized right-wing extremism.[29]

In addition to popular efforts to explain hooliganism, which include alcoholism, youth unemployment, and the supposedly excessive tolerance of the society, there were also various theories from the social and cultural sciences to explain the violence taking place in and around football stadiums.[30] Marxists depicted hooliganism, which was considered a new phenomenon of the 1960s, as resulting from the dissolution of the traditional working-class milieu, and the increasingly bourgeois nature and internationalization of football. Thus a subculture developed within the group of unemployed youth. They were inspired by the belief that club politics were once more democratic, and were opposed to the growing bourgeois element among the spectators at games, as well as the lifestyle of the highly paid stars.[31] This view is denoted as "soccer

27. Ibid., 177–81. Also see Dunning et al., *Hooligans Abroad: The Behaviour and Control of English Fans in Continental Europe* (London: Routledge, 1984).

28. For an overview of the scholarly and political discussions of the phenomenon of hooliganism from the 1960s until the 1990s, see Richard Giulianotti, "Social Identity and Public Order: Political and Academic Discourses on Football Violence," in *Football, Violence and Social Identity*, ed. Richard Giulianotti (London: Routledge, 1994), 9–36.

29. Dunning, *Roots*, 169–73. With regard to skinheads, also see Burkhard Schröder, *Rechte Kerle: Skinheads, Faschos, Hooligans* (Hamburg: Rowohlt, 1992).

30. See, for example, Christiane Eisenberg, "Rival Interpretations of Football Hooliganism: Figurational Sociology, Social History and Anthropology," in *Representations of Emotional Excess*, ed. Jürgen Schlaeger (Tübingen: Narr, 2000), 297–306; Jean Nicolai and Madjid Allali, *Violence et football: L'eurohooliganisme* (Marseille: Editions Autres Temps, 1998); Robert Braun and Rens Vliegenthart, "The Contentious Fans: The Impact of Repression, Media Coverage, Grievances and Aggressive Play on Supporters' Violence," *International Sociology* 23 (2008): 796–818.

31. Ian Taylor, "'Football Mad': A Speculative Sociology of Football Hooliganism," in *The Sociology of Sport: A Selection of Readings*, ed. Eric Dunning (London: Cass, 1976), 352–77; "Soccer Consciousness and Soccer Hooliganism," in *Images of Deviance*, ed. Stanley Cohen (Harmondsworth: Penguin Books, 1971), 134–64; John Clarke, "Football and the Working Class Fans: Tradition and

consciousness," borrowing the Marxist concept of "class consciousness." In this light, hooliganism is presented as a relic of proletarian resistance against the capitalist society, and the solidarity of the fan groups as a remnant of the workers' solidarity that supposedly once united the entire proletarian milieu. According to this theory, the violence of the hooligans played a role in making the employed elements of the working class responsive to the law-and-order slogans of the Conservatives and thus help to bring about the Thatcherite revolution with their ballots. The social division of the working class into the employed, the unemployed, and the unemployable thus had political consequences as well. It is argued against the Marxist interpretation that this view overestimates the one-time solidarity of the working classes and also ignores other earlier forms of hooliganism from the period before the First World War. In addition, the criticism has been raised that the existence of a soccer consciousness, on which this theory is based, has never been demonstrated in an empirically convincing manner.[32]

Another theory, largely connected with the Leicester School of Eric Dunning, which has developed in the context of research into hooliganism, borrows heavily from the sociologist Norbert Elias's theory of civilization. Elias set out the thesis in his essay *Über den Prozess der Zivilisation (The Civilizing Process)*, which was first published in 1939, that societal development (so-called socio-genesis) and individual development (so-called psychogenesis) are closely related and therefore can only be studied together. Elias believed that he could see an actual process of civilization taking place over the course of the past several centuries. Unlike other theoreticians, who saw this process taking place because of a process of discipline "from above,"[33] Elias argued that it was driven primarily by an increasing level of self-discipline among the people.[34] A fundamental marker of this process of civilization, according to Elias, was an increasing control by people over their emotions, and a concomitant

Change," in *Football Hooliganism: The Wider Context*, ed. Roger Ingham (London: Inter-Action Imprint, 1978), 37–60.

32. Dunning, *Roots*, 28–31.

33. See, for example, Sabine Vogel, "Sozialdisziplinierung als Forschungsbegriff?," *Frühneuzeit-Info* 8, no. 2 (1997): 190–94; and Michel Foucault, *Discipline and Punish: The Birth of the Prison*, trans. Alan Sheridan (New York: Vintage Books, 1975).

34. Norbert Elias, *Über den Prozess der Zivilisation: Sozio- und psychogenetische Untersuchungen* (2 vols.) (Frankfurt: Suhrkamp, 1976).

dramatic decline in violence. Building upon this foundation, the Leicester School developed the thesis that broad sections of the British working classes were only lightly affected by this civilizing process.[35] This was shown, for example, in the male-dominated relationship between the sexes and in the development of violent Maennerbund groups. Violence was exciting for hooligans, who suffered from limited growth in character, lack of life experiences, and poor education. This model saw several causes for the increase in violence during the 1960s, including a change in the relationship between the sexes, a modification in the intergenerational balance of power that led to a loss of "natural" authorities, the rising power of the working class, and the contemporaneous liberalization of legislation with a diminishing tolerance for deviant behavior, all of which put young workers on the defensive. This explanatory effort leaves itself open to the criticism that it tends to blame the root causes of hooliganism on hooliganism itself. The violence of the football fans is blamed on their lower level of civilization. This lower level of civilization, in turn, is demonstrated by acts of violence. Thus, the cat bites its own (theoretical) tail.

A further explanation, which is based more strongly on a social-psychological and ethnological approach, sees hooliganism as a form of ritualized aggression.[36] In this view, the violent acts of the hooligans are intended to humiliate the opponent, but not to injure him. Thus, there is a consensus about the appropriate means to achieve this goal. Breaking the rules is punished by one's own fan group. Truly serious violence only occurs when the ritual is disturbed from outside, as, for example, during an intervention by the police. This view has been criticized for presenting hooliganism as a harmless phenomenon, because rituals do not exclude real violence. Moreover, regulation is not the same thing as an absence of violence. In addition, this formulation only considers actions within the stadium, while much more violent confrontations often took place before and after the games.[37]

35. Dunning, *Roots*, 217–45.

36. See Peter Marsh, *Aggro: The Illusion of Violence* (London: Dent, 1978); Marsh et al., *The Rules of Disorder* (London: Routledge and Keegan, 1978); Marsh and Romano Harré, "The World of Football Hooligans," *Human Nature* 1, no. 10 (1978): 62–69; and Morris, *Spiel*, 262–71.

37. Dunning, *Roots*, 21–23; Dunning et al., "Anthropological versus Sociological Approaches to the Study of Football Hooliganism: Some Critical Notes," *Sociological Review* 39 (1991): 459–78.

It would appear that these theoretical efforts to embed hooliganism in "master narratives" such as the development of capitalist society or the civilizing process are not suitable for treating all aspects of a phenomenon that has been present for a long period not only in Great Britain but elsewhere as well.[38] It is now an open question whether it is appropriate to treat fan violence in Great Britain as exclusively a phenomenon of the lower classes. It is absolutely clear that such theories of hooliganism are not appropriate for continental Europe.[39] There is considerable evidence that it was the better-paid middle class that cherished the weekly "kick" of violence as a bright spot in an otherwise depressing daily existence. Those theories, which treat the phenomenon less in regard to the societal position of the fans and pay more attention to the issue of Maennerbund structures and the transnational learning process that is facilitated by media coverage, seem to be more appropriate for dealing with the range of variables that comprise hooliganism. Although social causes for fan violence cannot be discounted, the very different societal contexts in which the phenomenon appears with very similar characteristics point to the value of a gender-historical based analysis.

In sum, football appears to be a sport that is strongly characterized in various areas by a display of masculinity, and is marked by a large number of Maennerbund structures. At the same time, women's participation in football has a rather longer tradition than is usually recognized. It is to this topic that we now wish to direct our attention.

Women's Football and Male Resistance

For the most part, the history of women's football is a story of repression and exclusion. Although football-playing women can be seen just a few years after the establishment of the rules of the game by the Football Association, it was not until the early 1970s that many national football federations recognized women's football. Moreover, their acceptance by

38. Basic for the critiques of the grand narratives is Jean-François Lyotard, "Randbemerkungen zu den Erzählungen [1984]," in *Postmoderne und Dekonstruktion: Texte französischer Philosophen der Gegenwart*, ed. Peter Engelmann (Stuttgart: Reclam, 1990), 49–53.

39. For a comparative analysis of the composition of the audience for football matches, see Ivan Waddington et al., "The Social Composition of Football Crowds in Western Europe," *International Journal for the Sociology of Sport* 33 (1998): 99–113.

male football fans was a long time in coming, and remains something of an open question even today. In the following section, we will examine the mechanisms for exclusion in Great Britain and Germany and the arguments that were used to sustain them. We will also examine the societal contexts that led to the general recognition of women's football. Finally, we will consider the special case of the United States with its relatively gender neutral view of soccer.

Even before the regulation of modern football in the second half of the nineteenth century, there were women in Great Britain who encountered air-filled animal bladders. It was supposedly the custom in Inverness and Midlothian in Scotland in the eighteenth century that every year married women played a popular football game against the unmarried women in front of an audience of men who were interested in being married and used this game as a bride show.[40] During the second half of the nineteenth century, football was also played in some girls' secondary schools. In 1894 the London resident Nettie Honeywell founded the first women's football team, the British Ladies. When the first important women's football match took place on March 23, 1895, between northern and southern England, the newspaper commentators stressed the decorum and grace of the football-playing ladies.[41] As was true in other sports, such as cycling, the discussion turned to the question of what clothing was appropriate for women participating in athletics. Should they wear long but unpractical clothing, or more comfortable blouses and "masculine" short pants for their athletic activities? The so-called "rational dress movement" finally freed women from restrictive clothing regulations. As early as 1896, an English women's national eleven wished to make their debut. The planned game against a women's side from Sparta Rotterdam was blocked by the Royal Dutch Football Union.[42] In Scotland, the author, inventor, and activist for women's rights Lady Florence Dixey played a leading role in organizing benefit games between women's teams.[43] However, the Football Association was

40. David J. Williamson, *The Belles of the Ball: The Early History of Women's Football* (Devon: R&D Associates, 1991), 1.

41. Ibid., 5; and Philipp Heinecken, *Das Fussballspiel: Association und Rugby* (Hannover, 1898, reprinted Hannover: Schäfer, 1993), 12.

42. Schulze-Marmeling, *Fussball*, 99.

43. Ibid., 95.

by no means pleased by the increasing role of women. In 1902 the association issued a directive to its member clubs not to organize any games against "lady teams."

Women's football saw a major period of growth in Great Britain during the First World War. The worldwide battles led to a (temporary) weakening of the traditional division of gender roles. While men died heroes' deaths for their country in the trenches, women frequently took their places in the factories and in the fields.[44] There was a strong solidarity among the women working in factories. Firms frequently supported women's football for the same reasons that they supported men's football at the end of the nineteenth century. Sport kept the workers fit and healthy, and its support by the employers strengthened the paternalistic structure within the firm.[45] Munitions factories, in particular, became the breeding ground for organized women's football, which now suddenly received official support because of its "patriotic" orientation.

Women's teams largely played for charitable causes and to strengthen morale on the home front. A football club that was founded in Cardiff in 1917 and was composed of former hockey players grossed more than £2,000 for charitable purposes in the space of two years. Because the regular play of the Football League and the F.A. Cup were put on hold beginning in 1915, these women's games did not compete with established men's football. A competition for teams of women factory workers was established in northern England for the 1917–18 season, the Tyne, Wear & Tees Alfred Wood Munition Girls Cup. The best-known women's football team was the side founded in 1917 at Kerr's machine factory in Preston, Dick Kerr's Ladies.[46] Women's football was a big sensation that

44. See, for example, Gail Braybon, *Women Workers in the First World War* (London: Routledge, 1989); Arthur Marwick, *Women at War, 1914–1918* (Glasgow: Croom Helm, 1977); Laura Lee Downs, *Manufacturing Inequality: Gender Division in the French and British Metalworking Industries 1914–1939* (Ithaca, N.Y.: Cornell University Press, 1995); Deborah Thom, *Nice Girls and Rude Girls: Women Workers in World War I* (London: I. B. Taurus, 1998); Angela Woollacott, *On Her Their Lives Depend: Munition Workers in the Great War* (Berkeley: University of California Press, 1994); John Williams, *The Home Fronts in Britain, France and Germany, 1914–1918* (London: Constable, 1972); Gerard J. Degroot, *Blighty: British Society in the Era of the Great War* (London: Longman, 1996), 126–39.

45. Williamsson, *Belles*, 8–10; and Marwick, *Women*, 134.

46. Gail J. Newsham, *In a League of their Own! The Dick Kerr Ladies 1917–1965* (London: Paragon Publishing, 1997).

drew the masses to the stadium. However, the game could not escape its image as offering a spectacle. In some cases women's teams played against men, mixed teams played against each other, and there was even theater football with women in costumes.[47]

After the war, this boom continued at first. The first international meeting between two women's football teams took place in March 1920, as Dick Kerr's Ladies played four matches against Femina Paris, in front of a total audience of 61,000 paying spectators.[48] In October of the same year, the series was replayed, this time in France. A number of women's football teams also were established in Paris during the war, and they even held a championship in the 1918–19 season.[49] On Boxing Day 1920, 53,000 spectators attended a game between Dick Kerr's Ladies and St. Helen's Ladies. A further 10,000 hopefuls had to be turned away at the gates of Everton's Goodison Park.[50] It is thought that there were about 150 women's football clubs in England in 1921, most of them in the north and in the Midlands.

Despite the great popularity of women's football, there were also critics. There were discussions in both the press and public events about whether women really should play football. In addition to public rejection, there were also voices that sought to ridicule women's football. Others ignored women's football completely.[51] It soon became clear that some of these criticisms were based not only on concerns about the maintenance of traditional gender roles. There was an economic component as well. In 1921 there were suddenly widespread rumors about financial irregularities. It was claimed that receipts from admissions were falsified, and that individual players or even whole teams had received money for their appearance on the field. That this second charge was scandalous despite the fact that professionalism in men's football at this point had been legal for more than thirty years shows the fundamentally different nature that people were prepared to concede to women's football, under the best of circumstances. While people had come to accept that football could be a career for men, women were only permitted to play football for a good cause. David J. Williamson, a historian of

47. Williamsson, *Belles*, 11.
49. Wahl, *Archives*, 195–97.
51. Ibid., 47.

48. Ibid., 20.
50. Williamsson, *Belles*, 31.

women's football, claims that there were neither witnesses nor evidence for these charges of financial irregularities, and believes that they were part of a plot against women's football.[52] Since women's football was seen as competing with men's football, and particularly with the games of the lower professional divisions, the situation was comparable to that of women who had taken typically male positions in industry. After the end of the war, they also were expected to give up their places again to men, and there was a burning debate in the early 1920s about those women who refused to do so.[53]

The FA, which in the period immediately after the war generally had been willing to permit the women football players to use their stadiums, gradually returned the pre-1914 rejectionist stance. At first, targeted investigations stoked mistrust of women's teams. Then the decision came on October 21, 1921, that clubs could only make their stadiums available to women's football games if they had previously obtained the permission of the association. In addition, the clubs staging the games were made responsible for assuring that the income from admissions was correctly distributed, and had to make available the corresponding bookkeeping records to the association. On December 5 the FA banned women from using club stadiums. At the end of 1921, the association issued a general prohibition against women's football. This decision was based on the argument that it had become clear that the sport of football was completely inappropriate for women and should not be supported. In addition, it was alleged that a great part of the income from the spectators at women's football games was used to cover the cost of the matches, and a disproportionately small part was being used effectively for charitable purposes.[54]

This ban was to last for the next fifty years. However, the women football players immediately founded their own association, the English Ladies Football Association (ELFA), which organized its own cup competition for the 1921–22 season. In 1922 Dick Kerr's Ladies went to the United States and played nine games against entirely male teams in

52. Ibid., 59.

53. On this point, see Degroot, *Blighty*, 138; and Bernard Waites, *A Class Society at War: England 1914–1918* (Leamington Spa: Berg Publishers, 1987), 242.

54. Williamsson, *Belles*, 69.

Massachusetts, Rhode Island, New York, and Maryland, of which they won three and drew four.[55] However, it was clear that women's football had not been able to create deep ties in its homeland. The end of British women's football as a mass spectator sport was sealed by the decision of the FA in 1921. Women's football teams only made appearances in exceptional circumstances after this, when the gender order was set aside, at least temporarily. Thus in the carnivalesque atmosphere of the major seven-month mining strike in South Wales in 1926, there was a match between a men's and a women's team in Llwyncelyn, during which the men played with one arm tied behind their backs.[56] In addition, between 1937 and 1939, Dick Kerr's Ladies played against the Edinburgh City Girls three times for the Championship of Great Britain and the World.

British women's football enjoyed a small renewed boom in the period after the Second World War, although it was not comparable to the growth experienced between 1915 and 1922. In place of Dick Kerr's Ladies, it was now the Manchester Corinthians that dominated the game. The ban on English women's football was only lifted in 1971 under pressure from UEFA. Two years earlier an autonomous Women's Football Association had been established that included 44 member clubs at its founding and went on to organize several regional leagues and a countrywide cup competition in the 1970–71 season. In 1983, the women's football association joined the Football Association. The FA Women's Premier National League was finally established in 1991 as an analogue to the league structure in men's football. This was then replaced by the FA Women's Super League in 2011.

Germany also saw football played by girls in school during the pioneer stage of the late nineteenth century.[57] Philipp Heinecken mentions this specifically in his 1898 book *Das Fussballspiel* (*The Game of Football*) in order to weaken the argument of the gymnasts regarding the putative

---

55. Dirk Kerr's Ladies did not fold until 1965. By this time, the team had played more than 800 matches and had earned more than £70,000 for charitable causes.

56. Bruley, *Women*, 69.

57. The basic works on German women's football are Eduard Hoffmann and Jürgen Nendza, *Verlacht, verboten und gefeiert: Zur Geschichte des Frauenfussballs in Deutschland* (Weilerswist: Ralf Liebe, 2005); Carina Sophia Linne, *Freigespielt: Frauenfussball im geteilten Deutschland* (Berlin: Bebra-Wiss.-Verl, 2011); and *Frauenfussball in Deutschland: Anfänge-Verbote-Widerstände-Durchbruch*, ed. Markwart Herzog (Stuttgart: Kohlhammer, 2013).

brutality of the game in its two variants, soccer and rugby. Heinecken stressed that the schoolgirls playing football "are perfectly safe as they do so."[58]

The first women's football teams were established in the interwar period.[59] The first organized women's football game took place in Germany in 1922 in the context of the German university championships. The first Damen-Fussball-Club was established in Frankfurt in 1930 but was dissolved a short time later following numerous protests. Beyond that, there were very few efforts to establish women's football as a new sport. In general, the first efforts should be understood as part of a comprehensive experimental phase by women in a range of sports.

Just as was true in Great Britain, the First World War disrupted the traditional gender order in Germany.[60] Here too, women were brought into traditionally male occupations and were largely driven out of them after the armistice.[61] Important in this context, however, is that women's occupations shifted during the course of the 1920s. The percentage of service girls, maids, and agricultural laborers shrank, and the number of factory workers, and above all white-collar workers and civil servants increased. Overall, there was a growing concentration of women in the modern sectors of industry, trade, as well as in public and private services. There were now new "typically" female professions such as stenographers, assembly-line workers, sales clerks, primary school teachers, and social workers.[62]

58. Heinecken, *Das Fussballspiel: Association und Rugby*, 228.

59. Beate Fechtig, *Frauen und Fussball: Interviews-Portraits-Reportagen* (Dortmund: Edition Ebersbach, 1995), 22; and *Frau und Sport*, ed. Gertrud Pfister (Frankfurt: Fischer Taschenbuch Verlag, 1980), 179.

60. See, for example, *Home-Front: The Military, War and Gender in Twentieth-Century Germany*, eds. Karen Hagemann and Stefanie Schüler-Springorum (Oxford: Berg, 2002).

61. Ute Daniel, *The War from Within: German Working-Class Women in the First World War* (Oxford: Berg, 1997); "Fiktionen, Friktionen und Fakten—Frauenlohnarbeit im Ersten Weltkrieg," in *Der Erste Weltkrieg: Wirkung-Wahrnehmung-Analyse*, ed. Wolfgang Michalka (Munich: Piper, 1994), 530–62; Richard Bessel, "'Eine nicht allzu grosse Beunruhigung des Arbeitsmarktes': Frauenarbeit und Demobilmachung in Deutschland nach dem Ersten Weltkrieg," *Geschichte und Gesellschaft* 9 (1983): 211–29; Christiane Eifert, "Frauenarbeit im Krieg: Die Berliner 'Heimatfront' 1914–1918," *Internationale wissenschaftliche Korrespondenz zur Geschichte der deutschen Arbeiterbewegung* 21 (1985): 281–95; Williams, *The Home Fronts in Britain, France and Germany, 1914–1918*.

62. Following Peukert, *Weimarer Republik*, 101; and Ute Frevert, "Vom Klavier zur Schreibmaschine: Weiblicher Arbeitsmarkt und Rollenzuweisungen am Beispiel der weiblichen Angestellten in der Weimarer Republik," in *Frauen in der Geschichte: Frauenrechte und die gesellschaftliche*

Parallel to this phenomenon was the development of the image of the "new woman," who generally was thought of as an apolitical, consumption-oriented, white collar worker who was enthusiastic about the media. She had bobbed hair, a made-up face, wore stylish clothing, smoked cigarettes, and spent her free time in the cinema or dancing the Charleston.[63] During the second half of the Weimar republic, this image drew considerable criticism from two sources. The first of these was from the traditional women's rights movement that believed because women finally had achieved the right to vote and to stand for office, a concomitant political engagement was demanded from them to fight for equal rights in society and in the economy.[64] The second source of criticism was from conservative men and women, who held to the traditional bourgeois family and image of the mother.[65]

These social, cultural, and political processes provided the background for debates about women's sports in the interwar period. Women were suddenly trying all of the sports, including track and field, the strength sports, ski-jumping, mountain climbing, gliding, auto-racing, and even football.[66] One topical variety of the "new woman" in the 1920s was the "sport girl." One of the goals of these pioneers usually was to break out of traditional gender roles. In her doctoral thesis for the German University for Physical Education in Berlin, titled *Women and Sport*, Annemarie Kopp wrote in 1927 that "the task of sport should be to diminish as much as possible the artificially constructed division and alienation between the sexes. It should bring the sexes closer together on the basis of their pure humanity."[67]

Bitter opposition developed against these efforts and smoldered,

---

Arbeit der Frauen im Wandel: Fachwissenschaftliche und fachdidaktische Studien zur Geschichte der Frauen, eds. Annette Kuhn and Gerhard Schneider (Düsseldorf: Schwann, 1979), 82–112.

63. Peukert, *Weimarer Republik*, 104. Also see *Neue Frauen: Die zwanziger Jahre*, eds. Maruta Schmidt and Kristine von Soden (Berlin: Elefanten-Press, 1988).

64. See Florence Hervé, "Brot und Frieden—Kinder, Küche, Kirche: Weimarer Republik 1918/19 bis 1933," in *Geschichte der deutschen Frauenbewegung*, ed. Florence Hervé (Cologne: PapyRossa-Verlag, 1995), 85–110.

65. See, for example, Karin Hausen, "Mütter zwischen Geschäftsinteresse und kultischer Verehrung: Der 'Deutsche Muttertag' in der Weimarer Republik," in *Sozialgeschichte der Freizeit: Untersuchungen zum Wandel der Alltagskultur in Deutschland*, ed. Gerhard Huck (Wuppertal: Hammer, 1980), 249–80.

66. Gertrud Pfister, "Leibesübungen in der Weimarer Republik," in *Frau und Sport*, 27–46.

67. Annemarie Kopp, "Emanzipation durch Sport [1927]," in *Frau und Sport*, 69.

above all, on the question of women's participation in competitions.[68] Because it was, above all, "masculine" characteristics that were proven in competitive sports, this debate pointed to the core issue about the "nature" of the sexes, and was thus correspondingly emotional. The debate focused largely on the questions of the physical and psychological aptitude of women, as well as the aesthetics and moral ramifications of public appearances. The image of women as the "weaker sex" was universal in the interwar period, as it had been before and would continue to be. Numerous physicians warned—just as they had about the participation of men in competitive sports before the war—about the negative consequences to the body that would result from competitive sports, and particularly in those sports that required extended exertion, such as football.[69] Gynecologists claimed that sport cramped the musculature in the pelvic floor, and thus would made delivery more difficult. Women who participated in competitive sports frequently were defamed as "masculine women." These claims were vehemently rebuffed by female physicians, such as Alice Profé, who was also a member of the women's committee within the German National Committee for Physical Exercise. In 1928 Profé wrote: "The demonstrated sexual differences in the structure of the body, as they are known today, are so limited that they do not justify a different type of physical exercise."[70]

The opponents of women's competitive sports claimed that women lacked the necessary "fighting spirit," because as the "preservers of the species" they were caring and compassionate. Karl Ritter von Halt, one of the leading sports officials in the interwar period, said: "Battle is born in the man, it is alien to the nature of the woman. Thus, let us be done with the women's track championship."[71] Annemarie Kopp wrote against this argument in 1927: "It is necessary to reject the argument that women cannot participate in competition because it endangers their womanhood. The concepts that are generally thought of as applicable to women cannot properly bear this interpretation, because they actually designate broadly human attributes."[72]

68. Pfister, "Leibesübungen," 34–41.

69. John Hoberman, "'Mortal Engines': Hochleistungssport und die physiologischen Grenzen des menschlichen Organismus," in *Physiologie und industrielle Gesellschaft,* 496–500.

70. Alice Profé, "Frauensport aus ärztlicher Sicht [1928]," in *Frau und Sport,* 113.

71. Cited in Pfister, "Leibesübungen," 37.

72. Annemarie Kopp, "Wettkampf und Weiblichkeit [1927]," in *Frau und Sport,* 130.

However, in the final result the emancipatory ideas for the unwinding of this biological essentialism were not successful. This is demonstrated quite clearly in Germany, where, in contrast to Great Britain, professional sports also were frowned upon for men. Thus the reservations about women's sports, in general, and women's football, in particular, cannot be traced back to purely economic interests. It was much more the case that women playing sports touched on deep-seated convictions regarding the "nature" of the sexes and their roles in society, as well as their service for the *Volkskörper* (body of the people), as the concept was popularly expressed at that time. Football, as a particularly strongly "masculine" sport, remained a privilege of the "stronger" sex, even in the socialist workers' sport movement.[73]

Emancipatory ideas about sport were completely suppressed in the Third Reich.[74] The National Socialists placed sport completely in the service of military competence. The SA focused above all on "military sports," which included fighting games and scouting exercises.[75] Women's sports were reduced to joy in childbirth. "Masculine" sports such as football were forbidden to women.[76] The sex-specific polarization of sports thus reached a high point.

While the Second World War again shook the gender order, there was a rapid return to traditional conditions in the early years after the war, in parallel with the unfolding of the economic miracle.[77] The increased significance of football following the German victory in the 1954 World Cup was not lost on the female portion of the population. Numerous women's football teams were established in the immediate post-war period alongside the resurrected men's football teams and the German Football Union, which was reestablished in 1949. In 1955, the DFB debated wheth-

---

73. See, for example, Überhorst, *Arbeitersport- und Arbeiterkulturbewegung*, 181. The basic works on socialist women's sports are Sigrid Block, *Frauen und Mädchen in der Arbeitersportbewegung* (Münster: Lit, 1987) and Gertrud Pfister, "'Macht euch frei': Frauen in der Arbeiter-Turn- und Sportbewegung," in *Illustrierte Geschichte des Arbeitersports*, 48–57.

74. According to Fechtig, *Frauen*, 24.

75. Fischer, *Stürmer*, 22.

76. See Michaela Czech, *Frauen und Sport im nationalsozialistischen Deutschland: Eine Untersuchung zur weiblichen Sportrealität in einem patriarchalen Herrschaftssystem* (Berlin: Verlagsgesellschaft Tischler, 1994).

77. Eva Kolinsky, *Women in West Germany: Life, Work and Politics* (Oxford: Berg, 1989); Robert G. Moeller, *Protecting Motherhood: Women and the Family in the Politics of Postwar West Germany* (Berkeley: University of California Press, 1993).

er women's football should be brought into their structure. The result of these discussions was that the women's football teams were not permitted to join the DFB. Horst Schmidt, who was a member of the DFB staff at that time, said in a 1995 interview that the reason for this decision was that "at that time there were managers who traveled through the country earning money with breast-wobbling women. So we declined."[78] At a time when the DFB still held strongly to the defense of amateurism, it was doubly difficult for commercialized women's football.

Just as had been the case earlier, science also offered a number of arguments to the opponents of women's football. Sports physicians still maintained the view that the woman's body was not suited for football, and the psychologist Fred J. J. Buytendijk claimed in a study published in 1953 that football "was a demonstration of masculinity as we understand this on the basis of our traditional conception.... It has not yet been possible to permit women to play football, as they have played basketball, hockey, tennis, and so forth. The kick is specifically masculine. Whether being kicked is feminine is an open question. But certainly not kicking is feminine."[79] According to this view, women were unsuited to the sport of football both physically and psychologically.

However, despite the DFB prohibition, German women's football continued to develop. The West German Women's Football Association was founded in 1956, the German Women's Football Association followed in 1957, and the German Women's Football Union in 1958. In 1956, 18,000 spectators attended an international match between Germany and the Netherlands. The first international women's football association was established in 1957, the International Ladies Association (ILA). That same year, this association organized a European Championship in Berlin that included teams from England, the Federal Republic of Germany, Austria, Luxemburg, and the Netherlands. The Manchester Corinthians were the champions.[80] However, public interest was limited, and ten days after the final match, some officials were arrested for financial irregularities.[81]

78. Fechtig, *Frauen*, 25.

79. Fred J. J. Buytendijk, *Das Fussballspiel: Eine psychologische Studie* (Würzburg: Werkbund-Verlag, 1953), 20.

80. Schulze-Marmeling, *Fussball*, 98.   81. Fechtig, *Frauen*, 26.

German women's football expanded even further during the 1960s.[82] Important initiatives came from the outside, particularly from Denmark, the Netherlands, and Czechoslovakia, where early medical research had undermined the physiological arguments against women's football. Numerous women's football clubs had been founded in Germany by the end of the 1960s, and there were efforts to establish their own association. BSG Empor Dresden-Mitte, which was founded in 1968, was the first women's football team in the GDR.

The Confederation of Independent European Female Football (FIEFF) was established in November 1969. At the initiative of the beverage company Martini & Rossi, the first unofficial Women's World Cup took place in Italy in 1970 and was won by Denmark. A German squad from Bad Neuenahr/Illertissen took part in this tournament. A reporter from the *Münchner Abendzeitung*, Veit Mölter, accompanied the German team to the opening game against England and reported on it in the following manner:

Helga Walluga (28) from Bad Neuenahr, the "female sweeper" of the German eleven is going to the Women's World Cup in a rapidly undulating wave of blond hair. She is sitting with twelve football-playing comrades and a harsh-looking coach on a bus, which brought them to the stadium at Genoa. There, they tied on football boots and bodices, and a short time later began the first game of the world championship.

Admittedly, when the players were getting dressed there were problems with some of the journalists, who tried to "to get a look around the dressing rooms with all of the women," with the claim that this was common in international football. The Bavarian reporter was silent on the question of whether he was one of those types. A short while later, when both of the teams were on the field, "where the scent of the greater, wider football world awaited them: 5,000 curious Italians broke out in appreciative 'oh-ohs' when catching sight of the wondrous German calves," with which the "tree-trunk like calves of the British women" could not compete. "Then the national anthems were played, a pair of the German players handed over their head scarves to their chaperones on the sideline, and within 50 seconds the score was 1–0 in favor of

---

82. Fechtig, *Frauen*, 28–30.

England." The German team had no chance to avoid defeat as the game progressed. Mölter ascribed the defeat to the fact that "our eleven were committed to taking their breasts out of the line of fire when there was a hard kicked ball. Helga Walluga, in particular, played so that she could return intact to her marriage." Thus, the German sweeper, "who definitely would have been the first to be chosen as Miss Football Pitch ... shoveled more air than balls." By contrast, the British women "had long since ... overcome this handicap. They were all iron, and skillfully used their womanly weapons to stop the ball." In sum, the more attractive team had clearly lost.[83] It was apparently clear to the reporter that only masculine women could be successful in football. In any case, the athletic event was less interesting to him than the appearance of the players.

If some sections of the press did not take women's football seriously, as had been the case earlier as well, or simply ignored it, the tournament in Italy did lead several associations to lift their bans out of fear that independent national women's football organizations would be established. The French and German associations lifted their bans in 1970, and the English did so in the following year. However, in a poll conducted by FIFA of its member states in 1970, just 12 of the 90 national associations officially supported women's football.[84] In the context of the political and social atmosphere of the Federal Republic after 1968, which also saw the cultural end of the Adenauer era, legal discrimination by the association against women's football was no longer tenable in the face of a social-liberal policy of reform and the new women's movement. However, when it lifted its ban on women's football, the DFB put in place a series of special requirements making clear that it still was not convinced that the game of football was safe for women.[85] It became clear in the following period that most of these requirements were foolish or unenforceable, and they were subsequently lifted.[86] However, as late as the 1980s, women football players were prohibited from shirt advertising, apparently because it was feared that the advertisements would lead spectators to focus too much on the female anatomy.[87]

By 1971 there were 1,100 women's football teams in the Federal Re-

83. *Sport*, July 15, 1970.
85. Ibid., 33.
87. Pfister, "Leibesübungen," 40.

84. Fechtig, *Frauen*, 5.
86. Ibid., 34.

public. In 1982 there were 2,891. All state associations organized championship competitions for women in the 1972–73 season. But there was not yet an official German championship. There was a Gold Cup tournament at the end of the season for the champions of the individual states which was organized through a private initiative and served as an unofficial German championship. The next year, the DFB stepped in as the organizer of this tournament. The winner of the first official German women's football championship was TUS Wörrstadt, the same team as had won the first Gold Cup the year before.[88] The first official German national women's football eleven was organized in 1982. One year before, Germany had been represented at the unofficial Women's World Cup in Taiwan by series champion SSG 09 Bergisch Gladbach. The DFB would not reimburse the travel costs of the club, even though it won the tournament.[89]

The 1989 European championship in their own country was a landmark in German women's football both in an athletic context—the Germans won the tournament with a 4–1 victory in the final match against the defending champion Norway—as well as regarding the acceptance of women's football by the public. The final game was watched by 22,000 spectators in the stadium and was shown live on television, as was the semifinal against Italy. These games went a long way toward dispelling the cliché that women football players were "unfeminine."[90] The same year saw the establishment of a women's national league, which began playing games in the following season. However, despite various successes on the international stage, German women's football had only modest success in attracting an audience. During the 2012–13 season, games in the women's national league had an average attendance of 890 spectators, while the men's game attracted about 45,000.

Official recognition on the international level took even longer. It was not until 1991 that the first FIFA-organized World Cup for women's football took place, in China. Up until this point, FIFA had not taken a firm stance with regard to women's football. This policy was due, in no

88. See Hannelore Ratzeburg and Horst Biese, *Frauen-Fußball-Meisterschaften: 25 Jahre Frauenfußball* (Kassel: Agon, 1995).

89. Fechtig, *Frauen*, 37.

90. Ibid., 38–40.

small part, to the strong stance of many national associations against women's football. The survey taken in 1970, mentioned above, clearly showed the gap between Europe and part of Latin America, on the one hand, and the rest of Latin America as well as Africa and Asia, on the other. One Asian association answered the survey with a single sentence: "God save us from women's football!"[91]

However, the Women's World Cup was one means by which the United States became more thoroughly integrated into the business of football. Unlike in Europe, soccer in the United States long had been seen as a women's rather than as a men's sport. Masculinity traditionally was, and still continues to be represented by American football, which had developed in a variety of elite American schools from variants of British football. In 1873 representatives of Columbia, Rutgers, Princeton, and Yale established the Intercollegiate Football Association in order to carry out a refinement of the rules. Beginning in 1895, this exceptionally violent form of football also was played by professionals.

The first attempt to establish a professional soccer league for men took place in 1894, but it failed in its first season.[92] The American Soccer League (ASL) then operated between 1921 and 1933 as a professional association, and was very popular, proving to be a serious source of competition to the National Football League (NFL), which was founded in 1920 as the top professional league in American football.[93] The ASL collapsed during the Great Depression, and was immediately replaced by a second ASL, which stumbled along until the 1960s without receiving much attention. It was not until the 1966–67 season that two new leagues began playing, at first in competition with one another, and then joined together in 1967 to form the North American Soccer League (NASL). This league gained some attention during the 1970s thanks to the presence of aging stars from Europe and South America. However, the league was not able to sustain substantial public interest and ended play in 1984 for financial reasons. It remains an open question which factors played the greatest role in the failure of this league, whether internal problems,

91. Cited in Fechtig, *Frauen*, 35.

92. Roger Allaway et al., *The Encyclopedia of American Soccer History* (Lanham, Md.: Scarecrow Press, 2001).

93. Colin Jose, *The American Soccer League: The Golden Years of American Soccer 1921–1931* (Lanham, Md.: Scarecrow Press, 1998).

the structure of the game, the traditional advantages of the competing North American sports of football, baseball, ice hockey, and basketball, the struggle to obtain a piece of the advertising pie, or the fact that European football was seen as a culturally foreign import. One factor that should not be underestimated, however, is that the other sports in the United States fulfilled the need for a masculine-heroic identification. The following period saw the introduction of rival field and indoor football leagues. However, it was not until the 1993–94 season, with the establishment of the Major League Soccer (MLS), which was founded with an eye to expected growth in U.S. soccer resulting from hosting the World Cup in 1994, that there was again a national professional league. MLS began playing games in 1996.

At the same time, soccer enjoyed great popularity in both high schools and colleges among both sexes. It was precisely because men's soccer did not have an established structure with decades of tradition and that the gender order had been fixed in other sports that women's soccer could become established without male harassment. Thus in the 1990s, 40 percent of all people enrolled in the United States Soccer Federation (USSF) were women. At the end of the century, almost a third of all of the women registered as soccer players throughout the world came from the United States. It is therefore hardly surprising that the United States won the first Women's World Cup. Following American pressure, a women's soccer tournament took place for the first time at the 1996 Olympics in Atlanta. The final game, in which the United States defeated China, attracted more than 76,000 spectators. When the third Women's World Cup was held in the United States in 1999, no fewer than 90,000 people watched the final game live at the stadium, including the president of the United States. The viewing figures for the television broadcast, constituting 40 million Americans, was twice as high as the finals of the National Basketball Association, which had taken place two weeks earlier.[94]

However, the long-term institutionalization of a professional league for U.S. women's soccer has proven difficult. The USL W-League, which was founded in 1995, has included since its establishment both amateur teams as well as (largely foreign) professional players. But since the turn of the millennium, it has been reduced to a second-tier league. In April

94. Schulze-Marmeling, *Fussball*, 100.

2001 the Women's United Soccer Association League (WUSA League), which was founded the year before, began playing games. Its foundation came at the initiative of a number of leading women soccer players along with several media corporations, which together with other investors raised $40 million. However, the league folded for financial reasons in 2003. The next efforts to establish a professional league were the likewise short-lived Women's Professional Soccer, which operated in 2009–11, and the National Women's Soccer League, founded in 2012.

Women's football experienced enormous growth in other nations during the 1990s. By the end of the decade, more than half of FIFA member states had championships for women, and more than 30 million female players were registered worldwide.[95] During the 2001–2 season, a UEFA Women's Cup was established in response to the founding of the North American WUSA. In 2009 it was renamed to match the terminology of men's football: the UEFA Women's Champions League.

However, even during the 1990s there was resistance to women's football in Europe in which sexism crossed with the homophobia in football discussed above. For many men, gay football players were and are unthinkable. In an inversion of this view, football-playing women were seen as overwhelmingly lesbian. One example in which this view was manifested in a particularly dramatic fashion took place in Switzerland. On March 4, 1994, the representative of the women's branch of FC Wettswil-Bonstetten was summoned to an urgent meeting by the seven men who made up the governing committee of the club. At this meeting, it was decided that the women's team would immediately be dissolved. The justification for this action was that the team corrupted the youth and that it included too many lesbians, "who practiced their activities on the field and in the dressing room." In a press release, the governing committee stated that the club "was being used for the practice of 'abnormal predispositions' (lesbianism)."[96] Because the rules of the Swiss Football Association required at that time that women's teams had to be connected to a (male) football club, this meant that the team was finished. This case was

---

95. Schulze-Marmeling, *Fussball*, 101. Also see Sheila Scraton et al., "It's Still a Man's Game? The Experiences of Top-Level European Women Footballers," *International Review for the Sociology of Sport* 33 (1998): 99–113.

96. *Tages-Anzeiger*, April 2, 1994.

just what the media had been waiting for. The "sex scandal" around the "lesbian team" made it onto the front page of the leading tabloid *Blick*.[97] Swiss television aired a report with the title *Does Women's Football Corrupt the Youth?"*

In sum, the "gendered nature" of football demonstrates an astounding continuity over more than 150 years (or an even longer period, if one takes folk football into account). The basic connotation of football as masculine has proven even more persistent than the individual concepts of masculinity, which not only have changed over time, but even differ between social classes in the same period, as for example with regard to the question of emotionality. Interestingly, the different concepts of masculinity—the emotionless upper-class gentleman, the rough miner, or the hyper-potent rebellious young star—are all compatible with football, while the concepts of femininity have been excluded until very recently. Seen in the context of gender history, football is a mirror for the overall development of society and culture.

The various Maennerbund systems—clubs, associations, teams, fan groups (and one could include the sporting press here as well)—seem to have stabilized and reproduced themselves over the long course of football's history. The demonstration of masculinity on the playing field had a corresponding "masculinizing" effect on the spectators in the stands, which then went back to the players. The events on and around the pitch also marked the culture of the leadership echelons of the clubs and the associations. All three of these areas worked together in creating the societal image of the game. This process then played a central role in the recruitment of new players, coaches, officials, fans, and journalists, and thus worked to maintain the status quo so long as there were no major disruptions in the broader society.

In light of this background, the exclusion, distrust, repression, and mockery that are the hallmarks of the history of women's football are no longer surprising. Until very recently, women's football, so long as it was tolerated, was simply an appendage or an imperfect form of men's football. The images of female players followed in this same path. Because they presumed to play a man's sport, they were considered constitution-

97. *Blick*, April 2, 1994.

ally to be "manly women," and thus were seen as having a homosexual orientation. By placing football-playing women in the realm of the "abnormal," men's football was again brought into order. Female players who did not appear to fit this cliché were brought into line with the masculine world view of football through other strategies. Their feminine bodily charms were stressed, but at the same time their incompetence in playing football was highlighted so that their athletic activities could be made ridiculous and reinterpreted as an occasion for voyeurism.

How are the more recent trends to be interpreted? Are the increasing recognition of women's football and the increased presence of women in the stadiums evidence for the beginning of a de-gendering of football, or are they simply side effects of the general transformation of the football world in an age of globalization, a kind of modernization of the asymmetrical polarization of the sexes that does not really effect the basic "gendered nature" of the sport? The answer to this question cannot be separated from the broader societal environment, which clearly goes far beyond the scope of the current study. The future of the gender order in football may well be identical to the future of the gender order in society as a whole.

11 | *Conclusion*

AUTONOMY AND CONTEXT

This foray into aspects of the social and cultural history of modern football illustrates the private world of football, as well as the numerous external influences on the sport from society, culture, politics, economy, media, and science. Football exists, fundamentally, in a state of contingent autonomy. The results of a match cannot be precisely prognosticated even though games have always been manipulated for a highly varied set of reasons. The small always has a chance to defeat the great, and an entire championship can be decided in additional time. This autonomy, and the exceptionally emotional circumstances that arise from it, are at the heart of the private world of football. The sport is characterized by its own terminology and narrative, has developed its own formal and informal organizational structures, has generated its own geographical mental maps, and, not least, presides over its own distinct culture of memory.[1]

However, this autonomy does not exist in a vacuum, but rather communicates in a variety of different ways with its context. The societal place of football has changed in different places and different countries. But these changes have always taken place within the context of broader societal transitions and the processes of negotiation between various social groups and classes. The identification with a particular team and club often brought with it particular connotations of class as well as social-topographical or confessional attributions, without being completely subordinated to them. Contrasts between socioeconomic

1. See, for example, *Memorialkultur im Fußballsport: Medien, Rituale und Praktiken des Erinnerns, Gedenkens und Vergessens*.

centers and peripheries, both within countries and on the global level, are generally mirrored on the football stage.

From very early on, the economic realm has played an important role in the history of modern football. As soon as football made the transition from being the game of grammar school and university students into a mass spectator phenomenon, the processes of commercialization, professionalization, and media attention began. The symbiosis has been particularly close between football and mass media, whose technological and economic development has had an important impact on the sport, but which also used football's popularity for its own economic profit.

Politics has also had both direct and indirect influence on the history of football. Politicians from a range of backgrounds—democrats and dictators, both left and right—have attempted to use football for their own purposes in both peacetime and war, often (but not always) successfully. It is notable, however, that football developed along similar lines as a mass spectator phenomenon in very different political systems, and not always in a manner that pleased those in power.

Finally, football is a highly reliable seismograph for continuities and changes in the gender order of various societies. The long-enduring masculine-heterosexual dominance, as well as the occasional early feminine interventions, and finally the gradual transition toward greater gender equality in the final third of the twentieth century clearly mirror general societal and cultural trends. Thus, it is precisely the tense relationship between football's autonomous character and its complex cross-linkage with varied contexts that accounts for the fascination with the sport and makes the study of its history a worthwhile endeavor.

BIBLIOGRAPHY

Archives

Archive of the Swiss Football Association. Muri bei Bern.

City Archives Winterthur. Winterthur.

City Archives Worms. Worms.

International Institute of Social History. Amsterdam.

The National Archives. Kew.

Swiss Federal Archives. Bern.

Swiss Social Archives. Zurich.

Newspapers

Arbeiter-Zeitung. Basel.

Badener Tagblatt. Baden.

Berner Tagwacht. Bern.

Blick. Zurich.

Der Kämpfer. Zurich.

Der Landbote. Winterthur.

Der Spiegel. Hamburg.

Die Gartenlaube. Leipzig.

Die Rote Fahne. Berlin.

Frankfurter Allgemeine Zeitung. Frankfurt.

Freiheit. Basel.

Fussball-Woche. Berlin.

Gazette de Lausanne. Lausanne.

The Guardian. Manchester.

Journal de Genève. Geneva.

Krasnyi Sport. Moscow.

La Patrie valaisanne. Saint-Maurice.

Limmattaler Tagblatt. Altstetten-Zurich.

The Manchester Guardian. Manchester.

Manchester Times. Manchester.

Neue Zürcher Nachrichten. Zurich.

Neue Zürcher Zeitung. Zurich.

Neues Winterthurer Tagblatt. Winterthur.

The Observer. London.

Pall Mall Gazette. London.

Rundschau. Basel.

Schweizerische Fussball- und Athletikzeitung. Basel.

SonntagsZeitung. Zurich.

Sport. Zurich.

Tages-Anzeiger. Zurich.

The Times. London.

Völkischer Beobachter. Munich.

Volksrecht. Zurich.

Wrexham Advertiser. Wrexham.

Audiovisual Primary Sources

Schwarz, Martin H. *5 Jahrzehnte Fussball im Originalton: Die Geschichte des Fussballs in Deutschland*. 5 CDs. Hamburg: Hörbuch, 2000.

Bibliography

Published Primary and Secondary Sources

Ackermann, Jürg. *Fussball und nationale Identität in Diktaturen: Spanien, Portugal, Brasilien und Argentinien*. Berlin: Lit, 2013.

Aczel, Tamas, and Tibor Meray. *The Revolt of Mind: A Case History of Intellectual Resistance Behind the Iron Curtain*. New York: Praeger, 1959.

Aeschlimann, Daniel: "Der Tag, an dem das Wankdorf weltberühmt wurde." *Der Bund*, July 4, 2001.

Akten zur Deutschen Auswärtigen Politik 1918–1945. Serie D, vol. 8.1. Frankfurt: Keppler-Verlag, 1961.

Albonico, Rolf, and Katharina Pfister-Binz. *Soziologie des Sports: Theoretische und methodische Grundlagen*. Basel: Birkhäuser, 1971.

Alderman, George. "The Anti-Jewish Riots of August 1911 in South Wales." *Welsh History Review* 6 (1972): 190–200.

Alegi, Peter C. "Keep Your Eyes on the Ball: A Social History of Soccer in South Africa, 1910–1976." PhD diss., Boston University, 2000.

Allan, David. "Länderspiele England (1872–1900)." *Elf* 4 (1986): 62–74.

Allaway, Roger, et al. *The Encyclopedia of American Soccer History*. Lanham, Md.: Scarecrow Press, 2001.

Allison, Lincoln, ed. *The Politics of Sport*. Manchester: Manchester University Press, 1986.

———, ed. *The Global Politics of Sport: The Role of Global Institutions in Sport*. London: Routledge, 2005.

Allison, Maria T. "On the Ethnicity of Ethnic Minorities in Sport." *International Review for the Sociology of Sport* 15 (1980): 89–96.

Almond, Hely Hutchinson. "Football as a Moral Agent." *The Nineteenth Century* 34 (1893): 899–911.

Anderson, Thomas P. *The War of the Dispossessed: Honduras and El Salvador, 1969*. Lincoln: University of Nebraska Press, 1981.

Apraku, Eva, and Markus Hesselmann. *Schwarze Sterne und Pharaonen: Der Aufstieg des afrikanischen Fussballs*. Göttingen: Werkstatt, 1998.

Arbena, Joseph, ed. *Sport and Society in Latin America*. Westport, Conn.: Greenwood Press, 1988.

———, ed. *An Annotated Bibliography of Latin American Sport: Pre-Conquest to the Present*. Westport, Conn.: Greenwood Press, 1989.

Archetti, Edoardo P. "In Search of National Identity: Argentinian Football and Europe." *International Journal of the History of Sport* 12 (1995): 201–19.

———. "Playing Styles and Masculine Virtues in Argentine Football." In *Machos, Mistresses, Madonnas: Contesting the Power of Latin American Gender Imagery*, edited by Marit Melhuus and Anne Stølen, 34–55. London: Verso, 1996.

Armstrong, Gary, and Richard Giulianotti. *Entering the Field: New Perspectives on World Football*. Oxford: Berg, 1997.

———, eds. *Football Cultures and Identities*. Basingstoke: Macmillan, 1999.

———. *Fear and Loathing in World Football*. Oxford: Berg, 2001.

———. *Football in Africa: Conflict, Conciliation and Community*. Basingstoke: Palgrave, 2004.

Arnaud, Pierre, ed. *Les origines du sport ouvrier en Europe*. Paris: Harmattan, 1994.

Arnaud, Pierre, and Thierry Terret, eds. *Histoire du sport féminin: Le sport au féminin: Histoire et identité*. Paris: Harmattan, 1996.

Arnaud, Pierre, and Alfred Wahl, eds. *Sports et relations internationale: Actes du colloque de Metz-Verdun, 23–24–25 Septembre 1993*. Metz: Centre de Recherche Histoire et Civilisation de l'université de Metz, 1994.

Ash, M. "William Wallace and Robert the Bruce: The Life and Death of a National Myth." In *The Myths We Live By*, edited by R. Samuels and P. Thomson, 83–94. London: Routledge, 1990.

Assmann, Jan. *Das kulturelle Gedächtnis. Schrift, Erinnerung und politische Identität in frühen Hochkulturen*. Munich: Beck, 1999.

Axster, Felix, et al., eds. *Mediensport: Strategien der Grenzziehung*. Munich: Fink, 2009.

Baar, Arthur. *Fussballgeschichten—Ernstes und Heiteres: Hakoah Wien*. Tel Aviv: Brith Hakoah, 1974.

Bachrach, S. D. *The Nazi Olympics: Berlin 1936*. Boston: Little, Brown, 2000.

Back, Les, et al. *The Changing Face of Football: Racism, Identity and Multiculture in the English Game*. Oxford: Berg, 2002.

Bailey, P. *Leisure and Class in Victorian England: Rational Recreation and the Contest of Control*. London: Routledge, 1978.

Bairner, A. *Sport, Nationalism and Globalisation: European and North American Perspectives*. Albany, N.Y.: State University of New York Press, 2002.

Baker, Norman. "A More Even Playing Field? Sport during and after the War." In *Millions Like Us? British Culture in the Second World War*, edited by Nick Hayes and Jeff Hill, 125–55. Liverpool: Liverpool University Press, 1999.

Baker, W. S. "Muscular Marxism and the Chicago Counter-Olympics of 1932." *International Journal of the History of Sport* 9 (1992): 397–410.

Bale, John. "Sport and National Identity: A Geographical View." *International Journal of the History of Sport* 3 (1986): 18–41.

Balibouse, Guy, and Pierre Tripod. *Die Nationalmannschaft*. Lausanne: Sporama, 1976.

Ball, Alan. *Russia's Last Capitalists: The Nepmen, 1921–1929*. Berkeley: University of California Press, 1997.

Bamford, T. W. "Public Schools and Social Class, 1801–1850." *British Journal of Sociology* 12 (1961): 224–35.

Banks, Simon. *Going Down: Football in Crisis: How the Game Went from Boom to Bust*. London: Mainstream Publishing, 2001.

Barreaud, Marc. *Dictionnaire des footballeurs étrangers du championnat professionnel français (1932–1997)*. Paris: Harmattan, 1998.

Batchelor, Denzil. *Soccer: A History of Association Football*. London, 1954.

Bauer, Otto. "Die Arbeiterjugend und die Weltlage des Sozialismus." In *Werkausgabe*, by Otto Bauer, 2:867–83.Vienna: Europaverlag, 1976.

Bibliography

Baumann, Erich, et al. *Fussball-WM 1982 Spanien*. Künzelsau: Sigloch, 1982.

Baumeister, Willy. *50 Jahre Fussballclub Zürich 1896–1946*. Zurich: 1946.

Bausenwein, Christoph. *Geheimnis Fußball: Auf den Spuren eines Phänomens*. Göttingen: Werkstatt, 1995.

Bayer, Osvaldo. *Fútbol argentine*. Buenos Aires: Editorial Sudamericana, 1990.

Beck, Peter J. *Scoring for Britain: International Football and International Politics, 1900–1939*. London and Portland: F. Cass, 1999.

Becker, Frank. *Amerikanismus in Weimar: Sportsymbole und politische Kultur 1918–1933*. Wiesbaden: Deutscher Universitäts-Verlag, 1993.

Becker, Friedebert, ed. *Fussball-Weltmeisterschaft 1966*. Munich: 1966.

Belchem, John. "English Working-Class Radicalism and the Irish, 1815–1850." In *The Irish in the Victorian City*, edited by R. Swift and S. Gilley, 85–97. London: Croom Helm, 1985.

———. *Popular Radicalism in Nineteenth-Century Britain*. New York: St. Martin's Press, 1996.

Bellos, Alex. *Futébol: The Brazilian Way of Life*. London: Bloomsbury, 2002.

Ben-Porat, Amir. "National Building, Soccer and the Military in Israel." *International Journal of the History of Sport* 17 (2000): 123–40.

Berding, Helmut, ed. *Nationales Bewusstsein und kollektive Identität: Studien zur Entwicklung des kollektiven Bewusstseins in der Neuzeit*, vol. 2. Frankfurt: Suhrkamp, 1994.

———, ed. *Mythos und Nation: Studien zur Entwicklung des kollektiven Bewusstseins in der Neuzeit*, vol. 3. Frankfurt, 1996.

Bericht über den IV. Kongress zu Helsingfors, 5.–8. August 1927. s. l. 1927.

Bernett, Hajo. "Die nationalsozialistische Sportführung und der Berufssport." *Sozial- und Zeitgeschichte des Sports* 4, no. 1 (1990): 7–33.

Bessel, Richard. "'Eine nicht allzu grosse Beunruhigung des Arbeitsmarktes': Frauenarbeit und Demobilmachung in Deutschland nach dem Ersten Weltkrieg." *Geschichte und Gesellschaft* 9 (1983): 211–29.

Bette, Karl-Heinrich. *Systemtheorie und Sport*. Frankfurt: Suhrkamp, 1999.

Beuret, Charles, and Mario Marti, eds. *Stadion Wankdorf: Geschichte und Geschichten*. Bern: Benteli, 2004.

Biasi, R. de. *Le culture del calcio: Un' analisi comparativa dei rituali e delle forme del tifo calcistico in Italia e in Inghilterra*. Trent, 1993.

Binz, Roland. "'Borussia ist stärker': Zur Alltagsbedeutung des Fussballvereins, gestern und heute*. Frankfurt: Peter Lang, 1988.

Birbaum, Emile. *Rencontres sportives et voyages, 1904–1954*. Lugano: Tipografia, 1954.

Birley, Derek. *Playing the Game: Sport and British Society 1910–45*. Manchester: Manchester University Press, 1995.

Bitzer, Dirk, and Bernd Wilting. *Stürmen für Deutschland: Die Geschichte des deutschen Fußballs von 1933 bis 1954*. Frankfurt: Campus, 2003.

Blanchard, Kendall, ed. *The Anthropology of Sport: An Introduction*. Westport, Conn.: Bergin and Garvey, 1995.

Bibliography

Blaschke, Ronnie. *Versteckspieler: Die Geschichte des schwulen Fussballers Marcus Urban.* Göttingen: Werkstatt, 2008.

Blatter, Joseph S., ed. *90 Jahre FIFA: Jubiläumsschrift 1994.* Zurich: FIFA House, 1994.

Blazek, Helmut. *Männerbünde: Eine Geschichte von Faszination und Macht.* Berlin: Aufbau Taschenbuch Verlag, 2001.

Blees, Thomas. *90 Minuten Klassenkampf: Das Länderspiel BRD–DDR 1974.* Frankfurt: Fischer, 1999.

Block, Sigrid. *Frauen und Mädchen in der Arbeitersportbewegung.* Münster: Lit, 1987.

Blödorn, Manfred. *Fussballprofis: Die Helden der Nation.* Hamburg: Hoffmann und Campe, 1974.

Bock, Gisela. "Geschichte, Frauengeschichte, Geschlechtergeschichte." *Geschichte und Gesellschaft* 14 (1988): 364–91.

Bohlen, Friedrich. *Die XI. Olympischen Spiele: Berlin 1936: Instrument der innen- und aussenpolitischen Propaganda und Systemsicherung des faschistischen Regimes.* Cologne: Pahl-Rugenstein, 1979.

Bohstedt, John. "The Moral Economy of the Crowd and the Discipline of Historical Context." *Journal of Social History* 26 (1992–93): 265–84.

Booth, Michael R. "East End and West End: Class and Audience in Victorian London." *Theatre Research International* 2 (1977): 98–103.

Bortlik, Wolfgang. *Wurst & Spiele: Roman.* Hamburg: Nautilus, 1998.

Botz, Gerhard. *Nationalsozialismus in Wien: Machtübernahme und Herrschaftssicherung 1938/39.* Vienna: Mandelbaum, 1988.

Bourdieu, Pierre. *Outline of a Theory of Practice.* Cambridge: Cambridge University Press, 1977.

———. *Distinction: A Social Critique of the Judgement of Taste.* Cambridge, Mass.: Harvard University Press, 1987.

Bouvier, Beatrix, ed. *Zur Sozial- und Kulturgeschichte des Fußballs.* Trier: Friedrich-Ebert-Stiftung, 2006.

Bradley, Joseph M. "Football in Scotland: A History of Political and Ethnic Identity." *International Journal of the History of Sport* 12 (1995): 81–98.

———. "Integration or Assimilation? Scottish Society, Football and Irish Immigrants." *International Journal of the History of Sport* 13 (1996): 61–79.

Brändle, Fabian. "Toggenburger Wirtshäuser und Wirte im 17. und 18. Jahrhundert." In *Obrigkeit und Opposition: Drei Beiträge zur Kulturgeschichte des Toggenburgs aus dem 17./18. Jahrhundert,* edited by Fabian Brändle et al., 7–51. Wattwil: Toggenburger Vereinigung für Heimatkunde, 1999.

———. "Tennisbälle, Dolen und zerbrochene Scheiben: Zur Geschichte des Schweizer Straßenfußballs vor dem Zeitalter des Automobils (1920–1945)." *SportZeiten* 7, no. 3 (2007): 7–20.

———. "'Great Inconvenience': Zum traditionellen britischen Volksfussball und dessen Varianten." *SportZeiten* 8, no. 3 (2008): 57–77.

Brändle, Fabian, and Christian Koller. "'Ferdi National' oder 'Hugo International'? Radsport und Zeitgeist in der Schweiz der fünfziger Jahre." *Sozial- und Zeitgeschichte des Sports* 14 (2000): 7–25.

————. *4 zu 2: Die goldene Zeit des Schweizer Fussballs 1918–1939*. Göttingen: Werkstatt, 2014.

Brailsford, Dennis. *British Sport: A Social History*. Cambridge: Lutterworth, 1997.

Braun, Robert, and Rens Vliegenthar. "The Contentious Fans: The Impact of Repression, Media Coverage, Grievances and Aggressive Play on Supporters' Violence." *International Sociology* 23 (2008): 796–818.

Braybon, Gail. *Women Workers in the First World War*. London: Routledge, 1989.

Bredekamp, Horst. *Florentiner Fussball: Die Renaissance der Spiele: Calcio als Fest der Medici*. Frankfurt: Campus, 1993.

Brenner, Michael, and Gideon Reuveni, eds. *Emanzipation durch Muskelkraft: Juden und Sport in Europa*. Göttingen: Vandenhoeck und Ruprecht, 2006.

Briggs, Asa. *Victorian Cities*. Berkeley: University of California Press, 1993.

Brinker, Helmut. *Laozi flankt, Konfuzius dribbelt: China scheinbar im abseits: Vom Fussball und seiner heimlichen Wiege*. Frankfurt: Lang, 2006.

Bromberger, Christian. *Le Match de Football: Ethnologie d'une passion partisane à Marseille, Naples et Turin*. Paris: Maison des Sciences de l'Homme, 1995.

Broué, Pierre. *Histoire de l'Internationale Communiste 1919–1943*. Paris: Fayard, 1997.

Brüggemeier, Franz-Josef. *Zurück auf dem Platz. Deutschland und die Fußballweltmeisterschaft 1954*. Munich: DVA, 2004.

Bruley, Sue. *The Women and Men of 1926: A Gender and Social History of the General Strike and Miners' Lockout in South Wales*. Cardiff: University of Wales Press, 2010.

Brunotte, Ulrike. *Zwischen Eros und Krieg: Männerbund und Ritual in der Moderne*. Berlin: Wagenbach, 2004.

Bruns, Claudia. *Politik des Eros: Der Männerbund in Wissenschaft, Politik und Jugendkultur (1880–1934)*. Cologne: Böhlau, 2008.

Budd, A. *Sport and International Relations: An Emerging Relationship*. London: Routledge, 2004.

Buford, Bill. *Among the Thugs*. London: Vintage, 1990.

Bukey, Evan Burr. "Popular Opinion in Vienna after the Anschluss." In *Conquering the Past: Austrian Nazism Yesterday and Today*, edited by Fred Parkinson, 151–64. Detroit, Mich.: Wayne State University Press, 1989.

————. *Hitlers Österreich: "Eine Bewegung und ein Volk."* Hamburg: Europa-Verlag, 2001.

Bunzl, John. *Hoppauf Hakoah: Jüdischer Sport in Österreich von den Anfängen bis in die Gegenwart*. Vienna: Junius, 1987.

Burgener, Louis. *Sport Schweiz: Geschichte und Gegenwart*. Derendingen: Habegger, 1974.

Burke, Peter. *Popular Culture in Early Modern Europe*. London: Temple Smith, 1978.

Buschke, Jürgen. "Der Mythos von 1954." *Aus Politik und Zeitgeschichte* 24 (1994): 13–15.

Buytendijk, Fred J. J. *Das Fussballspiel: Eine psychologische Studie*. Würzburg, 1953.

Cachay, Klaus. *Sport und Gesellschaft: Sportspiel und Sozialisation*. Schorndorf: Hofmann, 1978.

Cachay, Klaus, et al. *"Echte Sportler"—"Gute Soldaten": Die Sportsozialisation des Nationalsozialismus im Spiegel von Feldpostbriefen*. Weinheim-Munich: Juventa, 2000.

Bibliography

Caillat, Michel. *Sport et civilisation: Histoire et critique d'un phenomene social de masse.* Paris: Harmattan, 1996.

Cante, Diego. "Propaganda und Fussball: Sport und Politik in den Begegnungen zwischen den italienischen 'Azzurri' und den 'Weissen' aus Wien in der Zwischenkriegszeit." *Zeitgeschichte* 26 (1999): 184–202.

Cappa, Angel. *La Intimidad del futbol.* San Sebastian: S.A. Tercera Prensa, 1996.

Caudwell, Jayne. "Women's Football in the United Kingdom: Theorizing Gender and Unpacking the Butch Lesbian Image." *Journal of Sport and Social issues* 23 (1999): 390–402.

Caysa, Volker, ed. *Sportphilosophie.* Leipzig: Reclam, 1997.

Chandler, Timothy J. L. "Games at Oxbridge and the Public Schools 1830–80: The Diffusion of an Innovation." *International Journal of the History of Sport* 8 (1991): 171–204.

Chehabi, Houchang E. "A Political History of Football in Iran." *Iranian Studies* 35 (2002): 371–403.

Cheska, Alyce T. "Ethnicity, Identity and Sport: The Persistence of Power." *International Review for the Sociology of Sport* 22 (1987): 99–109.

Childs, Michael J. *Labour's Apprentices: Working-Class Lads in Late Victorian and Edwardian England.* London: Hambledon Press, 1992.

Chmel'nickaja, I. B. *Sportivnye obščestva i dosug v stoličnom gorode načala XX veka: Peterburg i Moskva.* Moscow: Novyj chronograf, 2011.

Clark, Peter. *The English Alehouse: A Social History, 1200–1830.* Harlow: Longman, 1983.

Claussen, Detlev. *Béla Guttmann: Weltgeschichte des Fussballs in einer Person.* Berlin: Berenberg, 2006.

Clyde, Robert. *From Rebel to Hero: The Image of the Highlander, 1745–1830.* London: Tuckwell, 1995.

Cohen, Stan. *Folk Devils and Moral Panics: The Creation of the Mods and Rockers.* Oxford: Basil Blackwell, 1972.

Colley, Linda. *Britons: Forging the Nation 1707–1837.* London: Vintage, 1996.

Collins, Brenda. "The Origins of Irish Immigration to Scotland in the Nineteenth and Twentieth Centuries." In *Irish Immigrants and Scottish Society in the Nineteenth and Twentieth Centuries,* edited by T. M. Devine, 1–25. Edinburgh: John Donald Publishers, 1991.

Conn, David. *The Football Business.* London: Mainstream Publishing, 1997.

Cressy, David. *Bonfires and Bells. National Memory and the Protestant Calendar in Elizabethan and Stuart England.* London: The History Press, 1980.

Creveld, Martin van. *Technology and War: From 2000 B.C. to the Present.* New York: Free Press, 1989.

Critcher, Chris. *Football since the War: A Study in Social Change and Popular Culture.* Birmingham: Centre for Contemporary Cultural Studies, 1974.

———. "Football since the War." In *Working-Class Culture: Studies in History and Theory,* edited by Chris Critcher et al., 161–84. London: Hutchinson, 1979.

Crolley, Liz. "Real Madrid v. Barcelona: The State against the Nation? The Changing Role of Football in Spain." *International Journal of Iberian Studies* 10 (1997): 33–43.

Cronin, Mike. *Sport and Nationalism in Ireland: Gaelic Games, Soccer and Irish Identity since 1884*. Dublin: Four Courts Press, 1999.

———, ed. *Sport and Politics*. London: Sage, 2003.

Cronin, Mike, and David Mayall, eds. *Sporting Nationalisms: Identity, Ethnicity, Immigration and Assimilation*. London: Cass, 1998.

Crump, Ian. "Amusements of the People: The Provision of Recreation in Leicester 1850–1914." PhD diss., University of Warwick, 1985.

Czech, Michaela. *Frauen und Sport im nationalsozialistischen Deutschland: Eine Untersuchung zur weiblichen Sportrealität in einem patriarchalen Herrschaftssystem*. Berlin: Verlagsgesellschaft Tischler, 1994.

Dahlmann, Dittmar, et al., eds. *Überall ist der Ball rund: Zur Geschichte und Gegenwart des Fußballs in Ost- und Südosteuropa*. 3 vols. Essen: Klartext, 2006–11.

Dal Lago, Alessandro, and Roberto Moscati. *Regaletici un sogno: Miti e realità del tifo calcistico in Italia*. Milano: Bompiani, 1992.

Dalos, György. "Die ungarische Fussballkatastrophe von 1954." In *Ungarn: Vom Roten Stern zur Stephanskrone*, by György Dalos, 17–30. Frankfurt: Suhrkamp, 1991.

Daniel, Ute. "Fiktionen, Friktionen und Fakten—Frauenlohnarbeit im Ersten Weltkrieg." In *Der Erste Weltkrieg: Wirkung-Wahrnehmung-Analyse*, edited by Wolfgang Michalka, 530–62. Munich: Piper, 1994.

———. *The War from Within: German Working-Class Women in the First World War*. Oxford and New York: Berg, 1997.

Dankert, Harald. *Sportsprache und Kommunikation: Untersuchungen zur Struktur der Fussballsprache und zum Stil der Sportberichterstattung*. Tübingen: Tübinger Vereinigung für Volkskunde, 1969.

Darby, Paul. *Africa, Football, and FIFA: Politics, Colonialism, and Resistance*. London: Taylor and Francis, 2001.

Darwin, Charles. *On the Origin of Species* [1859]. Edited by Paul H. Barret and R. B. Freeman. London: Freeman, 1988.

David, Thomas, et al., eds. *Le football en Suisse: Enjeux sociaux et symbolique d'un spectacle universel*. Neuchâtel: CIES, 2009.

Davies, Nigel. *Die versunkenen Königreiche Mexikos*. Frankfurt: Ullstein, 1985.

Dawson, S. C. *The Modernization of Professional Football in England and the United States: A Comparative Analysis*. Eugene: University of Oregon Press, 1995.

Degroot, Gerard J. *Blighty: British Society in the Era of the Great War*. London: Longman, 1996.

Delhaye, Pascal, ed. *Making Sport History. Disciplines, Identities and the Historiography of Sport*. London: Routledge, 2014.

DeLillo, Don. *Underworld*. New York: Scribner, 1997.

Delius, Friedrich Christian. *Der Sonntag, an dem ich Weltmeister wurde*. Reinbek bei Hamburg: Rowohlt, 1994.

Delves, Anthony. "Popular Recreation and Social Conflict in Derby, 1800–1850." In *Popular Culture and Class Conflict 1590–1914*, edited by Eileen Yeo and Stephen Yeo, 89–127. Brighton: Harvester Press, 1981.

304

Bibliography

Dembowski, Gerd. "Zum Fussball als Männersache: Pädoyer für die bewusste Entdeckung der Männlichkeit in der auffälligen Fanscene." *Neue Praxis* 30 (2000): 87–92.

Derick, L. H. *The Political Olympics: Moscow, Afghanistan, and the 1980 U.S. Boycott.* New York: Praeger Frederick, 1990.

Deville-Danthu, Bernadette. *Le Sport en noir et blanc: Du sport colonial au sport africain dans les anciens territoires français d'Afrique occidentale (1920–1965).* Paris: Harmattan, 1997.

Devine, T. M. *The Scottish Nation 1700–2000.* London: Allen Lane, 2000.

Dierker, Herbert. *Arbeitersport im Spannungsfeld der zwanziger Jahre: Sportpolitik und Alltagserfahrung auf internationaler, deutscher und Berliner Ebene.* Essen: Klartext, 1990.

Die Schweizerische Grenzbesetzung 1914. Basel: Frobenius, 1916.

Dietschy, Paul. *Histoire du Football.* Paris: Perrin, 2010.

Diller, Ansgar. "Die erste Sportübertragung im deutschen Rundfunk." *Publizistik* 17 (1972): 315–25.

Dimeo, P., and J. Mill. *Soccer in South Asia: Empire, Nation and Diaspora.* London: Routledge, 2001.

Dobson, Stephen, and John Goddard. *The Economics of Football.* Cambridge: Cambridge University Press, 2001.

Doherty, Julian. "Dr. Arnolds Erben: Der Aufstieg und Fall des Amateurrugbys in Grossbritannien." *Sozial- und Zeitgeschichte des Sports* 4, no. 3 (1990): 46–55.

Dombrowski, Oda. *Psychologische Untersuchungen über die Verfassung von Zuschauern bei Fussballspielen.* Ahrenburg: Ingrid Czwalina, 1975.

Donaldson, W. *The Jacobite Song: Policital Myth and National Identity.* Aberdeen: Aberdeen University Press, 1988.

Downing, David. *Passovotchka: Moscow Dynamo in Britain 1945.* London: Bloomsbury Publishing, 1999.

———. *The Best of Enemies: England v. Germany, a Century of Footballing Rivalry.* London: Bloomsbury Publishing, 2000.

Downs, Laura Lee. *Manufacturing Inequality: Gender Division in the French and British Metalworking Industries 1914–1939.* Ithaca, N.Y.: Cornell University Press, 1995.

Dózci, Tamás. "Gold Fever (?): Sport and National Identity—The Hungarian Case." *International Review for the Sociology of Sport* 47 (2011): 165–82.

Dragowski, Jürgen, et al., eds. *Alive and Kicking: Fußball zwischen Deutschland und England.* Hamburg: Argument-Verlag, 1995.

Drews, Jörg. "Damals Moment siebenundvierzig jawohl: Sieben unwillkürliche Erinnerungen an eine Jugend am Fuss des Betzenberges." In *Netzer kam aus der Tiefe des Raumes: Notwendige Beiträge zur Fussballweltmeisterschaft*, edited by Ludwig Harig and Dieter Kühn, 63–65. Munich: Hanser, 1974.

Ducret, Jacques. *Das Goldene Buch des Schweizer Fussballs.* Lausanne: L'Age d'homme, 1994.

Düding, Dieter. *Organisierter gesellschaftlicher Nationalismus in Deutschland (1808–1847): Bedeutung und Funktion der Turner und Sängervereine für die deutsche Nationalbewegung.* Munich: Oldenbourg, 1984.

Duke, Vic, and Liz Crolley. *Football, Nationality and the State*. Harlow: Longman, 1996.

Dunning, Eric. "Industrialization and the Incipient Modernization of Football." *Stadion* 1 (1975): 103–39.

————. "The Development of Modern Football." In *The Sociology of Sport: A Selection of Readings*, edited by Eric Dunning, 133–51. London: Cass, 1976.

Dunning, Eric, and Kenneth Sheard. *Barbarians, Gentlemen and Players: A Sociological Study of the Development of Rugby Football*. Oxford: Martin Robertson, 1979.

Dunning, Eric, et al. *Hooligans Abroad: The Behaviour and Control of English Fans in Continental Europe*. London: Routledge, 1984.

Dunning, Eric, et al. *The Roots of Football Hooliganism: An Historical and Sociological Study*. London: Routledge, 1988.

Dunning, Eric, et al. "Anthropological versus Sociological Approaches to the Study of Football Hooliganism: Some Critical Notes." *Sociological Review* 39 (1991): 459–78.

Durham, William H. *Scarcity and Survival in Central America: Ecological Origins of the Soccer War*. Stanford, Calif.: Stanford University Press, 1979.

Dwertmann, Hubert. "Sportler-Funktionäre-Beteiligte am Massenmord: Das Beispiel des DFB-Präsidenten Felix Linnemann." *SportZeiten* 5, no. 1 (2005): 7–46.

Ebert, Friedrich. *Schriften, Aufzeichnungen, Reden*, vol. 2. Dresden: Carl Reissner, 1926.

Eco, Umberto. *Il Segno*. Milan: ISEDI, 1976.

————. *Apokalyptiker und Integrierte: Zur kritischen Kritik der Massenkultur*. Frankfurt: S. Fischer, 1984.

Edelman, Robert. "The Professionalization of Soviet Sport: The Case of the Soccer Union." *Journal of Sport History* 17 (1990): 44–54.

————. *Serious Fun: A History of Spectator Sports in the USSR*. Oxford: Oxford University Press, 1993.

————. "A Small Way of Saying 'No': Moscow Working Men, Spartak Soccer, and the Communist Party, 1900–1945." *American Historical Review* 107 (2002): 1441–74.

————. *Spartak Moscow: A History of the People's Team in the Workers' State*. Ithaca, N.Y.: Cornell University Press, 2009.

Eggenberger, Yves. *100 Jahre Grasshopper-Club Zürich*. Zurich: Grasshopper-Club, 1986.

Eggers, Erik. "Fussball in der Weimarer Republik." *Stadion* 25 (1999): 153–75.

————. *Fussball in der Weimarer Republik*. Kassel: Agon Sportverlag, 2001.

————. *Die Stimme von Bern: Das Leben von Herbert Zimmermann, Reporterlegende bei der WM 1954*. Augsburg: Wißner Verlag, 2004.

Ehalt, Hubert and Ottmar Weiss, eds. *Sport zwischen Disziplinierung und neuen sozialen Bewegungen*. Vienna: Böhlau, 1993.

Eifert, Christiane. "Frauenarbeit im Krieg: Die Berliner 'Heimatfront' 1914–1918." *Internationale wissenschaftliche Korrespondenz zur Geschichte der deutschen Arbeiterbewegung* 21 (1985): 281–95.

Eisenberg, Christiane. "Vom 'Arbeiter-' zum 'Angestelltenfußball'? Zur Sozialstruktur des deutschen Fußballsports 1890–1950." *Sozial- und Zeitgeschichte des Sports* 4, no. 3 (1990): 20–44.

————. "Football in Germany: Beginnings 1890–1914." *International Journal of the History of Sport* 8 (1991): 205–20.

———. "Massensport in der Weimarer Republik: Ein statistischer Überblick." *Archiv für Sozialgeschichte* 33 (1993): 137–78.

———. "Fussball in Deutschland 1890–1914: Ein Gesellschaftsspiel für bürgerliche Mittelschichten." *Geschichte und Gesellschaft* 20 (1994): 20–45.

———, ed. *Fussball, soccer, calcio: Ein englischer Sport auf seinem Weg um die Welt.* München: Deutscher Taschenbuch Verlag, 1997.

———. "Sportgeschichte: Eine Dimension der modernen Kulturgeschichte." *Geschichte und Gesellschaft* 23 (1997): 295–310.

———. *"English sports" und deutsche Bürger: Eine Gesellschaftsgeschichte 1800–1939.* Paderborn: Schöningh, 1999.

———. "Rival Interpretations of Football Hooliganism: Figurational Sociology, Social History and Anthropology." In *Representations of Emotional Excess,* edited by Jürgen Schlaeger, 297–306. Tübingen: Narr, 2000.

———. "The Rise of Internationalism in Sport." In *The Mechanics of Internationalism: Culture, Society, and Politics from the 1840s to World War I,* edited by Martin H. Geyer and Johannes Paulmann, 375–403. Oxford: Oxford University Press, 2001.

———. "From England to the World: The Spread of Modern Soccer Football 1863–2000." *Moving Bodies* 1 (2003): 7–22.

———. "International Bibiography of Football History." *Historical Social Research* 31 (2006): 170–208.

———. "Der Weltfußballverband FIFA im 20. Jahrhundert. Metamorphosen eines 'Prinzipienreiters.'" *Vierteljahrshefte für Zeitgeschichte* 54 (2006): 209–30.

Eisenberg, Christiane, et al. *100 Years of Football: The FIFA Centennial Book.* London: Weidenfeld and Nicolson Illustrated, 2004.

Elias, Norbert. *Über den Prozess der Zivilisation: Sozio- und psychogenetische Untersuchungen.* 2 vols. Frankfurt: Suhrkamp, 1976.

Elias, Norbert, and Eric Dunning. *Sport im Zivilisationsprozess: Studien zur Figurationssoziologie.* Edited by Wilhelm Hopf. Münster: Lit, 1982.

———. *"Elf Freunde müsst ihr sein!": Einwürfe und Anstösse zur deutschen Fussballgeschichte.* Freiburg: Haug, 1995.

Elwert, Georg. "Nationalismus und Ethnizität: Über die Bildung von Wir-Gruppen." *Kölner Zeitschrift für Soziologie und Sozialpsychologie* 3 (1989): 440–64.

Epstein, James. "Rituals of Solidarity: Radical Dining, Toasting and Symbolic Expression." In *Radical Expression: Political Language, Ritual, and Symbol in England, 1790–1850,* by James Epstein, 147–65. Oxford: Oxford University Press, 1994.

Erb, Andreas, and Dirk Leibfried. *Das Schweigen der Männer: Homosexualität im deutschen Fussball.* Göttingen: Werkstatt, 2011.

Eriksonas, Linas. *National Heroes and National Identities: Scotland, Norway and Lithuania.* Brussels: Lang, 2004.

Fabrizio, Felice. *Sport e fascismo: La politica sportiva del regime 1924–1936.* Florence: Guaraldi, 1976.

Fankhauser, Dominique Marcel. *Die Arbeitersportbewegung in der Schweiz 1874–1947: Beiträge zur Sozialen Frage im Sport.* Vienna: Lit, 2010.

Bibliography

Fasbender, Sebastian. *Zwischen Arbeitersport und Arbeitssport: Werksport an Rhein und Ruhr 1921–1938.* Göttingen: Cuvillier, 1997.

Fatheuer, Thomas. *Eigentore: Soziologie und Fussball.* Münster: Westfälisches Dampfboot, 1985.

Fechtig, Beate. *Frauen und Fussball: Interviews-Portraits-Reportagen.* Dortmund: Edition Ebersbach, 1995.

Fernández Santander, C. *El fútbol durante la guerra civil y el franquismo.* Madrid: San Martín, 1990.

Feldman, Gerald D. "Die Inflation und die politische Kultur der Weimarer Republik." In *Nation und Gesellschaft in Deutschland: Historische Essays,* edited by Manfred Hettling and Paul Nolte, 269–81. Munich: Beck, 1996.

Filter, Frank. "Fussballsport in der Arbeiter-Turn- und Sportbewegung." *Sozial- und Zeitgeschichte des Sports* 2 (1988): 85–93.

Finlay, Richard J. "Heroes, Myths, and Anniversaries in Modern Scotland." *Scottish Affairs* 18 (1997): 152–78.

———. *A Partnership for Good? Scottish Politics and the Union since 1800.* Edinburgh: John Donald, 1997.

———. "The Rise and Fall of Popular Imperialism in Scotland." *Scottish Geographic Magazine* 113 (1997): 98–114.

Finn, Gerry P. T., and Richard Giulianotti, eds. *Football Culture: Local Contests, Global Visions.* London: F. Cass, 2000.

Fisch, Jörg. "Zivilisation, Kultur." In *Geschichtliche Grundbegriffe: Historisches Lexikon zur politisch-sozialen Sprache in Deutschland,* edited by Otto Brunner et al., 7:679–774. Stuttgart: Klett-Cotta, 1992.

Fischer, Gerhard, and Ulrich Lindner. *Stürmer für Hitler: Vom Zusammenspiel zwischen Fussball und Nationalsozialismus.* Göttingen: Werkstatt, 1999.

Fishwick, Nicholas. *English Football and Society.* Manchester: Manchester University Press, 1989.

Foot, John. *Calcio: A History of Italian Football.* London: Harper Perennial, 2007.

Forster, David, et al. *"Die Legionäre": Österreichische Fußballer in aller Welt.* Münster: Lit, 2011.

Foucault, Michel. *Discipline and Punish: The Birth of the Prison.* Translated by Alan Sheridan. New York: Vintage Books, 1975.

François, Etienne, et al., eds. *Nation und Emotion: Deutschland und Frankreich im Vergleich—19. und 20. Jahrhundert.* Göttingen: Vandenhoeck & Ruprecht, 1995.

Frank, Wolfgang. "Was ist real an Real Madrid?" *ZEITmagazin* 40 (1973): 26.

Frevert, Ute. "Vom Klavier zur Schreibmaschine: Weiblicher Arbeitsmarkt und Rollenzuweisungen am Beispiel der weiblichen Angestellten in der Weimarer Republik." In *Frauen in der Geschichte: Frauenrechte und die gesellschaftliche Arbeit der Frauen im Wandel: Fachwissenschaftliche und fachdidaktische Studien zur Geschichte der Frauen,* edited by Annette Kuhn and Gerhard Schneider, 82–112. Düsseldorf: Schwann, 1979.

———. *Ehrenmänner: Das Duell in der bürgerlichen Gesellschaft.* Munich: Beck, 1991.

Bibliography

Friedemann, Horst, ed. *Sparwasser und Mauerblümchen: Die Geschichte des Fussballs in der DDR 1949–1991*. Essen: Klartext, 1996.

Friedrichs, Hans Joachim. *XI. Fussball-Weltmeisterschaft 1978 Argentinien*. Gütersloh: Bertelsmann, 1978.

Frykholm, Peter A. "Soccer and Social Identity in Pre-Revolutionary Moscow." *Journal of Sport History* 24 (1997): 143–54.

Fuller, J. G. *Troops Morale and Popular Culture in the British and Dominion Armies 1914–1918*. Oxford: Clarendon Press, 1990.

Furgler, Martin. *1879–1979—Ein Jahrhundert FC St. Gallen: Offizielles Jubiläumsbuch zum 100. Geburtstag des ältesten Fussballclubs der Schweiz*. Herisau: FC St. Gallen, 1979.

Fussball und Rassismus. Göttingen: Werkstatt, 1993.

Fussell, Paul. *The Great War and Modern Memory*. Oxford: Oxford University Press, 1975.

Galeano, Edoardo. *Der Ball ist rund*. Zurich: Unionsverlag, 2000.

Galisson, Robert. *Recherches de lexicologie: La banalisation lexicale: Le vocabulaire du football dans la presse sportive: Contribution aux recherches sur les langues techniques*. Paris: Nathan, 1978.

Gallagher, Tom. *Glasgow: The Uneasy Peace*. Manchester: Manchester University Press, 1987.

———. "The Catholic Irish in Scotland: In Search of Identity." In *Irish Immigrants and Scottish Society in the Nineteenth and Twentieth Centuries*, edited by T. M. Devine, 27–50. Edinburgh: John Donald, 1991.

Gamper, Michael. "Mythos Tour de France: Wie die Tour ihr Publikum fasziniert," in *Tour de France: Auf den Spuren eines Mythos*, 7–14. Zurich: AS Verlag, 1999.

Ganzenmüller, Jörg. *Das belagerte Leningrad 1941 bis 1944: Die Stadt in den Strategien von Angreifern und Verteidigern*. Paderborn: Schöningh, 2007.

Garland, Jon, et al., eds. *The Future of Football: Challenges of the Twenty-First Century*. London: Frank Cass, 2000.

Gastaud, Yves, and Stephane Mourlane, eds. *Le Footbal dans nos sociétés: Une culture populaire 1914–1998*. Paris: Autrement, 2006.

Geertz, Clifford. *Dichte Beschreibung: Beiträge zum Verstehen kultureller Systeme*. Frankfurt: Suhrkamp, 1997.

Gehrmann, Siegfried. "Fussball in einer Industrieregion: Das Beispiel F. C. Schalke 04." In *Fabrik-Familie-Feierabend: Beiträge zur Sozialgeschichte des Alltags im Industriezeitalter*, edited by Jürgen Reulecke and Wolfhard Weber, 377–98. Wuppertal: Hammer, 1978.

———. "Fritz Szepan und Ernst Kuzorra: Zwei Fussballidole des Ruhrgebiets." *Sozial- und Zeitgeschichte des Sports* 2, no. 3 (1988): 57–71.

———. *Fussball-Vereine-Politik: Zur Sportgeschichte des Reviers*. Essen: Hobbing, 1988.

———. "Ein Schritt nach Europa: Zur Gründungsgeschichte der Fussballbundesliga." *Sozial- und Zeitgeschichte des Sports* 6 (1992): 3–37.

———. "Fussballsport und Gesellschaft in historischer Perspektive: Ein Bericht zur Forschungslage in Grossbritannien." *Sozial- und Zeitgeschichte des Sports* 7, no. 2 (1993): 7–43.

————, ed. *Football and Regional Identity in Europe*. Münster: Lit, 1997.

Gehrmann, Thomas. *Fussballrandale: Hooligans in Deutschland*. Essen: Klartext, 1990.

Geyer, Martin H. *Verkehrte Welt: Revolution, Inflation und Moderne, München 1914–1924*. Göttingen: Vandenhoeck & Ruprecht, 1998.

Ghirelli, Antonio. *Storia del calcio in Italia*. Turin: Einaudi, 1990.

Giesen, Bernhard, ed. *Nationale und kulturelle Identität: Studien zur Entwicklung des kollektiven Bewusstseins in der Neuzeit*. Frankfurt: Suhrkamp, 1991.

Giordano, Ralph. *Die zweite Schuld oder Von der Last Deutscher zu sein*. Hamburg: Rasch und Röhring, 1987.

Giuliani, Markus. *"Starke Jugend—freies Volk": Bundestaatliche Körpererziehung und gesellschaftliche Funktion von Sport in der Schweiz (1918–1947)*. Bern: Lang, 2001.

Giulianotti, Richard. *Football: A Sociology of the Global Game*. Malden, Mass.: Polity Press, 1999.

————. "Built by the Two Valeras: Football Culture and National Identity in Uruguay." *Culture, Sport and Society* 2 (2000): 134–54.

Giulianotti, Richard, and John Williams, eds. *Game without Frontiers: Football, Identity and Modernity*. Aldershot-Brookfield: Arena, 1994.

Giulianotti, Richard, et al., eds. *Football, Violence and Social Identity*. London-New York: Routledge, 1994.

Glanville, Brian. *The Story of the World Cup*. London: Faber and Faber, 1993.

Goch, Stefan. "FC Schalke 04: Instrumentalisierung des Zuschauersports." In *Macht der Propaganda oder Propaganda der Macht? Inszenierung nationalsozialistischer Politik im "Dritten Reich" am Beispiel der Stadt Gelsenkirchen*, by Stefan Goch and Heinz-Jürgen Priamus, 81–92. Essen: Klartext, 1992.

Gödeke, Peter. *Tor! 100 Jahre Fussball*. Munich: Herbig, 1998.

Goksøyr, Matti. "'We are the best in the world! We have beaten England!' Norwegian Football's Function as a Carrier of Nationalism." In *Spiele der Welt im Spannungsfeld von Tradition und Moderne: Proceedings of the 2nd ISPES Congress, Berlin 1993, Teil I*, edited by Gertrud Pfister et al., 367–73. Sankt Augustin: Academia Verlag, 1996.

Golby, J. M., and A. W. Purdue. *The Civilization of the Crowd: Popular Culture in England 1750–1900*. New York: Schocken Books, 1985.

Goltermann, Svenja. *Körper der Nation: Habitusformierung und die Politik des Turnens 1860–1890*. Göttingen: Vandenhoeck & Ruprecht, 1998.

Goode, Eric, and Nachman Ben-Yehuda. *Moral Panics: The Social Construction of Deviance*. Oxford: Blackwell, 1994.

Gorsuch, Anne. *Youth in Revolutionary Russia: Enthusiasts, Bohemians, Delinquents*. Bloomington: Indiana University Press 2000.

Gotta, Ricardo. *Fuimos Campeones: La dictadura, el Mundial 78 y el misterio del 6 a 0 a Perú*. Buenos Aires: Edhasa, 2008.

Goulstone, John. "The Working-Class Origins of Modern Football," *International Journal of the History of Sport* 17 (2000): 135–44.

Gounot, André. *Die Rote Sportinternationale 1921–1937: Kommunistische Massenpolitik im europäischen Arbeitersport*. Münster: Lit, 1998.

Bibliography

————. "Sport or Political Organization? Structures and Characteristics of the Red Sport International, 1921–1937." *Journal of Sport History* 28 (2001): 23–39.

————. "Barcelona gegen Berlin: Das Projekt der Volksolympiade 1936." In *Der deutsche Sport auf dem Weg in die Moderne: Carl Diem und seine Zeit*, edited by Michael Krüger, 119–30. Münster: Lit, 2009.

Griffin, Emma. *England's Revelry: A History of Popular Sports and Pastimes, 1660–1830.* Oxford: Oxford University Press, 2005.

Gross, Hermann. *Körpererziehung und Sport in der Sowjetunion: Entscheidende Faktoren ihrer raschen Entwicklung.* Graz: Institut und Wissenschaftlicher Kreis für Leibeserziehung der Universität Graz, 1965.

Grotum, Thomas. *Die Halbstarken: Zur Geschichte einer Jugendkultur der 50er Jahre.* Frankfurt: Campus, 1994.

Grüninger, Paul. *25 Jahre F.C. Brühl St. Gallen.* St. Gall: SC Brühl, 1926.

Guggisberg, Philippe, ed. *75 Ans Swiss Football League—Ligue Nationale ASF.* Köniz: Ast und Jakob, Vetsch AG, 2009.

Guha, Ramachandra. "Politik im Spiel: Cricket und Kolonialismus in Indien." *Historische Anthropologie* 4 (1996): 157–72.

Guillain, Jean-Yves. *La Coupe du Monde de Football: L'œuvre de Jules Rimet.* Paris: Editions Amphora, 1998.

Güldenpfennig, Sven. *Der politische Diskurs des Sports: Zeitgeschichtliche Beobachtungen und theoretische Grundlagen.* Aachen: Meyer & Meyer, 1992.

Guttmann, Allen. *From Ritual to Record: The Nature of Modern Sport.* New York: Columbia University Press, 1978.

Gutzke, David W. *Protecting the Pub: Brewers and Publicans against Temperance.* Woodbridge: Boydell Press, 1989.

Hack, Fritz. *Spiele des Jahrhunderts.* Bad Homburg: Limpert, 1980.

Hafer, Andreas, and Wolfgang Hafer. *Hugo Meisl oder die Erfindung des modernen Fußballs: Eine Biographie.* Göttingen: Werkstatt, 2007.

Haffner, Sebastian. *Geschichte eines Deutschen: Die Erinnerungen 1914–1933.* Stuttgart-Munich: Deutsche Verlags-Anstalt, 2000.

Hagemann, Karen, and Stefanie Schüler-Springorum, eds. *Home-Front: The Military, War and Gender in Twentieth-Century Germany.* Oxford: Berg, 2002.

Halbwachs, Maurice. *La mémoire collective.* Paris: Presses universitaires de France, 1950.

Hale, William. *Turkish Foreign Policy 1774–2000.* London: Frank Cass, 2000.

Haley, Bruce. *The Healthy Body and Victorian Culture*: Cambridge, Mass.: Harvard University Press, 1978.

Hall, Stuart, et al., eds. *Policing the Crisis: "Mugging", the State and Law and Order.* London: Macmillan, 1978.

Hamilton, Aidan. *An Entirely Different Game: The British Influence on Brazilian Football.* Edinburgh: Mainstream Publishing, 1998.

Hammerich, Kurt, and Klaus Heinemann, eds. *Texte zur Soziologie des Sports.* Schorndorf: K. Hofmann, 1975.

Handelman, Don. *Models and Mirrors: Towards an Anthropology of Public Events.* Cambridge: Berghahn, 1990.

Handler, Andrew. *From Goals to Guns: The Golden Age of Soccer in Hungary 1950–1956.* New York: East European Monographs, 1994.

Handley, James E. *The Irish in Modern Scotland.* Cork: Cork University Press, 1947.

Hansen, Klaus. "Gott ist rund und der Rasen heilig: Quasi-religiöse Aspekte der Fussballfaszination." *Universitas* 55 (2000): 249–66.

Harding, John. *Football Wizard: The Story of Billy Meredith.* Derby: Breedon Books, 1985.

Hargreaves, John. *Sport, Power and Culture*: Oxford: Polity Press, 1986.

Harrison, Brian. *Drink and the Victorians: The Temperance Question in England, 1817–1872.* London: Faber and Faber, 1971.

Hart, Marie, ed. *Sport in the Sociocultural Process.* Dubuque, Iowa: W. C. Brown, 1981.

Hart-Davis, D. *Hitler's Games: The 1936 Olympics.* New York: Harper and Row, 1986.

Hartmann, Grit. *Goldkinder: Die DDR im Spiegel ihres Spitzensports.* Leipzig: Forum-Verlag, 1998.

Hausen, Karin. "Mütter zwischen Geschäftsinteresse und kultischer Verehrung: Der 'Deutsche Muttertag' in der Weimarer Republik." In *Sozialgeschichte der Freizeit: Untersuchungen zum Wandel der Alltagskultur in Deutschland*, edited by Gerhard Huck, 249–80. Wuppertal: Hammer, 1980.

Hausmann, Manfred. *Spiegel des Lebens: Gedanken über das Fussballspiel.* Zurich: Verlag der Arche, 1966.

Havemann, Nils. *Fußball unterm Hakenkreuz: Der DFB zwischen Sport, Politik und Kommerz.* Frankfurt: Campus, 2005.

———. *Samstags um halb 4: Die Geschichte der Fussballbundesliga.* Munich: Siedler, 2013.

Haynes, Richard. *The Football Imagination: The Rise of Football Fanzine Culture.* Aldershot: Arena, 1995.

Heiber, Helmut, ed. *Goebbels-Reden.* 2 vols. Düsseldorf: Droste, 1972.

Heidenreich, Frank. *Arbeiterkulturbewegung und Sozialdemokratie in Sachsen vor 1933.* Weimar: Böhlau, 1995.

Heinecken, Philipp. *Das Fussballspiel: Association und Rugby.* Stuttgart: 1898; reprinted Hannover: Schäfer, 1993.

Heinemann, Klaus. *Texte zur Ökonomie des Sports.* Schorndorf: Karl Hofmann, 1984.

———. *Einführung in die Soziologie des Sports.* Fourth edition. Schorndorf: Karl Hofmann, 1998.

Heinrich, Arthur. *Tooor! Toor! Tor! 40 Jahre 3 : 2.* Hamburg: Rotbuch Verlag, 1994.

———. "Tull Harder—Eine Karriere in Deutschland: Versuch einer Dokumentation." In *Antifaschismus*, edited by F. Deppe et al., 83–95. Heilbronn: Distel-Verlag, 1996.

———. *Der Deutsche Fussballbund: Eine politische Geschichte.* Cologne: PapyRossa-Verlag, 2000.

Heitmeyer, Wilhelm, and Peter Jörg-Ingo. *Jugendliche Fussballfans: Soziale und politische Orientierungen, Gesellungsformen, Gewalt.* Weinheim-Munich: Juventa-Verlag, 1992.

Henshaw, Richard. *The Encyclopedia of World Soccer.* Washington, D.C.: New Republic Books, 1979.

Herrmann, Hans Ulrich. *Die Fussballfans: Untersuchungen zum Zuschauersport.* Schorndorf: Karl Hofmann, 1977.

Hervé, Florence. "Brot und Frieden—Kinder, Küche, Kirche: Weimarer Republik 1918/19 bis 1933." In *Geschichte der deutschen Frauenbewegung*, edited by Florence Hervé, 85–110. Cologne: PapyRossa-Verlag, 1995.

Herzog, Markwart, ed. *Fussball als Kulturphänomen: Kunst-Kult-Kommerz*. Stuttgart: Kohlhammer, 2002.

———. *"Blitzkrieg" im Fußballstadion: Der Spielsystemstreit zwischen dem NS-Sportfunktionär Karl Oberhuber und Reichstrainer Sepp Herberger*. Stuttgart: Kohlhammer, 2012.

———, ed. *Frauenfussball in Deutschland: Anfänge-Verbote-Widerstände-Durchbruch*. Stuttgart: Kohlhammer, 2013.

———, ed. *Memorialkultur im Fußballsport: Medien, Rituale und Praktiken des Erinnerns, Gedenkens und Vergessens*. Stuttgart: Kohlhammer, 2013.

Herzog, Markwart, and Andreas Bode, eds. *Fußball zur Zeit des Nationalsozialismus: Alltag, Medien, Künste, Stars*. Stuttgart: Kohlhammer, 2008.

Hildebrand, Dieter. *... über die Bundesliga: Die verkaufte Haut oder Ein Leben im Trainingsanzug*. Frankfurt: Ullstein, 1981.

Hildebrand, Klaus. "Monokratie oder Polykratie? Hitlers Herrschaft und das Dritte Reich." In *Der "Führerstaat": Mythos und Realität: Studien zu Struktur und Politik des Dritten Reiches*, edited by Gerhard Hirschfeld et al., 73–97. Stuttgart: Klett-Cotta, 1981.

Hildenbrandt, Eberhard, ed. *Sport als Kultursegment aus der Sicht der Semiotik*. Hamburg: Czwalina, 1997.

Hilger, Gustav. *Wir und der Kreml. Deutsch-sowjetische Beziehungen 1918–1941: Erinnerungen eines deutschen Diplomaten*. Bonn: Athenäum, 1964.

Hill, Howard. *Freedom to Roam: The Struggle for Access to Britain's Moors and Mountains*. Ashbourne: Mooreland, 1980.

Hilton, Chistopher. *Hitler's Olympics: The 1936 Berlin Olympic Games*. Stroud: The History Press, 2006.

Hitler, Adolf. *Mein Kampf*. Munich: Zentralverlag der NSDAP, 1941.

Hitzler, Ronald. "Ist Sport Kultur? Versuch eine 'Gretchenfrage' zu beantworten." In *Soziologie des Sports. Theorieansätze, Forschungsergebnisse und Forschungsperspektiven*, edited by Joachim Winkler and Kurt Weis, 153–64. Opladen: Westdeutscher Verlag, 1995.

Holmes, Colin. *Anti-Semitism in British Society: 1876–1939*. London: Edward Arnold, 1979.

Holmes, Judith. *Olympiad 1936: Blaze of Glory for Hitler's Reich*. New York: Ballantine Books, 1971.

Hoberman, John. "'Mortal Engines': Hochleistungssport und die physiologischen Grenzen des menschlichen Organismus." In *Physiologie und industrielle Gesellschaft: Studien zur Verwissenschaftlichung des Körpers im 19. und 20. Jahrhundert*, edited by Philipp Sarasin and Jakob Tanner, 491–507. Frankfurt: Suhrkamp, 1998.

Hobsbawm, Eric J. *The Age of Capital 1848–1875*. London: Weidenfeld and Nicolson, 1975.

———. *Worlds of Labour: Further Studies in the History of Labour.* New York: Pantheon Books, 1984.

———. *The Age of Extremes.* London: Michael Joseph, 1995.

———. "Die Entstehung der Arbeiterklasse (1870–1914)." In *Ungewöhnliche Menschen: Über Widerstand, Rebellion und Jazz,* by Eric J. Hobsbawm, 80–102. Vienna: Hanser, 2001.

Hobsbawm, Eric J., and Terence Ranger, eds. *The Invention of Tradition.* Cambridge: Cambridge University Press, 1983.

Hochstrasser, Eugen, and Hans Stahel. *Jubiläumsschrift 75 Jahre FC Schlieren.* Schlieren: Fussball-Club Schlieren, 1996.

Hoffmann, Eduard, and Jürgen Nendza. *Verlacht, verboten und gefeiert: Zur Geschichte des Frauenfussballs in Deutschland.* Weilerswist: Ralf Liebe, 2005.

Hoffmann, Himar. *Mythos Olympia: Autonomie und Unterwerfung von Sport und Kultur.* Berlin: Aufbau-Verlag, 1993.

Holmes, Colin. *Anti-Semitism in British Society: 1876–1939.* London: Arnold, 1979.

Holt, Richard. *Sport and Society in Modern France.* London: Macmillan, 1981.

———. "Working Class Football and the City: The Problem of Continuity." *International Journal of the History of Sport* 3 (1986): 5–17.

———. *Sport and the British: A Modern History.* Oxford: Clarendon Press, 1989.

———, ed. *Sport and the Working Class in Modern Britain.* Manchester: Manchester University Press, 1990.

Holt, Richard, and Tony Mason. *Sport in Britain, 1945–2000.* Oxford: Blackwell Publishers, 2000.

Holt, Richard, et al., eds. *European Heroes: Myth, Identity, Sport.* London: Cass, 1996.

Holzweissig, Gunter, and Manfred Messing. *Diplomatie im Traingsanzug: Sport als politisches Instrument der DDR.* Munich: Oldenbourg, 1981.

Hong, Fan, and James Mangan, eds. *Kicking Off a New Era: Women's Football in the World: Progress and Problems.* London: Routledge, 2003.

Hopf, Wilhelm, ed. *Fussball: Soziologie und Sozialgeschichte einer populären Sportart.* Bensheim: Päd. Extra Buchverlag, 1979.

———, ed. *Die Veränderung des Sports ist gesellschaftlich.* Münster: Lit, 1986.

Horak, Roman, and Wolfgang Maderthaner, eds. "Vom Fussballspielen in Wien: Überlegungen zu einem popularkulturellen Phänomen der Zwischenkriegszeit." In *Philosophie, Psychoanalyse, Emigration: Festschrift für Kurt Rudolf Fischer,* edited by Cornelia Wegeler et al., 99–118. Vienna: WUV-Universitätsverlag, 1992.

———. *Mehr als ein Spiel: Fussball und populare Kulturen im Wien der Moderne.* Vienna: Löcker, 1997.

Horak, Roman, and Wolfgang Reiter, eds. *Die Kanten des runden Leders: Beiträge zur europäischen Fussballkultur.* Vienna: Promedia, 1991.

Hornby, Hugh. *Uppies and Downies: The Extraordinary Football Games of Britain.* Berkshire: English Heritage, 2008.

Hornby, Nick. *High Fidelity.* London: Gollancz, 1995.

———. *Fever Pitch.* London: Penguin Books, 1996.

Bibliography

Horne, John, et al., eds. *Sport, Leisure and Social Relations*. London: Routledge and Kegan Paul, 1987.

———. *Understanding Sport: An Introduction to the Sociological and Cultural Analysis of Sport*. London: E. and F. N. Spon, 1999.

Hortleder, Gerd. *Die Faszination des Fussballsports: Soziologische Anmerkungen zum Sport als Freizeit und Beruf*. Frankfurt: Suhrkamp, 1974.

Hortleder, Gerd, and Gunther Gebauer, eds. *Sport-Eros-Tod*. Frankfurt: Suhrkamp, 1986.

Houlihan, B. *Sport and International Politics*. New York: Harvester Wheatsheaf, 1994.

Howkins, Alan. "The Taming of Whitsun. The Changing Face of a Nineteenth-Century Rural Holiday." In *Popular Culture and Class Conflict: Explorations in the History of Labour and Leisure*, edited by Eileen Yeo and Stephen Yeo, 187–208. Brighton: Harvester Press, 1981.

Huba, Karl-Heinz, ed. *Fussball-Weltgeschichte: Von 1846 bis heute: Bilder, Fakten, Daten*. Munich: Copress Sport, 1996.

Hubacher, Helmut. "Einwurf: Der legendäre Sieg in Paris." *Tages-Anzeiger*, June 12, 1998.

Huberty, Ernst, and Willy B. Wange, eds. *Fussball-Weltmeisterschaft 1970*. Zurich: Lingen, 1970.

Huggins, M. "The Spread of Association Football in North-East England, 1876–90: The Pattern of Diffusion." *International Journal of the History of Sport* 6 (1989): 299–318.

Huizinga, Johan. *Homo Ludens. Vom Ursprung der Kultur im Spiel*. Hamburg: Rowohlt, 1987.

Humphries, Steven. *Hooligans or Rebels? An Oral History of Working Class Childhood and Youth, 1889–1939*. Oxford: Blackwell, 1981.

Hüttenberger, Peter. "Nationalsozialistische Polykratie." *Geschichte und Gesellschaft* 2 (1976): 417–42.

Hutton, Ronald. *The Rise and Fall of Merry England: The Ritual Year 1400–1700*. Oxford: Oxford University Press, 1996.

Impiglia, Marco. "The Volata Game: When Fascism Forbade Italians to Play Football." In *La comune eredità dello sport in Europa: Atti del primo Seminario Europeo di Storia dello Sport*, edited by Arndt Krüger and Angela Teja, 420–26. Rome: Coni, 1997.

———. "1934 FIFA World Cup: Did Mussolini Rig the Game?" In *The FIFA World Cup 1930–2010: Politics, Commerce, Spectacle and Identities,* edited by Stefan Rinke and Kay Schiller. Göttingen: Wallstein, 2014.

Ingham, Roger, ed. *Football Hooliganism: The Wider Context*. London: Inter-Action Imprint, 1978.

Irnberger, Harald. *Cesar Luis Menotti: Ball und Gegner laufen lassen*. Vienna: Werner Eichbauer, 2000.

Ittmann, Karl. *Work, Gender and Family in Victorian England*. New York: New York University Press, 1995.

Jaccoud, Christophe, et al., eds. *Sports en Suisse: Traditions, transitions et transformations*. Lausanne: Antipodes, 2000.

Bibliography

Jaeger, Franz, and Winfried Stier, eds. *Sport und Kommerz.* Zurich: Rüegger, 2000.

Jaun, Rudolf. *Preussen vor Augen: Das schweizerische Offizierskorps im militärischen und gesellschaftlichen Wandel des Fin de siècle.* Zurich: Chronos, 1999.

John, Michael. "Fussballsport und nationale Identität: Versuch einer historischen Skizze." *Historicum* (Winter 1998–99): 27–34.

———. "Aggressiver Antisemitismus im österreichischen Sportgeschehen der Zwischenkriegszeit: Manifestationen und Reaktionen anhand ausgewählter Beispiele." *Zeitgeschichte* 26 (1999): 203–23.

Johnes, Martin. *Soccer and Society: South Wales, 1900–1939: That Other Game.* Cardiff: University of Wales Press, 2002.

Jones, Stephen G. "The Economic Aspects of Association Football in England, 1918–39." *British Journal of Sports History* 1 (1984): 286–99.

———. *Sports, Politics and the Working Class: Organised Labour and Sport in Inter-War Britain.* Manchester: Manchester University Press, 1988.

Jose, Colin. *The American Soccer League: The Golden Years of American Soccer 1921–1931.* Lanham, Md.: Scarecrow Press, 1998.

Jost, Hans Ulrich. "Bedrohung und Enge (1914–1945)." In *Geschichte der Schweiz und der Schweizer,* edited by Beatrix Messmer et al., 731–819. Basel: Schwabe, 1986.

———. "Leibeserziehung und Sport im Rahmen des Vereinswesens der Schweiz." *Traverse* 5 (1998): 33–44.

Joung, James D. "Imperialism, Racism and the English Workers: Significance of the Race Riots in 1919." In *Internationale Tagung der Historiker der Arbeiterbewegung: 20. Linzer Konferenz (Linz, 11. bis 15. September 1984),* edited by Hans Hautmann, 171–96. Vienna: Europaverlag, 1989.

Jubiläumsschrift 50 Jahre Schweizer Fussball- und Athletik-Verband 1895–1945. Basel: Schweizer Fussball- und Athletik-Verband, 1945.

Judd, Mark. "'The Oddest Combination of Town and Country': Popular Culture and the London Fairs, 1800–1860." In *Leisure in Britain, 1780–1939,* edited by John K. Walton and John Walvin, 10–30. Manchester: Manchester University Press, 1983.

Jüdisches Museum Wien, ed. *Hakoah: Ein jüdischer Sportverein in Wien 1909–1995.* Vienna: Jüdisches Museum der Stadt Wien, 1995.

Jung, Beat, ed. *Die Nati: Die Geschichte der Schweizer Fussball-Nationalmannschaft.* Göttingen: Werkstatt, 2006.

Jung, Edgar J. *Die Herrschaft der Minderwertigen: Ihr Zerfall und ihre Ablösung durch ein neues Reich.* Berlin: Verlag Deutsche Rundschau, 1927.

Jürgs, Michael. *Der kleine Frieden im Großen Krieg: Westfront 1914: Als Deutsche, Franzosen und Briten gemeinsam Weihnachten feierten.* Munich: Bertelsmann, 2003.

Kapucinski, Ryszard. *Der Fussballkrieg: Berichte aus der Dritten Welt.* Frankfurt: Fischer Taschenbuch, 1990.

Karush, Matthew B. "National Identity in the Sports Pages: Football and the Mass Media in 1920s." *The Americas* 60, no. 1 (2003): 11–32.

Keller, Stefan. *Grüningers Fall: Geschichten von Flucht und Hilfe.* Zurich: Rotpunkt Verlag, 1998.

Kelly, Graham. *Terrace Heroes: The Life and Times of the 1930s Professional Footballer*. London: Routledge Chapman and Hall, 2005.

Kershaw, Ian. "Working towards the Führer: Reflections on the Nature of the Hitler Dictatorship." In *The Third Reich: The Essential Readings*, edited by Christian Leitz, 231–52. London: Wiley-Blackwell, 1999.

Keys, Barbara J. "The Internationalization of Sport, 1890–1939." In *The Cultural Turn: Essays in the History of U.S. Foreign Relations*, edited by Frank A. Ninkovich and Liping Bu, 201–20. Chicago: Imprint Publications, 2001.

———. "Soviet Sport and Transnational Mass Culture in the 1930s." *Journal of Contemporary History* 38 (2003): 413–34.

———. *Globalizing Sport: National Rivalry and International Community in the 1930s*. Cambridge, Mass.: Harvard University Press, 2006.

King, Anthony. "Football Fandom and Post-National Identity in the New Europe." *British Journal of Sociology* 51 (2000): 419–43.

———. *The End of the Terraces: The Transformation of English Football in the 1990s*. London: Bloomsbury Academic, 2002.

Kirkham, P., and D. Thoms, eds. *War Culture: Social Change and Changing Experiences in World War Two*. London: Lawrence and Wishart, 1995.

Kistner, Thomas. *Das Milliardenspiel: Fussball, Geld und Medien*. Frankfurt: Fischer, 1998.

Klein, Michael, ed. *Sport und Geschlecht*. Reinbek: Rowohlt, 1983.

Koch, Lutz. *Hinein ... Tor, Tor! Deutschlands Nationalelf in 135 Fussball-Schlachten*. Berlin: Deutscher Schriftenverlag, 1937.

Kocka, Jürgen. *Sozialgeschichte: Begriff-Entwicklung-Probleme*. Göttingen: Vandenhoeck und Ruprecht, 1986.

Köhler, Ulrich. "Das Ballspiel." In *Das alte Mexiko: Geschichte und Kultur der Völker Mesoamerikas*, edited by Hans J. Penn and Ursula Dyckerhoff, 273–81. Munich: Bertelsmann, 1986.

Kohn, Hans. "Father Jahn's Nationalism." *Review of Politics* 11 (1949): 419–32.

Kolinsky, Eva. *Women in West Germany: Life, Work and Politics*. Oxford: Berg, 1989.

Koller, Christian. "Zur Entwicklung des schweizerischen Firmenfussballs 1920–1955." *Stadion* 28 (2002): 249–66.

———. "Sport, Parteipolitik und Landesverteidigung: Die Auseinandersetzungen um die Subventionierung des schweizerischen Arbeitersports in der Zwischenkriegszeit." *SportZeiten* 3, no. 2 (2003): 31–71.

———. "Fussball und Stadt im deutschsprachigen Raum im späten 19. und frühen 20. Jahrhundert: Ein Forschungsbericht." *Informationen zur modernen Stadtgeschichte* 1 (2006): 84–96.

———. "Fussball und Immigration in der Schweiz: Identitätswahrung, Assimilation oder Transkulturalität?" *Stadion* 34 (2008): 261–84.

———, ed. *Sport als städtisches Ereignis*. Ostfildern: Thorbecke, 2008.

———, ed. *Sternstunden des Schweizer Fussballs*. Münster: Lit, 2008.

———. *Streikkultur: Performanzen und Diskurse des Arbeitskampfes im schweizerisch-österreichischen Vergleich (1860–1950)*. Münster: Lit, 2009.

———. "'Welch einmalige Gelegenheit, unter dem Deckmantel des Sports seine wahren Gefühle zu zeigen': Sport in der schweizerischen 'Geistigen Landesverteidigung.'" *SportZeiten* 9, no. 1 (2009): 7–32.

———. "Ein König und drei Diktatoren: Profifussball und 'Totalitarismus' in der Zwischenkriegszeit." *Stadion* 37 (2011): 259–83.

———. "Transnationalität und Popularisierung—Thesen und Fragen zur Frühgeschichte des Schweizer Fußballs." *Ludica* 17–18 (2011–12): 151–66.

———. "Glencoe 1692: Ein Massaker als komplexer Erinnerungsort." *Historische Zeitschrift* 296, no. 1 (2013): 1–28.

Koller, Christian, and Fabian Brändle. "'Man fühlte, dass die Eidgenossen eine Grosstat vollbracht hatten': Fussball und geistige Landesverteidigung in der Schweiz." *Stadion* 25 (1999): 177–214.

———, eds. *Fußball zwischen den Kriegen. Europa 1918–1939.* Münster: Lit, 2010.

Kopa, Raymond. *Mes matches et ma vie.* Paris: Pierre Horay, 1958.

Kopa, Raymond, and Pierre Katz. *Mon Football.* Paris: Calmann-Lévy, 1972.

Kopiez, Reinhard, and Guido Brink. *Fussball-Fangesänge: Eine Fanomenologie.* Würzburg: Königshausen und Neumann, 1998.

Korr, Charles. "West Ham United Football Club and the Beginnings of Professional Football in East London." *Journal of Contemporary History* 13 (1978): 211–32.

———. *West Ham United: The Making of a Football Club.* London: Duckworth, 1986.

Kowalski, Ronald, and Dilwyn Porter. "Political Football: Moscow Dynamo in Britain, 1945." *International Journal of the History of Sport* 14 (1997): 100–121.

Kreis, Georg. *Zensur und Selbstzensur: Die schweizerische Pressepolitik im Zweiten Weltkrieg.* Frauenfeld-Stuttgart: Huber, 1973.

Krockow, Christian von. *Sport, Gesellschaft, Politik: Eine Einführung.* Munich: Piper, 1980.

Krüger, Arndt. *Die Olympischen Spiele 1936 und die Weltmeinung: Ihre aussenpolitische Bedeutung unter besonderer Berücksichtigung der USA.* Berlin: Bartels & Wernitz, 1972.

———. "Deutschland, Deutschland über alles? National Integration through Turnen und Sport in Germany 1870–1914." *Stadion* 25 (1999): 109–29.

Krüger, Arndt, and William J. Murray. *The Nazi Olympics: Sport, Politics and Appeasement in the 1930s.* Urbana: University of Illinois Press, 2003.

Krüger, Arndt, and James Riordan, eds. *The Story of Worker Sport.* Champaign, Ill.: Human Kinetics, 1996.

Krüger, Michael. "Zur Geschichte und Bedeutung des Amateurismus." *Sozial- und Zeitgeschichte des Sports* 2 (1988): 85–93.

———. *Einführung in die Geschichte der Leibeserziehung und des Sports.* Vol. 2: *Leibeserziehung im 19. Jahrhundert: Turnen fürs Vaterland.* Schorndorf: Hofmann, 1993.

———. *Körperkultur und Nationsbildung: Die Geschichte des Turnens in der Reichsgründungsära.* Schorndorf: Hofmann, 1996.

Kuper, Simon. *Ajax, the Dutch, the War: Football in Europe during the Second World War.* London: Orion, 2003.

Kutsch, Thomas, and Günter Wiswede, eds. *Sport und Gesellschaft: Die Kehrseite der Medaille.* Königstein: Hain, 1981.

Kuzmics, Helmut, et al., eds. *Transformationen des Wir-Gefühls: Studien zum nationalen Habitus*. Frankfurt: Suhrkamp, 1993.

Lanfranchi, Pierre. "Football et modernité: La Suisse et la pénétration du football sur le continent." *Traverse* 5 (1998): 76–88.

Lanfranchi, Pierre, and Matthew Taylor. "Professional Football in World War Two Britain." In *Il calcio e il suo pubblico*, edited by Pierre Lanfranchi. Naples: Edizioni scientifiche italiane, 1992.

Langewiesche, Dieter. "Arbeiterkultur in Österreich: Aspekte, Tendenzen und Thesen." In *Arbeiterkultur*, edited by Gerhard A. Ritter, 40–57. Königstein: Verlagsgruppe Athenäum, 1979.

———. "'. . . für Volk und Vaterland kräftig zu würken . . .': Zur politischen und gesell-schaftlichen Rolle der Turner zwischen 1811 und 1871." In *Kulturgut oder Kör-perkult? Sport und Sportwissenschaft im Wandel*, edited by Ommo Grupe, 22–61. Tübingen: Attempto-Verlag, 1990.

Lawton, Tommy. *Football Is My Business*. Edited by Roy Peskett. London: Sporting Handbooks, 1946.

Lefebvre, Henri. *Die Revolution der Städte*. Frankfurt: Athenäum, 1990.

Leinemann, Jürgen. *Sepp Herberger: Ein Leben, eine Legende*. Berlin: Heyne, 1997.

Lenman, Bruce P. *The Jacobite Risings in Britain, 1689–1746*. London: Eyre Methuen, 1980.

Leo, Per. "'Bremsklötze des Fortschritts': Krisendiskurse und Dezisionismus im deutschen Verbandsfußball, 1919–1934." In *Die 'Krise' der Weimarer Republik: Zur Kritik eines Deutungsmusters*, edited by Moritz Föllmer and Rüdiger Graf, 107–37. Frankfurt: Campus, 2005.

Leonhard, Wolfgang. *Der Schock des Hitler-Stalin-Paktes: Erinnerungen aus der Sowjet-union, Westeuropa und USA*. Freiburg: Herder, 1986.

Lepsius, M. Rainer. "Parteiensystem und Sozialstruktur: Zum Problem der Demokra-tisierung der deutschen Gesellschaft." In *Die deutschen Parteien vor 1918*, edited by Gerhard A. Ritter, 56–80. Cologne: Kiepenheuer und Witsch, 1973.

Leser, Norbert. *Zwischen Reformismus und Bolschewismus: Der Austromarxismus als Theorie und Praxis*. Vienna: Europaverlag, 1968.

Lever, Janet. *Soccer Madness: Brazil's Passion for the World's Most Popular Sport*. Chicago: Waveland, 1983.

Levermore, R., et al., eds. *Sport and International Relations: An Emerging Relationship*. London: Routledge, 2005.

Lewis, George. "The Muscular Christianity Movement." *Journal of Health, Physical Education, and Recreation* 37 (1966): 27–42.

Lewis, Robert W. "The Genesis of Professional Football: Bolton-Blackburn-Darwen, the Centre of Innovation, 1878–85." *International Journal of the History of Sport* 14 (1997): 21–54.

Lindner, Rolf. *Der Satz "Der Ball ist rund" hat eine gewisse philosophische Tiefe: Sport, Kultur, Zivilisiation*. Berlin: Transit Buchverlag, 1983.

———. "Die wilden Cliquen zu Berlin: Ein Beitrag zur historischen Kulturanalyse." *Historische Anthropologie* 1 (1993): 451–67.

Bibliography

Lindner, Rolf, and Heinrich Bauer. *"Sind doch nicht alles Beckenbauers": Zur Sozialge-schichte des Fussballs im Ruhrgebiet.* Frankfurt: Syndikat, 1982.

Link, Jürgen, and Wulf Wülfing, eds. *Nationale Mythen und Symbole in der zweiten Hälfte des 19. Jahrhunderts: Strukturen und Funktionen von Konzepten nationaler Identität.* Stuttgart: Klett-Cotta, 1991.

Linne, Carina Sophia. *Freigespielt: Frauenfussball im geteilten Deutschland.* Berlin: Bebra-Wiss.-Verlag, 2011.

Lissina, Hartmut E. *Nationale Sportfeste im nationalsozialistischen Deutschland.* Mannheim: Palatium, 1997.

Longmate, Norman: *The Waterdrinkers: A History of Temperance.* Edinburgh: Hamilton, 1968.

Lopez, Sue. *Women on the Ball: A Guide to Women's Football.* London: Scarlett Press, 1997.

Lowerson, John R. *Sport and the English Middle Classes, 1870–1914.* Manchester: Manchester University Press, 1993.

Lowerson, John R., and J. Myerscough. *Time to Spare in Victorian England.* Brighton: Harvester Press, 1977.

Luchsinger, Fred. *Die Neue Zürcher Zeitung im Zeitalter des Weltkrieges 1930–1955.* Zurich: Neue Zürcher Zeitung, 1955.

Lüdtke, Alf. "Eigen-Sinn: Lohn, Pausen, Neckereien: *Eigensinn* und Politik bei Fabrikar-beitern in Deutschland um 1900." In *Fabrikalltag, Arbeitserfahrungen und Politik vom Kaiserreich bis in den Faschismus,* by Alf Lüdtke, 120–60. Hamburg: Ergebnisse Verlag, 1993.

Luh, Andreas. *Chemie und Sport am Rhein: Sport als Bestandteil betrieblicher Sozialpolitik und unternehmerischer Marketingstrategie bei Bayer 1900–1985.* Bochum: N. Brock-meyer, 1992.

———. *Betriebssport zwischen Arbeitgeberinteressen und Arbeitnehmerbedürfnissen: Eine historische Analyse vom Kaiserreich bis zur Gegenwart.* Aachen: Meyer & Meyer, 1998.

Luhmann, Niklas. "Der Fussball." *Frankfurter Allgemeine Zeitung,* July 4, 1990.

Lutz, Walter. *Die Saga des Weltfussballs.* Derendingen: Habegger, 1991.

———. "Rudolf Mingers Dank und 175 Franken: 1938—Das Wunder von Paris." *Sport,* May 31, 1991.

Lyotard, Jean-François. "Randbemerkungen zu den Erzählungen" [1984]. In *Postmod-erne und Dekonstruktion: Texte französischer Philosophen der Gegenwart,* edited by Peter Engelmann, 49–53. Stuttgart: Reclam, 1990.

Maase, Kaspar. *Grenzenloses Vergnügen: Der Aufstieg der Massenkultur 1850–1970.* Frankfurt: Fischer Taschenbuch Verlag, 1997.

Machatscheck, Heinz. *Sport—geboren im Feuer der Revolution: Körperkultur und Sport in der UdSSR.* East Berlin, 1966.

Maderthaner, Wolfgang. "Ein Dokument wienerischen Schönheitssinns: Matthias Sin-delar und das Wunderteam." *Beiträge zur historischen Sozialkunde* 3 (1992): 87–91.

Maderthaner, Wolfgang, and Lutz Musner. *Die Anarchie der Vorstadt: Das andere Wien um 1900.* Frankfurt: Campus, 2000.

Maguire, Joseph. "Sport, Racism and British Society: A Sociological Study of England's Elite Male Afro/Caribbean Soccer and Rugby Union Players." In *Sport, Racism and Ethnicity*, edited by Grant Jarvie, 94–123. London: Routledge, 1991.

Maguire, Joseph, and David Stead. "Border Crossings: Soccer Labour Migration and the European Union." *International Review for the Sociology of Sport* 33 (1998): 59–73.

Malcolmson, Robert. *Popular Recreations in English Society, 1750–1850*. Cambridge: Cambridge University Press, 1973.

Majumdar, Boris. "Sport in Asia: Soccer in South Asia—Review Essay." *International Journal of the History of Sport* 19 (2002): 205–10.

Malitz, Bruno. *Die Leibesübungen in der nationalsozialistischen Idee*. Munich: Eher, 1933.

Malz, Arié, et al., eds. *Sport zwischen Ost und West: Beiträge zur Sportgeschichte Osteuropas im 19. und 20. Jahrhundert*. Osnabrück: Fibre, 2007.

Mandell, Richard. *Hitlers Olympiade: Berlin 1936*. Munich: Heyne, 1980.

———. *Sport: Eine illustrierte Kulturgeschichte*. Munich: Nymphenburger Verlagshandlung, 1986.

Mangan, James A., ed. *Pleasure, Profit, Proselytism: British Culture and Sport at Home and Abroad 1700–1914*. London: Frank Cass, 1988.

———, ed. *Tribal Identities: Nationalism, Europe, Sport*. London: Frank Cass, 1996.

Mangan, James A., and Hong Fan. *Sport in Asian Society*. London: Frank Cass, 2003.

Manzenreiter, Wolfgang, and John Horne, eds. *Football Goes East: Business, Culture and the People's Game in China, Japan and South Korea*. London: Routledge, 2004.

Marías, Javier. *Alle unsere frühen Schlachten: Fussball-Stücke*. Stuttgart: Klett-Cotta, 2000.

Markovits, Andrei S. "Why Is There No Soccer in the United States?" *Leviathan* 15 (1987): 486–525.

Markovits, Andrei S., and Steven Hellermann. *Offside: Soccer and American Exceptionalism*. Princeton, N.J.: Princeton University Press, 2001.

Marschik, Matthias. *"Wir spielen nicht zum Vergnügen": Arbeiterfussball in der Ersten Republik*. Vienna: Verlag für Gesellschaftskritik, 1994.

———. "'Am Spielfeld ist die Wahrheit gewesen': Die Wiener Fussballkultur in der Zeit des Nationalsozialismus: Zwischen Vereinnahmung und Widerstand." *Österreichische Zeitschrift für Volkskunde* 50 (1996): 181–205.

———. *Vom Herrenspiel zum Männersport: Die ersten Jahre des Fußballs in Wien*. Vienna. Turia & Kant, 1997.

———. *Vom Nutzen der Unterhaltung: Der Wiener Fußball in der NS-Zeit: Zwischen Vereinnahmung und Resistenz*. Vienna: Turia & Kant, 1998.

———. "Between Manipulation and Resistance: Viennese Football in the Nazi Era." *Journal of Contemporary History* 34 (1999): 215–31.

———. *Frauenfussball und Maskulinität: Geschichte-Gegenwart-Perspektiven*. Münster: Lit, 2003.

———. *Sportdiktatur: Bewegungskulturen im nationalsozialistischen Österreich*. Vienna: Turia & Kant, 2008.

Marschik, Matthias, et al., eds. *Das Stadion: Geschichte, Architektur, Politik, Ökonomie*. Vienna: Turia & Kant, 2005.

Marsh, Peter. *Aggro: The Illusion of Violence*. London: Dent, 1978.

Marsh, Peter, and Romano Harré. "The World of Football Hooligans." *Human Nature* 1, no. 10 (1978): 62–69.

Marsh, Peter, et al. *The Rules of Disorder*. London: Routledge and Keegan, 1978.

Martin, John. *The Seduction of the Gullible: The Curious History of the Video "British Nasty" Phenomenon*. Nottingham: Fantasma Books, 1993.

Martin, Simon. *Football and Fascism: The National Game under Mussolini*. Oxford: Berg, 2004.

Marwick, Arthur. *Women at War, 1914–1918*. Glasgow: Croom Helm, 1977.

Mason, Tony. *Association Football and English Society, 1863–1915*. Brighton: The Harvester Press, 1980.

———. "Football on the Maidan: Cultural Imperialism in Calcutta." In *The Cultural Bond: Sport, Empire, Society*, edited by J. A. Mangan, 142–53. London: Frank Cass, 1992.

———. *Passion of the People? Football in South America*. London: Verso, 1995.

Matheja, Ulrich. "Soziale Aspekte des englischen Fussballs im 19. Jahrhundert." *Elf* 7 (1987): 11–24.

Mathias, Peter. "The Brewing Industry: Temperance and Politics." *Historical Journal* 1 (1958): 97–114.

McAleer, Kevin. *Duelling: The Cult of Honor in Fin-de-Siècle Germany*. Princeton, N.J.: Princeton University Press, 1994.

McAloon, John J. *Brides of Victory: Nationalism and Gender in Olympic Ritual*. Oxford: Berg, 1997.

McCarthy, Patrick. *Camus: A Critical Study of His Life and Work*. London: Hamilton, 1982.

McCutcheon, Robert. "'Edinburgh Football Association Cup (1875–1888)' and 'East of Scotland Football Association Challenge Shield' (1888–1900)." *Elf* 4 (1986): 90–92.

McGinniss, Joe. *Das Wunder von Castel di Sangrio: Ein italienisches Fussballmärchen*. Cologne: Ullstein, 1999.

McKanna, Claire V., Jr. *Homicide, Race, and Justice in the American West, 1890–1920*. Tucson: University of Arizona Press, 1997.

McKibbin, Ross. "Working-Class Gambling in Britain, 1880–1939." *Past and Present* 82 (1979): 147–78.

McKinley, Cynthia, and Arthur Cunningham, eds. *A Football Compendium: A Comprehensive Guide to the Literature of Association Football*. London: The British Library, 1995.

McMaster, Neil. "The Battle for Mousehold Heath, 1857–84: Popular Politics and the Victorian Public Park." *Past and Present* 127 (1990): 117–54.

McWilliam, Rohan. *Popular Politics in Nineteenth-Century England*. London: Routledge, 1998.

Mead, George Herbert. "The Problem of Society—How We Become Selves." In *Movements of Thought in the Nineteenth Century*, by George Herbert Mead, edited by Merrit H. Moore, 360–85. Chicago: University of Chicago Press, 1936.

———. *Mind, Self, and Society: From the Standpoint of a Social Behaviorist*. Edited by Charles W. Morris. Chicago: University of Chicago Press, 1972.

———. "Die objektive Realität der Perspektiven (1927)." In *Gesammelte Aufsätze*, by George Herbert Mead, edited by Hans Joas, 2:211–24. Frankfurt: Suhrkamp, 1983.

Medick, Hans. "'Missionare im Ruderboot'? Ethnologische Erkenntnisweisen als Herausforderung an die Sozialgeschichte." *Geschichte und Gesellschaft* 10 (1984): 295–319.

Meier, Marianne. *"Zarte Füsschen am harten Leder ...": Frauenfussball in der Schweiz 1970–1999*. Frauenfeld: Huber, 2004.

Merkel, Udo, and Walter Tokarski. *Racism and Xenophobia in European Football*. Aachen: Meyer & Meyer, 1996.

Mertin, Evelyn. *Sowjetisch-deutsche Sportbeziehungen im "Kalten Krieg"*. St. Augustin: Academia Verlag, 2009.

Metcalfe, Alan. "Organized Sport in the Mining Communities of South Northumberland, 1800–1899." *Victorian Studies* 24 (1982): 469–95.

———. "Football in the Mining Communities of East Northumberland." *International Journal of the History of Sport* 5 (1988): 269–91.

———. "Sport and Space: A Case Study of the Growth of Recreational Faciltes in North East Northumberland, 1850–1914." *International Journal of the History of Sport* 7 (1990): 258–64.

Meyer, Petra Maria, ed. *Acoustic Turn*. Paderborn: Fink, 2008.

Meyer, Werner H., ed. *Ereignis-Mythos-Deutung: Die Schlacht bei St. Jakob an der Birs*. Basel: Klingenthal, 1994.

Mignon, Patrick. *La Passion du Football*. Paris: Jacob, 1998.

Mildenberger, Florian. "Die Angst des Diktators vor dem Elfmeter: Sport und Politik bei der Fussballweltmeisterschaft 1974." *Sozial- und Zeitgeschichte des Sports* 14 (2000): 57–65.

Milward, Alan S. *War, Economy and Society, 1939–1945*. London: Lane 1977.

Minelli, Severino. "Meine 14 Jahre bei der Schweizer Fussball-Nationalelf 1930–1943." *Küsnachter Jahresblätter* (1968): 58–61.

Moeller, Robert G. *Protecting Motherhood: Women and the Family in the Politics of Postwar West Germany*. Berkeley: University of California Press, 1993.

Molnar, G. "Hungarian Football: A Socio-historical Overview." *Sport in History* 27 (2007): 293–317.

Moorhouse, H. F. "Scotland against England: Football and Popular Culture." *International Journal of the History of Sport* 4 (1987): 189–202.

———. "Ending Traditions: Football and the Study of Football in the 1990s." *International Journal of the History of Sport* 15 (1998): 227–31.

Moritz, Rainer, ed. *Doppelpass und Abseitsfalle: Ein Fussball-Lesebuch*. Stuttgart: Reclam, 1995.

Morris, Desmond. *The Soccer Tribe*. London: Jonathan Cape, 1981.

Morton, Graeme. "The Most Efficacious Patriot: The Heritage of William Wallace in Nineteenth Century Scotland." *The Scottish Historical Review* 77, no. 2 (1998): 224–51.

————. *William Wallace: Man and Myth*. Stroud: Sutton, 2001.

Moynihan, John. *Soccer Focus: Reflections on a Changing Game*. London: Simon and Schuster, 1989.

Muhs, Rudolf, et al. "Brücken über den Kanal? Interkultureller Transfer zwischen Deutschland und Grossbritannien im 19. Jahrhundert." In *Aneignung und Abwehr: Interkultureller Transfer zwischen Deutschland und Grossbritannien im 19. Jahrhundert*, edited by Rudolf Muhs, 7–20. Bodenheim: Philo Verlagsgesellschaft, 1998.

Muir, Edward. *Ritual in Early Modern England*. Cambridge: Cambridge University Press, 1997.

Muir, James Hamilton. *Glasgow in 1901*. Glasgow: White Cockade, 2001.

Müller, Hans Richard, ed. *Stadion Schweiz: Turnen, Sport und Spiele*, vol. 1. Zurich: Metz, 1947.

Murphy, Patrick, et al., eds. *Football on Trial: Spectator Violence and Development in the Football World*. London: Routledge, 1990.

Murray, Bill. *The Old Firm: Sectarianism, Sport and Society*. Edinburgh: John Donald Publishers, 1984.

————. *Football: A History of the World Game*. Aldershot: Scolar Press, 1994.

————. *The World's Game: A History of Soccer*. Chicago: University of Illinois Press, 1996.

Nairn, Tom. *The Break-up of Britain: Crisis and Neo-Nationalism*. London: NLB, 1977.

Nasaw, David. *Going Out: The Rise and the Fall of Public Amusements*. Cambridge, Mass.: Harvard University Press, 1999.

Naul, Roland, ed. *Turnen and Sport: The Cross-Cultural Exchange*. New York: Waxmann Minister, 1991.

Nerz, Otto, and Carl Koppehel. *Der Kampf um den Ball: Das Buch vom Fussball*. Berlin: Prismen Verlag, 1933.

Neuberger, Joan. *Hooliganism: Crime, Culture, and Power in St. Petersburg, 1900–1914*. Berkeley: University of California Press, 1993.

Newsham, Gail J. *In a League of Their Own! The Dick Kerr Ladies 1917–1965*. London: Paragon Publishing, 1997.

Nicolai, Jean, and Madjid Allali. *Violence et football: L'eurohooliganisme*. Marseille: Editions Autres Temps, 1998.

Niethammer, Lutz, ed. *Lebenserfahrung und Kollektives Gedächtnis: Die Praxis der "Oral History"*. Frankfurt: Syndikat, 1985.

————. *Kollektive Identität: Heimliche Quellen einer unheimlichen Konjunktur*. Reinbek: Rowohlt, 2000.

Niggli, Nicholas C. "Diplomatie sportive et relations internationales: Helsinki 1952, les 'jeux Olympiques de la Guerre froide'?" *Relations Internationales* 112 (2002): 467–85.

Nittnaus, Paul, and Michael Zink. *Sport ist unser Leben: 100 Jahre Arbeitersport in Österreich*. Vienna: Mohl Verlag, 1992.

Nora, Pierre, ed. *Les lieux de mémoire*. 7 vols. Paris: Gallimard, 1984–92.

————, ed. *Zwischen Gedächtnis und Geschichte*. Berlin: Wagenbach, 1986.

Bibliography

O'Gorman, Frank. "Campaign Rituals and Ceremonies: The Social Meaning of Elections in England 1780–1860." *Past and Present* 135 (1992): 79–115.

Olin, Halevi, ed. *Sport, Peace and Development: International Worker Sport, 1913–2013.* Vienna: CSIT, 2013.

Olson, Morgan A., ed. *Sport und Politik: 1918–1939/40: Kongressbericht der gleichnahmigen Veranstaltung vom 22. bis 26. Oktober 1984 in Oslo.* Oslo: Universitetsforlaget, 1986.

O'Mahony, Mike. *Sport in the USSR: Physical Culture—Visual Culture.* London: Reaktion Books, 2006.

Orwell, George. "The Sporting Spirit." *Tribune of London,* December 1945.

Oswald, Rudolf. "'Ein Gift, mit echt jüdischer Geschicklichkeit ins Volk gespritzt': Die nationalsozialistische Judenverfolgung und das Ende des mitteleuropäischen Profifußballs, 1938–1941." *SportZeiten* 2, no. 2 (2002): 53–67.

———. *"Fußball-Volksgemeinschaft": Ideologie, Politik und Fanatismus im deutschen Fußball 1919–1964.* Frankfurt: Campus, 2008.

Pawson, Tony. *The Goalscorers: From Bloomer to Keegan.* London: Cassell, 1978.

Payne, Stanley George. *The Franco Regime, 1936–1975.* Madison: University of Wisconsin Press, 1987.

Pearson, G. "'Paki Bashing' in a North East Lancashire Cotton Town: A Case Study and Its History." In *Working Class Youth Culture,* edited by G. Pearson and G. Mungham, 48–81. London: Routledge and Kegan Paul, 1976.

Peiffer, Lorenz. *Sport im Nationalsozialismus: Zum aktuellen Stand der sporthistorischen Forschung: Eine kommentierte Bibliografie.* Göttingen: Werkstatt, 2009.

Peiffer, Lorenz, and Dietrich Schulze-Marmeling, eds. *Hakenkreuz und rundes Leder: Fußball im Nationalsozialismus.* Göttingen: Werkstatt, 2008.

Peppard, Victor E. "The Beginnings of Russian Soccer." *Stadion* 8–9 (1982–83): 151–68.

Peppard, Victor E., and James Riordan. *Playing Politics: Soviet Sport Diplomacy to 1992.* London: JAI Press, 1992.

Pereira, Leonardo Affonso de Miranda. *Footballmania: Uma historia social do futebol no Rio de Janeiro, 1902–1938.* Rio de Janeiro: Nova Fronteira, 2000.

Peukert, Detlev J. K. *Die Weimarer Republik: Krisenjahre der Klassischen Moderne.* Frankfurt: Suhrkamp, 1987.

Pfister, Gertrud, ed. *Frau und Sport.* Frankfurt: Fischer Taschenbuch Verlag, 1980.

Pieth, Fritz. *Sport in der Schweiz: Sein Weg in die Gegenwart.* Olten: Walter, 1979.

Pietrow, Bianka. *Stalinismus-Sicherheit-Offensive: Das "Dritte Reich" in der Konzeption der sowjetischen Aussenpolitik 1933–1941.* Melsungen: Schwartz, 1983.

Pittock, Murray G. H. *Jacobitism.* London: Macmillan, 1982.

———. *The Invention of Scotland: The Stuart Myth and the Scottish Identity, 1638 to the Present.* London: Routledge, 1991.

———. *The Myth of the Jacobite Clans.* Edinburgh: Edinburgh University Press, 1995.

Pivato, Stefano. *Sia lodato Bartali: Ideologia, cultura e miti dello sport cattolico (1936–1948).* Rome: Edizioni Lavoro, 1985.

Plaggenborg, Stefan. *Revolutionskultur: Menschenbilder und kulturelle Praxis in Sowjetrussland zwischen Oktoberrevolution und Stalinismus.* Cologne: Böhlau, 1996.

Planck, Karl. *Fusslümmelei: Über Stauchballspiel und englische Krankheit.* Stuttgart: 1898; reprint, Münster: Lit, 2004.

Planert, Ute. "Vater Staat und Mutter Germania: Zur Politisierung des weiblichen Geschlechts im 19. und 20. Jahrhundert." In *Nation, Politik und Geschlecht: Frauen-bewegungen und Nationalismus in der Moderne,* edited by Ute Planert, 15–65. Frankfurt: Campus, 2000.

Pleil, Ingolf. *Mielke, Macht und Meisterschaft: Die "Bearbeitung" der Sportgemeinschaft Dynamo Dresden 1978–1989.* Berlin: Links, 2001.

Pöge, Alfredo W. "Der 'goldene Schuh'—posthum (Europas erfolgreichste Liga-Torschützen 1888–1900)." *Elf* 4 (1986): 14–40.

Polley, Martin. *Moving the Goalposts: A History of Sport and Society since 1945.* London: Routledge, 1998.

Poole, Steve. "'Til our liberties be secure': Popular Sovereignity and Public Space in Bristol, 1780–1850." *Urban History* 26 (1999): 40–54.

Prozumenščikov, Michail. *Bol'šoj Sport i bol'šaja politika.* Moscow: ROSSPEN, 2004.

Prudhomme-Oncet, Laurence. *Histoire du football féminin au 20e siècle.* Paris: L'Harmattan, 2003.

Prynn, David. "The Clarion Clubs: Ramblings and Holiday Associations in Britain since the 1890s." *Journal of Contemporary History* 11 (1976): 65–77.

Pujadas, Xavier, and Carles Santacana. *L'altra Olimpiada '36: Esport, societat i politica a Catalunya.* Barcelona: Llibres de l'Index, 1990.

———. "The People's Olympiad, Barcelona 1936." *International Review for the Sociology of Sport* 27 (1992): 139–49.

Purcell, Tim, and Mike Gething. *Wartime Wanderers: A Football Team at War.* London: Mainstream Publishing, 2001.

Pyta, Wolfram, ed. *Der lange Weg zur Bundesliga: Zum Siegeszug des Fußballs in Deutsch-land.* Münster: Lit, 2004.

———, ed. *Geschichte des Fussballs in Deutschland und Europa seit 1954.* Stuttgart: Kohl-hammer, 2013.

Race, Mike. *Public Houses, Public Lives: An Oral History of Life in York Pubs in the Mid-20th Century.* York: Voyager Publications, 1999.

Radenkovic, Petar. *Bin ich Radi....* Munich: Moewig-Verlag, 1965.

Ratzeburg, Hannelore, and Horst Biese. *Frauen-Fußball-Meisterschaften: 25 Jahre Frauenfußball.* Kassel: Agon, 1995.

Reader, W. J. *At Duty's Call: A Study in Obsolete Patriotism.* Manchester: Manchester University Press, 1988.

Reay, Barry. *Popular Cultures in England 1550–1750.* London: Routledge, 1998.

Redhead, Steve. *Post-Fandom and the Millennial Blues: The Transformation of Soccer Culture.* London: Routledge, 1997.

———, ed. *The Passion and the Fashion: Football Fandom in the New Europe.* Aldershot: Ashgate, 1993.

Reimann, Aribert. *Der grosse Krieg der Sprachen: Untersuchungen zur historischen Se-mantik in Deutschland und England zur Zeit des Ersten Weltkrieges.* Essen: Klartext, 2000.

Renkl, Thomas. "Der Boykott der Olympischen Spiele 1980 und die öffentliche Meinung." PhD diss., FU Berlin, 1983.

Reulecke, Jürgen. *"Ich möchte einer werden, so wie die ...": Männerbünde im 20. Jahrhundert*. Frankfurt: Campus, 2001.

Richter, Jörg, ed. *Die vertrimmte Nation oder Sport in rechter Gesellschaft*. Hamburg: Rowohlt, 1972.

Ridgwell, Stephen. "The People's Amusement: Cinema and Cinema-going in 1930s Britain." *The Historian* 52 (1996): 18–21.

Riha, Karl, ed. *Fussball literarisch oder Der Ball spielt mit dem Menschen: Erzählungen, Texte, Gedichte, Lieder, Bilder*. Frankfurt: Fischer Taschenbuchverlag, 1982.

Rindlisbacher, Rolf, and Brigitta Rindlisbacher. *20 Jahre Damenfussball in der Schweiz*. Zumikon: E. Streit, 1991.

Riordan, James. *Sport in Soviet Society: Development of Sport and Physical Education in Russia and the USSR*. Cambridge: Cambridge University Press, 1977.

———. *The Political Role of Sport in Britain and the USSR*. Manchester: Centre for Leisure Studies, University of Salford, 1980.

———. "The Strange Story of Nikolai Starostin, Football and Laverentii Beria." *Europe-Asia Studies* 46 (1994): 681–90.

———. "Sport under Communism and Fascism: Reflections on Similarities and Differences." *Stadion* 28 (2002): 267–74.

Riordan, James, and Arndt Krüger, eds. *International Politics of Sport in the 20th Century*. London: Taylor and Francis, 1999.

Rippon, Anton. *Gas Masks for Goal Posts: Football in Britain during the Second World War*. Stroud: The History Press, 2007.

Ritter, Andreas. *Wandlungen in der Steuerung des DDR-Hochleistungssports in den 1960er und 1970er Jahren*. Potsdam: Universitäts-Verlag, 2003.

Ritter, Lawrence S. *Lost Ballparks: A Celebration of Baseball's Legendary Fields*. New York: Studio, 1992.

Roberts, James. "The Best Football Team, the Best Platoon: The Role of Football in the Proletarinaziation of the British Expeditionary Force, 1914–1918." *Sport in History* 26 (2006): 26–56.

Robertson, Forrest C. "The Glasgow Merchants' Charity Cup (1877–1900)." *Elf* 47 (1986): 93–99.

Robins, D., and P. Cohen. *Knuckle Sandwich: Growing Up in the Working-Class City*. London: Penguin Books, 1978.

Rollins, Jack. *Soccer at War 1939–45*. London: Willow, 1985.

Romanov, Aleksej Osipovič. *Meždunarodnoe sportivnoe dviženie*. Moscow, 1973.

Rorty, Richard. *Achieving Our Country: Leftist Thought in Twentieth-Century America*. Cambridge, Mass.: Harvard University Press, 1997.

Rösch, Heinz-Egon. *Politik und Sport in Gegenwart und Geschichte*. Würzburg: Ploetz, 1980.

Rose, Lionel. *"Rogues and Vagabonds": Vagrant Underworld in Britain, 1815–1985*. London: Routledge, 1988.

Rosenwein, Barbara H. "Worrying about Emotions in History." *American Historical Review* 107 (2002): 821–45.

Roth, Philip. *The Great American Novel*. New York: Holt, Rinehart and Winston, 1973.

Rowe, William, and Vivian Schelling. *Memory and Modernity: Popular Culture in Latin America*. London: Verso, 1991.

Rüdlinger, Max, and Urs Frieden. "Vor 50 Jahren: Schweizer Fussballer missachten Verbot: 'Man spielt wieder mit uns.'" *Die WochenZeitung*, October 8, 1998.

Ruoff, Paul. *Das goldene Buch des Schweizer Fussballs*. Basel: Verlag Domprobstei, 1953.

Rürup, Reinhard, ed. *1936: Die Olympischen Spiele und der Nationalsozialismus: Eine Dokumentation*. Berlin: Argon-Verlag, 1996.

Rüschemeyer, Dietrich. "Professionalisierung: Theoretische Probleme für die vergleichende Geschichtsforschung." *Geschichte und Gesellschaft* 6 (1980): 311–25.

Russell, David. *Football and the English: A Social History of Association Football in England, 1863–1995*. Preston: Carnegie Publishing, 1997.

Rütten, Alfred. *Angewandte Sportsoziologie: Zwischen empirischer Forschung und Politikberatung*. Stuttgart: Naglschmid, 1992.

Samuels, Martin. *Command or Control? Command, Training and Tactics in the British and German Armies, 1888–1918*. London: Taylor and Francis, 1995.

Sarasin, Philipp. *Reizbare Maschinen: Eine Geschichte des Körpers 1765–1914*. Frankfurt: Suhrkamp, 2001.

Schaufelberger, Walter. *Der Wettkampf in der alten Eidgenossenschaft: Zur Kulturgeschichte des Sports vom 13. bis ins 18. Jahrhundert*. 2 vols. Bern: Haupt, 1972.

Scheidemann, Philipp. *Memoiren eines Sozialdemokraten*, vol. 2. Dresden: Reissner-Verlag, 1928.

Scher, A., and H. Palomino. *Fútbol: Pasión de multitudes y de elites*. Buenos Aires: CISEA, 1988.

Schiller, Kay. "Bundesligakrise und Fussballweltmeisterschaft 1974." In *Geschichte des Fussballs in Deutschland und Europa seit 1954*, edited by Wolfram Pyta, 139–55. Stuttgart: Kohlhammer, 2013.

Schirmer, Dietmar. "Politisch-kulturelle Deutungsmuster: Vorstellungen von der Welt der Politik in der Weimarer Republik." In *Politische Identität und nationale Gedenktage: Zur politischen Kultur in der Weimarer Republik*, edited by Detlev Lehnert and Klaus Megerle, 31–60. Opladen: Westdeutscher Verlag, 1989.

Schleppi, John Ross. "A History of Professional Association Football in England during the Second World War." PhD diss., University of Ohio, 1972.

Schlicht, Wolfgang, and Werner Lang, eds. *Über Fussball: Ein Lesebuch zur wichtigsten Nebensache der Welt*. Schorndorf: Hofmann, 2000.

Schmid, Jürg. *Schweizer Cup und Länderspiele: Nationalismus im Schweizer Fussballsport*. MA thesis, University of Zurich, 1986.

Schmidt, Maruta, and Kristine von Soden, eds. *Neue Frauen: Die zwanziger Jahre*. Berlin: Elefanten-Press, 1988.

Schoch, Andreas. "Die Schweizer Fussball-Nationalmannschaft 1904–1945: Fussball-Spitzensport und dessen politische Instrumentalisierung." MA thesis, University of Zurich, 2004.

Bibliography

Schönberger, Klaus. *Arbeitersportbewegung in Dorf und Kleinstadt: Zur Arbeiterbewegungskultur im Oberamt Marbach 1900–1933*. Tübingen: Tübinger Vereinigung für
Volkskunde, 1995.

Schröder, Burkhard. *Rechte Kerle: Skinheads, Faschos, Hooligans*. Hamburg: Rowohlt, 1992.

Schulze, Hagen. *Der Weg zum Nationalstaat: Die deutsche Nationalbewegung vom 18.
Jahrhundert bis zur Reichsgründung*. Munich: Deutscher Taschenbuch-Verlag, 1985.

Schulze-Marmeling, Dietrich, ed. *Der gezähmte Fussball: Zur Geschichte eines subversiven
Sports*. Göttingen: Werkstatt, 1992.

———. *Fussball: Zur Geschichte eines globalen Sports*. Göttingen: Werkstatt, 2000.

———, ed. *Davidstern und Lederball. Die Geschichte der Juden im deutschen und internationalen Fußball*. Göttingen: Werkstatt, 2003.

———, ed. *Die Geschichte der Fußball-Nationalmannschaft*. Göttingen: Werkstatt, 2004.

———, ed. *Strategen des Spiels: Die legendären Fussballtrainer*. Göttingen: Werkstatt,
2005.

———. "Juden und Antisemitismus im deutschen und europäischen Fußball." *SportZ-
eiten* 7, no. 2 (2007): 91–109.

Schumacher, Harald. *Anpfiff: Enthüllungen über den deutschen Fussball*. Munich: Droemer Knaur, 1987.

Schümer, Dirk. *Gott ist rund: Die Kultur des Fußballs*. Berlin: Suhrkamp, 1996.

Schwan, Heribert. *Tod dem Verräter! Der lange Arm der Stasi und der Fall Lutz Eigendorf*.
Munich: Droemer Knaur, 2000.

Schwarz-Pich, Karl-Heinz. *Der DFB im Dritten Reich: Einer Legende auf der Spur*. Kassel:
Agon Sportverlag, 2000.

Schwind, Karl Heinz. *Geschichten aus einem Fussball-Jahrhundert*. Vienna: Ueberreuter,
1994.

Scott, James C. *Domination and the Arts of Resistance: Hidden Transcripts*. New Haven,
Conn.: Yale University Press, 1990.

Scott, Joan W. "Gender: A Useful Category of Historical Analysis." *American Historical
Review* 91 (1986): 1053–75.

Scraton, Sheila, et al. "It's Still a Man's Game? The Experiences of Top-Level European
Women Footballers." *International Review for the Sociology of Sport* 33 (1998):
99–113.

Seitz, Norbert. *Bananenrepublik und Gurkentruppe: Die nahtlose Übereinstimmung von
Fussball und Politik 1954–1987*. Frankfurt: Scarabäus bei Eichborn, 1987.

———, ed. *Doppelpässe: Fussball und Politik*. Frankfurt: Eichborn, 1997.

Server, Lee. *Danger Is My Business: An Illustrated History of the Fabulous Pulp Magazines,
1896–1953*. San Francisco: Chronicle Books, 1993.

Shaw, D. *Fútbol y franquismo*. Madrid: Alianza Editorial, 1987.

Siemann, Wolfram. "Krieg und Frieden in historischen Gedenkfeiern des Jahre 1913."
In *Öffentliche Festkultur: Politische Feste in Deutschland von der Aufklärung bis zum
Ersten Weltkrieg*, edited by Dieter Düding et al., 298–320. Reinbek: Rowohlt, 1988.

Sillitoe, Alan. *Saturday Night and Sunday Morning*. London: W. H. Allen, 1958.

Silva, Ronaldo César de Oliveira. *Uma caixinha de surpresas: Apropriação do futebol pelas
classes populares (1900–1930)*. Londrina: Editora UEL, 1998.

Simmel, Georg. *Soziologie: Untersuchungen über die Formen der Vergesellschaftung.* Munich: Duncker & Humblot, 1923.

Sindall, Rob. *Street Violence in the Nineteenth Century: Media Panic or Real Danger?* Leicester: Leicester University Press, 1990.

Skornig, Lothar. "Chronik der deutsch-sowjetischen Sportbeziehungen bis 1937." *Theorie und Praxis der Körperkultur* 16 (1967): 885–900.

———. "Vor 50 Jahren: Die Moskauer Spartakiade 1928." *Theorie und Praxis der Körperkultur* 27 (1978): 670–78.

Smith, Adam. *An Inquiry into the Nature and Causes of the Wealth of Nations* [1776]. Edited by R. H. Campbell and A. S. Skinner. Indianapolis, Ind.: Liberty Fund, 1981.

Smith, Anthony D. *National Identity.* London: Penguin Books, 1991.

———. "The Nation: Invented, Imagined, Reconstructed?" *Millennium* 20 (1991): 53–68.

Smith, Tom. "'Bataille's Boys': Postmodernity, Fascists and Football Fans." *British Journal of Sociology* 51 (2000): 443–61.

Sobolev, P. *Sport in der UdSSR.* Moscow: Foreign Languages Publishing House, 1958.

Spaaij, Ramon. *Understanding Football Hooliganism: A Comparison of Six Western European Football Clubs.* Amsterdam: Amsterdam University Press, 2006.

Spencer, Herbert. *Education: Intellectual, Moral and Physical.* London: 1861.

———. *The Principles of Biology.* 2 vols. London: 1864–67.

———. *The Principles of Psychology.* 2 vols. London: 1870–72.

———. *The Study of Sociology.* London: 1874.

———. *First Principles.* London: 1875.

———. *The Principles of Sociology.* 3 vols. London: 1876–96.

———. *The Data of Ethics.* 2 vols. London: 1879.

———. *The Principles of Ethics.* London: 1892–93.

Spengler, Oswald. *Preussentum und Sozialismus.* Munich: Beck, 1920.

Spitzer, Giselher, et al., eds. *Schlüsseldokumente zum DDR-Sport.* Aachen: Meyer & Meyer Sport, 1998.

Springhall, John. *Youth, Popular Culture and Moral Panics: Penny Gaffs to Gangsta-Rap, 1830–1996.* London: Palgrave Macmillan, 1998.

Stamm-Kuhlmann, Thomas. "Humanitätsidee und Überwertigkeitswahn in der Entstehungsphase des deutschen Nationalismus: Auffällige Gemeinsamkeiten bei Johann Gottlieb Fichte, Ernst Moritz Arndt und Friedrich Ludwig Jahn." *Historische Mitteilungen* 4 (1991): 161–71.

Starr, Frederick. *Red and Hot: The Fate of Jazz in the Soviet Union.* Oxford: Oxford University Press, 1984.

Steinberg, David. "Die Arbeitersport-Internationalen 1920–1928." In *Arbeiterkultur,* edited by Gerhard A. Ritter, 93–108. Königstein: Verlagsgruppe Athenäum-Hain-Scriptor-Hanstein, 1979.

Stemmler, Theo. *Kleine Geschichte des Fussballspiels.* Frankfurt-Leipzig: Insel Verlag, 1998.

Stevenson, John. *Popular Disturbances in England, 1700–1832.* London: Routledge, 1992.

Stillwell, Stephen Joseph. *Anglo-Turkish Relations in the Interwar Era.* Lewiston, N.Y.: Edwin Mellen Press, 2003.

Stites, Richard. *Russian Popular Culture.* Cambridge: Cambridge University Press, 1992.

Bibliography

Stojanović, Danilo. *Čika Dačine uspomene.* Belgrade: Godina, 1953.

Storch, Robert D. "The Plague of Blue Locusts: Police Reform and Popular Resistance in Northern England 1840–57." *International Review of Social History* 20 (1975): 61–90.

———. "The Policeman as Domestic Missionary: Urban Discipline and Popular Culture in Northern England 1850–1888." *Journal of Social History* 9 (1976): 479–95.

Stritecky, Jaroslav. "Identitäten, Identifikationen, Identifikatoren." In *Formen des nationalen Bewusstseins im Lichte zeitgenössischer Nationalismustheorien*, edited by Eva Schmidt-Hartmann, 53–66. Munich: Oldenbourg, 1994

Strychatz, Thomas F. *Modernism, Mass Culture, and Professionalism.* Cambridge: Cambridge University Press, 1993.

Sudgen, John, and Alan Tomlinson. *FIFA and the Contest for World Football: Who Rules the Peoples' Game?* Cambridge: Blackwell, 1998.

———, eds. *Hosts and Champions: Soccer Cultures, National Identities and the US World Cup.* Aldershot: Ashgate, 1994.

Surette, Ray. *Media, Crime, and Criminal Justice: Images and Realities.* Pacific Grove, Calif.: Cengage Learning, 1992.

Swift, Graham. *Last Orders.* London: Picador, 1986.

Tauber, Peter. *Vom Schützengraben auf den grünen Rasen: Der Erste Weltkrieg und die Entwicklung des Sports in Deutschland.* Münster: Lit, 2008.

Taylor, Alan. "Common-Stealers, Land-Grabbers and Jerry Builders: Space, Popular Radicalism and the Politics of Public Access in London, 1848–1880." *International Review of Social History* 40 (1995): 383–407.

Taylor, Ian. "'Football Mad': A Speculative Sociology of Football Hooliganism." In *The Sociology of Sport: A Selection of Readings*, edited by Eric Düding et al., 352–77. London: Cass, 1976.

———. "Soccer Consciousness and Soccer Hooliganism." In *Images of Deviance*, edited by Stanley Cohen, 134–64. Harmondsworth: Penguin Books, 1971.

Taylor, Matthew. "Labour Relations and Managerial Control in English Professional Football, 1890–1939." *Sport History Review* 31 (2000): 80–99.

———. "Beyond the Maximum Wage: The Earnings of Football Professionals in England, 1900–39." *Soccer and Society* 2 (2001): 101–18.

———. *The Leaguers: The Making of Professional Football in England, 1900–1939.* Liverpool: Liverpool University Press, 2005.

———. *The Association Game: A History of British Football.* Harlow. Pearson Education, 2008.

———. *Football: A Short History.* Oxford: Shire Books, 2011.

Taylor, Matthew, and Pierre Lanfranchi. *Moving with the Ball: The Migration of Professional Footballers.* Oxford: Berg, 2001.

Taylor, Rogan. *Football and Its Fans: Supporters and their Relations with the Game, 1885–1985.* Leicester: Continuum International Publishing, 1992.

Taylor, Rogan, and Andreas Skrypietz. "'Pull the trigger—shoot the nigger': Fussball und Rassismus in England." In *Fussball und Rassismus*, 73–106. Reinbek: Rowohlt, 1994.

Taylor, Rogan, and Andrew Ward. *Kicking and Screaming: An Oral History of Football in England.* London: Robson Books, 1995.

Bibliography

Teichler, Hans-Joachim. *Internationale Sportpolitik im Dritten Reich*. Schorndorf: Hofmann, 1991.

Teichler, Hans-Joachim, and Irene Diekman, eds. *Körper, Kultur und Ideologie: Sport und Zeitgeist im 19. und 20. Jahrhundert*. Bodenheim: Philo, 1997.

Teichler, Hans-Joachim, and Gerhard Hauk, eds. *Illustrierte Geschichte des Arbeitersports*. Bonn: Dietz, 1987.

Tenfelde, Klaus. "Historische Milieus—Erblichkeit und Konkurrenz." In *Nation und Gesellschaft in Deutschland: Historische Essays*, edited by Manfred Hettling and Paul Nolte, 247–68. Munich: Beck, 1996.

Terraine, J., ed. *General Jack's Diary*. London: Eyre and Spottiswoode, 1964.

Thamer, Hans-Ulrich. "Monokratie—Polykratie: Historiographischer Überblick über eine kontroverse Debatte." In *Das organisierte Chaos: "Ämterdarwinismus" und "Gesinnungsethik": Determinanten nationalsozialistischer Besatzungsherrschaft*, edited by Gerhard Otto and Johannes Houwink ten Cate, 21–54. Berlin: Metropol, 1999.

Thiesse, Anne-Marie. *La création des identités nationales: Europe XVIIIe–XXe siècle*. Paris: Seuil, 1999.

Thom, Deborah. *Nice Girls and Rude Girls: Women Workers in World War I*. London: I. B. Taurus, 1998.

Thompson, E. P. *The Making of the English Working Class*. London: Victor Gollancz, 1963.

Thompson, R. R. *The Fifty-Second (Lowland) Division 1914–1918*. Glasgow: Maclehose, Jackson and Co., 1923.

Timmermann, Heinz. *Geschichte und Struktur der Arbeitersportbewegung 1893–1933*. Ahrensburg bei Hamburg: Ingrid Czwalina, 1973.

Tischler, Steven. *Footballers and Businessmen: The Origins of Professional Soccer in England*. London: Holmes and Meier Publishers, 1981.

Tokarski, Walter, et al., eds. *Two Players—One Goal? Sport in the European Union*. Aachen: Meyer & Meyer, 2004.

Tomlinson, Alan, ed. *Gender, Sport and Leisure: Continuities and Challenges*. Aachen: Meyer & Meyer, 1997.

———. *The Game's Up: Essays in the Cultural Analysis of Sport, Leisure and Popular Culture*. Aldershot: Ashgate, 1999.

Tomlinson, Alan, and Christopher Young, eds. *National Identity and Global Events: Culture, Politics and Spectacle in the Olympics and the Football World Cup*. Albany, N.Y.: State University of New York Press, 2005.

Tomlinson, Alan, et al., eds. *Sport and the Transformation of Modern Europe: States, Media and Markets 1950–2010*. London: Routledge, 2011.

Tranter, Neil L. "The First Football Club." *International Journal of the History of Sport* 10 (1993): 104–7.

———. "The Cappielow Riot and the Composition and Behaviour of Soccer Crowds in Late Victorian Scotland." *International Journal of the History of Sport* 12 (1995): 125–40.

———. *Sport, Economy and Society in Britain: 1750–1914*. Cambridge: Cambridge University Press, 1998.

Bibliography

Trykholm, Peter A. "Soccer and Social Identity in Pre-Revolutionary Moscow." *Journal of Sport History* 24 (1997): 143–54.

Tsoukala, Anastassia. *Football Hooliganism in Europe: Security and Civil Liberties in the Balance*. Hants: Palgrave Macmillan, 2009.

Tunis, J. R. "The Dictators Discover Sport." *Foreign Affairs* 14, no. 4 (1936): 606–17.

Ueberhorst, Horst, ed. *Geschichte der Leibesübungen*. 6 vols. Berlin: Bartels & Wernitz, 1972–89.

Ueberhorst, Horst, et al. *Arbeitersport- und Arbeiterkulturbewegung im Ruhrgebiet*. Opladen: Westdeutscher Verlag, 1989.

Unser, Margit. *Gelebte Geschichte: Alltagserfahrungen von Mannheimer Arbeitersportlern der Weimarer Zeit*. Mannheim: Landesmuseum für Technik und Arbeit, 1994.

Uridil, Josef. *Was ich bin und was ich wurde: Die Lebensgeschichte des berühmten Fussballers von ihm selbst erzählt*. Leipzig: R. Löwit, 1924.

Väth, Heinrich. *"Mir wor'n halt ein wilde Haufe ...": Die Sozialgeschichte des Fussballsports in einem Spessartdorf*. Bensheim: Päd. Extra Buchverlag, 1981.

———. *Profifussball: Zur Soziologie der Bundesliga*. Frankfurt: Campus, 1994.

Vamplew, Wray. "The Economics of a Sports Industry: Scottish Gate-Money Football, 1890–1914." *Economic History Review* 35 (1982): 549–67.

———. *Pay Up and Play the Game: Professional Sport in Britain 1875–1914*. Cambridge: Cambridge University Press, 1988.

Van Echtelt, Niels. "The Forgotten Front: The Multicultural War of 1914–1918 in Eyewitness Accounts from Flanders." In *World War I: Five Continents in Flanders*, edited by Dominiek Dendooven and Piet Chielens, 167–79. Tielt: Lannoo Publishers, 2008.

Vansina, Jan. *Oral Tradition as History*. Madison: University of Wisconsin Press, 1985.

Vartanjan, Akesel, ed. *Sto let Rossijskomu futbolu*. Moscow, 1997.

Vasili, Phil. *Colouring over the White Line: The History of Black Footballers in Britain*. Edinburgh: Mainstream Publishing, 2000.

Veitch, Collin. "'Play Up! Play Up! And Win the War!': Football, the Nation and the First World War 1914–15." *Journal of Contemporary History* 20 (1985): 363–78.

Vertinsky, Patricia, and John Bale, eds. *Sites of Sport: Space, Place and Experience*. London: Routledge, 2004.

Vinnai, Gerhard. *Fussballsport als Ideologie*. Frankfurt: Europäische Verlagsanstalt, 1970.

Vinokur, M. B. *More than a Game: Sports and Politics*. New York: Greenwood Press, 1988.

Vogel, Sabine. "Sozialdisziplinierung als Forschungsbegriff?" *Frühneuzeit-Info* 8, no. 2 (1997): 190–94.

Vogt, Ludgera. *Zur Logik der Ehre in der Gegenwartsgesellschaft: Differenzierung, Macht, Integration*. Frankfurt: Suhrkamp, 1997.

Vonnard, Philippe, and Grégory Quin. "Eléments pour une histoire de la mise en place du professionnalisme dans le football suisse durant l'entre-deux-guerres: Processus, résistances et ambiguïtés." *Schweizerische Zeitschrift für Geschichte* 62 (2012): 70–85.

Vorst, Hans. *Das bolschewistische Russland*. Leipzig: Der neue Geist, 1919.

Waddington, Ivan. "American Exceptionalism: Soccer and American Football." *Sports Historian* 16 (1996): 42–63.

Waddington, Ivan, et al. "The Social Composition of Football Crowds in Western Europe." *International Review for the Sociology of Sport* 33 (1998): 99–113.

Wagg, Stephen. *The Football World: A Contemporary Social History*. Brighton: Salem House Academic Division, 1984.

———, ed. *Giving the Game Away: Football, Politics and Culture on Five Continents*. Leicester: Continuum, 1995.

Wagg, Stephen, and David L. Andrews, eds. *East Plays West: Sport and the Cold War*. London: Routledge, 2007.

Wahl, Alfred. "Le footballeur français: De l'amateurisme au salariat." *Le mouvement social* 135 (1986): 7–30.

———. "Raymond Kopa une vedette du football." *Sport Histoire* 2 (1988): 4–6.

———. *Les archives du football: Sport et société en France, 1880–1980*. Paris: Gallimard, 1989.

———. *Il calcio: Una storia mondiale*. Trieste: Gallimard, 1994.

———. "Un professionalisme de résignation en France." *Sociétés et Représentations* 7 (1998): 67–75.

———, ed. *Football et histoire*. Metz: Centre de Recherche Histoire et Civilisation de l'Université de Metz, 2003.

Wahl, Alfred, and Pierre Lanfranchi. *Les footballeurs professionels des années trente à nos jours*. Paris: Hachette, 1995.

Wahlig, Henry. *Ein Tor zur Welt? Der deutsche Fussball und die FIFA 1945–1950*. Göttingen: Werkstatt, 2008.

Waites, Bernard. *A Class Society at War: England 1914–1918*. Leamington Spa: Berg Publishers, 1987.

Waller, Phillip J. *Democracy and Sectarianism: A Political and Social History of Liverpool 1868–1939*. Liverpool: Liverpool University Press, 1981.

———. *Town, City, and Nation: England 1850–1914*. Oxford: Oxford University Press, 1983.

Walter, Fritz. *Elf rote Jäger: Nationalspieler im Kriege*. Munich: Copress-Verlag, 1959.

Walter, Otto F. *Zeit des Fasans: Roman*. Reinbek bei Hamburg: Rowohlt, 1988.

Walters, Guy. *Berlin Games: How Hitler Stole the Olympic Dream*. London: Hodder and Stoughton, 2006.

Walvin, James. *Leisure and Society, 1830–1950*. London: Longman, 1963.

———. *Beside the Seaside: A Social History of the Popular Seaside Holiday*. London: Viking, 1978.

———. *Football and the Decline of Britain*. London: Palgrave Macmillan, 1986.

———. *The People's Game: The History of Football Revisited*. Edinburgh: Mainstream Publishing, 1994.

Wassermair, Michael, and Lukas Wieselberg, eds. *3 : 2 Österreich-Deutschland: 20 Jahre Córdoba*. Vienna: Döcker, 1998.

Wehler, Hans-Ulrich. *Die Herausforderung der Kulturgeschichte*. Munich: Beck, 1998.

Weis, Kurt, and Günther Lüschen, eds. *Die Soziologie des Sports*. Darmstadt-Neuwied: Luchterhand, 1979.

Bibliography

Weis, Kurt, and Joachim Winkler, eds. *Soziologie des Sports: Theorieansätze, Forschungsergebnisse und Forschungsperspektiven.* Opladen: Westdeutscher Verlag, 1995.

Weiser, Fedor. *Fussball als Droge? Psychosoziale und gesellschaftspolititische Aspekte der jugendlichen Fussballkultur beim Fussballverein Eintracht Frankfurt.* Giessen: 1990.

Welck, Gisela, and Karin Völger, eds. *Männerbande—Männerbünde: Zur Rolle des Mannes im Kulturvergleich.* Cologne: Rautenstrauch-Joest-Museum für Völkerkunde, 1990.

Wetzel, Horst. "Paris 1934—Internationaler Sportleraufmarsch gegen imperialistischen Krieg und Faschismus." *Theorie und Praxis der Körperkultur* 18 (1969): 961–65.

Wheeler, Robert F. "Organisierter Sport und organisierte Arbeit: Die Arbeitersportbewegung." In *Arbeiterkultur,* edited by Gerhard A. Ritter, 58–73. Königstein: Verlagsgruppe Athenäum, 1979.

White, Jerry. *The Worst Street in North London: Campbell Bunk, Islington, between the Wars.* London: Routledge and Kegan Paul, 1986.

Wilkie, Jim. *Across the Great Divide: A History of Professional Football in Dundee.* Edinburgh: Mainstream Publishing, 2000.

Williams, Graham. *The Code War: English Football under the Historical Spotlight.* Harefield: Yore Publications, 1994.

Williams, Jean. *A Game for Rough Girls? A History of Women's Football in England.* London: Routledge, 2003.

Williams, John. *The Home Fronts in Britain, France and Germany, 1914–1918.* London: Constable, 1972.

Williams, John, and Stephen Wagg, eds. *British Football and Social Change: Getting into Europe.* Leicester: Leicester University Press, 1991.

Williams, Raymond. *The Country and the City.* London: Chatto and Windus, 1973.

Williamson, David J. *The Belles of the Ball: The Early History of Women's Football.* Devon: R&D Associates, 1991.

Wodak, Ruth, et al. *Zur diskursiven Konstruktion nationaler Identität.* Frankfurt: Suhrkamp, 1998.

Wolle, Stefan. *Die heile Welt der Diktatur: Alltag und Herrschaft in der DDR 1971–1989.* Berlin: Links, 1998.

Woollacott, Angela. *On Her Their Lives Depend: Munition Workers in the Great War.* Berkeley: University of California Press, 1994.

Yallop, David A. *How They Stole the Game.* London: Constable, 2011.

Young, Percy. *A History of British Football.* London: Paul, 1968.

Zeller, Manfred. "Our Own Internationale, 1966: Dynamo Kiev Fans between Local Identity and Transnational Imagination." *Kritika* 12 (2011): 53–82.

Zunkel, Friedrich. "Ehre, Reputation." In *Geschichtliche Grundbegriffe: Historisches Lexikon zur politisch-sozialen Sprache in Deutschland,* edited by Otto Brunner et al., 2:1–63. Stuttgart: Klett-Cotta, 1975.

INDEX

Aachen, 158
Abegglen, Trello, 153, 155
Abel Xavier, 123
Aberdeen FC, 144, 148
Accrington, 75
AC Milan, 103, 118
Ademir, 131
Adenauer, Konrad, 170, 288
Admira Wien, 86, 119, 185
Aebi, Georges, 160
Aemisegger, Walter, 29
Afghanistan, 208, 212
Aguirre, José Antonio, 230
Aid to Russia Fund, 246
Ajax Amsterdam, 118
Akagündüz, Muhammet, 123
Albania, 139–40
Albert, Florian, 172
Albertini, Demetrio, 118
Algeria, 109, 115, 122
Allende, Salvador, 230
All-Union Council for Physical Culture, 201
Altobelli, Alessandro, 112
Amadò, Lauro "Lajo," 127
Amateur Athletic Association, 21
American Soccer League (ASL), 82–83, 290
Amnesty International, 235
Amoros, Manuel, 109–10, 112
Anderson, Viv, 38
Andrade, José Leandro, 116
Anglo-American Club Zurich, 27
Anglo-American Wanderers Zurich, 27
Angola, 123
Anquetil, Jacques, 113
Antognioni, Giancarlo, 111
Antwerp, 195
Arbeiter-Turnbund (ATB), 177–78
Arbeiter-Turn- und Sportbund (ATSB), 177–83
Ardiles, Oswaldo, 117
Argentina, 38, 82, 109, 114–15, 145, 200, 218, 223, 231, 234–36
Argentine Association Football League, 38

Arnold, Thomas, 15
Arsenal FC, 80, 100, 107, 144, 211
Asamoah, Gerald, 124
Ashbourne, 9–10
ASK Vorwärts Leipzig, 215
AS Laval, 124
AS Monaco, 112
AS Perugia, 124
AS Roma, 111
AS Saint-Etienne, 122, 259
Association of Amateur Football Clubs of
    Austria (VAFÖ), 185–86
Association of Workers and Soldiers Athletic
    Clubs (VAS), 184–85
Aston Villa, 54, 63, 73, 75
Asturias Club, 228
Athletic Club Bilbao, 227–28, 230
Atlanta, 291
Atlético Aviación, 228
Atlético Madrid, 128, 228
Australia, 40–41, 47, 231
Australian Football League, 40n103
Austria, 83–84, 86, 94, 123, 137, 152, 165, 172,
    176–77, 186, 189–90, 192, 195–96, 198,
    223–24, 256, 286
Austrian Football Association (ÖFV), 185
Austrian Football Union (ÖFB), 152, 185–86
Austrian Gymnastics and Athletic Front,
    187
Austria Wien, 84, 86–87, 119–20, 134
Austro-Hungarian Empire, 37, 184, 198
Aviación Nacional, 228
Azerbaijan, 207

Bad Neuenahr/Illertissen, 287
Baggio, Roberto, 126
Bahro, Rudolf, 4
Bakhramov, Tofiq, 108
Baku, 115, 207–8
Bale, Garreth, 97
Ballaman, Robert, 114
Baltača, Sergij, 219

Barbosa, Moacyr, 131–32
Barcelona, 124, 172, 194, 226, 228–29
Darcsi, Franco, 118
Bari, 119
Barmen, 182
Barnetta, Tranquillo, 123
Barnsley, 67
Barros, Rui, 125
Bartali, Gino, 113
Barthez, Fabien, 113
Basel, 25–26, 29, 35, 126, 154, 156–58, 161, 165,
  262
Basque National Party, 229
Batistuta, Gabriel, 127
Bats, Joël, 112
Battiston, Patrick, 109
Bauer, Otto, 184
Bauwens, Peco, 129, 164n79, 169
Bearzot, Enzo, 111
Bebeto, 113
Beck, Marcel, 140n4
Beckenbauer, Franz, 127, 216, 218–19
Becker, Peter, 269–70
Belanov, Igor, 118
Belfast, 149
Belfast City, 149
Belgium, 24, 41, 110, 124–25, 189–90, 259
Belgrade, 30, 133, 139, 149–50
Bellone, Bruno, 112
Bellos, Alex, 132
Belloumi, Lakhdar, 115
Ben Bella, Ahmed, 123
Benfica Lissabon, 117
Bensemann, Walter, 28–29
Bentley, J., 50
Bergamo, 29
Berger, Jörg, 219
Bergkamp, Denis, 68, 118
Beria, Lavrenty, 204
Berlin, 4, 33, 95, 129, 174, 182, 192–94, 200, 209,
  215, 226, 231, 239, 249–50, 252, 283, 286
Berlusconi, Silvio, 103
Bern, 116, 160, 162, 165–67, 170–71, 173–74, 251,
  256, 260–61
Bertoni, Daniel, 117
Beser, Joachim, 169
Best, George, 268
Betriebsgemeinschaft (BSG), 214
Bettega, Roberto, 125
BFC Dynamo, 215
Bickel, Fredy
Biermann, Wolf, 4
Birmingham, 18, 46, 49, 55, 61, 63
Blackburn, 61, 73

Blackburn Olympics, 74
Blackburn Rovers, 63, 74–75
Blackheath Club, 17
Blackpool, 46
Blanco, Cauthemoc, 127
Blazevic, Miroslav, 150
Blees, Thomas, 218
Blokhin, Oleg, 118
Bloomer, Stephen, 66, 119
Blue Stars St. Gall, 27
Blue Stars Zurich, 27
Boban, Zvonimir, 149
Bocquet, Roger, 114
Bogarde, Winston, 118
Bohemia, 121, 183
Bohemians, 119
Bolton, 61
Bolton Wanderers, 54, 75, 272
Bombay, 39
Boniek, Zbigniew, 110
Boninsegna, Roberto, 131
Bonn, 4, 163, 170, 216
Borussia Dortmund, 96, 103, 128
Borussia Mönchengladbach, 131, 219
Bosman, Jean-Marc, 101
Bossis, Maxime, 110
Bourdieu, Pierre, 6, 8, 22, 53
Bourgk, József, 164
Bozsik, József, 164
Bradford, 61, 99
Brady, Liam, 126
Brandt, Willy, 216
Brasilia, 232
Bratislava, 119, 252
Braunschweig, 31
Brazil, 38, 79n17, 82, 115, 123, 125, 131–32, 200,
  218, 231–33
Bregy, Georges, 126
Breitner, Paul, 112
Bremen, 182, 217
Briegel, Hans-Peter, 110
Briggs, Asa, 61
Bristol, 57, 65
Britannia Berlin, 35
British Championship, 141, 143–44
British Ladies, 277
British Workers' Sports Federation (BWSF),
  188–89
Brown, José Luis, 112
Brüggemeier, Franz-Josef, 171
Brussels, 99, 128
BSG Empor Dresden-Mitte, 287
Buchwald, Guido, 112
Budapest, 164, 171, 249, 256
Budzinski, Robert, 123

Index

Büechi, Traugott, 161
Buenos Aires, 38, 122, 235
Buenos Aires FC, 38
Bulgaria, 30, 172, 206, 259
Buli, Hugo, 30
Bundesliga, 95–98, 103, 130
Burevestnik, 201, 212
Burgener, Erich, 127
Burke, Peter, 118
Burnley, 73, 75
Burns, Robert, 142
Burson-Marsteller, 235
Bury, 75
Busby, Matt, 247
Busch, Christian, 250
Butcher, Terry, 128
Butragueño, Emilio, 127
Buytendijk, Fred J. J., 286

Cabrini, Antonio, 111
Calcutta, 39
Cambridge, 15–17, 19
Cameroon, 111, 117, 125
Campbell, Johnny, 142
Camus, Albert, 1
Canada, 40–41, 105
Canadian Football League, 41
Canadian Rugby Football Union, 41
Canário, 116
Caniggia, Claudio, 125
Cantona, Eric, 68
Cape Verde, 123
Cardiff, 278
Careca, 112
Catholic Union, 146
CDSA Moskow, 205
Celtic Glasgow, 1, 54, 56, 78, 145–49, 211
Central Commission for Workers Sports and
    Bodily Health, 177
Chad, 123
Championship of Great Britain and the World,
    281
Champions League, 102–4
Chapman, Herbert, 80
Chapuisat, Stéphane, 127
Charlton, Jackie, 119
Charlton Athletic FC, 104–5
Charrington, F. N., 242
Chelsea, 244
Chemnitz, 182, 216
Chicago, 193
Chilavert, José Luis, 133
Chile, 82, 95, 211, 227, 231
China, 8n2, 122, 157, 208, 289, 291

Chirac, Jacques, 135
Christ Church FC, 54
Churchill, Clementine, 246
Churchill, Winston, 246
CIA, 230
Clapham Rovers, 74
Clarion Cycling Club, 188
Cliftonville, 149
Clowes, Stan, 63
Coblenz, 33
Cole, Andy, 123
Collovati, Fulvio, 111
Cologne, 4
Colombia, 82, 132
Columbia, 290
Communist International (Comintern), 190,
    193, 205–6, 208
Communist Party of the Soviet Union, 202
Conen, Edward, 251
Confederation of Independent European
    Female Football (FIEFF), 287
Conservative Association of Everton, 51
Conti, Bruno, 111
Copa del Generalísimo, 228
Copenhagen, 170
Coppi, Fausto, 113
Córdoba, 114
Corinthians, 74–75
Corinthians São Paulo, 233
Cosmos New York, 117
Costacurta, Alessandro, 118
Costa, Rui, 113
Coubertin, Pierre de, 89
Country Brewers' Society (CBS), 51
Coupe Internationale Européenne, 82
Coutinho, 111
Creighton, Mandell, 62
Cricketer, 37
Croatia, 259
Croatia Zagreb, 150
Croy, Jürgen, 217
Crump, Ian, 62
Cruyff, Johan, 117, 218
Crystal Palace, 104
CSDKA, 201
CSIT World Sport Games, 196
CSKA, 213
Cuba, 227
Cyclist Touring Club, 189
Czech Communist Party, 209
Czechoslovakia, 81, 86, 133, 176, 206, 208, 211,
    223, 227, 287
Czibor, Zoltan, 164–65, 172

Da Costa e Silva, Artur, 232
Dalglish, Kenny, 117, 145
Darlington, 248
Darwen, 61
Darwin, Charles, 12–13, 19
Davies, John H., 51–52
Davitt, Michael, 147
Day of Physical Culture, 237
De Boer, Frank, 118
De Boer, Ronald, 118
De Gaulle, Charles, 122
Degeyter, Pierre, 192
DeLillo, Don, 265
Del Sol, Luis, 116
Delves, Anthony, 56–57
Denmark, 24, 41, 227, 252, 287
De Oliveira Figueiredo, João Baptista, 232
Derby, 9–10, 56
Derby County, 75
Derry, 149
Derry City FC, 149
Desailly, Marcel, 113
Deschamps, Didier, 113
De Souza Mello, Márcio, 232
Détari, Lajos, 172
Deutscher Fussballbund (DFB), 28–29, 35–36,
    86, 88, 90–93, 95–97, 129, 164, 169, 173,
    178–81, 183, 224–25, 235, 247–50, 256, 262,
    285–86, 288–89
Deutscher Fussball- und Cricket-Bund, 35
Deutscher Reichsbund für Leibesübungen,
    87, 93
Deutscher Sportausschuss (DS), 213–14
Deutsche Turnerschaft (DT), 32, 177
Deutscher Turn- und Sportbund (DTSB), 214,
    218
DFC Germania, 35
DFC Prague, 35, 37
Dick Kerr's Ladies, 278–81
Didi, 111
Dieguito, 130
Diem, Carl, 35
Dienst, Gottfried "Gotti," 108
Dirceu, 126
Di Stéfano, Alfredo, 116, 229
Divisione Nazionale, 220
Dixey, Florence, 277
Dobrovol'nye sportivnye obščestva (DSO), 212
Dorchester, 192
Dortmund, 124
Dresden, 173, 182, 218
Dresdner SC, 251
Drews, Jörg, 167
DSV 1910 Dresden, 183

Dublin, 40
Ducadam, Helmut, 124
Dundee, 145, 148
Dundee Harp, 147
Dunga, 113
Dunkirk, 101
Dunning, Eric, 274
Düsseldorf, 166, 181
Dylan, Bob, 116
Dynamo, 201, 205, 213–14
Dynamo Dresden, 215
Dynamo Kiev, 118, 213
Dynamo Moscow, 205, 210
Dynamo Tiflis, 210
Dynamo Zagreb, 149–50

Earle, Steve, 116
Ebi, Fritz, 161
Eder, 111, 127
Edinburgh, 17, 61, 143–44, 148
Edinburgh City Girls, 281
Edward II, 10
Egypt, 16, 247
Eigendorf, Lutz, 219
Eindhoven, 218
Eintracht Frankfurt, 95–96, 116
Eisenberg, Christiane, 23, 140
Elias, Norbert, 274
El Salvador, 240
Elsener, Charly, 173
Empor Lauter, 215
Energie Cottbus, 151
England, 3, 8n2, 26–27, 39–40, 41n106, 47–48,
    50–52, 61, 65, 67, 71, 75–76, 86, 88, 96, 99–
    100, 118–19, 130, 141–45, 164, 176, 189,
    203, 211, 243–44, 246–47, 264, 277–79,
    286–88
English Ladies Football Association (ELFA),
    280
Enrique, Luiz, 130
Escobar, Andrés, 132
Essen, 165–67, 180
Eton, 10, 15–17
European Champion Clubs' Cup, 95, 99, 115–16,
    118, 229
European Championship, 123, 125, 127, 130,
    133–34, 139, 211, 229, 286, 289
European Court, 101
European Cup Winners' Cup, 96, 173, 213, 215,
    218
European Union, 101
Eusébio, 117, 123
Euzkadi ta Askatasuna (ETA), 230
Everton FC, 51, 75, 100, 279

Index

Excelsior Zurich, 27
Eyre, Charles, 147

Facchinetti, Giacinto, 131
FA cup, 18–19, 73, 75–76, 79–80, 244–45, 247, 278
Falcão, Paulo Roberto, 111
Faroe Islands, 115
Fascist Party, 220–21
Fashanu, Justin, 269
Faszekas, Laszlo, 134, 172
Fatherland Front, 187
Fatton, Jackie, 114, 131
FA Women's Premier National League, 281
FA Women's Super League, 281
FC Aarau, 128
FC Airdrieonians, 144
FC Au, 138
FC Barcelona, 29, 149, 173, 226–30
FC Bari, 29
FC Basel, 26–27, 114, 126
FC Bayern München, 71, 91, 96, 115, 126–27, 133, 136, 172, 253
FC Bologna, 29
FC Cantonal Neuchâtel, 254
FC Grandson, 161
FC Hansa Rostock, 151
FC Kitzbühel, 239
1. FC Köln, 109, 134
FC Lugano, 127
FC Lyon, 29
1. FC Magdeburg, 215, 218
FC Mönchengladbach/Rheydt, 91
FC Nantes, 147
1. FC Nürnberg, 91
FC Porto, 115
FC Santos, 117
FC Schalke 04, 90–91, 97, 124, 172, 175, 239, 252
FC St. Gall, 24, 27
FC St. Pauli, 105, 135–36
FC Wacker München, 91
FC Wettswil-Bonstetten, 292
FC Wiesloch, 262
FC Winterthur, 29, 161
1. FC Wuppertal, 91
FC Yverdon, 27
FC Zürich, 29, 126
Federal Commission for Radio and Press, 261
Federal Department of the Military, 258–59
Federal Office for Wartime Food Production, 259
Federal Republic of Germany (FRG), 4, 96, 108, 164, 169–71, 215–19, 286, 288–89
Fédération Internationale de Football Association (FIFA), 41–42, 86, 153, 192–93, 207, 209–10, 217, 222, 226, 231, 233, 235–36, 262, 288–89, 292
Femina Paris, 279
Ferencvaros Budapest, 172
Ferguson, Alec, 144
Fernandez, Luis, 112, 123
Ferretti, Lando, 220
Ferrol, 238
Fignon, Laurent, 113
Figo, Luis, 113
Finger, Edi, 114
Finke, Volker, 136
Finland, 190, 259
Finney, Tom, 247
Fiorentina, 133
Fire Flies, 27
First Vienna Football Club, 37, 84–85, 119, 252
Fischer, Klaus, 110, 127
Fishwick, Nicholas, 55
Fleming, Harold, 65–66, 119
Floridsdorfer Athletiksportklub, 37
Fontaine, Just, 171
Foot, Michael, 169
Football Association (FA), 17–18, 21–23, 26, 30, 34–35, 38–41, 43, 67, 73, 77, 101, 189, 242–45, 276–77, 280–81
Foot-Ball Club, 17
Football League (FL), 21, 50, 52, 75–76, 79, 99–100, 244–45, 278
Foreign Office, 227
Förster, Karl-Heinz, 112
Fortuna Düsseldorf, 91, 165
Forza Italia, 103
France, 9, 39, 41, 81, 113, 121–23, 136, 150–51, 158, 162, 176, 178, 189–90, 194, 204, 206, 208, 227–28, 256, 259–60, 279
Francescoli, Enzo, 126
Franco, Francisco, 194, 226–30
Frank, Wolfgang, 116
Frankfurt am Main, 83, 91, 174, 190, 218, 282
Frauenfeld, 25
Freie Deutsche Jugend (FDJ), 214
Freier Deutscher Gewerkschaftsbund (FDGB), 214
Friaça, 131
Friedländer, Hans-Peter, 260
Friedrichs, Hanns Joachim, 115
Friends of Nature, 184
Front de Libération Nationale (FLN), 122
FT Jessitz, 183
Fürth, 166

Gaelic Athletic Association (GAA), 40
Galeano, Eduardo, 133

Index

Gallacher, Hugh, 144
Gallipoli, 241
Galton, Francis, 12
Gamper, Hans "Joan," 29
Garrincha, 111, 127, 133
Gascoigne, Paul, 135
Geertz, Clifford, 3
Gehrmann, Siegfried, 180–81, 197
Geisel, Ernesto, 232
Gelsenkirchen, 91, 180
Gemmill, Archie, 145
General Federation of Trade Unions (GFTU), 77
Geneva, 25, 28, 160–61, 165, 169, 256–57
Genghini, Bernard, 109
Genoa, 29
Genova, 287
Gentile, Claudio, 111, 130
Gento, Francisco, 116, 127
George II of Greece, 246
George V, 242
German Democratic Republic (GDR), 4, 151, 170–71, 213–15, 216–19, 231, 287
German Institute for Technical Labor Education (DINTA), 180
German National Commitee for Physical Exercise, 284
German University for Physical Education, 283
German Women's Football Association, 286
German Women's Football Union, 286
Germany, 12, 30–31, 34, 36, 85–86, 88, 91, 94–95, 98, 109, 118–20, 122, 127, 136, 146, 151–56, 158, 160, 162–64, 166, 169, 176–77, 190–92, 195–98, 200, 206, 208–10, 224–25, 227, 231, 238, 242, 247–52, 257, 259–62, 277, 281–82, 285–87, 289
Gestapo, 225
Ghiggia, Alcides, 132
Gibraltar, 148
Gijón, 109
Giordano, Ralph, 163n76
Giresse, Alain, 109–10
Giro d'Italia, 113
Girondins de Bordeaux, 110
Gladstone, William, 51, 142
Glasgow, 1, 46, 56, 61, 116, 141–43, 145–46, 148, 150
Glasgow Rangers, 1, 56, 78, 145, 147–48
Glass, John, 146
Goebbels, Joseph, 224–25, 239, 251, 253, 261
Göhring, Hermann, 225
Götz, Falko, 219
Globocnik, Odilo, 121
Goicoechea, Andoni, 130

Gold Cup, 289
Gomes, Nuno, 113
Gómez, Juanito, 135
Goodall, John, 51
Gornik Zabrze, 119
Gorst, John, 63
Gotha, 33
Grasshopper Club Zürich, 6, 26–29, 127, 136, 162
Graziani, Francesco, 111
Great Britain, 5–6, 8–9, 11–12, 24, 34, 39, 41–44, 46, 54, 65, 71, 76, 82–83, 85, 100, 175–76, 187, 190, 198, 206, 210–11, 220, 223, 242–43, 246–48, 263, 272, 276–78, 282, 285
Great Lever, 73
Greaves, Jimmy, 127
Greece, 172
Griffith, Tom E., 26
Grimshaw, Henry, 62
Grini, 129
Grobelaar, Bruce, 130
Grosics, Gyula, 166, 170
Grüninger, Paul, 136
Guadeloupe, 123
Guernica, 227
Guillaume, Günter, 216
Guisan, Henri, 257, 260
Gullit, Ruud, 118, 123
Guttmann, Béla, 84

Haakon VII of Norway, 246
Hadji, El Moustafa, 130
Haffner, Sebastian, 88, 90, 238
Hagi, Gheorge, 126
Hahn, Arie, 127
Hallaton, 10
Halt, Karl von, 284
Halvorsen, Asbjørn, 129
Hamann, Erich, 217
Hambach, 174
Hamborn, 180
Hamburg, 31, 105, 129, 182, 216, 219
Hamburger SV, 91, 96, 110, 112, 114, 129, 179
Hamilton Foot Ball Club, 41
Hanappi, Gerhard, 114
Hanau, 32
Handelman, Don, 68
Hannah, David, 142
Hannover, 129
Hansen, Alan, 117
Happel, Ernst, 114
Harder, Otto Fritz "Tull," 129
Harper, Bill, 144
Harrow, 17, 19

Hartwig, Jimmy, 124
Harvie, Johnny, 142
Hauser, Fritz, 159
Havelange, João, 233, 235
Havemann, Nils, 92
Heart of Midlothian, 78, 244
Heidelberger Flaggen-Club, 35
Heinecke, Helga, 217
Hegel, Georg Wilhelm Friedrich, 176
Heighway, Steve, 135
Heinecken, Philipp, 281–82
Heinrich, Arthur, 164
Heisserer, Oskar, 136
Hellas Verona, 124
Hellmann, Rudolf, 216
Hellström, Ronnie, 125
Herald, William, 38
Herberger, Sepp, 164, 168, 170, 251
Herrera, Helenio, 117
Hertha BSC Berlin, 4, 91
Hess, Rudolf, 225
Hibernian Edinburgh, 144, 147
Hidalgo, Michel, 109
Hidegkuti, Nándor, 164, 172
Hildebrand, Dieter, 3
Hills, Arnold E., 53
Hinault, Bernard, 113
Hirsch, Julius, 136
Hitler, Adolf, 94, 121, 136, 152, 157, 163, 166, 195, 225, 253
Hobsbawm, Eric J., 50, 59, 74, 139, 140n4
Hoeness, Uli, 71, 216
Hogg, James, 38
Hogg, Thomas, 38
Holmes, Robert, 67–68
Holt, Richard, 21, 55, 68, 118
Honduras, 240
Honecker, Erich, 4
Honeywell, Nettie, 277
Honved Budapest, 172
Horak, Roman, 119
Hornby, Nick, 107
Höttges, Horst-Dieter, 217
Hottiger, Marc, 173
Houlding, John, 51, 61
Hrubesch, Horst, 110
Hubacher, Helmut, 154
Huddersfield, 61
Huddersfield Town, 80
Hueppe, Ferdinand, 31
Hügi, Seppe, 114
Humphries, Stephen, 62
Hungary, 81, 83, 86, 113, 161, 163, 170, 172–73, 176, 179, 223, 256, 259

Hunt, Henry, 57
Hurst, Geoff, 107–8

Iceland, 219
Impiglia, Marco, 223
Independent Labour Party, 188
India, 16, 39
Indian Football Association, 39
Intercollegiate Football Association, 290
Intercontinental Cup, 117
Inter Departmental Committee on Physical Deterioration, 64
International Labour Sport Federation (CSIT), 195–96
International Ladies Association (ILA), 286
International Olympic Committee (IOC), 210
International Socialist Association for Physical Education (ASIEP), 189
International Summer Festival of the Workers' Sports Cultural Cartel, 192
International Workers' Association for Sport and Physical Culture, 190
Internazionale Milano, 29, 112, 117, 131
Inverness, 277
Iran, 1
Iraq, 122
Ireland, 39, 47, 83, 145, 149
Iribar, José Ángel, 230
Irish Free State, 40
Irish Republican Army (IRA), 148
Iron Front, 183
Iselin, Walter, 128
Italian Football Association, 221
Italian Olympic Committee, 220–21, 223
Italy, 29, 94, 96, 118, 123, 125–26, 130, 136, 151, 172–73, 191, 193, 195, 200, 220, 222, 226–27, 230, 256, 259, 261, 287–89

Jackson, N. Lane "PA," 75
Jahn, Friedrich Ludwig, 31
Jairzinho, 111
Japan, 8n2
Jarni, Robert, 150
Jennings, Pat, 125
Jeremies, Jens, 130
Johnston, Maurice, 147
Jones, Stephen G., 188
Jordan, 122
Jungdeutschlandbund, 36
Junior, 111
Jung, Edgar J., 89
Jürgens, Udo, 114
Juventus Turin, 4, 111, 125

Index

Kaiserslautern, 165–67, 171
Kampfgemeinschaft für Rote Sporteinheit (KG), 182
Karlsruhe, 136, 262
Karlsruher FV, 136
Karlsruher SC, 97
Keegan, Kevin, 4
Kempes, Mario, 117
Kenya, 38
Kershaw, Ian, 224
Kharkov, 189
Kickers Zurich, 27
Kiev, 189, 227
Kilmarnock, 148
Kimslau, 136
Kiprich, József, 172
Kirsten, Ulf, 127
Klein, Michael, 267
Klemperer, Viktor, 165
Klinsmann, Jürgen, 130
Klöti, Emil, 161
Knudsen, Knud, 115
Knup, Adrian, 127
Koblet, Hugo, 113
Koch, Konrad, 31, 34
Koch, Lutz, 94
Kocsis, Sándor, 164, 172
Koeman, Ronald, 127
Kohlmeyer, Werner, 171
Koller, Jan, 125
Komsomol, 201, 203–5
Koncilia, Friedl, 114
Kopa(czewski), Raymond, 121–23, 171
Kopp, Annemarie, 283–84
Koppisch, Richard, 177
Korr, Charles, 53–54
Kosarev, Aleksandr, 204–5
Kosovo, 150
Kostedde, Erwin, 124
Krankl, Hans, 114, 127
Krool, Ruud, 218
Kubitschek, Juscelino, 232
Kucker, Fritz, 137
Kübler, Ferdinand "Ferdi," 113
Kuhn, Gustav, 29
Kuhn, Köbi, 126
Kuper, Simon, 247
Kuzorra, Ernst, 153

Labour Party, 68, 169, 188, 198
Lacombe, Bernard, 109
Ladies Gaelic Football Association, 40
Lanfranchi, Pierre, 24, 122
Lantos, Mihaly, 172

Larsson, Henrik, 147
Lato, Grzegorz, 119
Lauck, Reinhard, 217
Laudrup, Brian, 127
Laudrup, Michael, 126
Lausanne, 25, 28–29, 114
Lausanne Football and Cricket Club, 24, 27
La Villa Longchamp Ouchy, 27
League of Nations, 33, 208
Leeds, 61
Le Havre AC, 25, 30
Leicester, 62
Leighton, Jim, 125
Leipzig, 32, 35, 178, 182, 215, 218
LeMond, Greg, 113
Leningrad, 189, 204, 210
Le Pen, Jean-Marie, 123
Liberal Party, 51, 142
Libuda, Reinhard "Stan," 127
Libya, 122
Liebrich, Werner, 164
Lienen, Ewald, 135
Lima, 236
Lineker, Gary
Linfield FC, 149
Linnemann, Felix, 93
Linz, 184
Lippens, Willi "Ente," 133
Lippmann, Frank, 219
Lipton, Thomas, 38
Lithuania, 85
Litmanen, Jari, 118
Littbarski, Pierre, 109, 127
Liverani, Fabio, 124
Liverpool, 4, 18, 46, 52, 63, 141, 145
Liverpool FC, 52, 54, 61, 63, 99–100, 117, 131, 135
Lloys, Treytorrens de, 254
Llwyncelyn, 281
Lobanovskyi, Valeriy, 118
Locarno, 178
Lofthouse, Nathaniel "Nat," 68
Lokomotiv, 201, 212
Lombardo, Attilio, 125
London, 17–19, 43, 44n4, 46–47, 49, 53, 57, 61, 73, 76, 104, 107, 143–44, 173, 188–89, 243, 245–46, 254, 272, 277
Londonderry, 149
Lorant, Gyula, 172
Los Angeles, 126, 193, 212
Lucerne, 160, 190
Lucerne International (LSI), 190, 192–93
Luchsinger, Fred, 152
Lüdtke, Alf, 45
Luhmann, Niklas, 105

Luque, Leopoldo, 117
Luther, Martin, state secretary, 252
Luxemburg, 286
Lyon, 123, 193, 256

MacDonald, Ramsay, 188
Maderthaner, Wolfgang, 59, 119
Madjer, Rabah, 115
Madrid, 194, 226
Magath, Felix, 112
Maier, Sepp, 114, 133–34, 217
Major League Soccer (MLS), 269, 291
Maldini, Paolo, 118, 125
Mali, 123
Manchester, 28, 46, 50, 61–62, 68, 77, 128n27, 169
Manchester City, 68, 128
Manchester Corinthians, 281, 286
Manchester United, 49, 51, 68, 77, 100, 103, 145
Mangan, J. A., 118
Manganiello, Raffaele, 223
Mannheim, 182
Maradona, Diego, 119, 125, 130, 151
Marías, Javier, 116, 135
Marquitos, 116
Marschik, Matthias, 199
Marseilles, 29, 123, 136
Marx, Karl, 42
Mason, Tony, 48, 55, 67
Matildas, 264
Matthews, Stanley, 125, 127
Mazzola, Sandro, 131
McCoist, Ally, 127
McGowan, Shane, 116
McGregor, William, 76, 271
McKibbin, Ross, 50
McKillop, William, 147
McLeod, Alistair, 145
McLeod, Murdo, 128
McQueen, Thomas, 145
Mead, George Herbert, 140
Medellín, 132
Médici, Emílio Garrastazu, 232–33
Meier, Geni, 173
Meisl, Hugo, 82
Mekloufi, Rachid, 122–23
Menotti, César Luis, 117, 235–36
Meredith, William "Billy," 68, 77
Mesked, 207
Metcalf, Alan, 50
Mexico, 82, 128, 172, 227–28, 233
Mexico City, 112
Middlesborough, 46
Middlesborough Ironopolis, 61
Midlothian, 277

Mihajlovic, Sinista, 130
Milan, 29
Mildner, Fritz, 93
Milla, Roger, 111, 125
Millar, Jimmy, 142
Millionarios de Bogotá, 229
Mills, Mickey, 117
Milward, Alan S., 241
Minelli, Severino, 153
Minger, Rudolf, 159, 162
Ministry for State Security (MfS), 214, 216
Minsk, 227
Mitropa Cup, 82, 86
Mitrović, Stefan, 140
Mödling, 184
Mölter, Veit, 287–88
Molyneux, D. D., 49
Monnier, Henry, 28
Montgomery, Bernard, 246
Montreux FC, 28
Moorhouse, H. F., 143
Morgarten, 160
Morlock, Max, 165
Morocco, 122, 194, 208
Morris, Desmond, 267
Moscow, 37, 189–90, 192–93, 202–4, 206, 208, 211–13, 227, 231, 235
Motherwell, 148
Motherwell FC, 148
Mozambique, 123
Müller, Gerd, 126, 217
Muller, 127
Munich, 112, 166, 169, 178, 262
Musner, Lutz, 59
Mussolini, Benito, 195, 220–22

Nachtweih, Norbert, 219
Nagy, Imre, 172
Naples, 28, 151
Napoleon, 32
National Banner Black-Red-Gold, 183
National Basketball Association (NBA), 291
National Football League (NFL), 265, 290
National League, 257–58
National People's Army (NVA), 214
National Socialist Party of Austria, 87
National Union for Physical Education, 224
National Women's Soccer League (NWSL), 292
National Workers' Sports Association (NWSA), 189
NATO, 135
Neal, Phil, 117
Neeskens, Johan, 218
Nerz, Otto, 95

Netherlands, 41, 98, 113, 123, 125, 134, 173, 218, 286–87
Netzer, Günter, 125, 131, 219
Neuberger, Hermann, 235
Neuchâtel, 152, 160
Neuengamme, 129
Newcastle United, 61, 142, 145
Newcastle-upon-Tyne, 47, 57
New York Yankees, 102
New Zealand, 40, 66
Nier, Willi, 91
Nigeria, 38
Nîmes, 28
N'Kono, Thomas, 111
Nora, Pierre, 4, 173
Nordau, Max, 85
North American Soccer League (NASL), 290
Northern German Football Association, 249
Northern Ireland, 125, 149, 246
North Vietnam, 122
Norway, 195, 208, 210, 225, 227, 289
Norwegian Workers' Sport Association, 193
Norwich, 57
Nottingham, 55, 57, 61
Nottingham Forest, 117
Notts County, 75
Nyliasi, Tibor, 172

Oberhuber, Karl, 224
Obilic Belgrade, 150
Ocwirk, Ernst, 114
Odermatt, Karl, 126
Oertel, Heinz-Florian, 217
Österreichischer Fussballverband (ÖFV), 37
Ogris, Andreas, 127
Old Boys Basel, 27, 255
Old Carthusians, 74
Old Etonians, 74
Oldham, 131
Olympic Games, 42, 170, 193, 196, 200, 210, 212, 225, 235, 291
Olympique Marseille, 123
Ortiz, Oscar, 117
Orwell, George, 238
Oslo, 129
Osmanovski, Yksel, 123
Oswald, Rudolf, 93–94
Overmars, Marc, 118
Oxford, 19, 31, 74
Oxford City, 62
Oxford United, 270

Pahl, Jürgen, 219
Palermo, 29

Palestine, 85, 208
Pallas, David, 123
Panathinakos Athens, 172
Panenka, Antonin, 133–34
Pan-German League, 31
Paraguay, 82
Paris, 157, 160, 162, 193, 208, 227, 279
Paris St. Germain, 112
Partisan Belgrade, 149
Paoli, Silvio, 127
Pascolo, Marco, 123
Passarella, Daniel, 117
Pelé, 111, 117, 119, 125, 232
Peñarol Montevideo, 117
People's Olympics, 194
People's Police, 215
Perdigão, Pedro, 132
Perez, Valdir, 111
Perón, Juan, 234
Persia, 207–8, 210
Pertini, Sandro, 111
Peru, 82
Petit, Emmanuel, 113
Pezzey, Bruno, 114
Piñeiro y de Queralt, Enrique, 228
Pinochet, Augusto, 212, 230–31
Pinto, João, 115
Planck, Karl, 34
Platini, Michel, 109, 112, 113n4, 119, 123, 125
Poland, 85, 111, 121, 172, 216, 227
Polgar, Alfred, 84
Polster, Toni, 127, 134
Poole, William, 38
Portsmouth, 272
Portugal, 123, 228, 259
Poulidor, Raymond, 113
Pozzo, Vittorio, 28
Prague, 31, 35, 209
Premier League, 101
Preston, 51, 61, 278
Preston North End, 51, 68, 73, 75
Princeton, 290
Profé, Alice, 284
Professional Footballer's Association (PFA), 77
Prohaska, Herbert, 114, 126
Prosinecki, Robert, 150
Pro Vercelli, 127
Prussia, 32
Puskás, Ferenc, 116, 164–65, 172, 174

Race, Mick, 48
Racing Paris, 1, 204, 208
Racing Strasbourg, 136
Racing Universitaire d'Alger, 1

Index

Radencovic, Petar, 133–34
Rahn, Helmut, 165–67, 171
Ramuz, Charles-Ferdinand, 253
Rapallo, 206–8
Rapid Wien, 4, 37, 84–86, 114, 119–20, 184
Rappan, Karl, 153, 260
Rasensport Strassburg, 136
Rauch, Louis, 29
Raúl, 127
RC Liège, 101
Real Madrid, 96–97, 116–17, 121, 135, 172, 228
Real Sociedad San Sebastian, 135, 230
Red Cross, 246, 255, 257
Red Sport International (RSI), 190, 192–93, 195, 206
Red Star Belgrade, 149–50
Reichenau, Walter von, 249
Reiziger, Michael, 118
Renner, Karl, 184
Rensenbrink, Robert, 126
Republican Protective Union, 187
Republik Euskadi, 227
Revolutionäre Gewerkschaftsopposition (RGO), 182
Rexach, Carlos, 229
Rhodesia, 38
Richmond, 18
Rijkaard, Frank, 118, 123
Rimet, Jules, 153
Rimini, 196
Rio de Janeiro, 79n17, 82, 131
Ripon, 16
Rivaldo, 113
Rivelino, Roberto, 111, 126
River Plate Buenos Aires, 229, 235
Rochetau, Dominique, 109
Rodrigues, Nelson, 132
Roggers, Robbi, 269
Rohr, Oskar, 136–37
Rolff, Wolfgang, 112
Romania, 81, 85
Romario, 113
Rorschach, 25
Rose, William, 67
Rossi, Paolo, 111–12, 127
Rostock, 215
Roth, Philipp, 265
Rovers, Neuchâtel, 27
Royal Air Force, 247
Royal Army, 247
Royal Dutch Football Union, 277
Royal Engineers, 19, 74
Rudel, Hans-Ulrich, 235
Rudolfshügel, 37

Rufer, Wynton, 66
Rugby, 14–18, 31
Rugby Football Union (RFU), 18, 21–22, 30
Rugby League, 21
Ruggieri, Oscar, 130
Rummenigge, Karl-Heinz, 110
Russia, 37, 42, 136, 207
Rutgers, 290

SA, 285
Saint-Louis, 206
Saldanha, João, 233
Salzburg, 116
Sampdoria Genoa, 125, 173
Sanchez, Hugo, 127
Santiago de Chile, 231
Santos, Djalma, 111
Santos, Marcio, 113
Santos, Nílton, 111
São Paulo, 82, 131
SAS, 148
Savicevic, Dejan, 118
Scarfoglio, Michele, 28
Scarfoglio, Paolo, 28
Schachner, Walter, 114
Schaffhausen, 25
Scheidemann, Philipp, 42
Schiaffino, Juan Alberto, 131
Schinz, Konrad, 30
SC Brühl St. Gall
SC Freiburg, 136
SC Lorbeer 06 Hamburg, 181
SC Ostmark Wien, 87
Schlegel, Dieter, 219
Schlieren, 262
Schmeichel, Peter, 125
Schmidt, Horst, 286
Schneider, Werner, 216
Schön, Helmut, 251
Schröder, Gerhard, 173–74
Schulze-Marmeling, Dietrich, 44
Schumacher, Toni, 109–10, 112, 130
Schuster, Bernd, 126, 130
Schwan, Heribert, 219
Schwarz, Emmanuel, 87
Schwarzenbeck, Hans-Georg "Katsche," 127
Schweizerischer Fussballverband, 28, 159, 160n62, 262, 292
Schweizer Wehraktion, 161
Scifo, Enzo, 126
Scirea, Gaetano, 111
Scotland, 19, 40, 47, 52, 71, 76, 86, 128, 141, 144–46, 148, 244–46, 264, 277
Scotland Yard, 188

Scott, Jack, 142
Scott, Walter, 142–143
Scottish Football Association (SFA), 144, 148
Scottish Football League (SFL), 77–79, 144, 147
Sebes, Gusztav, 171
Seeler, Ewrin, 179, 181
Seeler, Uwe, 127, 179
Seitz, Karl, 184
Senderos, Philippe, 123
Senegal, 123
Serbia, 139, 150
Servette FC, 26, 114, 152, 160, 162, 257
Sesa, Davide, 123
Sesta, Schasti, 119
Sétif, 122
Seville, 109, 112, 228
Sforza, Ciriaco, 123
Shankley, Bill, 100
Sheffield, 18, 49, 61, 80
Sheffield FC, 17
Sheffield United, 63, 67, 244
Shilton, Peter, 125
Signori, Beppe, 125
Sillitoe, Alan, 55, 60
Silva, Mauro, 113
Sindelar, Matthias, 119–21
Singen, 166
Sinn Féin, 40, 148
Six, Didier, 109–10
SK Hakoah Wien, 84–87, 119
Slavia Prague, 119
Slezak, Leo, 84
Sligo, 146–47
Slovakia, 252, 259
Smith, Adam, 13, 19
Smith, David, 55, 65
Smolarek, Włodzimierz, 110
Sochaux, 109
Social Democratic Party of Germany (SPD),
    177, 182–83
Social Democratic Party of Switzerland (SPS),
    154
Socialist Unity Party (SED), 215–16, 218
Socialist Workers Sport International (SASI),
    185, 188, 190, 193, 195
Sócrates, 111–12, 233
Sounes, Graeme, 117
South American Cup, 130
South German Association for Professional
    Football Matches, 93
Soviet Union, 172, 182, 189–90, 193, 195, 200–
    201, 206–13, 215, 219, 227–28, 231
Spain, 41, 81, 118, 123, 125, 131, 157, 172, 195,
    200, 206, 219, 226, 228, 230, 259

Spanish Football Association, 226
Spartacus Games, 192–93, 208, 212
Spartak, 201, 205, 212
Spartak Moscow, 204, 211
Sparta Prague, 119
Sparta Rotterdam, 277
Sparwasser, Jürgen, 4, 217–19
*Specializirovannaja detsko-junošeskaja
    sportivnaja škola olimpijskogo rezerva*, 212
Spencer, Herbert, 12–13, 19
S.-Peterburgskij Kružok Ljubitelej Sporta, 30
Spiez, 167
Sportfreunde Basel, 227
SS, 87, 129, 136
SSC Napoli, 151
SSG 09 Bergisch Gladbach, 289
SS Strassburg, 136
Stade de Reims, 121, 173
Stade Helvétique de Marseille, 29
Stalin, 202–5, 211
Stalingrad, 210, 239, 252
Standard Liege, 124
Starostin, Nikolaj, 204
Stasi, 215, 219
Steaua Bucharest, 124
Stein, Jock, 128
St. Gall, 29, 136, 262
St. Helen's Ladies, 279
Stielike, Uli, 110
Stiles, Nobby, 127
St. Jakob an der Birs, 156
Stockholm, 135, 261
Stoitchkov, Hristo, 127
Stoke City, 63, 65, 75, 125
Stoke-on-Trent, 63
St. Petersburg, 30, 37, 272n22
Strachan, Gordon, 127
Strasbourg, 136
Strummer, Joe, 116
Stuttgart, 91, 261–62
Suddell, William, 51
Suker, Davor, 150
Sunderland, 73
Sunderland FC, 61, 63, 142
Suñol, Josep, 226
Sutter, Alain, 125, 135
Sutter, Hans, 160
Sweden, 41, 83, 121, 131, 135, 171, 173, 208, 210,
    251, 259, 261–62
Swift, Graham, 60
Swindon, 47, 65–67
Swiss Cup, 128
Swiss Football and Athletic Union, 155, 159, 259
Swiss Football Association, 27

Index

Switzerland, 24, 26–28, 30, 41, 81, 86, 119, 123, 126, 131, 136–38, 150–56, 158, 160–62, 164–65, 172, 176, 206, 225–26, 228, 242, 254, 261–62, 292
Szarmach, Andrzej, 134
Szepan, Fritz, 153

Taffarel, Claudio, 113
Taiwan, 289
Talinn, 196
Tapie, Bernard, 130
Tarantini, Alberto, 117
Tardelli, Marco, 111–12
Tassotti, Mauro, 130
Tauber, Peter, 249
Teague, Bert, 65
Tehran, 208
Tell, William, 160
Tetzlaff, Alfred, 216
Thatcher, Margaret, 45, 99, 144
Thommen, Ernst B., 262
Thompson, E. P., 45
Thuram, Lilian, 113
Tiflis, 227
Tigana, Jean, 109–10
Tipperary, 40
Thames Ironworks, 53
Tilkowski, Hans, 108
Torberg, Friedrich, 84
Torres, José Augusto, 117
Tostão, 111
Tottenham, 49
Totti, Francesco, 134
Toulouse, 123
Tour de France, 113
Trautmann, Bernd, 128
Trésor, Marius, 109–10, 123
Trogen, 25
Trudovye Rezervy, 201, 212
Tschammer Cup, 253
Tschammer und Osten, Hans von, 93, 225, 250–52
TSV München 1860, 96, 133, 253
Tudjman, Franjo, 150
Türkyilmaz, Kubilay, 123
Tunisia, 122
Turati, Augusto, 221
Turek, Toni, 4, 165–66, 168, 173
Turin, 4, 28
Turkey, 124, 164, 208–9
TUS Wörrstadt, 289
Tyne, Wear & Tees Alfred Wood Munition Girls Cup, 278

UEFA. *See* Union of European Football Associations
UEFA Cup, 215
UEFA Women's Champions League, 292
UEFA Women's Cup, 292
Uganda, 38
Ukraine, 103, 192, 213
Union Berlin, 151
Union Franco-Musulmane de Sétif, 122
Union Internationale Amateur de Football Association (UIAFA), 42
Union of European Football Associations (UEFA), 211, 281
United Irish League, 147
United States, 1, 5, 12, 34, 40, 42, 82, 84, 102, 115, 125, 208, 232, 264, 277, 280, 290–91
United States Soccer Federation (USSF), 291
Urban, Marcus, 269
Uridil, Josef, 119
Uruguay, 38, 79n17, 82, 131, 165, 192, 232, 234
US Bastia, 151
USL W-League, 291
Utley, George, 67

Valdez, Francisco, 231
Valencia, 228
Valley Party, 104
Vampley, Wray, 78
Van Basten, Marco, 118, 127
Van de Kerkhof, René, 218
Van de Kerkhof, Willy, 218
Van der Sar, Edwin, 118
Van Zandt, Townes, 116
Vargas, Gétulio, 231–32
Varna, 196
Vasco da Gama, 131
Vava, 111
Vega, Ramon, 123
Veitch, Fred, 48
Venice, 29
Vernati, Sirio, 160
Vernède, R. E., 242
Versailles, 152
Vevey, 257
VfB Stuttgart, 110
VfL Leipzig, 35
Viareggio, 220
Vichy, 136
Victoria Hamburg, 181
Victorian Football Association, 40
Videla, Jorge Rafael, 234, 236
Videoton Székesfehérvár, 172
Vidigal, José Luis, 123

Vienna, 37, 81, 84, 87, 119–21, 179, 183, 186, 191–92, 199, 249, 256
Vienna Cricket and Football Club, 37
Viera, Patric, 113
Viktoria Wien, 37
Vodnik, 212
Vogts, Berti, 114, 217
Volkssturm, 252
Vollenweider, Eduard, 30
Von der Goltz, Colmar, 248
Vorwärts, 213–14
Vorwärts Frankfurt, 217
Vsevobuč, 201
Vukovar, 150

Wacker Wien, 119–20
Wagner, Theodor, 114
Wahl, Alfred, 122
Walacek, Génia, 152–53
Wales, 46, 63, 77, 128, 246, 281
Walfrid, 146
Wallace, William, 143
Waller, J. P., 61
Walluga, Helga, 287–88
Walsall Swifts, 73
Walter, Des, 123
Walter, Fritz, 165–67, 171, 174
Walter, Ottmar, 171, 174
Walvin, James, 55, 57
Wanderers, The, 19, 74
War Cup, 245–46
Watson Hutton, Alexander, 38
Weber, Max, 118
Weber, Wolfgang, 108
Weimar, 174
Weissweiler, Hennes, 131
West Bromwich Albion, 63, 75
West German Women's Football Association, 286
West Ham United, 53–54, 85, 108
Westrup, Zenon Stanislas, 261
Whiteside, Norman, 125
Wiener Amateur-Sportverein, 85, 184
Wiener Athletik-Sportclub, 37
Wiener Neustadt, 183–84
Wiener Sportclub, 37
Wilhelm II, 33
Williamson, David J., 279
Winchester, 14
Winter, Aaron, 123
Winterthur, 28–29
Witschge, Richard, 118
Wolverhampton Wanderers, 67, 75, 211, 246
Women's Football Association, 281
Women's Professional Soccer (WPS), 292
Women's United Soccer Association League (WUSA League), 292
Women's World Cup, 287, 289–91
Woodcock, Tony, 127
Woolwich Arsenal, 76
Workers Football European Championship, 192
Workers Football World Championship, 193
Workers Olympics, 179, 186, 190–92, 195–96, 208, 227
Workers Union for Athletics and Physical Culture (ASKÖ), 185
World Cup, 86, 94–96, 98, 108–9, 111–13, 115–17, 121–23, 125–28, 130–32, 134–36, 145, 150–53, 157–58, 164–65, 169, 172–73, 192, 211–12, 215–16, 222, 224–25, 230–35, 240, 257, 261, 272, 285, 291
Worms, 39
Wortmann, Sönke, 174
Wright, Ian, 123

Yad Vashem, 137
Yakin, Hakan, 124
Yakin, Murat, 124
Yale, 290
Yashin, Lev, 124–24
York, 48–49
Young Boys Bern, 6, 27, 173
Young Communist League, 188
Young Fellows Zurich, 27–28
Young German Union, 248
Yugoslavia, 119, 149, 164, 169, 259

Zamoskvoretskij, 206
Zenit, 201, 212
Zentralausschuss für Volks- und Jugendspiele, 31
Zico, 111, 125
Zidane, Zinedine, 113, 123
Zimmermann, Herbert, 165–66
Zitouni, Mustapha, 123
Zoetemelk, Joop, 113
Zoff, Dino, 111, 125
Zola, Gianfranco, 68
Zurich, 25–26, 28, 126, 152, 154–55, 157, 160–61, 225, 261–62